The Invention of George Washington

The Invention of
George Washington

Paul K. Longmore

UNIVERSITY OF CALIFORNIA PRESS
Berkeley • Los Angeles • London

University of California Press
Berkeley and Los Angeles, California

University of California Press, Ltd.
London, England

© 1988 by
The Regents of the University of California

Library of Congress Cataloging-in-Publication Data

Longmore, Paul K.
    The invention of George Washington / Paul K. Longmore.

        p.   cm.
    Bibliography: p.
    Includes index.
    ISBN 0-520-06272-8 (alk. paper)
    1. Washington, George, 1732–1799—Influence.   2. Washington,
George, 1732–1799—Public opinion—History—18th century.   3. Public
opinion—United States—History—18th century.   4. Presidents—
United States—Biography.   I. Title.
E312.17.L84   1988
973.4′1—dc19   87-34272
                                                                CIP

Printed in the United States of America

1 2 3 4 5 6 7 8 9

for Mom and Dad

Contents

Preface

The title *The Invention of George Washington* has three significations. It refers first of all to the historical process by which the revolutionary generation of Americans made an individual leader into an heroic personage who incarnated their republican and nationalist beliefs. That is the story of how a man became a myth, a myth not in the colloquial sense of a fantastic and "untrue" story, but in the technical sense of a story which combines factual and fictional elements to express a people's fundamental aspirations and convictions.

Second, the title calls attention to Washington's conscious and purposeful role in that process, his intentional shaping of his public and historic self. Finally, it denotes his inventiveness as a political actor and leader, a talent, I would argue, amounting to genius. Ironically, precisely because of his skillful embodiment of contemporary ideals, this is perhaps his least recognized and least appreciated gift.

This study recounts the interaction between Washington's public career and public image from his entry onto the historical stage during the Seven Years' War, through the years of mounting political crisis in the 1760s and 1770s, climaxing with the outbreak of revolution and the Declaration of Independence. It combines political biography and intellectual history in an attempt to explain how an ambitious frontier soldier and provincial politician became the "Father of his Country." It seeks to trace the connection between his image and the cultural values and political ideology of the revolutionary generation. It tries to demonstrate his own deliberate part in these historical events, recounting his increasing skill and sophistication as a political leader and his growth as an American nationalist and republican revolutionary.

What emerges is a Washington different from the one his biographers have presented; politically shrewd, closely in touch with the beliefs, aspirations, and fears of his contemporaries, a consummate political leader and public actor who sought to embody and to be perceived as embodying their highest ideals. That revised biographical understanding in turn helps illuminate what he meant to the generation who fought the Revolution and founded the nation, not only what they thought, but how they felt about him.

CHAPTER ONE

The Country of His Fathers

Throughout his life, the ambition for distinction spun inside George Washington like a dynamo, generating the astounding energy with which he produced his greatest historical achievement, himself. Even before the Revolution, that hunger for recognition prodded him to great exertions. In his twenties, he ceaselessly promoted his "interest," presenting himself to the attention of influential and powerful men. His surviving letters make plain his motive. He strove to separate himself from the "*common run*."[1] Indefatigably, he sought honor from his country and the good opinion of leading men in Virginia and the British military establishment.

Born in February 1732, George was the eldest child of the second marriage of Augustine Washington, an up-and-coming planter who left it to his sons from both marriages to continue the family's rise to the top rank of Virginia's gentry. In 1743, when the lad was eleven, his father died. Thereafter, his mother, Mary Ball Washington, seems to have expected him to make her needs his main concern. Especially later in her life, their relationship was often strained. She apparently never encouraged his ambitions or praised his accomplishments. As for his connection with his father, despite the fables of Parson Weems depicting the close ties between them, scant evidence exists to shed light on that fundamental and formative relationship. It is nearly impossible to determine the influence of the father or the memory of him on the son. Washington's voluminous writings yield little mention of him, by one count, only three references. Unsurprisingly but incorrectly, some historians have concluded that Augustine Washington and his absence had little effect on his son.[2]

It is intriguing that, having lost his natural father early on, through-out the first half of his life George Washington sought the patronage and, more important, the approbation of older men of prominence. He took them as his models and patterned his conduct after theirs. Nor was he above practicing the ingratiating manner of the courtier to win their attention. Of course, many young men on the make have endeav-ored to insinuate themselves into the good graces of men of status and influence, but George wanted more than their aid in his advancement. He yearned for their approval and frequently fretted that he had lost it. In the end, when the leaders of the British imperial establishment re-fused to acknowledge or reward his merits, he reacted with bitter rage.

Perhaps we can see in the loss of his father the origins of his extraor-dinary drive for public fame. Yet, by itself, that explanation seems sim-plistic. Many boys have been bereft of their fathers without developing such a hunger.

Washington's striving for recognition might also readily be explained in terms of Anglo-Virginian gentry values. That competitive culture fanned his ambitious energies, while its ethos of honor instructed him to seek public validation of his social merit and character. The basic contours of "Southern honor," as described by Bertram Wyatt-Brown, character-ized colonial Virginia. Honor involved an "inner conviction of self-worth," but that estimate was not to be the verdict of an autonomous conscience. The individual must lay the claim of his "self-assessment before the public." The public, the community, would then appraise that claim by examining his behavior. In that sense, a gentleman's honor meant his public reputation. The most important component would be his reputation among other honorable gentlemen. To hold securely one's own sense of honor, one's self-assessment must concur with the com-munity's assessment. Personal identity was, then, inseparable from pub-lic reputation.[3]

George Washington lived by the ethos of honor. That ethos taught him to seek the approbation of his society and especially "the esteem of the truly valuable part of mankind," gentlemen of the first rank. He strove, therefore, not only to act honorably, but to cultivate a reputation for doing so. An inner conviction might try to reassure him that he had conducted himself as a virtuous and honorable gentleman, but always nagging was the internalized cultural need for public validation. Throughout his life he would grow uneasy when his hard-won reputation was questioned or put into jeopardy.[4] And so he quested after honor, first from Virginia and then from all America.

As with the psychological analysis of Washington's ambition, this cultural explanation has its limits. The honor he pursued far exceeded the imperatives of provincial culture. His effort finally became an heroic exertion to attain historical fame. One might argue that he belonged to a revolutionary generation whose members ceaselessly tried to outdo each other in deeds of valor and patriotic sacrifice. The difficulty is that that impulse had incessantly prodded him long before the Revolution.

In the end, historical circumstances, culture, and psychology all appear insufficient to explain fully Washington's yearning for public honor. For this study of his career and the public response to it, it is enough to note that the desire gnawed at him throughout his life, never giving him rest from his historic labors.

Washington's ambitions and outlook were shaped in other ways by the reigning social and political ideology. Virginians conceived of society, not as a collection of competing interest groups, but as a stratified organic whole. This social order, distinguishing sharply between rulers and subjects, used its rituals and trappings and symbols to express and reinforce the notions of hierarchy and monarchy as natural and God-ordained.

For instance, the dictates of honor applied to white gentlemen. They referred only indirectly to women, poor white men, and black slaves. Such people were defined as inherently irresponsible and beyond the influence of community judgment. White gentlemen established their honor in part by the manner in which they related to, looked after, and managed these social inferiors. Thus, the code of honor helped to rationalize and perpetuate the hegemony of white gentlemen.

Closely related was a cluster of beliefs about patriarchy. The culture that nurtured young George supplied many substitute "fathers" for the one he had lost. It had developed a many-faceted metaphorical conception of fatherhood encompassing far more than biological paternity. Masters of slaves and servants oversaw them as "fathers" over "children." A young man intent on success would seek the protection and guidance of a patron, the word itself from the same root as father. The governing authorities of commonwealths ruled their subjects as "fathers." In 1775, Virginians praised Peyton Randolph, Speaker of the House of Burgesses, as the "father of his Country."[5] Britons addressed their king as the "Father of all his People." Their religion described the Creator of the Universe in paternal language.

These varying images of fatherhood shared certain fundamental elements. They again assumed the existence of a natural hierarchical order balancing authority and deference, governance and submission, and entailing on either side duties and benefits. All "fathers" were expected to provide for and protect their "children," to guide them by precept and example, to punish and reward them according to their deserts and for their welfare.

Patriarchal notions were essential to the self-image of Virginia's leading gentlemen. They thought of their plantation workers as composing extended "families" over which they themselves presided in paternal fashion. Their lands were tilled by scores of black slaves and, in such areas as the Northern Neck, by white tenants as well. Slave artisans and indentured servants practiced every craft. The great estates were, in many ways, self-sustaining agricultural communities. "Like one of the patriarchs," declared William Byrd II, "I have my flocks and my herds, my bond-men and bond-women, and every soart of trade amongst my own servants, so that I live in a kind of independence on every one, but Providence."[6]

Independence: that was the ideal and the goal of the great planters. Peyton Randolph and Landon Carter, using identical language, each proclaimed his estate an "excellent little Fortress . . . built on a Rock . . . of *Independency*." Anglo-American culture has always placed a high value on personal independence. Virginia's slave-based way of life intensified that concern among white men. Gentlemen like Carter and Randolph aimed ultimately at complete personal autonomy. This meant far more than material self-sufficiency. Fundamentally, it was a social and moral condition. Gentlemen freeholders seated securely on their own properties, in their self-contained plantation "fortresses," were thought to be insulated from any external influence or power.[7]

These assumptions had important political implications. Those without property, those subject to the will of another (indentured servants, tenants, propertyless adult sons) lacked the autonomy necessary for full participation in civic affairs. Those regarded as having emotional, physical, or "natural" "disabilities" (women, slaves, minors, people with various handicaps) were thought incapable of real self-control and therefore incompetent for such involvement. Full political rights should belong only to men with sufficient property to free them from, in John Locke's words, "depending upon the wills of any other man. . . ."[8]

The great planters' landed wealth supposedly made them especially fit for leadership by guaranteeing the independence and integrity of their political judgment. They were beyond lures or manipulations, it was said, and could not be bought or pressured. Conventional wisdom held that this ensured their trustworthiness with governing power. It would also enable them to withstand imperial encroachments upon colonial rights. Propertied independence was, then, the source of public virtue.

Concern with independence was also a major theme of what historians have sometimes called English "Country Party" political thought. Most prominent among these dissenting writers were the radical Whigs John Trenchard and William Gordon and the radical Tory Henry St. John, Lord Viscount Bolingbroke. They warned against the deliberate "corruption" of the English constitutional system by Crown ministers intent upon undermining both the independence of the British legislature and the moral and political independence of the English landed gentry. The "Country" writers had widespread influence in America, probably because their analysis seemed to fit the colonials' experience with Crown officials. In particular, Bolingbroke's almost mythic picture of agricultural patriarchy matched the self-image of Virginia's great planters.[9]

That self-image of rural retirement and virtuous independence included, of course, an element of fiction, even of self-deception. Gentlemen wanted political power. They coveted the honors of office. They fully intended to safeguard their property and their position. They relished the game of politics. With the exception of Washington's influential neighbor and colleague George Mason, whose temperament and preference exactly fit the ideal of independent retirement, the leading gentlemen of Virginia lived much of their lives on public stages and preferred a public life. Leadership they considered their obligation, their prerogative, and their favorite pastime.

Gentrymen fiercely guarded both their personal and political independence. "[T]hey are haughty and jealous of their liberties," said the English traveler Andrew Burnaby in 1760, "impatient of restraint, and can scarcely bear the thought of being controuled by any superior power." This disposition was grounded in the daily experience of managing their estates and in half a century of provincial political practice. It was reinforced by the explanatory power of political ideology.[10]

But the great planters' posture and self-image contained the seeds of crisis. They depended on the outside world far more than they cared to admit. They needed and, increasingly, wanted English manufactured goods. Their prosperity was tied to a fluctuating international tobacco market they only vaguely understood. And their province was still a subordinate unit of the British Empire. With each decade, their way of life became more enmeshed with, more dependent upon, that larger world. If the operation of the political and commercial system turned against their interests, it could strip away the illusion of autonomy and call into question the moral, social, and political identity of Virginia's ruling class.

In this culture young George Washington developed. Like his models and mentors, he would seek to become an independent and virtuous landed gentleman, a great planter ruling over his flocks and fields and bondservants, a "father" on his estate, in his neighborhood, and of his country.

When George was a boy, his father frequently left the family, energetically pursuing his business ventures, repeatedly voyaging to London. In 1735, Augustine Washington settled his second family at Hunting Creek, a plantation on the Potomac that would later be renamed Mount Vernon. In about 1740, he moved them to the new town of Fredericksburg. When Augustine died in 1743, eleven-year-old George was sent back to Mount Vernon to live with his half-brother Lawrence, who became largely responsible for the lad's upbringing.

That same year, Lawrence married Anne Fairfax, forming a connection with the powerful Fairfax clan that proved important for himself and a key aid to the early career of young George. Anne's father, Colonel William Fairfax, sat on the Council of the colony and served as agent for the vast Fairfax land grant. Belvoir, the Fairfax family seat, was within sight of Mount Vernon. George often visited there. Lawrence Washington and William Fairfax became, in effect, his teachers and models in business, social intercourse, and public responsibility.

Probably George's father had hired a tutor to instruct him privately, intending to send him to school in England later, as he had the sons of his first marriage. The elder Washington's death put an end to that plan. Instead, when the boy went to live at Mount Vernon, he apparently attended a school in the neighborhood for a time.[11]

His studies included mathematics, covering arithmetic, geometry, trigonometry, and surveying. He learned to calculate the cubic volumes of timber and stone and liquids. One of his school exercise books contains "forms of Writings and Rules of Civility." The first section of this bound volume provides specimens of frequently used legal forms, including a bill of exchange, a tobacco receipt, a bail bond, a servant's indenture, a short will, a land conveyance, a land lease, and a Virginia land patent. The latter part of the book is the famous "Rules . . . of Civility & Decent Behaviour in Company and Conversation," a selection of 110 maxims from the English translation of a sixteenth-century French handbook of gentlemanly deportment. Probably one of his teachers required him to copy it over as practice in penmanship and instruction in social etiquette.[12]

Most of the "rules" prescribe considerate behavior in the presence of others: Rule 1, "Every Action done in Company, ought to be with Some Sign of Respect, to those that are Present." Rule 100, "Cleanse not your teeth with the Table Cloth Napkin Fork or Knife but if Others do it let it be done wt. a Pick Tooth[.]" Rule 18, "[C]ome not near the Books or Writings of Another as to read them unless desired or give your opinion of them unask'd also look not nigh when another is writing a Letter." Rule 21, "Reproach none for the infirmaties of Nature, nor Delight to Put them that have in mind thereof."

Many rules establish proper conduct suited to the social rank of the other person: Rule 28, "If any one comes to Speak to you while you are Sitting Stand up tho he be your inferiour, and when you Present Seat let it be to every one according to his Degree[.]" Rule 40, "Strive not with your Superiers in argument but always, Submit your Judgment to others with Modesty[.]" Rule 52, "[K]eep to the Fashion of your equals. . . ."

Although most of these maxims prescribe decorous and deferential manners, a few command the student to cultivate moral integrity and good repute: Rule 48, "Wherein . . . you reprove Another be unblamable yourself; for example is more prevalent than Precept[.]" Rule 56, "Associate yourself with men of good Quality if you Esteem your own Reputation; for t's better to be alone than in bad Company[.]" Rule 109, "Let your Recreation be Manfull not Sinfull." Rule 110, "Labour to keep alive in your Breast that Little Spark of Celestial fire Called Conscience."[13]

As he copied over this code of manners and morals, the Virginian youth inscribed it in his memory. It established the foundation that would guide his conduct. Half a century and more later, he reiterated to his nephews and to his step-grandson the substance of the ethical dicta. In adulthood, he also acquired a copy of Lord Chesterfield's widely popular *Letters to His Son*. These essays taught him more of the art of elegant self-presentation. An English visitor would note with some surprise that the American first magistrate had improved upon his natural dignity by adding to it "perfect good breeding, & a correct knowledge" of even courtly etiquette, "how acquired heaven knows. . . ."[14]

Near the end of his formal schooling, young Washington studied geography and astronomy, gaining an elementary knowledge of the continents, the globe, and the heavenly constellations. This whetted a lifelong appetite for books on geography and travel and spawned a kind of hobby of collecting a wide variety of maps, an interest unsurprising in a land speculator and soldier.[15]

To what extent his academic training included instruction in composition and grammar the scanty records fail to show. Apparently George himself thought it insufficient, because within a year or two of leaving school he acquired the third edition of James Greenwood's *The Royal English Grammar*. This manual claimed to contain "what is necessary to the Knowledge of the English tongue . . . , Shewing the Use of the Parts of Speech, and joining Words together in a Sentence."[16]

Washington's collected correspondence reveals that he worked throughout his career to improve his writing. He progressively polished his grammar and corrected his spelling. He even altered his penmanship, on the eve of the Revolution replacing his rather ornate early style with a simpler, clearer hand. Most important, he straightened out his sometimes convoluted syntax, rid himself of a tendency to use florid phrasing, and developed into a writer of usually direct, forcible prose.[17]

This composed George's formal education. Unlike many sons of the Virginia gentry, he missed the opportunity to complete his preparation at the College of William and Mary. He supplemented his schooling with excursions into literature, history, and geography. At the age of sixteen, he was reading *The Spectator* and an unspecified history of England. In the next few years, he acquired Sir Richard Steele's *The Guardian*, Henry Fielding's *Tom Jones*, Tobias Smollett's *The Adventures of Peregrine Pickle*, Daniel Defoe's *A Tour through the Whole Island of Great Britain*, and *A Compleat History of the Piratical State of Barbary*. Doubtless at the instance of Lawrence Washington and William Fairfax, the eager youth became acquainted with Roman classicism by reading Sir Roger L'Estrange's popular version of Stoic philosophy, *Seneca's Morals*, as well as Julius Caesar's *Commentaries* in translation and perhaps the writings of other Roman generals.[18]

Despite its limitations, George's schooling supplied practical preparation for a young man intent on rising in Virginia's ruling class. It imparted the legal and business knowledge and the surveying skills necessary to a would-be planter and land speculator. It inculcated the social graces and the sense of social roles essential to a gentleman. The supplemental tutelage of Lawrence Washington and William Fairfax held up for his emulation models of Roman patriotism and virtue, thereby instructing him in the public responsibilities of the landed gentry and in the nobility of character proper to a man of his station. Such an education aimed, not at training in scholarship, but at preparation for practical leadership, at the continued dominion of the sons of Virginia's propertied elite.

The stress on gentlemanly breeding, the acute attention to social rank and to one's own place within that ranking, and the earnest cultivation of personal and public virtue were the ethical and behavioral concerns of an honor-based culture. Washington sought to adhere to these standards because his culture upheld them as ideals of behavior. From his youth, his preceptors and reading had propounded to him the code by which he would win or lose good repute.

If education and etiquette were badges of gentility, so too was dress. The code of honor held that a man's appearance reflected not only his social standing, but his inner worth as well. George early began to take great care in the selection of his clothes. In 1748 at the age of sixteen, he wrote a memorandum to himself to have a coat made according to his specifications. It totaled 152 words. That same year, listing items he would need for a visit to Fairfax County, he included nine shirts, six linen waistcoats, a cloth waistcoat, and other wearing apparel.[19]

Correspondence between outward appearance and inward reality was not inevitable, though. An individual might display the veneer of a gentleman while lacking the character of one. To some Virginians, it seemed that too many gentrymen were cultivating externals and ignoring essentials. They were merely keeping up appearances. These critics called for restoration of genuine honor and virtue. One of them, Landon Carter, who was also one of George's mentors, advised him "always . . . [to] regard the inward Man. . . ."[20] Thus the young Virginian was taught to put on the character and not just the clothes of a gentleman.

Eighteenth-century Virginia was a provincial culture attempting to emulate English metropolitan culture. This was another reason for the gentry's attention to proper etiquette, fashion, and self-presentation. Washington copied the "Rules of Civility" and read *The Spectator* and, later, Lord Chesterfield and the *Country Magazine* because he too based his deportment and style of life on the model of the English country gentleman. He would plan Mount Vernon's architecture and landscaping in imitation of English estates. For instance, he would never give up trying to grow "live fences," hedgerows, even though the heat and frequent droughts of Chesapeake summers always thwarted him.[21]

During the era of George's youth and early adulthood, Americans, especially members of the colonial elite, manifested divided feelings about English civilization. They measured themselves and their societies against its standards and found both wanting. Yet increasingly they resented metropolitan disdain of their provincialism, and more and more they thought the New World morally superior to the Old. All of this, the imitation, the sense of inferiority, the resentment, and finally the assertion of superiority based on native standards marked the social and cultural maturation of colonial America. Still dependent, it was seeking, in both that imitation and that rejection, to fashion an independent identity.[22]

As a gentleman and a soldier, Washington would work tirelessly to match English standards. To his bitter distress, imperial leaders would refuse to acknowledge fully his attainment of them. He would never entirely let go of English ideals, but he *would* labor to redefine his identity in American terms. Ultimately, he would conduct that redefinition publicly in collaboration with his countrymen. They, in turn, would make him the exemplar of the new nation's values.

The colonial Virginia of George's early years was a highly competitive society. Mundane activities became means to win personal and social distinction. His biographers have reported his reputation in his own day as an excellent horseman and an eager and energetic dancer. What they have failed to recognize is the contemporary cultural and social significance of that reputation.

Horses were a means of personal display. Virginians talked of them endlessly, talked of horse breeding and horse racing and horsemanship. Virtually everyone rode and virtually everyone, even the poorest, kept horses. Horses, said an English traveler, were the Virginians' "pleasure and pride." They became extensions of their owners, "adjunct[s] to virile self-presentation. . . ." In horsemanship as in all else, gentlemen tried to distinguish themselves from lesser folk. They fashioned a style of riding commonly called "a Planter's Pace, . . . a good sharp hand-Gallop." This manner of passage through the social and physical landscape impressed and even awed social inferiors, as it was meant to do. In a society that gave such attention to equines and equestrianism, George Washington became known as a superb horseman.[23]

Dancing was another primary mode of self-assertion and competition. The gentry employed dancing masters to instruct themselves and their young people in the fashionable dances current in Britain and Europe. By this means, they further marked the difference between themselves and the lower orders. Equally popular with all ranks of Virginians were vigorous and highly competitive jigs. Solo dancers contended for the approval of the audience as the onlookers repeatedly eliminated competitors until it was determined who was the "best of the ball." At other times, these individual performers would vie with the fiddler in contests of endurance. Even at play, Virginians expressed the fundamental character of their culture. It is unsurprising, then, to find that George Washington studied formal dancing as a teenager and enjoyed attending balls through much of his life. Most important, this young man, eager for public recognition, acquired a name as an energetic and skillful dancer.[24]

It was undoubtedly George's skill as a dancer and horseman that, when added to his natural strength and prowess, made him lithe in all his movements. His physical grace was an important part of the personal presence that from early on so vividly impressed those who met him. Once again, the ethos of honor took external appearance as a sign of inner merit.[25]

The social life of colonial Virginians provided many occasions for dramatic self-presentation. Horse races and even ordinary horseback riding, dances and other social gatherings, court days and election days and public meetings, all served as stages on which individuals, and especially gentrymen, might act out their claims to public honor and have them validated by the community. As his career advanced, Washington became an increasingly skillful public actor. An enthusiastic patron of the theater throughout his life, he may have learned something of the relationship between a performer and his audience by watching professional actors practice their art.[26]

Prowess on the dance floor or on horseback could momentarily boost a public reputation. Only wealth in land and slaves could secure a gentleman's honor. Gentlemen would, of course, display breeding and some learning. What truly distinguished the great planters was their patriarchal way of life and their skill in the difficult art of tobacco cultivation. Here was the fiercest competition of all. Not only their prosperity was at stake. Among the major planters, as T. H. Breen has shown, growing the finest tobacco and obtaining the best prices for it was an object of public scrutiny and a matter of personal honor. "I cannot allow myself to come behind any of these gentlemen in the planter's trade," anxiously declared Robert "King" Carter, the most successful planter of his day. For a time, George Washington would emulate his elders, working tirelessly to make himself a "crop master." Eventually, he would break with the traditional tobacco culture and economy, finding other means to establish his honor and independence.[27]

Douglas Southall Freeman called the Virginia of Washington's day "an ambitious landed society."[28] Even more fundamentally than tobacco, land was the foundation of the wealth, independence, and honor of the leading gentlemen. To that end, they built their great estates, consciously modeling them on the country seats of the English gentry. They also acquired other plantations and properties scattered throughout the province, and they speculated in western lands. Again, the competition among them was strenuous, and again young Washington would follow their example.

The men in whose presence he developed, the men who shaped his outlook, were among the most energetic speculators in Virginia. They pursued even more than wealth and status. They quested after a vision of landed empire. During George's boyhood, a group of enterprising gentlemen emerged as the dominant force in the economy and politics of the upper Potomac River Valley. They spearheaded British penetration of the Ohio Valley, undertaking to direct the Indian fur trade, land speculation, and white settlement of the interior. To make this imperial dream a reality, they were ready for Britain to make war on both the Indians and the French.

This group of adventurers included members of the Lee and Mercer families, George Mason, and, most important, the rich and powerful Fairfaxes. Thomas, Lord Fairfax, had inherited a grant of some five million acres, encompassing nearly one-fourth of the province east of the mountains, all of the Northern Neck, and an enormous territory west of the mountains. His cousin, Colonel William Fairfax, served as proprietary agent.

One scheme of this group was a speculative venture called the Ohio Company, a plan to take up half a million acres in the Ohio Valley and settle them with farm families. Lawrence Washington served as president of the company during the last years of his life. The founding members also included Robert Dinwiddie, Virginia's lieutenant governor, and the Hanbury brothers, prominent London merchants. With these connections at the seat of the empire, the company secured an arrangement obtained by no other group of land speculators: a ten-year exemption from quitrents on all cultivated lands.

Lawrence and several members of the Fairfax clan were also trustees of the new town of Alexandria, across the Potomac from the site of the future District of Columbia. From the beginning, the founders and boosters of Alexandria intended to make it the hub of commerce in the Potomac River Valley and the link between the Ohio country and the Atlantic world. George seized that vision early and pursued it throughout his life.

Lawrence Washington and William Fairfax, who had instructed George in the character of a gentleman, also gave him his start in surveying and land speculation. In 1747 and early 1748, when he was not yet sixteen years of age, he ran the boundaries of lands owned by Lawrence and other relatives who lived along the Potomac. During the spring of 1748, he accompanied Lawrence's brother-in-law, George William Fairfax, on a journey over the mountains to survey in the western portion of the Fairfax Proprietary. The following spring, he acted as assistant surveyor in the layout of Alexandria.[29]

In July 1749, the youth qualified as a county surveyor and soon assumed the office of surveyor of Culpeper County. It was unusual for a seventeen-year-old to snare such an appointment. Young men typically began as apprentices or deputy county surveyors. Perhaps it was thought that George already had sufficient experience to qualify him. More likely, he got the post because of his ties with the Fairfaxes. Culpeper County lay entirely within Lord Fairfax's proprietary.[30]

Surveying was a profession of some status in mid-eighteenth-century Virginia. Surveyors were reckoned the social equals of doctors, attorneys, and clergymen. Most were gentlemen. Surveying could also yield a substantial income. In a little over three years, George probably cleared close to £400. Most important, surveyors, particularly on the frontier, had the chance to seek out and secure for themselves the finest lands. Probably for that reason, George made only one survey in Culpeper. From 1749 until 1752, he did most of his surveying in the less settled frontier county of Frederick, also within the Fairfax grant. Here again his Fairfax connection gave him a boost. Lord Fairfax had authority to permit official surveyors to make public surveys outside their designated counties in any county within his proprietary.[31]

In the autumn of 1749, young Washington enlisted to serve another phase of the cause of expansionism and empire. Again traveling westward, he took charge of surveying tracts for the Ohio Company. In October 1750, at the age of eighteen, he bought his first plantation and the following spring made his first essay as a land speculator, advertising for sale two lots in Fredericksburg.[32] By May of 1753, through purchase and grant, he had acquired more than 2500 acres in Frederick County alone.

His Fairfax connection gave young George his start in the contest for land and wealth. Later it would make him uneasy to seek favors from and grant the requests of great men, especially when they ignored merits he thought deserving of reward. But for now, he willingly followed the practice of a deferential society and made use of his ties with the Fairfaxes. He later acknowledged to his younger brother Jack: "[T]o that Family I am under many obligations, particularly to the old Gentleman," William Fairfax.[33]

Whether in business or play, colonial Virginia society urged its members to contend for advantage and success. This reinforced George's gnawing hunger for distinction. But perpetual promotion of competition threatened the bonds of community. The economic and social striving of Virginians and their geographic dispersion were undermining the traditional hierarchical social order. Probably in part to counter these centrifugal tendencies, Virginians turned to "Country Party" political ideology with its emphasis on public virtue and communal harmony. The gentlemanly code of manners and public duties, too, attempted to mitigate the effects of egotism and rivalry even while perpetuating the social hierarchy.

The fear of the social destructiveness of untrammeled egotism and ambition, and the related fear of the insatiable appetite of men for political power, stemmed from a larger fear of the turbulence of human passions. In the eighteenth century, the view was widespread that human beings fundamentally acted from nonrational motives. Perpetually they deluded themselves that they were guided by reason, but this simply rationalized their biased outlook and selfish grasping for advantage and arbitrary power. Uncontrolled emotion might lead to excesses disruptive of communal harmony and unity; it might lead to social anarchy. Passions must be mastered and managed.

This view of human nature made sense to inhabitants of the British North American colonies, where tradition and social authority were weak and social, economic, and political competition was fierce. Hence the popularity of books like L'Estrange's version of *Seneca's Morals*. In it, readers sought, not instruction on the path to philosophic detachment and calm, but a way to restrain their surging, socially dangerous emotions. Young Washington read that work less as a student of Roman Stoicism than as a son of his own culture. The older men whose approval he sought reiterated the same lessons. Landon Carter strove for self-mastery throughout his life and urged George to cultivate that virtue.[34]

Anglo-Virginia society thus communicated to young men like Washington two contradictory imperatives: they should strive to outdo one another in the contest for social distinction and material rewards, but they should constrain the antisocial passions unleashed by such competition. They were admonished to cultivate personal virtue and to shoulder public responsibilities as a way of offsetting the simultaneous message of their culture to vie with one another for position, wealth, and honors.

George Washington exerted himself to excel and yearned to win the regard of others. He aimed at public honor as his culture taught him he ought to do. He was also a man of the strongest passions. For the first four decades of his life, he struggled to gain mastery over his emotions in order to attain the self-command upheld by his culture as a social virtue and a manly ideal. That culture also declared that men in command of themselves were most fit for political leadership.

Politics was yet another arena of contest among gentlemen, yet another source of honor, yet another means by which they marked the distinction between themselves and the "common" planters. Lawrence Washington probably first whetted his younger brother's appetite for it by his own example. In 1744, Fairfax County elected Lawrence as one of its first two representatives to the House of Burgesses in Williamsburg. Four years later, he sought reelection among a crowded field of five candidates. Sixteen-year-old George probably watched with excitement on that summer day in 1748 as the freeholders, hearing the clerk call their names, stepped forward to announce their votes publicly. The voting began with Thomas, Lord Fairfax, and Colonel William Fairfax, who both announced for Colonel Colville and Major Washington. To the admiring youth's delight, the voters returned his brother to office. That day, if not before, the fever of politics got into George's blood and never cooled. Lawrence kept a copy of the poll, the list of who voted and how, probably to use for his canvass at the next election. When Lawrence died a few years later, George saved the paper among his own.[35]

Besides his other interests, George developed an enthusiasm for soldiering. Service as an officer in the colonial militia was an additional important measure of one's social status. The gentry monopolized the officer ranks, claiming for themselves the respect due such military personages. Militia service was also a principal means of displaying one's personal virtue and public spirit. "Country" political ideology viewed arms-bearing by the citizenry as a sign of the moral health and social cohesiveness of the community.

Yet George wanted more than the respect accorded a leader of the county militia. Lawrence Washington probably supplied added inspiration. He served as a captain of Virginian forces on the British expedition against Cartagena in the early 1740s. Returning home, he named his plantation on the Potomac after his commander, Admiral Edward Vernon. Subsequently, he ascended to the post of adjutant-general of the province. Doubtless all of this stirred heroic dreams in the imagination of an admiring younger brother.[36]

In all he did, young Washington shaped himself to the pattern prescribed by his culture. From early on, he labored to win the position and fortune that not only would establish him as an independent, virtuous, and honorable gentleman, but would rank him with the great Virginia planters. Yet gentlemanly deportment and attire, skill as a horseman and dancer, wealth in land and slaves, leadership in local politics and the local militia could never give him the eminence he wanted. Virginia boasted many rich gentlemen colonels. He must find a means to greater glory. He turned his ambitious energies to arms. Soon he would have his own war to fight in quest of military renown.

CHAPTER TWO

"Honour and Glory"

Throughout his early military career (1753–58), the desire for distinction, the yearning for public recognition, fired George Washington's actions. As Lawrence Washington lay dying at Mount Vernon early in 1752, Virginia's leaders decided that, rather than replacing him as adjutant-general, they would divide the province into four military regions. George, despite his total lack of soldierly experience at age twenty, angled for the adjutancy of the Northern Neck. The post paid £100 a year. For half that sum, a deputy carried out the duties. Plainly put, the appointment was a sinecure, a salaried office with little actual work. The British Empire was filled with such patronage positions. American revolutionaries would later condemn them as useless charges on the public that supported political cronyism. Washington himself would refuse a salary as Continental Army commander-in-chief, but in 1753 the young man accepted the values of the political system within which he hoped to rise.

Instead of the Northern Neck, the Executive Council appointed him to the adjutancy of the Southern District. Dissatisfied with this post far from his residence on the Potomac, he besought the intervention of powerful members of the Council to have his office transferred. In mid-1753, his friends put through the desired change of appointment, shifting him to the Neck.[1]

George moved rapidly along other avenues of advancement as well. The French had been building forts in the Ohio Valley, challenging British claims to that region and threatening the interests of the Ohio Company. In recent years, both empires had begun to think more seriously about securing control of the interior. Throughout Washington's career, in his military service, business ventures, and political activities, the strategic, economic, and political importance of this region remained a primary preoccupation.

In October 1753, London ordered Virginia's Governor Robert Dinwiddie to send a messenger who should command the French to clear out of British-claimed territory. If they ignored this warning, Dinwiddie was to "drive them off by Force of Arms." Learning of these instructions, probably from Council member William Fairfax, George seized the opportunity. According to the Journal of the council, he "offered himself to go" as envoy to the French.[2]

Some thought it extraordinary, Washington recalled more than three decades later, "that so young and inexperienced a person should have been employed on a negotiation with which subjects of the greatest importance were involved." If his Fairfax connection had helped him snare the appointment, his execution of it vindicated the trust. Carrying the provincial rank of major, he set out with a small party through the threatening bleakness of a wilderness winter, gathered important intelligence, delivered his message to the French commandant, received that officer's bold refusal to withdraw, and returned to Williamsburg after a three-months' absence, having survived attempted assassination by an Indian guide and near-drowning in an ice-choked river. In his report to Governor Dinwiddie, his most important recommendation was construction of a fort at the strategic forks of the Ohio River. His "Aim," he admitted, had been to win the governor's approbation.[3]

The adventure gave him his first public recognition outside his home province. If some Virginia skeptics believed he had magnified the French threat in order to promote the Ohio Company's schemes, many throughout the colonies and in Britain thought his account the most important intelligence to date verifying aggressive French intentions. Governor Dinwiddie wrote to other provincial executives about the danger, enclosing copies or summaries of Washington's Journal. That report was published as a pamphlet in Williamsburg and London. Accounts of his embassy and reactions to it appeared in colonial newspapers and in the *Gentleman's Magazine* of London, the *Scots Magazine* of Edinburgh, and other British publications. Into the spring, the American press reported news of the Ohio country and of Major Washington's activities.[4]

His diligence not only earned him this small measure of renown, it secured him command of a militia force to protect the English settlements on the Ohio. Within a few months, he sought and won a commission as lieutenant colonel and second in command of the Virginian troops. To Council member Richard Corbin, he explained, "I neither look for, expect, nor desire" the "command of the whole forces . . . it is a charge too great for my youth and inexperience. . . ."⁵ There is something audacious in the disclaimer itself.

Awaiting the arrival of his superior, Colonel Joshua Fry, Washington exercised command as senior officer. He also fought his first battle, really only a skirmish, but a victory nonetheless. Warned of the surreptitious approach of a small enemy party, his force of Virginians and Indians surprised the intruders and killed or captured them in their camp. The surviving French officers claimed that their fallen commander, one Jumonville, had come on a diplomatic embassy, much like Washington's mission of the previous winter. Displaying official papers to support this assertion, they protested that the Virginian had violated the sacred character of an ambassador and his retinue.

At first, Washington dismissed this story as a disguise of their actual intent to spy out the country. Then he began to worry that his civilian superiors might believe it. He probably also feared that instead of praising his military success, they would censure his haste in advancing before reinforcements arrived. Hurriedly he reeled off a somewhat nervous refutation of the French case.⁶

Most people on the British side apparently discounted the enemy claim. In 1756, as the North American struggle expanded into a worldwide conflict, French propagandists would resurrect the charges in their campaign to blame the war on the British. Anxious to protect his reputation, Washington would again try to refute them.⁷ During the Revolution, Tory and British writers revived the tale once more to discredit the American cause. Even some historians have said that Washington, too quick on the trigger, had provoked war with France. But the plain fact is, the French and the British, both imperially ambitious to control North America and other parts of the world, had already been preparing to fight. The Jumonville incident simply provided a justification for what would have happened anyway. George's error was that he precipitated the fighting before Virginia was ready.

In 1754, the public adulation fed the fledgling soldier's appetite for honor. Friends in Williamsburg congratulated him and reported the general praise. Colonial newspapers and British magazines published this new accomplishment. At first, the accounts made little mention of the killing of Jumonville. Instead they dwelt on the capture of M. La

Force, described as a skillful officer with great influence among the Indians. By seizing him, Lieutenant Colonel Washington supposedly had "rivetted the Indians to the British interest." [8]

The *London Magazine* accompanied its account with George's letter to his younger brother Jack. With boyish, one even might say callow, enthusiasm he exclaimed: "I heard the bullet's whistle, and believe me, there is something charming in the sound." Said King George II, "He would not think so, if he had been used to hear many." Horace Walpole later called the ambitious young colonial a *fanfaron*, a braggart, and observed that he soon "learned to blush for his rodomontade." [9]

Washington's star climbed higher still when Colonel Fry, his superior, fell from a horse and died before reaching the frontier. On 4 June 1754, Governor Dinwiddie promoted George to the provincial rank of colonel and commander of the Virginia Regiment. Continued prosecution of "Your usual Conduct and Prudence . . . ," Dinwiddie assured, "must recomend You to the favor of His Majesty and Your Country." [10] Colonel George Washington was now charged to hold the line against the French. He had just turned twenty-two.

Even in this moment of triumph, George confronted vexations that would plague him repeatedly during his early quest for distinction. In mid-May, one of the South Carolina Independent Companies had arrived in Virginia, soon to be followed by two New York contingents. The officers all held regular army commissions and received regulars' pay. The provincial commander and his officers complained to Governor Dinwiddie that their lower pay was discriminatory. Already Washington had felt insulted by the small compensation for his wilderness embassy and had argued with Dinwiddie about his pay as lieutenant colonel. William Fairfax had dissuaded him from resigning. He would stay on out of a sense of patriotic duty and personal honor, he said, but he requested permission to serve as a volunteer.

Dinwiddie gently but firmly rebuked George's "ill timed Complaints" and inappropriate support of his officers' murmuring. Washington replied with renewed gratitude for the governor's favors and promised to do his duty. Then he launched into a lengthy justification of his previous protest. William Fairfax and Assembly Speaker John Robinson had promised to support his position, he said. Again he asked permission to serve as a volunteer, declaring that his only motive was to obtain honor. Only after pages of such self-exculpation did he report the encounter with Jumonville. [11]

If discriminatory pay galled Washington and his officers, they bridled even more at discriminatory distinctions of rank and commission. As a provincial colonel, George stood below even captains in the regular army. Governor Dinwiddie hoped Washington and Captain James Mackay of the South Carolina Independents would "not . . . let some Punctillio's about Command" obstruct the expedition. But the newly commissioned provincial colonel had no intention of subordinating himself to the regular captain. "I hope Captn MacKay will have more Sense than to insist upon any unreasonable distinction," he said. Dinwiddie had somewhat calmed George's anxiety about Mackay by urging that his continued good conduct would win him imperial attention. Washington eagerly took this as "assurance . . . of His Majesty's favour," in other words, a royal commission.[12]

When Mackay and the South Carolina Independents arrived, official friction started immediately. Mackay refused to allow his men to join the Virginians in road-building because Washington could not pay them the extra wages guaranteed to regulars for such labor. He kept his company separate and distinct from the provincial regiment. He rejected any communications from the Virginian that could be construed as commands, nor would Colonel Washington take orders from Captain Mackay. George urged the governor to settle the matter speedily. "[T]his is what we always hop'd to enjoy," he said, "the Rank of Officers which to me Sir is much dearer than the Pay." It was an issue of honor, public recognition of his merit.

He accompanied this complaint with an ominous announcement. Partly to avoid additional clashes, he had decided to move his small force farther west, closer to the threatening French.[13]

More than a matter of honor spurred this foolhardy advance. Washington wanted more glory. For weeks, he had been reporting rumors that the French were moving or preparing to move in his direction in force. He boasted of his patriotic fervor, his willingness to defend British rights "to the last remains of Life." His small victory over Jumonville made him even cockier. If all of the French behaved "with no more Risolution than this chosen Party . . . we shall have no gt [great] trouble in driving them" to Montreal. At the Great Meadows, his soldiers had built a little palisaded fort "in which with my small Number's I shall not fear the attack of 500 Men." He commanded fewer than a third as many. In response to such youthful bravado, Dinwiddie urged "Prudence & resolution," but the militarily inexperienced governor failed to command a halt to await reinforcements.[14]

Another development helped provoke George's reckless advance.

Dinwiddie had appointed Colonel James Innes, a Scot immigrant to North Carolina, as commander-in-chief of all the forces, provincial and regular. On 10 June, in the letter announcing his decision to move farther west, Washington rejoiced to the governor "that I am likely to be happy under the command of an experienced Officer and Man of Sense. . . ." A revealing portion of this letter, long missing and unknown to Washington's biographers, shows that in fact the Innes appointment worried him.[15]

He told Dinwiddie, "The approbation you have expressd of my conduct has given me more pleasure than any thing wch has happen'd since my Imbarking in this Expedition . . . for I assure you Sir I have expected nothing but your disapprobation; such unfortunate circumstances have Interven'd to Eclipse, or Cloud the Face of things and turn them to my disadvantage: and now I shall not have it in my power to convince yr Honr, my Friends, and Country of my diligence, and application to the Art Military, as a Head will soon arrive to whom all Honour and Glory must be given."[16] He had strained to win public honor. Now a new commander would displace him from the principal role in defending Virginia's frontier. He feared he would soon disappear in the shadow of another man.

This same day, he had pursued the mirage of another victory, hoping to win a few more plaudits before Innes arrived. Misunderstanding the report of a scout, he had marched out with one hundred thirty men expecting to confront ninety of the enemy, "full with hope of procureing another present of F[renc]h p[risone]rs for your Honour[;] then judge my disappointment at meeting 9 only, and those coming for protection[.]" He had already garnered praise for capturing M. La Force. Now he was "plodding [*sic*] a Scheme" to seize Captain Joncaire, the Indian interpreter. If the plan succeeded, "it will be glorious to have a Man of his Importance. . . ."[17]

Washington had decided to march farther west even before Mackay and the South Carolina Independents showed up. The dispute over rank and command only added another reason. With inadequate munitions and supplies, without reinforcements, and against the advice of his Indian allies, he was nevertheless determined to advance toward the enemy alone. According to one militia officer, he planned "to attack the F. [French] Fort."[18] He apparently hoped to beat the French singlehanded.

On 16 June 1754, Washington and his small force moved out of Fort Necessity, the encampment they had dug at the Great Meadows, to continue the painfully slow work of clearing a road over the mountains. This arduous labor broke the wagons and most of the horses. By 28 June, they were still short of their goal, Redstone Creek, but were within two days' march of the Ohio Forks and the French. Reliable intelligence reported the approach of a large force of French and Indians. Washington and his staff initially decided to throw up an entrenchment and meet the enemy on that spot. When Mackay and the South Carolinians arrived the next day, the combined leadership decided more prudently to retreat to Wills Creek, bypassing even Fort Necessity.

With few field horses and wagons left to transport the baggage and swivel guns, the escape proved as costly as the advance. Men became beasts of burden. The spent soldiers reached the Great Meadows on 1 July and could march no farther. Resorting to the flimsy protection of Fort Necessity, they probably hoped reinforcements would arrive in time. There the French and Indians caught them and on 3 July 1754 compelled their acceptance of an ignominious surrender.[19]

The Articles of Capitulation confessed to the "assassination" of Jumonville and virtually admitted a British invasion of French territory. Washington and his fellow officers accused a Dutch captain in the regiment named Van Braam of having treacherously mistranslated "assassination" as "death" or "loss" or "killing," they could not remember which. Undoubtedly he had misconstrued the word as he read the terms of surrender by flickering light on that rain-soaked evening, translating as he went along. But just as surely, the fatal slip was an error rather than a betrayal. He had enjoyed Washington's confidence up to now. Unfortunately, the French had carried him off as one of their hostages. Upon his return from captivity several years later, he seems to have convinced the Virginia Assembly of his innocence, for they voted to reimburse him for his lost time and hardship.[20]

Meanwhile, though Virginians accepted the officers' explanation, young Colonel Washington himself was not off the hook. His friends and patrons in the provincial aristocracy might praise his courage. They might blame his defeat on Van Braam's perfidy, Governor Dinwiddie's failure to supply and reinforce him adequately, the governor's supposed bias in favor of fellow Scots, or the lack of support from other colonies.[21] To the north and in London, less friendly judges evaluated his conduct more critically.

John Huske's popular tract "The State of the British and French Colonies in North America" (London, 1755) called the Articles of Capitulation "the most infamous a British Subject ever put his Hand to."[22]

Harsh comment came also from within the imperial establishment, from the very men who had it in their power to encourage or block the royal commission George yearned to win. Governor Horatio Sharpe of Maryland assured Washington that he blamed the dishonorable surrender on Van Braam's treachery, but to other correspondents he attributed the reckless advance to the "pique" over rank between the Virginia and the South Carolina officers. Thomas Penn, proprietor of Pennsylvania, felt concern at Washington's "imprudent conduct." Baron Calvert, proprietor of Maryland, laid the defeat to "his unmilitary Skill." Lord Albemarle thought this proved that colonials, though brave, knew nothing of the military art, were undependable, and must be led by regular officers. Perhaps the most perceptive criticism came from William Johnson of New York, another provincial frontier officer. He surmised that Washington's incautious advance had resulted from his "being too ambitious of acquiring all the honour, or as much as he could, before the rest Joined him. . . ."[23]

Washington's letters in the weeks leading up to the defeat at Fort Necessity, especially the letter to Dinwiddie of 10 June, support Johnson's conclusion. He had shown courage and the capacity to lead his men, most of them raw recruits, under the most hazardous conditions. He had labored with inadequate supplies and insufficient reinforcements. Given these nearly impossible circumstances, the costly cutting of a road through that rugged terrain, when considered by itself, stands as a notable military achievement. Yet that accomplishment also involved a reckless movement into the neighborhood of an enemy superior in both numbers and armament. His violation of fundamental strategic precepts led directly to the defeat at Fort Necessity. Taking into account his difficulties, his professional inexperience, and his evident promise, historians have tended to exculpate his rash behavior somewhat.[24]

Rather than evaluating his military leadership, the purpose here is to understand Washington's motivations. He complained of discriminatory pay, clashed with Captain Mackay, and finally decided to put some distance between his regiment and the royally commissioned regulars. But that foolish and fateful advance also stemmed from his worry that when Colonel Innes and reinforcements arrived he would lose his chance to win the applause of his country and the attention of influential men. He feared he would miss a glorious opportunity to lay claim to public honor. This presaged much that was to come.

"The chief part of my happiness"

For decades, gradually, unsystematically, and usually with the unthinking acquiescence of the Crown, the Virginia House of Burgesses had been augmenting its authority. The Seven Years' War offered the greatest opportunity yet for it and the other provincial lower houses deliberately to expand their role in governance. It also marked the historical moment when imperial officials began to recognize and resist these bids for power.

The first years of Washington's military career coincided with the Pistole Fee Dispute. The controversy flared in 1753 when Governor Dinwiddie tried to collect that small sum each time he affixed his seal to land patents. His real aim was to stop speculators from postponing patenting and thus payment of quitrents. But the dispute quickly became a constitutional issue as well, because the governor had usurped the Burgesses' long-held authority to set all fees. Though Washington is not known to have expressed his opinion of the controversy, he showed his interest by obtaining Landon Carter's pamphlet attacking the constitutionality of Dinwiddie's action.[1]

Another dispute developed after Washington's report of French incursions into the Ohio Valley. In February 1754, the House appropriated £10,000 for military purposes but required that a legislative committee oversee its expenditure. This was the first of a series of joint Burgess-Council military committees, all dominated by Speaker and Treasurer John Robinson, all part of an effort to hedge the power of the royal governor and augment that of the House. The Crown in turn granted Virginia £20,000 for defense but, against Dinwiddie's advice, required the province to repay it out of tobacco export tax revenues. It also put its expenditure under the governor's control. These moves aroused the ire of the colony's leaders. Through his friends in Williamsburg, Washington kept abreast of these developments.[2]

Meanwhile, he himself kept clashing with royally commissioned officers. Throughout mid-1754, provincials and regulars disputed about rank and the Virginians complained about the regulars' higher pay.[3] In October, Governor Dinwiddie decided to reorganize the Virginia Regiment as independent companies. This would put all officers' commissions and pay on the same footing, since all would belong to the royal military establishment. It would also solve the problem of disciplining the troops, by placing the soldiers under the regular army's Articles of War.

But the plan required recalling all of the higher commissions in the Virginia Regiment, substituting captaincies in the new independent companies. Colonel Washington may have hoped his regiment would simply be incorporated into the regular army and that at the age of twenty-two he would obtain a regular colonelcy. At the very least, he probably expected to be made a regular major. Instead, his superiors offered to reduce his rank and to subordinate him to those with royal captaincies of earlier date, the very officers he had thought it his right to command as a provincial colonel.[4]

The other provincial officers acquiesced in the demotions, but Washington, on the advice of his friends, refused to accept this slight to his honor. He angrily resigned from the service. He blamed the new arrangements on bias against provincials in the regular army and the imperial establishment. His opinion was confirmed when the king issued orders again subordinating provincials to regular officers. The chief military merit of many regulars was a family wealthy enough to buy them a commission. Understandably, then, the royal instructions rankled Washington and other capable provincial officers.[5]

Governor Sharpe of Maryland, commander-in-chief of operations in the Middle Colonies, offered to allow George to retain his provincial colonelcy. The proud young man brusquely rejected this "empty" commission, because it could carry neither the rank nor the pay of a regular colonel. But he had no real wish "to leave the military line," he said. "My inclinations are strongly bent to arms."[6]

Washington tried to satisfy that inclination again early in 1755. General Edward Braddock was heading a full-scale expedition to recapture the Ohio Forks. George congratulated him on his safe arrival but then allowed powerful friends to solicit Braddock's favor. He was soon offered a position on the general's staff. The appointment would avoid all difficulties about rank and commission. George would report directly to the general. He had acquired essential knowledge of the frontier. Braddock probably thought him a useful man to have along.[7]

Washington had hoped for a regular army commission, but Braddock could grant nothing higher than a brevet captaincy. His sense of honor required George to go as a volunteer. He enlisted, he said, for the "laudable desire . . . to serve (with my poor abilitys) my King & Country . . ." and to seek once more the "regard & esteem" of his friends and province. Perhaps he could also gain soldierly experience and form "an acquaintance" which might be useful, "if I can find it worth while pushing my Fortune in the Military way." Meanwhile, he urged his brother Jack to visit the Fairfax family "often," "as it is in their power to be very serviceable upon many occasion's to us as young beginner's." [8]

Even as he set out to win more military glory, George pursued other ambitions. He had never sought a merely military reputation. The ordinary course of advancement in Virginia politics proceeded from minor local office to county court justice to Burgess, but George Washington was no ordinary young man. He had already attained command of the province's military forces at the age of twenty-two. At age twenty-three, election to the Assembly seemed the appropriate next step in his rise.

John Carlyle, a prominent merchant from Alexandria and a son-in-law of William Fairfax, asked if he were interested in standing for the Burgesses in the upcoming election. Carlyle then tantalizingly hinted that Washington's friends might nominate him in any case. In May 1755, while on the march with Braddock's army, George asked his brother Jack to sound out the leading men in Fairfax County regarding his political prospects. He should discover their sentiments "witht disclosing much of mine. . . ." If they seemed "inclinable to promote my Interest" and the situation required immediate action, "you then may declare my Intentions & beg their assistance." If they favored someone else, drop the matter. "[C]onduct the whole . . . with an air of Indifference & unconcern; after that you may regulate your conduct accordingly." [9]

He had grown up among the men who dominated politics in the Northern Neck and who held a major share of power in Virginia at large. From them he had grasped the fundamental axioms of politics:

Find out as much as you can about the aims and plans of others; reveal as little of your own as possible. Attach yourself to those who can do you the most good, those with political clout. Assess your support and your prospects. If the situation seems favorable, act decisively. Otherwise, avoid wasting your political capital, namely, the goodwill of the populace and your standing with political leaders. Apparently Jack sent back word that the time was not yet ripe. George sat out the election.

Meanwhile, the Braddock expedition reiterated to Washington his status as a Virginia provincial. "[F]requent breaches of Contracts" by army suppliers gave the general a low opinion of colonials. George warned that he might "represent us [at] home in a light we little deserve; for instead of blameing the Individuals as he ought, he charges all his Disappointments to a publick Supineness. . . ." The two men argued heatedly and often. William Fairfax showed George's letter "to our particular Friends" in Williamsburg. Braddock's "unreasonable Impatience and the unmerited Censure of our Want of public Zeal" worried them. He might determine his needs; they would judge Virginia's ability to supply him.[10]

Another development also distressed Washington. His associates in trade and land speculation intended Virginia to dominate the postwar fur trade and settlement of the Ohio country. A group of Pennsylvanians with the same idea lobbied Braddock to have part of the army march through Maryland. Instead, the general chose a Virginia route, but the Pennsylvanians convinced him that, once recaptured, the Ohio Forks should be supplied by a road to be opened across their province. Learning of this, George unconsciously showed his own provincial bias by fuming about the Pennsylvanians' lack of patriotism.[11]

Braddock seems to have excluded his young staff officer from his condemnation of colonials. He also heeded George's counsel to transport supplies by pack horse instead of wagon and to divide the army, sending ahead a lightly equipped force. The former recommendation showed that Washington had learned from his experiences of the previous year; the latter advice was perhaps questionable. Still, Braddock respected and liked the young man and promised to assist him in obtaining a regular army commission.[12]

The campaign of 1755 boosted Washington's fame without advancing his fortune in quite the way he had hoped. On 9 July, the expected conquest of the French turned into a massacre of the British. Many of the regular and provincial officers fell. Braddock himself was mortally wounded. Despite several near misses, George emerged unscathed.

Barely recovered from a serious fever, he urged the general to let him lead provincial troops in irregular fashion against the hidden enemy, a proposal Braddock rejected. Later, he supervised the removal of his dying commander from the field. He then carried a message to the troops in the rear. He never forgot that ride through infernal darkness amid the hellish cries of the dying who lay along the bloody road of retreat. Three days later, he presided over the burial of the general. He had survived, he said, because of "the miraculous care of Providence, that protected me beyond all human expectation. . . ."[13]

British and, particularly, American critics condemned Braddock's refusal to heed colonial advice on the art of forest fighting. Some criticized the regular soldiers' supposed cowardice. Many praised the Virginia provincials for the courage and skill that, they believed, had prevented an even bloodier loss.[14]

For conspicuous gallantry, they singled out George Washington. One dispatch described him as a "Gentleman much respected, who went out a Voluntier, and was appointed one of the General's Aide de Camp's. . . ." Another widely circulated report told how he had "begged the General, when he was first attacked, to let him draw off about 300 in each wing to scour the woods: but he refused it, and obstinately persisted in the form of a field-battle, his men standing shoulder to shoulder. . . ."[15] In accounts published in nearly every colony, Captain Robert Orme, Braddock's aide and protégé, campaigned to safeguard the reputation of his fallen patron. Though he changed few minds, one of his assertions readily won public acceptance: "Mr. Washington had two Horses shot under him and his Cloaths shot thro' in several Places, behaving the whole Time with the greatest Courage and Resolution."[16]

The reports of George's heroism triggered an explosion of acclaim. "[O]ur Brave Colo. Washington," wrote one Virginia gentleman, ". . . came off with great applause." That applause reverberated in letters of congratulation from Governor Dinwiddie, William Fairfax, Councillor Philip Ludwell, and other members of Virginia's ruling class. Outside the province, a Charlestown, South Carolina, newspaper published his praises, and in Pennsylvania, said a friend, "Yor Name is more talked off . . . then any Other person of the Army. . . ." "I cannot sufficiently speak the merit of Washington," proclaimed Dr. Alexander Hamilton of Annapolis. "He is a person well deserving and ought to be distinguished and taken notice of. . . ."[17]

From across the ocean came more praise. George's uncle in Stratford, England, lauded his nephew and reported, "Every Body Blames his

[Braddock's] Rash Conduct" and "Commends the Courage of the Virginians and Carolina men. . . ." Wrote Lord Halifax, "I know nothing of Mr. Washington's character, but, that we have it under his own hand, that he loves the whistling of Bullets, and they say he behaved as bravely in Braddocks action, as if he really did."[18]

The best-remembered words spoken of Washington on this occasion came from the Presbyterian preacher and later president of Princeton College, Samuel Davies. During the French and Indian War, the idea spread from New England throughout the colonies that God had chosen America to model civil and religious liberty to the world. He had chastised the provinces with the Braddock catastrophe, it was said, because of their unfaithfulness in living up to that mission. Nonetheless, He would stand with them if they resisted French slavery and Catholic idolatry. This was precisely the point of a sermon Davies preached following the debacle.

In that sermon, Davies noted thankfully that the Lord of Hosts had pleased "to diffuse some Sparks of his Martial Fire" in Virginia. "As a remarkable instance of this, I may point out to the Public that heroic Youth Col. Washington, who I cannot but hope Providence has hitherto preserved in so signal a Manner for some important Service to his Country."[19] This passing reference was the first linking of Washington with belief in America's providential political mission.

The legend of Braddock's defeat connected Washington's name with another powerful American myth. British colonials, deeply suspicious of professional armies, had long avowed faith in the superiority of militia over regular troops. Supposedly, militia fought better because they defended their homes, families, and communities, while professional soldiers fought only for pay. The reported cowardice of the regulars and the courage of the colonials at the battle on the Monongahela confirmed this conviction. In the almost instantaneous folklore recounting the event, Washington was made the embodiment of this interpretation. Ironically, he himself had been striving to learn from and to match the standard of the professional British regulars.

Compounded with this ideological interpretation was an incipiently nationalist one. Colonials had proved themselves more expert than the British at conducting warfare in their unique New World environment. Braddock had scorned the advice of provincials experienced in frontier fighting. The regulars had panicked; the colonials had kept their heads. The brave provincial colonel George Washington had prevented the complete annihilation of the British forces. Again, he became a native hero symbolizing the superiority of American over European ways.[20]

In truth, the British officers and troops were familiar with irregular warfare and, until the last day, had been on the alert against enemy ambush. That one lapse cost Braddock his expected victory, his life, and his reputation.[21] American critics ignored these facts. Braddock's outspoken disdain of colonials made him a highly visible example of Crown officers' anticolonial bias. His failure gave Americans a convenient target for attacking that prejudice and affirming themselves.

Two decades later, on the eve of the war with Britain, delegates to Congress from throughout the continent would remember Washington as the hero of Braddock's massacre. Some Americans would blend the nationalist, ideological, and providentialist interpretations of that event and count the words of Samuel Davies as prophecy.

Washington had sought the esteem of his fellow Virginians. Now he had won the applause of all the colonies and of Britain as well. He noted the exaggeration of some of the praise and observed, with sympathy and uneasiness, the abuse heaped upon the fallen Braddock. Doubtless he found this moment of glory satisfying, but where could he go from here? He had served as a volunteer, without rank or pay, and the man who had promised to help him secure a royal commission now lay in an unmarked grave in the wilderness of western Pennsylvania.[22]

In August 1755, Washington got another chance to push his "Fortune in the Military way." The remnants of Braddock's army had retreated all the way to Philadelphia, in midsummer going into winter quarters. With Virginia's frontiers entirely exposed, Governor Dinwiddie had to act quickly. He had thrown over his plan of the previous fall to reorganize the colony's regiment as independent companies. In a province with a paucity of experienced military men, he had few options.[23]

Some leaders thought confidence in Washington would boost enlistments and support for the war effort throughout the Middle Colonies. In Pennsylvania, said a friend, "every body Seems willing to Venture under Your command. . . ." Both Benjamin Franklin and Richard Peters, Secretary of the Pennsylvania Executive Council, believed a request from him for assistance "would now get it Sooner than any one in Amerrica." Likewise in his home province, "People . . . seem very desirous of serving under the brave Colo. Washington, and want nothing more to encourage 'em out, but yr Declaration of going to command them. . . ."[24]

Philip Ludwell, Speaker John Robinson, George's brother Augustine, and others were pressing the governor and the Assembly to put him in charge of Virginia's defenses again. They wanted him to come to Williamsburg to lobby for the appointment, especially as there was another "warm Sollicitation. . . ." Possibly it came from the outsider, the regularly commissioned Colonel James Innes. This was neither the first nor the last time provincial politicians supported Washington in their continuing struggle to defend the interests and powers of Virginia's internal leadership. Whatever misgivings the governor may have had, he offered George the post as colonel of the regiment. To it was now added the command of all Virginia's military forces.[25]

Washington's handling of this affair reveals him beginning to establish a pattern that would mark his later career. He had actively sought his first commissions as district adjutant, diplomatic courier, and lieutenant colonel. Altering the strategy, he had brought himself to Braddock's attention but then had let his political patrons promote his selection as a staff officer.

This time he decided against soliciting the appointment. He told one acquaintance, ". . . I am unequal to the Task . . . it requires more experience than I am master of. . . ." To another, more influential friend, he confessed that he definitely was interested in the new command but would never put up with the vexations of the year before. He refused to risk his health or his reputation without certain guarantees. Most important, he wanted a voice in the selection of his subordinate officers and financial arrangements protecting him from personal loss. To offer himself and at the same time issue these provisos, he realized, "woud *look* a little incongruous [emphasis added], . . . as if I imagin'd there were not other's equally, (if not more) capable of conducting the affair than myself; But if the command should be offerd, the case is then alter'd. . . ."[26]

Four tactics emerge here that would reappear in Washington's later, more sophisticated and subtle performances at the times of his appointment to command the Continental Army, his selection as a delegate to the Constitutional Convention, and his two elections to the presidency. He carefully regards appearances; how will his audience perceive and interpret his conduct? He protests his inadequacy. He avoids actively soliciting the job. And finally, by making the offer come to him, rather than promoting himself, he increases his influence and authority.

One other feature of his conduct would also recur throughout his career: anxiety about his reputation. Even if the colony's government met his terms, he still feared that no one, under the present conditions, could lead its defense without incurring the censure of the public and a consequent loss of honor. He worried that he would lose "what at present constitutes the chief part of my happiness, i.e. the esteem and notice the Country has been pleasd to honour me with." But he feared even more that to decline an appointment offered on honorable terms would reflect greater discredit on him.[27] This solicitude for his public reputation was not the fretfulness of an egocentric personality. It reflected again the values of an honor-based culture. A gentleman's claim to merit, indeed, his very sense of self-worth, must obtain public validation.

He avoided mentioning that the provincial post again offered the possibility of securing a royal commission. A sense of public responsibility, fear of public disfavor, and the undiminished ambition for distinction prodded him once more. Washington accepted command of the regiment and the new and greater responsibility to head the colony's defenses.[28] He was twenty-three years old.

CHAPTER FOUR

"The service done . . . merits reward"

During his next three and one-half years as chief of Virginia's defenses (1755–8), Colonel George Washington would wrestle with a horde of vexations. The unpopularity of the war with many Virginians kept recruitment low and prompted some legislators to resist voting adequate military appropriations. Repeatedly he would complain of lack of clothing, blankets, and other essentials, low or late pay of the troops, and inadequate provision for disabled soldiers. Voluntary enlistments failed to fill the ranks. Nor did a draft of the landless and voteless work. Poor young white men, aided by the common folk, deserted in droves. Even after the colonel hanged two deserters as an example and warning, the conscripts kept running off.[1]

Each year, he had to build the regiment virtually all over again. He also had trouble getting legal authority from the Assembly to discipline his troops and to control the often insubordinate militia. This was one reason he kept hoping for a regular army commission. Under such conditions, how could he be expected to defend the frontier? How could he hope to win public honor? Within one month after accepting the command the second time, he threatened to resign.[2]

Washington's concern about his own pay also continued to grate him. This was something more than an urge to make money. It was again an issue of honor. To his brother Augustine, he complained:

"I was employ'd to go a journey in the Winter (when I believe few or none woud have undertaken it) and what did I get by it? my expences borne! I then was appointed with trifling Pay to conduct an handfull of

Men to the Ohio. What did I get by this? Why, after putting myself to a considerable expence in equipping and providing Necessarys for the Campaigne—I went out, was soundly beaten, lost them all—came in, and had my Commission taken from me . . . under *pretence* of an Order from home. I then went out a Volunteer with Genl Braddock and lost all my Horses and many other things but this being a voluntary act I shoud not have mention'd it, was it not to shew that I have been upon the loosing order ever since I enterd the Service, which is now near two Year's; so that I think I can't be blam'd, shou'd I, if I leave my Family again, endr [endeavor] to do it upon such term's as to prevent my sufferg (to gain by it, is the least of my expectation)."[3]

The talk is of money, but just below the surface throbs the anger and hurt of an ambitious young man who felt that his countrymen had failed to appreciate his sacrifices on their behalf, had failed to validate his claim to social merit.

He also expected the benefits befitting his station. He demanded and won the right to appoint for himself an aide-de-camp and a secretary. Governor Dinwiddie complained, "its the first Colo. of a Regiment that ever had an Aid de Camp. . . ." Some Burgesses agreed, opposing these appointments as "extraordinary." In 1757, Washington asked a regular army colonel about officers' allowances for servants and provisions in the Royal American Battalions. Then he lobbied Assembly leaders to have cuts in his perquisites restored. The pay and privileges of a regular officer were a form of social distinction.

He was looking out for his financial interests, though. Under the terms of his new commission and with his sinecure as district adjutant of the Northern Neck, he profited enough to enlarge his holdings in land and slaves. Despite what he told Augustine, he did intend to augment his wealth.[4]

The ambitious young provincial also kept chasing the mirage of a royal commission. Ever it rippled tantalizingly. Ever it vanished as he clutched for it. Recurrent rumors teased that the Crown would soon incorporate the regiment into the regular establishment. His friends in the Assembly secured a vote recommending such appointments for him and the other field officers. Dinwiddie too repeatedly made that recommendation. He did so at George's instance and to mollify his politically powerful supporters, but also because he believed Washington "a Man of great Merit and Resolut'n," whom Braddock "w'd have recomended . . . to the Royal Favo." had he lived.[5]

To fit the regiment for such a commission, the colonel pushed them to match the standard of the regular army. Repeatedly he exhorted his officers to set aside time for study of such works as Humphrey Bland's widely used *Treatise of Military Discipline*. Having "no opportunities to improve from example," he said, "let us read. . . ." Expertise in their profession could not "be attained without application; nor any merit or applause to be atchieved without a certain knowledge thereof." Many regular officers made little such effort. George took as his models those who reached for the highest standards.[6]

Because the officers were "Gentlemen of Family," Washington appealed to their sense of honor and ambition for distinction. The soldiers, on the other hand, came from the lower ranks of Virginia society. Some were vagrants, wandering poor young men without property or social standing and without a stake in this war for empire. Drafted against their will, they willingly deserted. Occasionally Washington called upon their patriotic zeal or their desire for his good opinion of them. Mostly, though, he agreed with the typical upper-class conviction that common soldiers could be controlled only through fear of punishment. His experience commanding the revolutionary republican army would alter these attitudes somewhat. For now, he expected disciplining the troops and exhorting the officers to ready his regiment for regular commissions.[7]

He also thought a fit appearance essential. He designed for his regimental officers a uniform of blue, the coat faced and cuffed with scarlet and trimmed with silver, the waistcoat of scarlet trimmed with silver. The dress even of common soldiers drew his attention: what effect would their outfits have on allied and enemy Indians?[8]

Even while on military duty, George kept up his eager involvement in politics. In December 1755, elections were held throughout the province. At Alexandria he campaigned actively for his friend George William Fairfax. In the heat of the contest, he and William Payne, a supporter of another candidate, exchanged angry words, and Payne knocked the colonel to the ground. It seems that the next day Washington wrote a note of apology to Payne. He worked continually to constrain his fierce temper. To govern and lead others, a gentleman must first be master of himself. He also wrote down and alphabetized the poll of the election in Fairfax County, keeping it among his papers. One day he would use it on behalf of his own ambitions.[9]

In Frederick County that same December, friends did exactly what John Carlyle had jokingly suggested they might do. They put his name up as a candidate for Burgess, it seems without his knowledge. This last-minute nomination garnered only forty votes. Given the lack of planning, a friend thought this tally "not despicable." With even "a Weeks Notice," he felt sure, "you would have gone Unanimously. . . ." Washington saved a copy of the Frederick poll, biding his time, awaiting a better chance.[10]

By now, the colonel was embroiled in another dispute with an officer who claimed the prerogatives of a regular. John Dagworthy held only a provincial captaincy from Maryland, but, asserting authority from a defunct royal commission, he contested Washington's command of colonial troops operating out of Fort Cumberland in that province. Washington and Dinwiddie protested to Maryland's Governor Sharpe but without effect. It seemed to George that Sharpe was backing Dagworthy. Hoping a royal brevet commission would soon arrive, he stayed away from the fort to avoid a confrontation. He vowed to resign rather than subordinate himself to Dagworthy.[11]

Dinwiddie asked Governor William Shirley of Massachusetts, acting commander-in-chief for North America, to settle the squabble. When this effort failed, Washington obtained Dinwiddie's permission early in 1756 to carry his protest all the way to Boston. He wanted Shirley to prevent future difficulties by incorporating his regiment into the regular army. Once again, he took his complaints to the Assembly's leaders, and once again, they backed him. He probably shared Speaker Robinson's hope that he rather than Governor Sharpe might win command of the next offensive against the French fort on the Ohio. The dispute with Dagworthy had caused such resentment in Virginia, Dinwiddie told Shirley, that the Burgesses might withhold support of the war effort.[12]

On this journey, the young colonel intended to impress those he met with his status as Virginia's commander-in-chief. His entourage comprised two aides and two servants, the latter dressed in livery of the Washington colors and riding horses bedecked with the Washington coat-of-arms. And the hero of the Monongahela did attract public notice in Philadelphia, New York, and Boston. The most prominent inhabitants welcomed him as their guest. Boston's *Gazette* described him as "a Gentleman who has deservedly a high Reputation for Military Skill, Integrity, and Valor; tho' Success has not always attended his Undertakings." Reportedly he would "consult" with General Shirley about "measures" regarding the Southern Indians.[13]

Though Shirley vindicated the colonel's superiority to Dagworthy, he failed to alter the status of the Virginian troops. Nor did he grant brevet commissions to the officers as Dinwiddie had urged. Worse, he put Governor Sharpe in charge of the next intercolonial assault on the Ohio Forks. George apparently had entertained some pretensions to head that expedition himself. He certainly would never subordinate himself to a man he considered the source of his recent distresses. He "went to Williamsburg fully resolved to resign. . . ."[14]

His ambition quickly overcame his anger, though. Instead of resigning, he applied to Shirley for appointment as second-in-command of the new offensive and asked Sharpe to endorse him. Happily, both governors readily assented. Unhappily, news arrived almost simultaneously that a new commander-in-chief, Lord Loudoun, would replace Shirley.[15] The aspiring soldier must labor all over again to establish his "interest."

No sooner had Washington returned from Boston in the spring of 1756 than accusations burst in Williamsburg against the regimental officers at Fort Cumberland. Allegedly they had committed irregularities in recruiting, neglected discipline, and practiced and permitted drunkenness and immorality. Governor Dinwiddie reported that the Assembly was "greatly inflamed." Councillor Fairfax said they might conduct an inquiry. Speaker Robinson urged George to go to the post and put a stop to the misconduct.[16]

These criticisms particularly distressed Washington because they came just when French and Indian ravages had whipped the frontier into a panic. Confessing that he had stayed away from Fort Cumberland to avoid a confrontation with Captain Dagworthy, he protested that he had "never failed to send" proper orders to regulate the contingent there. In the future, he would enforce discipline rigorously. He saw little prospect "of gaining Honor and Reputation," he said. He implied he might resign but because of the desperate situation on the frontier promised to stay on for now.[17]

His Williamsburg patrons reassured George that no one blamed him for the misconduct of some of his officers. They did think, though, that a small knot of unnamed political enemies wanted to engineer his replacement. Still, "a very great majority of our House would prefer you to any Person," said the influential Charles Carter, "and in order to prev[en]t a superior command are determind the men to be raisd by lot shall not be marchd out of the Colony." He should ignore attacks upon him, advised his friends; his merit would receive its due reward.[18]

Through the rest of the spring and into the summer of 1756, Washington kept warning of the jeopardy of the frontier. Speaker Robinson and Councillor Fairfax thought the Assembly at last was awakening to that danger. Regard for him remained high, they said. "Our hopes Dear

George," wrote Robinson, "are all fixed on You. . . ." Meanwhile, the
frontier settlers, "[d]espairing of assistance and protection from below
. . . talk[ed] of capitulating and coming upon terms with the French and
Indians. . . ." To the patriotic Washington, these were thoughts "unworthy . . . of a British Subject."[19]

His countrymen were deeply suspicious of soldiers: armies, they
feared, would sooner maraud civilians than fight the enemy. So, the
colonel cracked down on his troops. He ordered his officers to keep the
soldiers from plundering the people, to stop swearing, gambling, drunkenness, brawling, and desertion, to maintain orderly behavior and appearance.[20] Despite these attempts to forestall further criticism, in September the censure he feared struck like a bolt of lightning.

Since April, the *Virginia Gazette* had been publishing a series of essays by "The Virginia Centinel." Reprinted in other colonies, they were
perhaps the most widely read periodical articles in British North
America before 1764. They denounced laggard support of the war and
exhorted patriots to resist the French Catholic enemy. "Centinel No. I"
lamented "that even such an acceptable and popular Officer as Col.
Washington" had been unable to rouse adequate enlistments. That must
have offered George some comfort. But "Centinel No. III" asserted that
militia troops inspired and properly trained by gentlemen officers could
answer "all the Purposes of a standing army, without the Expence to
the Country. . . ." This was a reflexive declaration of Whig faith and a
backhanded way of saying Virginia could do without Washington's
regiment.[21]

Then in September, "Centinel No. X" charged that men devoid of
military experience who had mismanaged their private affairs had secured regimental commissions and promotions through influential connections. Abusing their authority, these officers mistreated the soldiers,
discouraged the militiamen from striving for a share of public honor,
and permitted and practiced idleness and vice. Worst of all, "sculking
in Forts," they made no attempt to stop the enemy as it "ravaged in
their very Neighborhood. . . ." "Censure cannot be silenced," said the
"Centinel," "nor can the Public receive much Advantage from a Regiment of such dastardly debauchees."[22]

The criticism of the quality of appointments was undoubtedly aimed
at Governor Dinwiddie. Virginia leaders, including Northern Neck
neighbors of Washington, had privately accused him of favoring Scottish cronies while neglecting worthy members of the provincial gentry.
Though the "Centinel" omitted mention of Colonel Washington, the

charges of disorder and immorality and particularly of cowardice could hardly have left the commander-in-chief untouched.

George wanted to defend his honor in the public prints. He wanted to resign. But his friends in Williamsburg counseled him to keep mum and do his duty. Above all, he should not resign. The Burgesses and the public still supported him. Besides, the criticism was aimed more at others.[23] Washington would apply this advice when his actions were assailed during the Revolution and his presidency. At the moment, he had trouble seeing its wisdom. Despite his best efforts, he seemed to lose honor instead of winning it.

If he resigned, George's political supporters believed, Dinwiddie would replace him with his fellow Scot, Colonel James Innes. Dinwiddie's appointment of Innes in 1754 to take command of colonial troops had provoked the foolhardy advance which had ended with Washington's humiliation at Fort Necessity. Since then, there had been no love lost between the two. Innes's appointment now, wrote brother Augustine from Williamsburg, would be "disagreeable . . . to the whole colony (a few Scotchmen excepted) & I must believe as much so to you as any in particular." Hang on, he urged, until George could learn from Lord Loudoun "what prospect you stand to be put on the British establishment. . . ." If he resigned, the officers would quit, the common soldiers would desert, the province would stand defenseless, and "you will be blamed by your Country more for that than every other action of yr life."[24]

As if to confirm Augustine's warning, the indignant regimental officers gave notice that unless the Assembly repudiated the charges of the "Centinel," they would resign en masse. Colonel Washington skillfully quelled their ire. Though deeply wounded himself and still threatening to turn in his own commission, he heeded his friends' advice and stayed on.[25] By keeping his complaints private and sticking to his duty, he showed not only greater maturity, but a shrewder sense of his own best interests.

Meanwhile, Washington started a campaign to win the attention of Lord Loudoun. He already had Governor Shirley's endorsement to appoint him second-in-command on the next Ohio offensive. At his request, Governor Dinwiddie again recommended him for a royal commission, pointing out his merits, his hardships, and his popularity in Virginia. George himself penned a petition to his Lordship in the name of the regiment. Though not endorsed officially from Williamsburg, this effort had the support of his political patrons. Expecting Loudoun to visit Virginia, he intended to whip his troops into shape. He also backed Dinwiddie's recommendation of a new drive to recapture the Ohio Forks.[26]

Confronted with both the desperate situation on the frontier and criticism of his conduct, Washington grew increasingly impatient.[27] The effort to gain Loudoun's ear seemed wasted. His Lordship announced no offensive against Fort Duquesne. Nor did he acknowledge that Virginia's officers merited regular commissions. Instead, he had brought orders to raise troops in America and place them under officers imported from Europe. What more proof did Washington need of bias against colonials? Worse, a dispute over military policy pitted Colonel Washington against, not only Dinwiddie and the Executive Council, but Loudoun himself.

Throughout the last half of 1756, Washington argued with the governor and Council against keeping Virginia troops at Fort Cumberland in Maryland. He thought the place useless because of its distance from Virginia's frontier. He preferred to have it demolished to prevent its capture by the enemy. If it must be maintained, Maryland should shoulder the burden of a citadel in its own province. The present policy weakened his defensive plan, a chain of frontier stockade forts and a major fortress at Winchester. Dinwiddie and his councillors disagreed. General Braddock had established Fort Cumberland; only another imperial official could order its destruction. Until such time, Virginia must help maintain it, and Washington must keep part of his force there.[28]

As in other cases, Washington maneuvered around the governor to enlist the support of influential Burgesses.[29] In this disagreement over Fort Cumberland, in the concern to prevent Colonel Innes or any other outsider from replacing George as commander of the colony's troops, in the preference for him rather than Governor Sharpe to head the next expedition to the Ohio, these politicians and Washington connived to defeat actions of the governor and Crown they thought harmful to Virginia's interests. Their collaboration was another phase of the continuing struggle for control of Virginia's government which pitted provincially based political leaders against agents of the imperial administration and their local allies.

As soon as Washington had made his case against Fort Cumberland to Governor Dinwiddie, he wrote to Speaker Robinson. Mr. Speaker convened a House committee to investigate, but Dinwiddie remained adamant.[30] From August through November 1756, Washington fought the policy. Finally, on 10 December, Dinwiddie reported Lord Loudoun's rejection of the colonel's plan. He had ordered evacuation of the frontier stockades, required reinforcement of Cumberland, and warned that George's previous failure to do so "will have a bad Effect as to the Dominion: & will not have a good Appearance at Home." Washington carried out these commands but made sure the settlers knew that abandonment of the frontier had been against his advice.[31] During the Revolution, he would never disparage his civilian superiors to the public.

George complained to his confidant Robinson that these foolish instructions had come just when his measures had begun to calm the panicked settlers. His advice was "disregarded as idle & frivolous; my propositions and measures, as partial & selfish. . . . My Orders are dark, doubtful and uncertain; *to day approved, tomorrow condemned.* . . ." Once again, it seemed Crown officials were ignoring the province's military experts and defensive needs while insisting upon their own authority and ill-conceived policies. Yet George vowed to "bear up under all the embarrassments some time longer; in hope of better Regulation on the arrival of Lord Loudoun; to whom I look for the future fate of Virginia."[32]

He feared, though, that Dinwiddie had misrepresented his views, had prejudiced Loudoun against him. He decided to go over the governor's head. He must advocate personally both his past military measures and the right of the regimental officers to royal commissions. Dinwiddie gave reluctant and rather exasperated consent for him to go to Philadelphia.[33]

Washington had already written a lengthy report outlining Virginia's military situation, describing his problems of supply, discipline, and desertion, and sharply criticizing the Assembly's failure to support adequate defensive measures. Originally he had included Dinwiddie in his strictures but then prudently decided to delete those comments. He also pressed for an offensive against Fort Duquesne as the only means of removing the threat to the frontier. Presently, he sent this able analysis along to Loudoun. His Lordship appeared duly impressed. The colonel intended this paper not simply to inform the commander-in-chief of conditions in Virginia, but also to display his own expertise and to seek preferment for the regimental officers and, particularly, for himself.[34]

Washington hoped to find in "your Lordship our Patron. . . . Altho' I have not the Honour to be known to Your Lordship: Yet, Your Lordship's Name was familiar to my Ear, on account of the Important Services performed to His Majesty in other parts of the World—don't think

My Lord I am going to flatter. I have exalted Sentiments of Your Lordships Character, and revere Your Rank . . . my nature is honest, and Free from Guile[.]"

Getting to the point, he explained that the Virginia officers, tantalized to anticipate "a better Establishment," had waited "in tedious expectation. . . ." The ill-fated General Braddock had promised Washington himself "preferment equal to my Wishes. . . . General Shirley was not unkind in His Promises" either, but he had gone to England. Complimenting the great man further on his "Ability and Experience," the eager petitioner hoped he would "condescend to point out the way" toward redress of these grievances. He also composed a flowery address in the name of "The Officers of The Virginia Regiment," soliciting Loudoun's patronage. Neither report nor address directly requested incorporation into the regular army, but that was Washington's object.[35]

To James Thomas Flexner, Washington's "clumsy" try at flattery showed he "lacked . . . the necessary turn of mind for a courtier."[36] In fact, he eventually overcame this early awkwardness, later displaying the graceful courtly skills and verbal finesse of a diplomat, albeit in a distinctively republican American fashion. More important, these addresses to Loudoun, when read alongside a letter Washington sent simultaneously to Dinwiddie, reveal a significant development in his political identity and thinking. The letter written to the governor on behalf of the Virginia officers does not shuffle with the bowing and scraping of the addresses to Lord Loudoun. It states their complaints bluntly, even bitingly.

The Virginia regiment, begins that remonstrance, "was the first in arms of any Troops" in British America. It had served continuously ever since, while other colonials took the field only seasonally. Matching the regulars in enlistment, training, discipline, equipage, and service, declared Washington, "we want nothing but Commissions from His Majesty to make us as regular a Corps as any upon the Continent. . . . [W]e labour under every disadvantage, and enjoy not one single benefit which regulars do." The colonel was not simply boasting. At least some regular officers distinguished the Virginia troops he had trained from other provincials.

Aiming a barb Dinwiddie's way, he suggested that the Crown had neglected the Virginia officers because "our Services are slighted, or have not been properly represented to His Majesty: otherwise the best of Kings would have graciously taken Notice of Us in turn. . . ." This was unfair. The governor had repeatedly recommended royal commissions, particularly praising Washington's merit. No matter. The Virginian felt increasingly certain, and not without cause, that he and his fellow officers had suffered discriminatory treatment because they were colonials.

"We cant conceive, that being Americans shoud deprive us of the benefits of British Subjects; nor lessen our claim to preferment: and we are very certain, that no Body of regular Troops ever before Servd 3 Bloody Campaigns without attracting Royal Notice." He rejected as "whimsical & absurd" the argument that they defended their "own properties." "We are Defending the Kings Dominions. . . . Some boast of long Service as a claim to Promotion—meaning I suppose, the length of time they have pocketed a Commission. . . . It is the service done, not the Service engag'd in, that merits reward. . . ." The provincial colonel felt, he noted sarcastically, "as equitable a right to expect something for three years hard & bloody Service, as for 10 spent at St. James's &ca where real Service, or a Field of Battle never was seen."[37]

Washington's anger at unequal treatment of colonials was not new, but it was intensifying. More important, he was beginning to connect that grievance to the entire British system of deference, dependence, and patronage, as his jibe about St. James's shows. Ambitious and patriotic, this young colonial Englishman was coming to believe that the Empire rewarded those with "interest," in modern parlance "connections," not those with merit. To press forward his career, to gain public honor, he was having to play the deferential game again by soliciting the support of Lord Loudoun.[38]

Significantly, the memorial to Loudoun in the name of the officers is an edited version of the letter to Dinwiddie, but with a remarkable change of tone. The peremptory manner of the letter virtually demands Crown commissions as a rightful reward. The memorial, shorn of the complaints of colonial discrimination, "humbly" begs Loudoun's patronage to redress their grievances. The letter is a step toward republicanism and nationalism. The memorial is another attempt to operate within the British imperial system, a system whose justice Washington was beginning to doubt.

Loudoun received the memorial and Washington's report but offered no promise of royal commissions. Also, there would be no expedition against Fort Duquesne during 1757. On the bright side, henceforth Maryland would garrison Fort Cumberland, while the Virginia troops maintained Fort Loudoun and the chain of frontier forts. This decision in effect endorsed Colonel Washington's previous measures.[39] But he and his officers counted Loudoun's failure to act on their petition as another instance of anticolonial discrimination, denying them the reward merited by faithful service.

"Be distinguished from the common run"

By the autumn of 1757, Washington had become convinced that Governor Dinwiddie was helping to block a regular commission for him. Dinwiddie not only found this accusation unfair, he was angered by George's conniving with Assembly leaders against him. "My Conduct to Yo. from the Begining was always Friendly," said Dinwiddie, "but Yo. know I had g[rea]t Reason to suspect Yo. of Ingratitude. . . ." "I do not know," rejoined Washington, "that I ever gave Your Honor cause to suspect me of ingratitude, a crime I detest, and would most carefully avoid." [1]

Here again is the language of a deferential political order. As Washington's powerful "friend" and patron, Dinwiddie would bestow favors upon him for which Washington would show his "gratitude" by pledging his service. Reciprocal obligations and expectations bound superior and subordinate by ties of patronage and deference.

Though Washington had gotten his start through the "friendly" aid of Dinwiddie and other patrons, he felt increasingly ambivalent about the system of deference and dependence. William Fairfax now wanted regimental lieutenant's commissions for his sons Bryan and Billy. Washington wriggled uncomfortably under these requests. Granting them would supersede veteran ensigns who had earned promotions. He asked the governor to order Billy Fairfax's appointment so that he could distance himself from the decision.

More and more, he resisted patronage appointments as an injustice which provoked the discontent of experienced officers. He advocated appointment and promotion based on merit, seniority, and service. Requesting authority to fill up vacancies himself, he pledged to observe "the strictest justice." Already he was beginning to practice that impartiality for which he would later receive such high praise. Still, Washington willingly acted as the patron and benefactor of his own friends. Some of these favors he justified because he was helping regimental officers he thought deserving of advancement and regular army commissions. The fact was, his interventions succeeded less through their merit than through his position and connections.[2]

This contradictory conduct reflected something deeper than a double standard. It indicated an important ideological transition taking place in the minds of many colonials. Washington's "impartiality" was not simply a laudable trait of personal character, as his biographers have thought. It represented a shift in social values. His handling of regimental appointments and promotions shows a movement away from an ideology of deference, "interest," and honor, toward an ideology espousing reward of individual talent and service according to supposedly objective criteria. He never intended to level the social hierarchy. The lower orders should defer to their superiors. But within the governing classes, he was coming to believe, men should rise on the basis of their personal merits.

In the long run, Americans would celebrate Washington's "impartiality" as a way of affirming their belief that their society lived up to its ideals of individualistic meritocracy. In the mid-1750s, ambitious young colonials like Washington were taking the first steps toward those convictions. Meanwhile, he must try to operate within the existing deferential system. This partly explains the seeming contradiction between his impartiality regarding regimental appointments and his efforts to gain "interest" for himself and his friends with Lord Loudoun and others.

Washington's impartiality also expressed a "professional" military ethic. Despite his protest about "ingratitude," he was coming to think of himself less as a subordinate seeking favors and more as a patriotic and expert soldier who had earned advancement. His pledge to reward merit and to administer discipline evenhandedly was part of his effort to bring the regiment up to regular army standards. The memorial to Lord Loudoun asserted attainment of that goal. The regiment's improved performance in 1757–8 bore out his claim and justified his methods.[3]

Washington had apparently given up any hope of a royal commission, but he continued his quest for public honor. At last, imperial authorities had decided to launch another offensive in 1758 against Fort Duquesne, this time under Brigadier General John Forbes. He sought no favors from the general, Washington declared. Still, he "would gladly be distinguished in some measure from the *common run* of provincial officers. . . ." This could "hardly be deemed an unreasonable request. . . ." After all, "I have been much longer in the service than any provincial officer in America." Disappointingly, Forbes offered him nothing.[4]

On this expedition, Washington again clashed repeatedly with regular officers. He and his fellow Virginians strenuously resisted cutting a new road directly across Pennsylvania. They favored the somewhat longer but already existing Virginia route opened by Braddock's army. Washington disagreed partly because of an honest difference of opinion regarding a difficult military decision, but intercolonial rivalry also entered into the argument, as it had on Braddock's expedition. Virginians and Pennsylvanians interested in the Ohio Valley Indian trade and land speculation favored the respective routes that would channel postwar business to their own provinces. Influenced by this partisanship, Washington concluded that General Forbes and the other regulars had been dupes "or something worse" of "P-s-v-n [Pennsylvanian] Artifice." "It has long been the luckless Fate of Poor Virginia," he complained, "to fall a Victum to the views of her Crafty Neighbours. . . ."[5]

From June through October 1758, he and the Virginian officers rattled out a drumfire of dissent against the Pennsylvanian route.[6] Only in late September, after General Forbes had rebuked him and Colonel William Byrd of the Second Virginia Regiment, did he even begin to mute his criticism. Then shifting his ground, he urged Forbes to supply Fort Duquesne, once it was captured, by Braddock's road.[7]

A third motive throbbed behind Washington's strenuous opposition. If he had given up his hope of military preferment, he had yet to slake his thirst for public honor. His vision of military glory had long centered on reclaiming the Ohio Forks for the British Crown. Now he fretted that Forbes's decision would thwart him once more. It seemed that the stubborn and stupid refusal of British regulars to heed the advice of experienced provincials perpetually blocked him from winning the distinction for which he strove. Perhaps the general would decide to send ahead "a Body of light Troops," as Washington recommended. If so, he prayed Colonel Bouquet's "Interest . . . to get my Regiment and myself Included. . . ." On 2 September 1758, his rage spilled over:

"That appearance of Glory once in view, that hope, that laudable Ambition of serving Our Country, and meriting its applause, is now no more!"[8]

The excruciatingly slow advance as the army hacked its way through the rain-drenched autumn woods fed these fears. In the second week of November, a council of war confirmed them when it decided to postpone the final assault until spring. Just then, three captured prisoners reported the weakness of Fort Duquesne. Seizing the moment, Forbes selected 2500 men to march rapidly to the Forks. He divided them into three temporary brigades. Regular officers headed the first two. Washington received command of the third.

Here at last was distinction, if only for this one operation. Perhaps the general intended merely to recognize the colonel's seniority among provincial officers rather than his merit. Even so, no other colonial attained such a rank, and, as Douglas Southall Freeman observed, "many a Colonel of the regular establishment, twice his age, had aspired in vain" to the status of brigadier general.[9]

Washington's contingent of provincials spearheaded this urgent movement. Despite the prisoners' encouraging report, the calendar still threatened failure. Although the Assembly had extended the pay of the Second Virginia Regiment until January, their enlistments legally ended on 1 December. The ill-clad soldiers could choose to head home at that time. Meanwhile, Maryland, Pennsylvania, and North Carolina had failed to appropriate funds for their forces after that date.[10] Unless Forbes's advance brigades flew to meet the suddenly less formidable enemy, a substantial number would dissolve before his eyes. With them would go the general's hope of immediate victory and Washington's dream of a final moment of glory to cap his performance in the war.

On 24 November 1758, the select troops camped just twelve miles short of the goal and prepared for the final assault. But that night, startling news! Scouts returning from the Forks announced that the French and their Indian allies had evacuated Fort Duquesne, burned it to the ground, and fled down the river. The next day's march confirmed this intelligence.[11]

Friends had wished for Washington to return from the campaign crowned with laurels. That hope now lay in a heap of ashes in the western wilderness. Colonial and British periodicals had hardly noticed his presence on the expedition. Returning to Virginia in December, he finally did what he had threatened so many times. He resigned his commission.[12]

Despite the vexations of the past five and one-half years, Washington had matured strikingly as a soldier and leader, demonstrating a remarkable capacity to grow in response to each new and greater challenge. This is particularly noteworthy because he largely taught himself. Learning from his mistakes, he made sure to avoid the foolish and disastrous errors of the spring of 1754. From 1755 on, his letters show he had outgrown his earlier cocksureness and bravado. Guided by military books and occasional service with regulars, he molded his regiment into an efficient fighting force. His reports to his superiors skillfully analyzed frontier conditions and proposed measures that, despite an almost endless series of problems, generally proved effective.[13]

Still, Washington had much to learn about military leadership, most especially about the role of soldiers in colonial American society. His adherence to an ethos of military professionalism was at odds with the thinking of most provincials. He had chafed under the constraints of civilian authorities. "Chimney Corner Politicians," he called them. They had denied him the full means to defend the province, including emergency authority to appropriate civilians' goods and to quarter his soldiers in civilians' houses. Circumstances had at times compelled extralegal actions, he asserted, but the legislators, "tenacious of Liberty, and prone to Censure; condemn all Proceedings that are not strictly Lawful, never considering what Causes may arise to make it necessary and excusable."[14] Though Washington had tried to keep his troops orderly, he was not yet fully attuned to the deep-seated fear in his society of military abuses of power.

Meanwhile, lobbying vigorously on behalf of his regiment and frontier defense, he aligned himself with provincial politicians in their bid to expand the power of the lower House. But he also played the governor and the Burgesses against one another and criticized all of them to Lord Loudoun. This less than full respect for his civilian superiors would contrast sharply with the conduct of the American commander-in-chief two decades later.

One must avoid exaggerating the impact of this friction and of Washington's occasional outbursts against his superiors. He inspired admiration and support among Virginia's rulers and gained the confidence, even the attachment, of the frontier settlers and the regimental officers. "In our earliest Infancy you took us under your tuition," said his officers, "trained us up in the Practice of that Discipline, which alone can constitute good Troops." The very language of this "humble address" shows that in Virginia's deferential society the twenty-six-year-old had already risen to become one of the "fathers" of his country.[15]

The confidence he inspired, the willingness of others to follow his lead, partly flowed from the impression Washington made on them. His friend George Mercer's contemporary description captured that impression:

"He may be described as being as straight as an Indian, measuring six feet two inches in his stockings, and weighing 175 pounds. . . . His frame is padded with well-developed muscles, indicating great strength. . . . His head is well shaped though not large, but is gracefully poised on a superb neck . . . blue-gray penetrating eyes, which are widely separated and overhung by a heavy brow. . . . A pleasing, benevolent, though a commanding countenance. . . . His features are regular and placid, with all the muscles of his face under perfect control, though flexible and expressive of deep feeling when moved by emotions. In conversation he looks you full in the face, is deliberate, deferential and engaging. His voice is agreeable rather than strong. His demeanor at all times composed and dignified. His movements and gestures are graceful, his walk is majestic, and he is a splendid horseman."[16]

Throughout his career, those who met George Washington noted these same features and qualities. They believed the man's physical appearance and manner expressed his character. Few realized that he presented his audience with a studied performance. He had taken his natural endowments and was carefully cultivating them.

He stood a full head taller than most of the soldiers he commanded.[17] He also repeatedly demonstrated his physical strength and stamina, particularly on the arduous embassy to the French in the winter of 1753, but he was no mere muscular giant. He took dancing lessons, studied fencing, and became, as Mercer said, "a splendid horseman." He moved with agile grace and dignity whether afoot or on horseback.

He would never have said clothes make the man, but he and his culture believed they told much about his social status and inner worth. And so he spent considerable time and money selecting his apparel. He intended to make his appearance reflect a particular image of his personal and social character.

He also continued to train himself in the art of social intercourse, skills he had first learned when copying over the "Rules of Civility" as a youth. The driving ambition and the anxiety about his reputation apparent in his letters perhaps convey the misimpression of a difficult and disagreeable young man. He confined these complaints to private correspondence. His companions found him congenial: in George Mercer's words, "deferential and engaging," and in the words of the regimental officers, "affable." His approaches to social superiors in the imperial establishment, men such as General Shirley and Lord Loudoun, were the awkward initial attempts of a man who became increasingly skillful in courtly manners.

In all of this, Washington labored to fashion for himself a public persona. In this honor-based culture, such self-presentation was the means by which a gentleman registered and won community validation of his claim to social merit. Thereby, he also established his sense of self-worth. Yet Washington's effort exceeded the requirements for attaining public honor. His quest for military glory and meticulous molding of his public self already displayed a hunger for wider fame.

His careful creation of a public self additionally demonstrated his talents as a political actor. By combining a remarkable natural physical endowment, an acute sense of other people's responses to him, and an actor's craftsmanlike understanding of how to shape his performance, he had begun to create the majestic "presence" that would constitute one of his chief assets. This ability was perhaps his most important political gift.

These years of military service also changed Washington's perception of the British Empire and of his relation to it. He and other Virginians felt imperial administrators had neglected their province's needs, violated its rights, and thwarted its interests. He remained unaware of the extent of his own provincialism. His disputatiousness over Braddock's and Forbes's routes, his concern to protect Virginians' stake in western lands and the fur trade, and his collaboration with Williamsburg politicians to control military policy all advocated local interests. His views of military strategy, too, remained local, ignoring that the greatest threat to the British provinces came from French Canada, just above New England. He expected imperial officials to make the capture of Fort Duquesne a major priority. If they paid too little attention to the danger on Virginia's frontiers, for his part he had too weak a grasp of the overall war effort.

In the long run, though, Washington's wartime experience had begun to break down his parochialism. After the Ohio Forks had been recaptured, he recommended that Virginia superintend its fur trade to prevent rascals from alienating the Indians and to win for the colony a "large share" of that commerce. He also proposed that commissioners from the concerned provinces fashion a "general system" to bar one colony or its unscrupulous traders from undermining the Indian trade of other colonies.[18] To be sure, he meant to safeguard Virginia's economic interests and military security, but instead of merely denouncing Pennsylvania's rivalry as unpatriotic selfishness, he was considering how to accommodate the competing interests of neighboring colonies. He had begun to think that his province's safety and prosperity might lie in intercolonial cooperation.

Much of his "schooling" in these years taught Washington a far more painful lesson about his place in the British Empire. In the early days of the war, he burned to rouse "the heroick spirit of every free-born Englishman to assert the rights and privileges of our king (if we don't consult the benefit of ourselves) and resque [rescue] from the invasions of a usurping enemy, our majesty's property, his dignity, and lands." His eagerness to defend his "King and Country" expressed his identity as a British American, or, more accurately, an American Briton.[19]

When he and his contemporaries, including Governor Dinwiddie, referred to Virginia as "our country," they never implied a distinctive nationality. In the eighteenth century, the term *country* was primarily a geographical designation. For Virginians, "the country" might also mean the provincial government. Washington viewed Virginians as members of the British nation. He thought of himself as an Englishman in America, "Defending," as he put it, "the Kings Dominions."[20]

He saw no conflict between these professions of patriotic zeal and his ambition for public honor. His patrons had taught him that faithful service would reap the reward of royal favor.[21] For several years now, supporters in Virginia, in other colonies, and even in the regular army had shared his hope that at long last the Crown would recognize and reward his merits. They agreed that imperial officials had unjustly neglected him. Some had even suggested that if his services, as well as his advice, continued to be ignored, he might find retirement at Mount Vernon more satisfying.[22]

In his quest for a Crown commission Washington never specified the rank he wanted. Nor did he say if he intended to pursue a military career after the war and outside Virginia. He only said, "My inclinations are strongly bent to arms."[23] If his larger dreams remain obscure, he made unmistakably clear his eagerness for appointment as a regular officer.

Considering his age, his brief time in the service, and his lack of connections in England, some historians have concluded that he prob-

ably sought a majority. Anything higher would have been unrealistic.
But young Washington had always aimed high. He rated his regiment
as equal in every respect to any regular unit. Likewise, he considered
his provincial colonelcy equivalent to a royal commission of the same
rank. From at least August 1755 on, when he took the command the
second time, he seems to have expected imperial officials simply to incorporate the Virginia regiment into the regular army and to exchange
the officers' colonial commissions for Crown appointments. He never
offered to buy a commission of any rank. His sense of honor required
that he receive one in recognition of his patriotic and meritorious
service.[24]

Unsurprisingly then, the disdain of many regular officers for their
provincial counterparts infuriated him. The refusal of Crown officials
to recognize his services and reward his merits embittered him. This
collision with anticolonial bias started an important change in his sense
of himself and of his colony in relation to the mother country. It produced in him a kind of negative identity as a British colonial. He concluded that the powerful men who had thwarted his rise and neglected
his province were relegating him and his fellow colonials to an inferior
status within the Empire. Other Americans were having similar thoughts.
Washington had begun to question the justice of the British political
system. As so often happens in history, what became political resistance
started with a personal grievance.[25]

Ironically, Washington had won much the sort of public honor he
had originally aimed for. Most of his fellow Virginians held him in high
esteem. Early in the war, he had achieved a few moments of glory and
one of acute embarrassment. Throughout the continent and across the
ocean, powerful men had taken note of him. Although the rest of his
wartime service received less attention outside his native province, he
had compiled a distinguished record. He had risen far and fast, but had
failed to attain the full glory for which he yearned. As his first military
career neared its end, he expressed his long-held belief that an irresist-
ible "destiny" controlled human affairs.[26] If this conviction gave him
hope that an overruling power might have greater things in store, his
deep feeling of injustice smothered the comforting thought.

He received the plaudits of his countrymen with as much grace as he
could muster under the circumstances. Although the wider war went on
and a new threat from the Cherokees arose on Virginia's southwestern
frontier, the greatest menace to the colony had fallen with Fort Du-

quesne. He could resign without fear of censure. He "quit [the] Military Life" hoping, he said, "to find more happiness in retirement than I ever experienc'd amidst a wide and bustling World. . . ."[27] Late in December 1758, with a bitter sense of accumulated grievance, George Washington brought to an end his career as a soldier. Two months later, he observed his twenty-seventh birthday.

CHAPTER SIX

"I deal little in Politics"

Disappointed in his dream of military glory, Colonel George Washington retired as commander of Virginia's provincial regiment in December 1758 and shifted the direction of his propulsive ambition. Taking at face value his declaration henceforth to seek satisfaction in retirement, his biographers have usually assumed he now turned his back on public life. For the next decade and a half, the standard interpretation goes, he gave himself over primarily to the care of his plantation "family," to the promotion of his business ventures, and to the needs of his neighborhood. He made provincial politics a secondary concern, pushed events in the larger world to the periphery of his mind. Douglas Southall Freeman and other biographers have concluded that private experiences during this interim (1758–75) between the Seven Years' War and the Revolution worked a remarkable change in him. Personal challenges constituted a kind of spiritual schooling. They caused him to mature emotionally, preparing him for his later public service.[1]

A fresh look at the evidence suggests that Washington's biographers have misunderstood his ambitions and development during these years. He remained active in provincial politics and attentive to colonial-imperial relations. He continued to develop his skills and style as a leader. Contrary to Freeman's opinion, he underwent a transformation not so much of personal character as of political perspective. At least as important as his emotional maturation was his increasing political sophistication. Contemporary political events and ideology drastically altered his outlook. They also taught him to tailor his conduct and his presentation of himself so that he could satisfy his still burning desire for public honor.

Even before he retired from military service, Washington had been planning to advance his political ambitions. In spring 1758, Virginia's new governor, Francis Fauquier, dissolved the Assembly and called for elections. At the time, Colonel Washington was at Fort Cumberland readying his troops to join General Forbes's army. Even so, he decided to stand for the Burgesses. Virginia law permitted a man to vote and hold office in any county in which he owned sufficient property. Washington chose to run, not in his home county of Fairfax, but in the newer and more westerly Frederick County, where he was looked up to as the protector of the frontier. He and Colonel Thomas Bryan Martin, Lord Fairfax's nephew and his land agent in the county, would challenge the incumbents. In Washington's absence, his friends conducted the politicking on his behalf.

The key to success in Virginia's class-based politics was one's "interest" with other gentrymen. Washington's supporters included the leading gentlemen of the Northern Neck. To manage his campaign, he selected the two most active and influential politicians in that region. Gabriel Jones, known as the "Valley Lawyer," represented several counties in the Assembly over three decades and held a host of local offices. Colonel James Wood was a founder and leading citizen of Winchester, Frederick's county seat, and a proponent of Potomac River Valley development. On election day, Wood sat on the bench in Winchester to take the poll for Washington. Jones and John Hite, another leader in the county and an active town-builder, worked the crowd making sure that yeomen who had pledged their support voted as promised.

During the campaign and on election day, important personages from Fairfax County who owned land in Frederick came up to exert their influence among the small farmers and common planters with whom they had personal connections. These gentlemen included Washington's patron, Colonel William Fairfax; Fairfax's son, Colonel George William; and Colonel John Carlyle, a Fairfax son-in-law and prominent Alexandria merchant. Officers of the regiment stationed at Winchester also worked on behalf of their commander.[2]

Washington needed more than the backing of propertied gentlemen. Election of Burgesses was the only occasion on which Virginia's yeomen could select public officeholders. Though excluded from major offices themselves, they had a voice in deciding which gentrymen would sit in the Assembly. Typically they followed the lead of the most prominent local gentlemen, but as the eighteenth century wore on that deference became less automatic, especially in frontier areas like Frederick. To ensure victory, gentlemen candidates must renew their "interest" with ordinary freeholders, must reaffirm the reciprocal obligations between them.

The votes of yeomen "goe as farr as those of men of sence," complained one of Washington's friends in exasperation. Gabriel Jones and John Kirkpatrick thought they detected a slippage among precisely these voters. "[T]he promises of the Vulgar," warned Kirkpatrick, "are too precarious to build your hopes upon. . . ." James Wood saw no such decline, but experience had convinced him, "there is no relying on the promises of the common herd, the promise is too often forgot when the back is turned." All three agreed on the importance of the colonel's presence at least on election day, to bolster wavering voters. Lord Fairfax, showing his interest in the election, anxiously observed that young Washington would be "very hard pushed."[3]

Some freeholders feared the colonel could not attend the Assembly and defend them at the same time. His supporters responded not only by praising their candidate's character, but by trumpeting his "Superior interest, both here & in the House." In other words, they argued that Washington's property, business dealings, military service, and personal ties gave him a stake and influence in Frederick County. At the same time, his connections, expertise, and position carried clout in Williamsburg.[4]

The campaigners vigorously pressed Washington's cause in his absence. Still, they urged that he come to Winchester on election day. Heeding their advice, he requested a brief leave. His superior, the regular colonel Henry Bouquet, granted it, but Adam Stephen, Washington's lieutenant colonel, reported from the Raystown camp that Bouquet had hesitated because he was attached "to regularity, duty & discipline" and thought "himself answerable for What happens in your Absence." Taking this private intelligence into account, Washington immediately wrote back to Bouquet. He felt obligated for the favor, he said, but "at this juncture I can hardly perswade myself to think of being absent from my more immediate Duty, even for a few days." He would withhold a final decision until he got further word from his political advisers in Winchester.[5]

Washington expected this update within a day. It is usually assumed that reassuring information about the election and his devotion to duty convinced him to stay with his regiment. But another motive has gone unnoticed: his continuing quest for military glory. He worried that he might miss out on a final moment of victory in the war. He chose, he said, "to leave the management of [his election] to the care of my Friends, than be absent from my Regiment when there is a probability of its being call'd upon." News on 21 July 1758 "that a Body of light Troops may soon move on" seemed to confirm this decision. "I pray your Interest, most Sincerely, with the General," he solicited Bouquet, "to get my Regiment and myself Included in the Number."[6]

Although his military endeavors during the succeeding five months would leave him frustrated and furious, the next few days brought a satisfying political victory. The voters of Frederick County came to Winchester on 24 July. Election day was one of the chief ceremonies of colonial Virginia culture. The act of voting was itself a political ritual that reinforced the hierarchial social order. When called by name, each man qualified by property to vote in the county pressed forward and announced for all to hear the two candidates he supported to sit as Burgesses.

Thomas Lord Fairfax, proprietor of the Fairfax grant, county lieutenant of Frederick, senior justice of the County Court, and specially designated justice of the peace for every county in the Northern Neck, cast the first vote. He swung his considerable influence behind his nephew Thomas Bryan Martin and his young protégé George Washington. Second came the leading cleric in those parts, William Meldrum, an Anglican. He too announced for Washington and Martin. Then followed Colonel James Wood. He sat on the bench throughout the election to receive votes on Washington's behalf and to express the candidate's gratitude to each voter personally. This customary political sacrament reiterated the reciprocal ties and obligations between the ruling elite and the people. Wood, of course, voted for Washington, but chose the incumbent Hugh West rather than Martin. Fourth to vote was Colonel John Carlyle, who voted for Washington and Martin.

The poll sheets identified five voters as gentlemen. All gave their support to Washington and Martin. One was Fielding Lewis, "Esqʳ," husband of Washington's sister Betty and a resident of Fredericksburg in Spotsylvania County. Apparently he had come up to use his influence on behalf of his brother-in-law. In addition to the Rev. Mr. Meldrum, two other ministers, a Baptist and a Presbyterian, also voted for the candidates. Another supporter was Dr. James Craik, Colonel Washington's lifelong friend and physician, who, incidentally, named one of his sons George Washington Craik. Eight voters were colonels, captains, or lieutenants in the provincial regiment or one of the county militias. Seven went for Washington, six for Martin. Virtually the entire ruling class of Frederick County and some of the most prominent and wealthy gentlemen of northern Virginia consolidated behind the two candidates.

Led by these propertied gentlemen and under the expert management of Colonel Wood and Lawyer Jones, Washington's and Martin's supporters voted early, putting the two out in front from the first. Washington's enormous popularity as a military hero and defender of the Virginia frontier, the weight of his powerful backers, and the skill of his political handlers won him 309 of the 397 votes cast. The only contest lay between Martin and the incumbent West, who received 240 and 198 votes, respectively. The fourth candidate, Thomas Van Swearingen, also an incumbent Burgess, got a meager 45 votes.[7]

Candidates commonly "treated" the voters to liquid and other refreshments. This violated the election laws but had become customary. It signified a gentleman's "liberality," betokened his sense of class obligation to look after his social inferiors, and reinforced the fact of his economic and social superiority. It probably also bolstered support in frontier counties where class authority had yet to solidify.

Lieutenant Charles Smith managed the alcoholic phase of Washington's campaign, buying and freely dispensing some 160 gallons of wine, rum, punch, and cider. The bill came to more than £39, a sum considerably above the minimum property requirement for voters. The leading candidate had no complaints about the cost of victory. He feared, rather, that Smith might have spent too sparingly.[8]

The new Burgess evidenced his future political ambitions by retaining two copies of the poll sheets among his papers. The first simply listed the voters and their votes in the order in which they came forward. To make this information more useful, Washington himself laboriously alphabetized the poll in four columns, one for each candidate. This would make canvassing the voters much easier when he stood for reelection. These were hardly the actions of a man who intended, as his biographers claim, to withdraw into private life.[9]

The biographers also mistakenly concluded that after his resignation from the regimental command Washington lost interest in military affairs. He certainly had not lost his fascination with military heroes. He wanted to decorate his mansion with busts of Alexander the Great, Julius Caesar, Charles XII of Sweden, and Frederick II, but was unable to obtain them. He did acquire a biography of Oliver Cromwell and later would purchase lives of Charles and Frederick.[10]

The retired colonel also remained concerned about the course of the current war. Relatively few letters written by him during the latter half of the Seven Years' War survive. Most of the extant correspondence went to English merchants. Nevertheless, it not infrequently mentioned wartime developments and Indian troubles on the frontier.

In the very letter in which he asserted his intention to find happiness in retirement, Washington noted that the struggle for control of North America had shifted in favor of Britain. As in subsequent letters, he omitted details because "[t]woud be folly in me to attempt particularising their Action's since you receive Accts. in a Channel so much more direct than from hence." He continued to comment to his trading partners on the progress of British arms and to offer them his observations on the chances of pacifying the Indians. He was also closely following the course of the war in other parts of the world and keeping track of peace negotiations. He knew full well that both the war and the peace would determine the British Empire's prosperity and his own.[11]

Washington kept up to date on military developments not only by reading the gazettes, but also by staying in close contact with the officers who had served under him. Some of them he tried to assist in advancing their military careers. They provided him with intelligence of regimental affairs and of the colony's defensive posture.[12] Most important, the officers considered him their advocate in the Assembly. That role he willingly undertook.

During his first years in the House, Washington played a minor part. Some have incorrectly inferred a lack of interest in the business of the Burgesses. On the contrary, in his usual methodical manner he was learning how that institution worked. He was serving a necessary apprenticeship in the politics of legislation. Session by session through the next decade and a half, one can see him scaling the ladder of power within the House.

He first took his seat in the Assembly in February 1759, on his twenty-seventh birthday. The leadership immediately placed him on the Committee of Propositions and Grievances, which oversaw matters of business and government. He probably also concerned himself with local bills respecting Frederick County and with petitions and accusations regarding provincial officers and soldiers. He sat on several special committees to review some of these claims. Doubtless his fellow Burgesses consulted the House's new resident military expert about legislation continuing the regiment and providing for additional defensive measures. Washington made his interest in that bill clear, staying in Williamsburg for the vote on it and then immediately requesting leave to go home.[13]

In the session of November 1759, the Assembly again passed measures for the defense of Virginia. Although the House Journal fails to indicate what part Washington played in their passage, the records do mention his service on three special committees to consider petitions from an army supplier and two soldiers; in the latter two cases he sat as chair.[14]

Washington missed the brief session of 4–11 March 1760 that planned an expedition against the Cherokees. He stayed home not, as has been thought, because of preoccupation with his farm work, but because he failed to receive timely notice of the meeting. The Assembly met again for three weeks in October. In deciding to raise the regiment to full strength and to maintain it until the following spring, the Burgesses undoubtedly relied on his expertise. They also designated him to wait upon the governor and Council with an address concerning reimbursement of prisoners of war recently released by the French.[15]

During the next Assembly session, in the spring of 1761, Washington made unmistakably clear his concern about military matters. On 12 March, Captain Robert Stewart of the Virginia Regiment wrote him two letters which indicate that the retired commander was exerting his influence on behalf of his former troops. Having recently met with Washington, at his request Stewart wrote a lengthy analysis of the regiment's need for new equipment and supplies and for a fresh recruiting drive. He thought Washington's "Military Knowledge" and legislative position made him "the properest person to represent" these matters to the Burgesses. On 27 March, Washington wrote Stewart from Williamsburg. He expected the House to take positive action. In early April, the legislature authorized the desired recruiting effort to bring the force up to full strength. It also provided for funding and supply of the regiment until 1 December 1761 and planned for its deployment against the Cherokees.[16]

In this session, Washington again sat on the standing Committee of Propositions and Grievances. Facing reelection, he spearheaded measures of concern to his Frederick County constituents. On five occasions, he carried messages from the House up to the Council.[17]

The November 1761 session was convened to vote supplies in case the Cherokees kept up their war. Washington believed the Indians neither wanted this war to go on, nor were "prepard for it," as they had been "solliciting" peace for some time. In this Assembly meeting, he chaired a special committee to examine the petitions of several disabled veterans and introduced a bill to establish the town of Strasburg in the Shenandoah Valley. Because of illness, however, he had to turn over management of the bill to another Burgess.[18]

He stayed home from the one-week session of January 1762, but not, as Freeman thought, out of apathy. Probably he wanted to avoid a recurrence of the illness from which he had recently recovered and which had prevented him from doing full service in the previous gathering. Those Burgesses who did brave the winter weather voted further measures for defense of the colony and recompense of the regimental officers. The latter act fell far short of the officers' expectations, Captain Stewart told Washington, but they had "the great satisfaction to see the most eminent Men in the Country" espouse their cause. Still, he added, "we miss'd your Friendly Offices excessively. . . ."[19]

Washington did make it to the nine-day meeting in March–April 1762 at which the old regiment was disbanded and a new one established. Before going down to Williamsburg for the November–December session, he visited his constituency in Frederick County, probably to familiarize himself with their current requirements. Again he sat on the Committee of Propositions and Grievances and served on several special committees to hear petitions of former soldiers and an officer of the regiment; in the latter case he chaired the committee.[20]

Washington was by no means a key leader during his first four years in the House. But neither were public and, particularly, military affairs matters of marginal interest to him, as his principal biographers have maintained. The assemblyman's most important contributions were his soldierly expertise and his legislative advocacy of the regiment and its officers. During the remaining thirteen years of the colonial era, as subsequent chapters will show, he would become an increasingly influential Burgess.

It has usually been assumed that Washington sought membership in the Assembly reluctantly and only out of a sense of gentlemanly duty. He himself provided the clearest evidence to the contrary in his bare-knuckled 1761 reelection campaign.

Thomas Bryan Martin, the other Frederick County incumbent, chose to retire. Captain George Mercer, who had served in the Virginia Regiment from 1754 to 1760, for a time as Colonel Washington's aide, decided to run for Martin's seat. Following the war, Mercer worked energetically on behalf of the Ohio Company. From 1763 to 1770, he would travel repeatedly to England and live there as the company's London agent. The Mercers belonged to the clique of Northern Neck land barons which included the Washingtons. Eighteenth-century Virginia had no "tickets" or political "parties" in the modern sense of those words, but gentlemen candidates might legitimately "join" their "interests." Washington and Mercer deliberately campaigned together.

The only other serious candidate was Adam Stephen, formerly Washington's lieutenant colonel. The colonel had at times felt annoyed and even angry with his subordinate's conduct. It seems he eventually lost all respect for the man. His biographers have misperceived Washington's vigorous 1761 campaign as a defense of his incumbency against the threat from Stephen. It is unlikely that Stephen intended to challenge his onetime commander. Washington remained popular, his seat secure. One friend foresaw "every appearance of your going with a greater Majority at the next than you did at the last Election. . . ."[21] Because the voters would select two Burgesses, Stephen was probably making his race against Mercer. The biographers have failed to see that Washington aimed his efforts at ensuring Mercer's victory.

As in 1758, Washington's supporters mainly feared that the "common herd" would follow the wrong leader. In February 1761, Captain Robert Stewart wrote from Winchester that Stephen was "traversing this County" and using "every method of making Interest with it's Inhabitants for Electing him. . . ." He promised to sponsor "various Commercial Schemes" to bring Frederick greater prosperity. These plans seemed "strange & chimerical" to Stewart, but they "attracted the attention of the Plebeians, whose unstable Minds are agitated by every Breath of Novelty, whims and nonsense. . . ."[22]

Stephen's approach to the voters flatly violated the gentry code of election etiquette. Gentlemen did not campaign on what modern democratic politics calls "issues." They did not pledge to support particular measures or to follow their constituents' wishes. They promised only to use their own best independent judgment. Their platforms were their character and reputation. The average voters, white men of small property, had the almost passive function of choosing which of the gentlemen they would trust with power.[23]

That was the pattern of traditional deferential politics. But eighteenth-century Virginia was an expanding society in which lower-class acquiescence to upper-class authority was not unquestioning, especially in the more recently settled western and Southside counties.[24] The social and political order of the Northern Neck was comparatively stable. Common folk typically yielded to their "betters." Yet, even in the Neck, elements appeared of what would become a more popular post-revolutionary politics. Stephen's 1761 campaign promises were part of that trend.

Those were the seeds of future politics. What still counted now was the "joining of interests." Washington's alliance with Mercer connected gentlemen from two of the Northern Neck's most prominent families. Support among the other gentry was also essential. Stephen's seeming success had made Stewart uneasy "till I was certain that the Leaders and all the Patrician Families remains firm in their resolution of continuing for You. . . ." The leading gentlemen still favored Washington. In turn, their "interest" among the yeomen, often quasi-feudal retainers of the great planters, would almost guarantee victory. But "to fix it beyond the most distant doubt," Stewart advised, the incumbent should canvass the county himself.[25]

Stewart was an eager political campaigner: "I need not tell you how happy McNeill and I are in arriving at a Juncture when the Flame of Burgessing kindles every Breast." He came down to Mount Vernon to plot strategy and then returned to Winchester to talk with "our particular Friends." In mid-March 1761, three of them planned to make "an excursion to the lower part of the County." Stephen "continues indefatigable," reported Stewart, but by now he felt sure Washington's interest had been "immutably establish'd."[26]

A Burgess might proclaim his independence and his gentlemanly devotion to his constituents' well-being. A shrewd provincial politician also took care of business. In April 1761, candidate Washington went to Williamsburg, where he sponsored legislation vital to Frederick County. Drawing on the report from Captain Stewart mentioned earlier, he promoted measures to bolster frontier defense. He also chaired a special committee to prepare a bill to establish the town of Woodstock. With the help of Edmund Pendleton, one of the Burgesses' legal experts, he drafted legislation to preserve the water of Winchester by preventing hogs from running wild, a plan for sanitation vital to that community.[27]

In early May, the candidate came up for a campaign "tour" of the county. He went to a cockfight and a wedding and at various other stops canvassed the voters. On such occasions, gentlemen did not directly solicit votes. Their presence was meant to display solicitude for common folk, while their manner and dress reinforced their higher status.[28]

If his own seat remained secure, Washington showed that he took Stephen's challenge to Mercer very seriously indeed. Stephen had become embroiled in some sort of controversy in the streets of Winchester. What happened has been forgotten, but at the time Stephen worked earnestly to persuade voters of his innocence. Washington tried to convince them otherwise. He circulated material, now missing, that was detrimental to Stephen. Three days before the election, he offered it to the sheriff of the county, Captain Thomas Van Swearingen.

As sheriff, Van Swearingen had the duty of managing the election. He set its date and decided on the qualifications of individual voters. He himself could vote only in case of a tie. He opened the poll, and he closed it when, in his opinion, the freeholders had had sufficient opportunity to come in and cast their votes. This gave him enormous power, power the law instructed him to exercise impartially. But sheriffs might wield their authority, as some did, on behalf of favored candidates.[29]

Ignoring the law, Washington sent the sheriff the anti-Stephen ammunition. "[Y]ou may, if you think it expedient, communicate the contents to your Neighbours and Friends . . . ," he said. "His [Stephen's] conduct throughout the whole is very obvious to all who will be convinced, but I find there are some that do not choose to have their Eyes opened." Washington hoped his own "Interest" in Van Swearingen's "Neighbourhood still stands good, and as I have the greatest reason to believe you can be no Friend to a Person of Colo. Stephens Principles; I hope, and indeed make no doubt that you will contribute your aid towards shutting him out of the Public trust he is seeking. . . ."

Washington had a suggestion as to just what form that aid might take. He wanted to use the same strategy that had worked so successfully for him during the voting in 1758. "[C]ould Mercer's friend's and mine be hurried in at the first of the Poll it might be an advantage," he urged Van Swearingen, "but as Sheriff I know you cannot appear in this, nor would I by any mean have you do any thing that can give so designing a Man as Colo. Stevens the least handle."[30]

Apparently Sheriff Van Swearingen went along with these tough-minded tactics. The hotly contested race climaxed in Winchester, the county seat, on 18 May 1761. Both sides mobilized a large turnout. Supporters of Washington and Mercer dominated the early voting, building a momentum for Mercer that Stephen found it impossible to overcome. When the sheriff closed the poll, 603 freeholders had voted. Five hundred and five had announced for Washington, 400 had gone for Mercer, 294 for Stephen. Significantly, several of the leading gentlemen of the county, including Thomas Bryan Martin, Washington's fellow candidate in 1758, disagreed with his harsh opinion and voted for

Stephen. The day after the election, Washington paid Mercer fifty pounds for campaign expenses. As in the past, he kept a copy of the poll.[31]

In this election, Washington violated not only the law, but also the custom that gentlemen refrained from canvassing the voters. These and other features of the code of the eighteenth-century Virginia gentry actually worked to the advantage of men of property. As the historian Charles Sydnor pointed out: "Gentlemen, let it plainly be said, wanted office despite their hostility to aggressive electioneering. But gentlemen knew how to seek support with such delicacy of phrase as to avoid the appearance of doing so. . . ." Still, when it seemed necessary, as in Frederick County in 1761, custom gave way to practical politics.[32]

The dominant Whiggish code also demanded that Washington keep ambitious motives hidden. He must present himself as participating in politics only in a spirit of disinterestedness. Two months after his re-election, replying to a travel writer who had visited Mount Vernon, Washington mentioned a recent illness, an illness he had acquired while campaigning. He could find few occurrences worth reporting. "I deal little in Politics," he said, "and what to advance under the articles of news I really know not."[33]

Here began the myth of Washington as reluctant politician. It started with Washington's own attempt to present himself as satisfying contemporary political mores. His biographers, taking his words at face value, have perpetuated that myth.[34]

CHAPTER SEVEN

"A free mind"

Despite his vexations with imperial officials and the regular army, Washington felt a strong emotional attachment to England and the Empire. For many years, he had had a "longing desire" to visit London, "the great Matrapolis of that Kingdom." Unfortunately, the responsibilities of his new marriage and family made such a voyage impossible. Still, he wished for nothing more "ardently," he said, than "a trip to England. . . ."[1]

But in his commercial enterprises he found himself increasingly at odds with the purposes and practices of the British Empire. Imperial theorists and policymakers declared frankly that the colonies existed for the sake of the mother country and not the other way around. They were to serve as suppliers of raw materials and markets for manufactured goods. A complex system of regulations implemented this policy, encouraging agriculture and other extractive industries and discouraging manufacture of finished goods. These rules required shipment of most colonial products to British ports, even if the ultimate market was on the Continent. To give British manufacturers a competitive edge, European goods bound for America must first go to Britain, where they incurred import duties and additional shipping charges. All shipping must utilize British vessels.

As the colonies matured economically and politically, Americans chafed more and more under their yoke of subordination. Washington, like many other Virginia planters, felt that this system not only slighted his interests, but exploited him.

During his military service, his tobacco crops had suffered from the poor supervision of hired managers and relatives. He also thought London and Bristol consignment merchants had neglected his interests, selling his tobacco at low prices and shipping goods carelessly. Resuming direction of his affairs early in 1759, he resolved that things would be different. He would invest in improvements on the Mount Vernon farms, buy more land in the neighborhood and near his other plantations, expand his tobacco acreage, and purchase more slaves for the painstaking work of cultivating that crop. He intended to grow the finest leaf and to grow it profitably.[2]

Washington was determined to maximize his profits. In mid-1759, he switched most of his business to a new set of trading partners in London and tried a shipment to a different merchant in Bristol. Later he would experiment with small consignments to houses in Liverpool and London. Twice he severed commercial relations with merchants he had dealt with for years. Repeatedly he threatened to break his ties with Robert Cary and Company of London, his principal agents during these decades. He stuck with them to avoid the charge of "fickleness," he said, but he also knew from experience that he was unlikely to find better prices for his tobacco elsewhere. Even after he had given up tobacco as his major enterprise, he meant to get the highest prices going.[3]

New agents proved no more satisfactory than the old ones. Year after year, he complained of the low prices they obtained for his crop. Why had they sold it quickly instead of waiting for a rise in the market? Why should his tobacco sell for less than that of some of his neighbors? "Certain I am no Person in Virginia takes more pains to make their Tobo. fine than I do and tis hard then I shoud not be as well rewarded for it."[4]

If the prices for his tobacco were often too low, the cost of the goods he ordered was frequently exorbitant and the quality inferior. He thought ". . . many Shop keepers, and Tradesmen in London when they know Goods are bespoke for exportation . . . palm[ed] sometimes old, and sometimes very slight and indifferent Goods upon Us taking care at the same time to advance 10, 15 or perhaps 20 pr. Ct. upon them." In a shipment of plows, "many of the most material parts" were missing, he complained in 1762, making them entirely useless. The small and narrow hoes sent to one of his plantations in 1763 were all worthless for farm work and had to be returned.[5]

Throughout the early 1760s, Washington made growing tobacco his major enterprise. He experimented with different varieties. His experiments all failed. Mount Vernon's soils were simply unsuited to cultivating the superlative product he wanted identified with his name. On top of that, bad weather, bad crops, bad prices, shipwrecks, costly expansion, a costly way of life, fluctuations in an unpredictable market, and a commercial system designed primarily to serve the economic interests of an English merchant rather than a Virginia planter all combined to skew his balance sheet.[6]

This failure meant more than financial loss to Washington, for among the great Tidewater planters tobacco was more than a cash crop. It was another source of honor. T. H. Breen has shown that cultivation of the highest-quality product was central to a gentleman's public reputation and personal identity. Growing fine tobacco requires meticulous care, literally leaf-by-leaf attention. Even a skilled and experienced planter needs a good deal of luck to escape the vicissitudes of nature. Virginia planters grappled with an enormous element of chance, not only from weather, but from the uncertainties of the international tobacco market. Still, they persuaded themselves that in the long run a "crop master" would prove himself equal to the challenges of both nature and the market. Here was another component of the gentrymen's self-image of personal autonomy. Constantly, the leading planters measured their crops, their work, their material and moral worth against one another's achievements. The prices a grower obtained and the opulent life-style his profits purchased became the most convenient yardsticks of success and thus chief sources of reputation and self-esteem.[7]

No wonder, then, that Washington fretted about the prices his tobacco brought. His social as well as financial worth was at stake. As ever, he expected his pursuit of honor to yield both moral and material rewards. In 1762, after three years of using "my utmost endeavours," he found to his surprise that he still failed to "partake of the best prices that are going. . . ." Perhaps, he confessed, it is "an Art beyond my skill, to succeed in making good Tobo. . . ."[8]

Despite this apparent admission, he did not think he had failed. He recognized that his product fell short of the standard he had set, but he attributed this to misfortunes, not his own shortcomings. Anyway, he felt certain his tobacco matched his neighbors' in quality. He blamed his low returns primarily on the merchants who marketed it in England. Why else would his tobacco and his stepson Jacky Custis's, both grown on the same Custis estate lands by the same manager using the same methods, sell at different prices, with Jack's profits higher than his?[9]

Washington and many colonials felt at the mercy of merchants thousands of miles away. This stemmed from the basic conditions of a colonial economy. Hard money, indeed any circulating medium of exchange, was chronically scarce in Virginia. English and Scottish tobacco merchants supplied a partial remedy, offering easy credit to large planters and small. That credit financed the spread of the tobacco regime into the Piedmont. It enabled Washington to expand his tobacco production, buying much more land and many more slaves. But easy credit had its adverse side. Virginia's was a developing staple economy, short of capital and dependent on British credit for its expansion. Thus, fundamental economic decisions were made, not in Alexandria or Norfolk, but in Glasgow and London. These economic arrangements, the classic relationship between an imperial power and one of its colonies, kept Virginia in a state of dependency.

Easy credit also supported Washington's and other great planters' opulent (by colonial standards) way of life. It enabled even small planters to purchase English manufactured goods. After 1750, Virginians with any disposable income bought consumer items on a massively increased scale. Gentry families indulged in an orgy of spending. Washington, too, spent lavishly on luxuries. He bought expensive toys for his stepchildren. He sent for a six-horse chariot harness with his family crest on it. He ordered suits of livery for his body servant and one of young Jacky Custis's, describing both outfits in great detail. He purchased fine clothes for himself and his stepson. These expenses were necessary, he felt, to support the dignity of his social station. A gentleman's style of living was one measure of his social worth.[10]

Rising consumer spending and economic expansion built on easy credit, along with fluctuations in the international tobacco market, vastly increased private debt in Virginia. Debt among the great planters reached unprecedented levels, at times ruining family fortunes. Many gentlemen tried to keep up appearances by maintaining their extravagant way of living, but in neighborhoods where everyone's business quickly became common knowledge, it was hard to mask one's financial distress for long. According to gentry values and the predominant "Country Party" political ideology, debt compromised a gentleman's honor and his independence. When a planter had to plead with an English consignment merchant to carry his debt for another season and then another, he had difficulty sustaining the fiction of his complete personal autonomy. Virginia's landed gentlemen, it turned out, were not so independent after all. The increasingly unavoidable realities of debt and colonial economic dependence were beginning to undermine the gentry's corporate self-image.[11]

His mounting debts certainly jarred George Washington's self-image. From 1759 to 1763, he had deliberately relied on credit, increasing his indebtedness in order to put Mount Vernon back in shape, to buy land and slaves, to grow more tobacco. In the summer of 1761, his London creditors, Cary and Company, announced that he owed them nearly £2000. Since the Custis estate's credit balance was almost that high, Washington did not worry. But in mid-1764, he found himself, despite his constant exertions, almost as deeply in debt as three years earlier.[12]

In August 1764, he sent Cary a lengthy and impassioned defense of himself and the state of his accounts, losing control of his syntax as he often did when he had lost control of his temper. By pressing him for payment, they had, he felt, questioned his integrity. He had fallen so much in arrears through "Mischances rather than Misconduct . . . ," he protested. He repeated the litany of bad weather, bad luck, bad prices, bad debts owed him, and costly purchases of land and slaves that was his explanation to himself of his failure to grow tobacco profitably. He had no intention of piling up more debt. He thought he had already made that plain. Cary might, of course, charge him interest until he paid off what he owed. If they refused to wait for him to pay out of the returns on future crops, he would "hit upon a method" he preferred to avoid that would "discharge the Debt" immediately and "effectually remove me from all further mention of it. . . ." His slighted honor provoked a sharp complaint. ". . . I did not expect that a corrispondant so steady, and constant . . . woud be reminded in the Instant it was discovered how necessary it was for him to be expeditous in his payments. . . . [I]t is but an irksome thing to a free mind to be anyways hampered in Debt. . . ."[13]

Despite his best efforts, profit and honor as a tobacco planter lay beyond Washington's grasp. His prosperity depended, he felt, on men an ocean away who put their interests above his. Worse, he knew that deepening debt undermined his vaunted autonomy. Debt could turn him from a morally and politically independent landed gentleman into the dependent creature of English creditors. To maintain his identity as an honorable gentleman, "a free mind," he must wipe out that debt. He determined to cut back on expensive purchases, but frugality alone could never keep him out of debt. He began to think that he must free himself from the enslaving economics of tobacco. He must find other profitable crops and enterprises on which to build his independence.

Washington had left the military life to escape the vexations of his subordinate provincial status within the imperial establishment. But as a civilian planter, he kept butting up against what he considered biased arrangements. He began to relate his personal frustrations to a larger problem, the developing constitutional and political crisis between the mother country and the colonies.

To understand the imperial-colonial conflict, he turned to political pamphlets. During the eighteenth century, essay tracts were a chief means of public discussion and debate. Washington made them an essential part of his reading. His friend and mentor Landon Carter was a frequent polemicist in the pre-revolutionary published debates. Carter's "A Letter to the Right Reverend Father in God, Lord B——p of L——n" (Williamsburg and London) fired one of the opening salvos of the Parsons' Cause in 1760. Richard Bland, who had defended Washington and the regiment against the aspersions of the "Centinel," joined that debate the same year with "A Letter to the Clergy of Virginia" (Williamsburg). In 1764, Carter reentered the controversy with "The Rector Detected" (Williamsburg), while from the other side the Rev. Mr. John Camm shot back "A Review of The Rector Detected: or the Colonel Reconnoitred" (Williamsburg, 1764). Washington owned all of these tracts.[14]

The Parsons' Cause flared after the Burgesses, to relieve the economic distress caused by poor tobacco harvests, altered the method of paying Anglican clergymen's salaries. When the clerics convinced London to disallow this legislation, the matter billowed into a constitutional and political dispute between the colony and the Crown. Governor Fauquier's superiors instructed him to veto all legislation omitting a suspending clause, a provision that statutes would take effect only upon Crown approval. The Burgesses had left out such clauses because the economic emergency had required an immediate short-term solution.

Making Virginia's constitutional case, Carter and Bland claimed that royal instructions applied only to the royal governor, not to the provincially elected legislators. They also challenged the constitutionality of the suspending clause when it came to emergency legislation. The Assembly must remain free to decide what best served the colony's needs and interests. The Crown could not constitutionally require it to follow instructions harmful to Virginia. These arguments struck at two of London's chief instruments for controlling colonial governments. They took an important step toward demanding colonial self-determination by asserting, in Carter's words, that the Burgesses were Virginia's "Parliament."

In May 1763, another constitutional dispute arose. "Our Assembly is suddenly called," reported Washington, "in consequence of a Memorial of the British Merchts. to the Board of Trade representing the evil consequences of our Paper emissions, and their Lordships report and order's thereupon. . . ."[15] The scarcity of hard money in the colonies deprived them of a medium of exchange adequate to the demands of internal trade and the recurring eighteenth-century wars for empire. Colonial legislatures turned time and again to paper money. To meet the unprecedented requirements of the Seven Years' War, the Burgesses reluctantly but then repeatedly issued such currency. They also made it legal tender; creditors could not refuse it. In all, Virginia emitted some £440,000 of paper money during the war.

The rapid depreciation of this currency alarmed British merchants trading with the colony. They feared Virginians would force them to take depreciated paper in payment of debts. In 1759 the merchants persuaded the Crown to order payment of sterling debts in sterling. With gold and silver still scarce, the Burgesses simply ignored the instructions and kept issuing paper money as wartime demands dictated. Landon Carter defended their actions in "A Letter to a Gentleman in London from Virginia" (Williamsburg, 1759). Washington obtained this pamphlet.[16]

In 1762, the merchants again protested the legal-tender provision, and in February 1763, the Lords of Trade sternly reprimanded the Burgesses, repeating their previous orders. Those were the orders that caused the Assembly to meet now. "I suppose," said Washington, this "will set the whole Country in Flames. . . ." Meeting late in May, the House defended its paper emissions as necessary to comply fully with Crown military requisitions. It argued that the legal-tender provision and one authorizing the courts to resolve disputes over rates of exchange ensured justice to debtors and creditors alike. It refused to bow to the imperial instructions. Washington thought the merchants' "stir . . . ill timed" and feared its effects.[17]

The consequences quickly became apparent. Rebuked by the Board of Trade and prorogued by the governor, the Burgesses were ignored that summer when Indians invaded Virginia's frontiers during Pontiac's uprising. Acting alone, the governor and Council relied on the militia, a defensive force Washington considered too costly and wholly inadequate. He knew Virginia could never mount a proper defense as long as its Assembly was prohibited from issuing paper money.[18] Once again, imperial officials had rejected colonial solutions to colonial problems.

In January 1764, the House established a commission to review and certify for payment the accounts of the militia forces that had fought Pontiac's warriors. Washington accepted the difficult chairmanship of this body. At the next session (October–December 1764), he delivered its report. He also served as usual on the standing Committee of Propositions and Grievances.[19] Meanwhile, the Burgesses' continued defiance about paper money provoked a vigorous response from the British ministry. In April, Parliament adopted the Currency Act of 1764. Ignoring the desperate shortage of hard money in the colonies, it prohibited them from issuing paper bills as legal tender.

The Currency Act was part of a comprehensive new imperial policy designed to impose closer control over the North American provinces. With the Seven Years' War over and the French threat removed, the Crown meant to bring the colonies to heel. The policy marked a new phase in imperial-colonial relations. It also began a new stage in George Washington's relationship with Britain and with America.

As part of its postwar policy, the ministry decided to impose revenue-raising taxes on the colonies. The Stamp Act of March 1765 required the use of officially stamped paper for all legal documents, pamphlets, and newspapers. The revenues would help pay to supply regular troops stationed in the colonies. This assertion of parliamentary authority struck at the heart of colonial legislative power, the power of the provincial assemblies to levy taxes. It also rejected the theory of the British constitution upon which American lower Houses had implicitly been operating. Increasingly they had come to think of themselves as coordinate legislatures, in effect, the colonial equivalents of Parliament. Anticipating the Stamp Act, the Burgesses in December 1764 had claimed sole jurisdiction in matters of "internal polity" and taxation. The crisis over the act forced colonial leaders to begin to spell out an ideology of American political self-determination.

Washington attended the Assembly session of May 1765. Probably, along with the majority of Burgesses, he had left Williamsburg before his Fairfax neighbor, the distinguished attorney George Johnston, moved that the House consider a response to the Stamp Act. That motion led to Patrick Henry's famous resolutions, an action in which Johnston had an intimate part.[20] From the beginning, Fairfax County supplied leadership in the movement of colonial resistance.

Because of the Stamp Act Resolves, the governor dissolved the Assembly and called for new elections that summer. When for reasons of health Johnston decided against seeking reelection, Washington seized the chance to switch his constituency from Frederick to his home county. Undoubtedly he first secured the support of the gentlemen who dominated politics in Fairfax, the men who would make it a center of colonial opposition to the Crown. Already popular in the county, he led the July voting in what he himself called "an easy and creditable poll." He again signified his political ambitions by saving a copy of the poll and alphabetizing it.[21]

Meanwhile, Washington had been altering his plans to achieve his financial ambitions. He had begun to reduce his purchases from England in order to decrease his debts. Cutting expenses would not be enough, though. He needed new sources of income. In 1764, he had started to grow more wheat for the Alexandria market and had begun to develop some plantation industries, such as brandy-making, hoping they would yield a small profit. Then in February 1765, Cary and Company reported that again in 1764 his tobacco had done poorly on the market. He knew now more certainly than ever that he must find alternatives to tobacco.

Washington's reply to Cary in September 1765 evinces a major development in his thinking about the relationship between the colonies and Great Britain. In this revealing letter, he began to trace connections between his distresses as a tobacco planter and the Crown's new colonial policy. He was also considering means for the colonies to attain greater self-determination. He had definitely determined to increase his own independence.[22]

He complained sharply about the "pitifully low" prices Cary had gotten for his crop, prices below what some Potomac neighbors had gotten for "common Aronoke" tobacco. He himself found better returns at Liverpool on "the meanest sort" of tobacco grown by his tenants, the kind Cary had once called "the worst of Maryland and not Saleable." He was incredulous that his and Jacky Custis's tobacco had "so much depreciated in quality as not only to sell much below" quality crops, "but actually for less . . . than the commonest kinds do. . . ." Nor could he understand how his own tobacco had netted "a good deal less" than Jacky's, when both crops had been grown on the same lands according to the same directions.

"Can it be otherwise than a little mortifying then to find, that we, who raise none but Sweet-scented Tobacco, and endeavour . . . to be careful in the management of it, however we fail in the execution, and who by a close and fixed corrispondance with you, contribute so largely to the dispatch of your Ships in this Country shoud meet with such unprofitable returns? Surely I may answer No!" Tobacco prices had fallen in the past year or two, so he did not expect his and Master Custis's crops to "fetch their usual prices." He did think, though, that they should have "come in for a part of the good prices that are going," partly because he believed the quality of their tobacco "not so much inferior to some that still sells well. . . ." He also expected that "so considerable a Consignment, when confined in a manner to one House . . . woud lay claim to the best endeavours of the Merchant in the Sales. . . ."

Low prices undercut Washington's reputation as a tobacco planter. He knew his product failed of his intentions, but he felt sure it was closer to the mark than the sales indicated. Significantly, he blamed Cary, not himself, for his poor returns.

He also thought Cary and other merchants failed to use their "best endeavours . . . in the return of Goods." He paid "exceeding heavily" for many articles and yet often received the wrong items. He could not simply return them, as Cary had once suggested. How could a colonial who imported necessities do without them for a year? Also, some orders had been sent to the wrong Virginia river, incurring additional shipping charges and causing damage to the goods. This could be avoided if Cary took care to send his purchases only in vessels bound to the rivers Washington's invoices specified. Plainly he thought London merchants overcharged and exploited him, injuring him financially. "[S]elling of our Tobacco's well, and purchasing of Our Goods upon the best Terms," he declared, "are matters of the utmost consequence to our well doing. . . ."

Justice to himself and his ward, he warned, might compel him to take his business elsewhere. In fact, several months earlier he had made trial of a Liverpool partnership, Crosbies and Trafford, sending a small tobacco consignment and ordering goods from them. He would find no greater profit there, though.[23]

He had concluded that he could never do well growing tobacco. He had decided to substitute another cash crop. Until he found one, he would, of course, have to continue with tobacco, so he was sending forty-eight hogsheads. He had been experimenting, though as yet unsuccessfully, with hemp and flax. He asked Cary and other English agents about shipping costs and possible profits regarding these commodities and inquired about the parliamentary bounty on hemp.[24]

George Washington had come to a major turning point in his life. Growing the finest tobacco profitably was a principal avenue to honor among Tidewater gentlemen. For seven years, he had pursued that form of honor, but without success. Now he had decided to seek other means to establish his fortune and reputation. He made the shift because more essential to his honor than cultivating high-quality tobacco was maintaining his personal independence. The economics of tobacco and, from his viewpoint, British merchants' practices had yielded only meager profits, excessive expenses, mounting debts, and subjection to consignment agents. Control of his ultimate financial well-being, he felt, had been taken out of his hands. Economic independence was the basis of a gentleman's moral integrity and political autonomy. Washington required both material prosperity and economic self-determination to maintain his self-image and public reputation as an independent, virtuous gentleman. He had vowed to fashion new means to that end.[25]

Of even greater significance, Washington had begun to link his private economic difficulties with the British Empire's political and commercial arrangements. In particular, he connected his problems with the Stamp Act and the Crown's new colonial policy. The last third of his letter to Cary emphatically set forth his views.

He called the Stamp Act an "unconstitutional method of Taxation[,] . . . a direful attack upon their Liberties" "imposed on the Colonies by the Parliament of Great Britain." Clearly he already believed that, at least when it came to taxes, Parliament's proper and sole sphere of authority was the British Isles. Following repeal, he used stronger language still, labeling it an "Act of Oppression."[26]

He also criticized the "late restrictions of our Trade and other Acts to Burthen us." Undoubtedly he referred mainly to the Currency Act and the Plantation Act of 1764 (known in America as the Sugar Act). The former, as noted above, prohibited paper money at a time when the colonies lacked hard money and desperately needed a circulating medium for trade. The latter tightened enforcement and expanded the scope of the Navigation Laws and Acts of Trade. The Crown intended thereby to increase customs revenues and to further protect metropolitan commerce with the colonies from foreign competition.

With regard to the Sugar Act, Washington predicted, "the advantages accruing to the Mother Country will fall far short of the expectations of the Ministry. . . ." Duties on British goods would induce the colonists to cut back on imports. "[T]he whole produce of our labour hitherto has centred in Great Britain—what more can they desire? . . . The Eyes of our People, (already beginning to open) will perceive, that many of the Luxuries" bought from Britain "can well be dispensed with whilst the Necessaries of Life are to be procurd (for the most part) within ourselves." He regarded revenue-raising duties as a form of taxation. If Britain loaded her exports "with Heavy Taxes," he warned, it would simply introduce frugality into America, reduce colonial imports, stimulate colonial industry, and hurt British manufacturers. "Where then lies the utility of these Measures?"

As for the Stamp Act itself, most immediately, he prophesied, it would put a stop to all judicial proceedings. Even if the colonists were willing to enforce the law, they could not comply, because it required them to pay for the stamps with the hard money they lacked. The inevitable closing of provincial courts would prevent collection of debts owed British creditors. When that happened, said Washington pointedly, "it may be left to yourselves, who have such large demands upon the Colonies, to determine who is to suffer most in this event—the Merchant, or the Planter." To another correspondent, he predicted that, once debt collection had been halted, "the Merchants of G. Britain trading to the Colonies will not be among the last to wish for a Repeal. . . ."[27]

Washington spoke of "the Colonies," but his comments clearly also reflected his own experience. His own eyes had opened to the need to reduce imports and develop plantation industries. His own debts to Cary lay behind his remarks about debt collection. As the earlier part of the letter shows, he was already moving toward a personal policy of economic self-sufficiency and independence.

At the same time, he was locating his private problems within a larger pattern of colonial economic and political subordination. English merchants increased their profits by scouting this Virginia planter's interests. Now they would lose much of his business. Shortsighted commercial policies aimed to squeeze more revenue out of the colonies. Instead, they would force cutbacks in colonial trade. Parliament encroached on the provincial assemblies' constitutional prerogatives with the "illjudged" Stamp Act and other forms of taxation. British creditors would suffer the consequences. Even more clearly than in the past, Washington perceived representatives of the metropolitan culture as ignoring colonial needs, colonial realities, and colonial leaders. Now he was considering how he and his countrymen could counter this pervasive and intensifying discrimination and move toward greater self-determination.

Washington's comments also reveal important aspects of his developing political style. He omitted ideological arguments, but not because

he thought them unimportant. Rather, he knew the Crown would withdraw the Stamp Act once British merchants felt the economic effects of
colonial resistance. One might argue that his dispassionate tone showed
he had yet to arrive at the militancy of a Patrick Henry. But for the rest
of his career, even when discussing issues about which he felt strongly,
he usually assumed this same voice of detachment, seemingly speaking
from above the swirl of events. Amid the turbulence of a revolutionary
era, his tone would reassure his fellow citizens that George Washington
yet stood calm, unshakable, certain of himself and of his cause.

That dispassionate voice also would help persuade Americans of his
trustworthiness with power. They praised patriotic zeal, but they feared
fierce passions once unleashed. Emotional anarchy might end in political tyranny. Washington would prove his fitness to lead a revolution by
his mastery of himself. Eventually, he would make that voice an integral
part of his public persona. At this point, in 1765, he was still fashioning
it, still testing it out.

His objective tone also reflected one of his foremost political gifts,
the capacity to keep a part of his judgment aloof from the tumult of
circumstances in order to grasp their meaning. Deftly he read public
opinion and discerned the direction of events. This ability to sift political situations with some degree of detachment, the product of both in-
stinct and experience, was an essential aspect of his genius as a leader.

Just as Washington had foreseen, in November 1765 the requirement
of stamped paper closed the provincial courts. He knew this would in-
jure not only British creditors, but local creditors and debtors as well.
In December, he discussed the problem with his neighbors George William Fairfax and George Mason, the latter one of Virginia's most brilliant political thinkers and most reluctant politicians. They agreed that
Mason should draft and Washington introduce in the Assembly a legislative proposal to resolve the dilemma by circumventing the stamp
law. Repeal of the Stamp Act a few months later made the plan unnecessary, but its formulation marked the beginning of a political collaboration that extended over the next ten years. Mason would serve as the
draftsman, the man of words and ideas, Washington as the public advocate, the political leader lending his prestige and influence to pro-
grams they had combined to produce.[28]

The Crown withdrew the Stamp Act when, as Washington had predicted, British merchants felt the pinch of colonial resistance. He rejoiced in repeal, "for had the Parliament of Great Britain resolvd upon
enforcing it the consequences I conceive would have been more direful

than is generally apprehended both to the Mother Country and her Colonies." Now he hoped to see a thorough reform of British commerce. As long as the colonies concentrated on extractive industries, they would naturally provide ready markets for British manufactured goods, and American wealth would flow to Britain. The economic advantage to Britain of equitable arrangements seemed obvious to Washington. The necessity of harmonious relations between mother country and colonies seemed equally plain. But as with his complaints about ill-treatment by British merchants, his labeling of the Stamp Act as an "Act of Oppression" by "the Parliament of Great Britain" expressed his persisting sense of discrimination against American provincials.[29]

Provincial polemicists blamed the Stamp Act Crisis on a ministerial conspiracy to deceive the king. They accused corrupt counselors of trying to weaken the trust between George III and his people, but nothing, they asserted, could separate them from their love of their sovereign. The Stamp Act Congress professed inviolable attachment to "the best of Kings." When George installed a new ministry under the Marquis of Rockingham that brought about withdrawal of the law, colonials attributed to their monarch a primary role in repeal. Many towns celebrated it on the king's birthday. These beliefs bore almost no relation to political reality, but it mattered little. George III's stock in his American colonies, already high, rose higher still.[30]

By 1766, Washington had served eight years as a respected, though not a prominent, Burgess. A small group led by Speaker and Treasurer John Robinson had long dominated lower House proceedings. Exposure of misappropriation of public funds by the deceased Robinson now provoked calls for reform. Though he was much beloved, his censurable dealings proved again the dangers of concentrating power. The reform group demanded separation of the offices of Speaker and Treasurer. They also won wider distribution of power within the House. Washington and other younger leaders began to acquire more influence. He had long sat on the permanent Committee of Propositions and Grievances. In November 1766, he also joined the standing Committee of Privileges and Elections, the powerful instrument of the House to supervise admission to its membership and to protect its prerogatives. Carrying out his initial special service on that committee, he waited upon the governor with new writs for elections in Frederick and Hampshire counties.[31]

Washington had decided that to maintain his status as an independent gentleman, "a free mind," he must emancipate himself from the oppressive tobacco regime. In 1766, he stopped growing the leaf at

Mount Vernon. He grew only enough on his portion of the York River Custis plantations to trade for English goods. Eventually he would consider discontinuing even those small crops. He also gradually shifted most of his tenants from paying rents in tobacco to payment in other commodities or cash.[32]

He grew much less tobacco, but he still expected the best prices and the best effort from Cary and Company. Throughout the late 1760s, he barraged them with complaints about the way they handled his consignments. They sold his higher-quality tobacco for less than the inferior grade shipped by some of his neighbors. They even sold it in England for less than he could have earned in Virginia. They ignored his instructions and sold it quickly when prices were down, instead of holding it until prices had risen again. He, one of their steady customers, had to pay higher freight than planters who dealt with the company irregularly. In one instance, the carelessness of a ship's captain ruined some and damaged much of a tobacco shipment by allowing it to stand in twelve to fifteen inches of rainwater in the hold.[33]

As in the past, he also griped that he paid excessive prices for the goods he ordered, some of which he could have gotten cheaper in Virginia. And as before, he complained that tradesmen sent the wrong items. For instance, the wheat riddles he had received were "so entirely useless that I shall be under a necessity of sending them back, or keeping by me as useless lumber." This could have been avoided if his directions had been followed. If the tradesmen and shopkeepers had no intention of doing so, it would be better if they sent no goods at all. Complain as much as he did year after year, his English trading partners seemed simply to ignore his strictures.[34]

Washington had kept track of the Stamp Act debate by acquiring pamphlets. For instance, he obtained a copy of Benjamin Franklin's parliamentary testimony opposing it. He also indicated his intention to move toward economic self-sufficiency by purchasing John Wily's "A Treatise on the Propagation of Sheep, the Manufacture of Wool, and the Cultivation and Manufacture of Flax" (Williamsburg, Virginia, 1765).[35]

Colonials had begun to see, said Washington, that they need not watch their economic "substance" drain off to Britain. They could cut back on duty-laden and costly British manufactured goods. "Many Luxuries" they could dispense with. The "necessaries of Life" they could mostly make themselves. In 1764 he had begun to manufacture some of these "necessaries" at Mount Vernon. He set his blacksmiths to fashioning ironware. He had his spinners and weavers make cloth to outfit his hundreds of slaves. By 1770, this had become a small factory producing a variety of fabrics for sale. Such enterprises may never have proved profitable, but he apparently hoped they eventually would.[36] In thus pursuing his own economic interests, he was subverting the goals of the British Empire: He denied English merchants a colonial market they had hitherto monopolized. He developed "domestic" industries imperial policymakers had systematically sought to restrict.

To free himself from debt and dependence, the Virginia planter knew he must do more than replace costly imports with cheaper home manufactures. The chief cause of his financial bondage to English creditors was the economics of tobacco. He had determined to shift to other cash crops. He continued to experiment with hemp and flax. Most successfully, he turned to growing and processing wheat. In 1764, he sold a mere 257 bushels in Alexandria. Within three years, he had increased his yield more than tenfold. By the end of the decade, he produced and sold nearly twenty-five times as much. He built flour mills in various parts of Virginia, processed other farmers' wheat and corn, and marketed his own brand of flour. He sold his second-rate wheat as ship's biscuit. Within the province and in the West Indies, he also sold corn and corn meal, staples in the diet of slaves. As always, he intended to distinguish himself by the quality of his products. He had failed to make the finest tobacco. He succeeded with wheat flour. The "G. Washington" brand, a Norfolk merchant told him in 1773, "has the preference of any at this market."[37]

Washington made fishing the Potomac another profitable enterprise. For years, he had had his "people" catch shad and herring to supplement their diet. In 1769, he experimented with fishing as a commercial venture, sending a small consignment to Antigua. The returns proved encouraging. In 1770, his seines caught 473,000 herring; by 1771, 679,000; by 1772, 900,000. Here again though, his search for profit and economic self-determination was hampered by imperial policy. To promote fishing by the Northern and Middle Colonies, the Crown allowed them to import salt directly from southern Europe. Wanting the southern provinces to grow only staple crops, it required them either to use poorer-quality American or English salt or to pay the high cost of importing European salt indirectly through Britain or other British colonies. Chesapeake commercial fishermen resented these restrictions which they considered discriminatory. Washington ordered salt from Liverpool, though he knew the best salt for curing fish came from Lisbon. In fact, he had difficulty obtaining any salt at all. Once more, he found himself mistreated by English merchants.[38]

Despite such hindrances, Washington profitably sold both fish and flour in Alexandria and Norfolk and, through those ports, to the West Indies. He acquired his own schooner and, later, a brig for shipping his products. He also tried selling his flour in the Madeira Islands and, on the eve of the Revolution, inquired about the London wheat market. Some of the West Indian profits he spent to buy slaves. He needed more field workers to expand his farming operations. He intended to put thousands of acres under grain cultivation. He no longer relied solely on an uncertain tobacco market. Diversified enterprises protected him from losses in any one business. They also made him more independent of the English market.[39]

Other planters besides Washington sought an alternative crop to escape the economic restrictions of the tobacco trade and the soil exhaustion caused by tobacco. Hemp became for a time a second major staple in Virginia. Many Chesapeake farmers also switched to wheat in response to burgeoning European and West Indian markets. After mid-century, the growing population of Europe increased demand beyond the capacity of Continental agriculture. This pushed prices up, prompting American farmers to grow more wheat. Food shortages also created a demand in the West Indian islands. A coastal trade developed among the British North American colonies.

Profits from the export of foodstuffs stayed in American hands, because colonial entrepreneurs, not British merchants, controlled this commerce. These economic leaders created a more complex and extensive infrastructure of processing, marketing, and shipping. Urban centers expanded. New York and Philadelphia spurted ahead of Boston in shipping, population, and wealth. They became major transshipment points for the commerce of the grain-growing Middle Colonies and Chesapeake. In the upper South, towns and cities grew up that had remained stunted under the tobacco regime. The region that had always drawn Washington's closest attention as soldier and speculator, planter and politician, became heavily involved in this trade. The frontier farmers of western Virginia sold their surpluses of grain and livestock for consumption abroad. Along the upper Potomac, market towns developed to handle this business. Alexandria swelled and prospered.

All of this marked a movement toward economic self-determination, the sort of independence Washington wanted for himself and had begun to envision for the colonies. By the early 1770s, he had almost unshackled himself from debt. Like his fellow colonials, he still hoped to find justice within the Empire, and like the most militant of them, he was getting ready to use more vigorous, more defiant measures. Meanwhile, he continued his rise to prominence and power within Virginia's ruling class.

"Some thing shou'd be done"

George Washington was a methodical man. "System in all things should be aimed at," he said, "for in execution, it renders every thing more easy." "[T]o establish good rules, and a regular system, is the life, and the soul of every kind of business." Whether that business was farming or commerce, military command or politics, he acted methodically. He once observed his slave carpenters to calculate how much work they could do in a day, depending on the amount of daylight and the type of wood they worked with. Another time, he burned a spermaceti candle and a tallow candle simultaneously to determine their relative costs. He even alphabetized the poll lists for his initial elections to the House of Burgesses from Frederick and Fairfax counties.[1] As a young man, an ambitious young man in a hurry, he had sometimes stepped rashly and to his embarrassment. With maturity, he showed increasing prudence, planning carefully, moving deliberately. There was nothing flashy or flamboyant in him. In all things, he calculated how to achieve his aims.

From 1765 to 1774, Washington pressed his advancement to wealth, position, and power within Virginia's ruling class. In Fairfax County, he joined the small circle of planter–merchant–land speculators who dominated politics. They visited one another, hired a dancing master for their children, and rode to hounds together. They sat as justices of the county court and as vestrymen in Fairfax and Truro parishes. They decided whom they would collectively support in the election of Burgesses. Washington intended to move to the center of this self-selected, self-perpetuating group.

In 1762, he had first been elected a vestryman of Truro Parish. From then until the outbreak of the Revolution, he held that position continuously, helping to select the site of a new church and to "view and examine" its construction. For a time, he also shared with George William Fairfax the duties of churchwarden of the parish. In the newly constructed Pohick Church, the Washington family owned one of the most prominent pews.[2]

The wealthier and more genteel families had the pews in the front of the church sanctuary. Other parishioners, white and black, occupied the places on the main floor and in the balcony appropriate to their ranks in society. It was probably customary in Washington's neighborhood, as in other parts of Virginia, for the local gentlemen to enter the church in a body after the worship service had begun. In the same manner they exited, while women and men of lower degree waited and watched until they had departed. The arrangement of seating, the rituals of entry and exit, the self-perpetuating government of the vestries by twelve gentlemen, all expressed and reinforced the values and practices of a hierarchical society.[3]

In eighteenth-century Virginia, county court justices served by appointment of the governor with the advice of the Executive Council. In practice, the courts themselves recommended replacements to fill vacancies. By this means, the gentry maintained their monopoly of the extensive powers of local government respecting property. In September 1768, Washington took the oath of office as a justice of the Fairfax County Court. In November, he sat on the court for the first time.[4]

In many counties, the justices were notorious for their lack of legal training. Fairfax distinguished itself by the quality of the legal minds sitting on its bench, among them George Mason and George Johnston. Perhaps spurred by their example as well as his own usual desire to excel, Washington obtained copies of legal works, including Richard Burn's *The Justice of the Peace and Parish Officer*. This popular handbook went through numerous editions because of its useful explanations of the functions and duties of local office.[5]

Elections to the Assembly offered the only opportunity for rank-and-file voters to render a verdict on their leaders. Occasionally someone from outside the tightly knit Fairfax oligarchy challenged a sitting Burgess, but no incumbent ever lost a race for reelection. In December 1768, Washington faced the Fairfax freeholders for the second time. The first time out, he had spent only a little over £9 for campaign expenses, principally "treating" the voters. This time around he spent more than £27, most of it on a ball in Alexandria. This sum exceeded the minimum qualification to vote. Once more he won easily, leading the poll. In September 1769 and again in December 1771, he and his fellow incumbent John West encountered no opposition. They were declared elected without the trouble of a poll. Following the 1771 election, Washington again sponsored a ball.[6]

Meanwhile, strife between the North American colonies and the mother country heated up again. The British ministry had given up the tax on stamped paper, but the Declaratory Act of 1766 still asserted Parliament's authority to raise a revenue in the American colonies. In 1767, Parliament passed the so-called Townshend duties. These taxes on tea, paper, glass, red and white lead, and painter's colors imported to the colonies would pay the administrative costs of a centralized Board of Customs Commissioners for North America. Remaining funds would go toward the support of military defense and royally appointed civil officials. The Crown had long wanted to make the colonies pay for their own military protection. Now it also sought to establish a colonial civil list. Deriving their salaries from duties on imports, governors and other imperial officials would stand independent of the colonial legislatures. At the same time, Parliament suspended the New York Assembly for failing to appropriate additional supplies for the regular army contingents stationed there.

These measures provoked stiff resistance in the colonies. The Virginia Burgesses, meeting briefly in March–April 1768, petitioned both Parliament and the king for repeal of the Townshend duties. They also pledged George III "the warmest assurances of their most cordial and inviolable attachment to your sacred Person and Government" and implored his "Fatherly goodness and Protection."

During the next months, militants in Boston, New York, and Philadelphia took a stronger stand. They formed nonimportation associations to press for repeal of the revenue-raising duties. In March 1769, merchants in Philadelphia urged fellow traders in Annapolis to follow their example. The Marylanders replied that a boycott in their province must comprehend different articles from those enumerated for Pennsylvania. More important, the private "Gentlemen & Planters" who conducted the bulk of trade must be convinced to join them. To enlist such support, the Annapolis merchants sent a circular letter throughout the colony. They enclosed the papers from the Philadelphia association and their own reply. When Dr. David Ross of Bladensburg on the Potomac received this packet, he had the materials copied and transmitted them across the river to his friend George Washington.[7]

After reading the documents, Washington passed them along to George Mason, unaware that Ross had also sent them to him. These decisive plans of action set Washington's blood to surging. His covering letter of 5 April 1769 makes clear that in just three years his willingness to test parliamentary authority and imperial policy had risen sharply.[8]

"At a time when our lordly Masters in Great Britain will be satisfied with nothing less than the deprication[9] of American freedom, it seems highly necessary that some thing shou'd be done to avert the stroke and maintain the liberty which we have derived from our Ancestors; but the manner of doing it to answer the purpose effectually is the point in question." Just how far his thinking had developed he made plain in his next sentence.

"That no man shou'd scruple, or hesitate a moment to use a-ms in defence of so valuable a blessing, on which all the good and evil of life depends; is clearly my opinion; yet A-ms I wou'd beg leave to add, should be the last resource; the denier [*dernier*: Fr. "last"] resort. Addresses to the Throne, and remonstrances to parliament, we have already, it is said, proved the inefficacy of; how far then their attention to our rights and priviledges is to be awakened or alarmed by starving their Trade and manufactures, remains to be tryed.

"The northern Colonies, it appears, are endeavouring to adopt this scheme. In my opinion it is a good one, and must be attended with salutary effects, provided it can be carried pretty generally into execution. . . ." At the time of the Stamp Act Crisis, Washington had warned English merchants with whom he did business that such boycotts could only hurt them and help the colonists. The difficulty, as he had just remarked to Mason, was how to ensure compliance. The diffusion of trade in the tobacco colonies increased that problem even more, but, he thought, "not insurmountably . . . if the Gentlemen in their several Counties" would "explain matters to the people, and stimulate them" to adhere to a nonimportation agreement. Nonassociators and those violating the association "ought to be stigmatized, and made the objects of publick reproach.

"The more I consider a Scheme of this sort, the more ardently I wish success to it . . . ," said Washington. Debts owed British creditors had grown enormously. Many families had been reduced almost to penury. To protect their honor, some insolvent planters were desperately propping up the facade of prosperity. Mounting debts were undermining the moral integrity, social authority, and political independence of Virginia's ruling class.[10] A nonimportation scheme, Washington believed, would promote frugality and bring an end to the current economic distress. Since the time of the Stamp Act Crisis, in order to reduce his own debts, he had been manufacturing cloth and ironware at Mount Vernon rather than purchasing those goods from England. He was also committed to promoting greater economic self-determination for himself and the colonies. His own energies increasingly went into marketing flour and fish and expanding his milling operations. He advocated a boycott now partly to promote colonial manufacturing.

With regard to manufacturing, he had long thought that "by virtue of the same power" under which Parliament assumed the right to levy a revenue-raising tax, it might "attempt at least to restrain our manufactories; especially those of a public nature. . . ." Clearly, he saw a link between the constitutional dispute and commercial arrangements. The authority Parliament used to squeeze tax revenues out of colonials might just as easily justify keeping them a captive market for British goods. He thought Americans should test whether Parliament would claim such a further measure of "arbitrary power."

Back of this letter piled fifteen years of grievances, fifteen years of discrimination and ill-treatment at the hands of regular army officers and imperial officials and English merchants and Crown policymakers. Half a decade earlier, reacting to a perceived threat to his personal independence, Washington had quit tobacco and turned to enterprises that gave him more control over his economic destiny. He had also begun to see his problems as more than personal wrongs done him, more even than evidence of bias against colonials. He had called the Stamp Act an "Act of Oppression." A series of postwar colonial policies put his private difficulties and those of his fellow Virginians into a larger context, a *pattern* of oppression. The Parliament of Great Britain seemed intent on curtailing colonial autonomy. He was concluding that it meant to hold the colonies in a state of economic and political servitude.

Few of his countrymen had reached such conclusions as yet. Many now realized, as he had in 1765, that pervasive private indebtedness constituted a collective public experience. But most still separated the constitutional dispute with Parliament from the commercial system and the debt crisis confronting tobacco planters.[11]

Though couched in his usual dispassionate tone, Washington's opinions had grown markedly more militant. Petitions to Parliament and even to the king he thought useless. He was ready to take up arms, if necessary, but that time had yet to come. First, Americans should try economic coercion, strike the British in their pocketbooks. A commer-

cial boycott would reduce indebtedness, promote domestic manufacturing, and move the provinces toward economic self-sufficiency. It would
also reveal just how far Parliament was willing to go to keep the colonies in line. He indicated how far he was willing to go in the present
situation to discipline fellow colonials: he would subject violators of the
boycott to public stigma. Six years before the outbreak of revolutionary
war, he was ready to use or consider using fierce measures, at least social coercion, if necessary, physical violence.

On the details of a nonimportation plan for Virginia, he sought the
advice of his neighbor. Should they set a scheme in motion now or
merely communicate their "sentiments to one another" and wait until
the May Assembly session when the Burgesses could fashion a "uniform
plan" for the colony?

Mason replied that same day. He agreed entirely that adoption of a
"regular Plan of the Sort proposed" must await the meeting in Williamsburg when "Gentlemen" from throughout the province could confer
and act in concert. Meanwhile, it might "be necessary to publish something preparatory to it in our Gazettes, to warn the People at least of
the impending Danger, & induce them the more readily & chearfully
to concur in the proper Measures to avert it. . . ." He had begun to draft
such a piece for the press, but one of his recurring medical disorders
had incapacitated him for the moment. He would write to his colleague
at Mount Vernon or endeavor to see him. "[I]n the mean Time pray
commit to Writing such Hints as may occur."

As yet, Mason did not share Washington's desire for economic self-
sufficiency. Once the colonists had obtained redress of their grievances,
they should "no longer discontinue our Importations," although they
should never import any article bearing a revenue-raising tax. He
thought it against "the Interest of these Colonys to refuse British Manufactures: our supplying our Mother-Country with gross Materials, &
taking her Manufactures in Return is the true Chain of Connection
between us; these are the Bands, which, if not broken by Oppression,
must long hold us together, by maintain[in]g a constant Reciprocation
of Interest. . . ." But, to tighten the pressure on the ministry, Virginia
planters might stop making tobacco, "by which the Revennue wou'd
lose fifty times more than all their Oppressions cou'd raise here."[12]

Mason might favor militant means, but ultimately he wished for a
restoration of the old and harmonious relationship of colonial dependency on the mother country. Washington was already close to a different conception of the empire, one in which the self-directing North

American provinces were connected to Britain as partners rather than dependents.

Two and a half weeks later, on 23 April 1769, Mason sent Washington a copy of a proposed nonimportation association for Virginia. Someone else had drafted it, possibly Richard Henry Lee. In a brief memorandum, Mason suggested alterations. Washington wrote all but one of these into his own copy of the proposal. On 30 April, he set out for the Assembly session in Williamsburg.[13]

During his first three days in the capital, Burgess Washington dined with the Executive Council; Speaker Peyton Randolph; the new governor, Lord Botetourt; and Councillor Robert Carter, one of the wealthiest men in Virginia. Later he would again share meals with the governor and the Speaker, as well as with Treasurer Robert Carter Nicholas and George Wythe, Clerk of the House and a prominent attorney. In Williamsburg, he regularly dined with the most powerful men in the province. Others were noticing his growing importance in the Assembly and began to seek his assistance there.[14]

One indication of Washington's increasing importance as a provincial leader was his appointment to legislative committees that dealt with the chronic scarcity of hard money. That problem continued to plague Virginia and the other colonies. Their populations were swelling, their economies expanding, but their money supply was always far below their needs. Nonetheless, the Currency Act of 1764 and subsequent ministerial directives enforced a rigid policy prohibiting legal-tender paper money. Finally in 1773, the ministry would agree to allow paper currency in payment of taxes and other public debts, but not private debts. These stubbornly enforced policies kept reminding colonials that their economies and their legislatures were subservient to imperial prerogatives.[15]

At the March–April 1767 Assembly meeting, Washington had served on a conference committee with members of the House and the Council to consider a new plan for emitting paper money. This was his first appointment to a conference committee on a major bill. In July 1771, he would sit on another committee to examine the redemption of paper currency issued during the French and Indian War.[16]

When the Assembly convened on 8 May 1769, Washington as usual received appointment to the powerful committees of Propositions and Grievances and of Privileges and Elections. A week later, he was put on the newly created standing Committee for Religion. This marked another significant step in his rise in the House. For the remainder of his membership, he would serve on these three standing committees. He was becoming an increasingly influential and prominent Burgess. Washington now stood in the second circle of power, just outside the central core of leadership.[17]

Signs of corruption alarmed Virginia's leaders: the Robinson scandal, the sensational Chiswell murder case, pervasive materialism among the gentry, a consequent massive increase in private debt, reputedly widespread immorality among the Anglican clergy, declining influence of the established church, and the rise of disruptive religious sects. The Committee for Religion was established to combat these ominous trends. It included leading members of the House: Colony Treasurer Robert Carter Nicholas (Chair), Attorney General John Randolph, Richard Bland, Benjamin Harrison, Patrick Henry, Richard Henry Lee, Edmund Pendleton, and George Washington. The last six would serve in Virginia's delegation to the first Continental Congress.[18]

The committee worked to police the established church by regulating parish vestries. It drafted plans to block a proposed Anglican episcopate and keep the church under indigenous control. It sought to defuse the divisive question of religious dissent by preparing legislation that would extend toleration to Baptists. In short, its actions were part of the effort to restore communal unity and public virtue at a time when both seemed in jeopardy. This task was essential as the province confronted the Crown. Virginia's unified front from 1769 to 1775 suggests that the effort succeeded. It was no coincidence that the colony's leaders created the Committee for Religion at the same time they fashioned means to resist the Townshend duties and other recent arbitrary measures.[19]

The remonstrances of the Virginia Assembly in 1768 against the Townshend duties had angered Crown officials. They had sent a new governor, Lord Botetourt, to enforce imperial policy vigorously. Unbeknownst to Virginians, he carried instructions either to persuade provincial leaders to stop their protests against parliamentary authority, or, failing that, to dissolve the Assembly and call for new elections. Meanwhile, the House of Lords, probably at the instigation of Lord Hillsborough, invoked a statute from the reign of Henry VIII to threaten the leading militants in Massachusetts with transportation to England to face charges of treason.[20]

The Burgesses took up consideration of this dangerous law as well as Parliament's other attempts to suppress colonial protests. On 16 May 1769, without dissent, they passed four bold resolves: First, that constitutionally the Assembly of Virginia had "the sole Right of imposing

Taxes on the Inhabitants" of the colony. Second, that Virginians had an "undoubted Privilege . . . to petition their Sovereign for Redress of Grievances . . . [and] to procure the Concurrence of his Majesty's other Colonies. . . ." Third, that all trials for treason or any other crime committed in Virginia should take place within the colony "according to the fixed and known Course of Proceeding" and that transportation of any accused person "beyond the Sea to be tried is highly derogatory of the Rights of *British* Subjects. . . ." Fourth, that they would present "an humble, dutiful, and loyal Address" to King George III, "to assure him of our inviolable Attachment to his sacred Person and Government; and to beseech his Royal Interposition, as the Father of all his People. . . ."[21]

The next day, 17 May, the House approved the petition to the king. They had moved on to other business when Governor Botetourt summoned them to the Council Chamber. Speaking briefly, one might say bluntly, he adhered to the letter of his instructions: "Mr. Speaker, and Gentlemen of the House of Burgesses, I have heard of your Resolves, and augur ill of their Effect. You have made it my Duty to dissolve you; and you are dissolved accordingly."

But the "late Representatives of the People" refused to acquiesce in this summary dismissal. Most of them walked down the street and reconvened unofficially in the Apollo Room of Anthony Hay's Raleigh Tavern. With Speaker Randolph as their moderator, they launched into an open and full discussion of the "distressed Situation" of the colony and of means to defend its "true and essential Interests." Deciding to form a nonimportation association, they appointed a committee, which included Washington, to draft a plan for presentation the following morning.

The deposed Burgess from Fairfax dined with the influential colony treasurer Robert Carter Nicholas and then spent the entire evening huddled with the committee hammering out the Virginia Association. As they considered the draft proposal that he, Mason, and others had been examining during the preceding weeks, Washington proposed the amendments he and Mason had discussed. Virtually all were adopted. Additional amendments were added, but the proposal remained substantially the same.[22]

The following morning, 18 May, the committee delivered its report. Approving of the plan as presented, "a great Number of the principal Gentlemen of the Colony" in attendance signed the nonimportation Association. They avowed their "inviolable and unshaken Fidelity and Loyalty to our most gracious Sovereign" and their "Affection" for their

fellow British subjects, but they protested "the Grievances and Distresses, with which his Majesty's *American* Subjects are oppressed. . . ."

The Associators were especially concerned about the state of commerce, most importantly the enormous debt owed for British goods and
the increasing precariousness of its payment. Underlying this expressed
concern lay deep anxiety about the gentry's apparent corruption and
loss of independence. Greed for British goods had enervated Virginia
morally. The nonimportation plan aimed as much to restore public virtue as to defeat the Townshend duties.

The signatories blamed the economic crisis on "Restrictions, Prohi-
bitions, and ill advised Regulations, in several late Acts of Parliament,"
in particular "the late unconstitutional Act . . . for the sole Purpose of
raising a Revenue in *America*." Their "many earnest Applications" for
redress had availed nothing. Therefore, they subscribed to the commercial boycott. They would refuse to import or purchase any articles bearing revenue-raising duties, as well as an additional long list of products,
until Parliament had repealed the unconstitutional taxes.[23]

"The Business being finished, the following Toasts were drank. . . .
The King. The Queen and Royal Family. . . . A speedy and lasting Union
between Great-Britain and her Colonies. The constitutional British Liberty in America, and all true Patriots, the Supporters thereof." After
half a dozen more such libations, "the Gentlemen retired." Washington
went and purchased John Dickinson's *Letters from a Farmer in Pennsylvania*. The following evening he and a "numerous and polite company" attended "a splendid ball and entertainment at the Palace" given
by the governor in honor of the queen's birthday.[24] In all of this, the
protesters saw no contradiction between their vigorous assertion of colonial rights and their repeated professions of loyalty and affection to
George III and the British nation.

For his own part, Washington carefully instructed his trading partners in London that if he had mistakenly ordered any products "Tax'd
by Act of Parliament for the purpose of Raising a Revenue in America,
it is my express desire and request, that they may not be sent. . . ." He
intended "to adhere religiously" to the Association and feared he might
have "unwittingly" included some such items in his invoice. Indeed he
had sent for a number of taxed articles, which suggested that the terms
of the boycott were perhaps a bit too complicated and cumbersome and
foreshadowed the difficulties that would arise in its enforcement. Still,
Washington had taken one more decisive step in asserting his and his
fellow colonials' constitutional rights.

This same letter to Cary and Company reiterated another way in which he continued to pursue self-determination. He was shipping only seventeen hogsheads of tobacco. He had grown no tobacco at his plantations on the Potomac, had "made none for two or three years past and believe I never shall again."[25]

In New England and the Middle Colonies, nonimportation sharply reduced British imports. To the south, observance was lax and importation apparently actually increased. Although the boycott seems to have had little effect on imperial policymakers, colonials active in the resistance movement avowed their faith in such militant measures. More important, the communication among the various associations promoted intercolonial cooperation. Meanwhile in Parliament in April 1770, a new administration headed by Lord North engineered repeal of all the Townshend duties except the levy on tea. The strategy was to undercut the basis of the nonimportation pacts while upholding parliamentary authority. Pragmatic colonials called this partial repeal a victory; ideologues and radicals argued that to yield even to the small tax on tea would give away the whole cause.

In Virginia, geographical dispersion made enforcement of the Association difficult. Whether inadvertently or deliberately, violations were widespread. On 22 May 1770, at a general meeting in Williamsburg, the Virginia Associators appointed a committee of twenty, including Washington, to rewrite the pact.

When the committee met on 25 May, they differed so sharply there seemed scant possibility of agreement. Robert Carter Nicholas and Edmund Pendleton headed the moderates "who were for meeting the Parliament half" way. It had repealed most of the duties. Virginians should end the boycott or moderate its terms as a conciliatory gesture. To fierce ideologues such as Nicholas's uncle, Landon Carter, this was "Fine language . . . just as if there could be any half way between Slavery and freedom." Thus split, the committee wrangled till 11 P.M. the night of 28 May and till 1 A.M. on 31 May.[26]

Probably because of this division within the committee, the general meeting of the Association reconvened at the Capitol on 1 June. For five hours that evening, the discussion dragged on. At last, they decided to invite "all Gentlemen[,] Merchants, Traders, and others," to gather in Williamsburg on 15 June to consider revision of the Association.[27]

Richard Henry Lee, one of the proponents of a more rigorous association, sought George Mason's advice. Mason too favored strict enforcement. The "Names of such Persons as purchase or import Goods contrary to the Association should be published, & themselves stigmatized as Enemys to their Country," he said. They should be ostracized in business and common life. Committees in the various counties should enforce the regulations by looking into imports and publicizing violations.[28]

In late June 1770, 164 Associators, including Washington, endorsed a compromise boycott plan. While allowing the importation of more items and prohibiting mainly luxuries, the new Association sought stricter observance by adopting Mason's proposal for local enforcement committees. After the signing, the company adjourned to the Raleigh Tavern where they celebrated with a head-spinning seventeen toasts, the first being: "The King."[29]

It is difficult to assess Washington's precise role in the formation of the new Association. Most likely, he acted as a bridge between the militants and the moderates. Clearly, he intended to keep the lines of communication open while the two factions thrashed out a compromise. He dined twice with the leader of the moderates, Treasurer Nicholas, and shared meals with Speaker Peyton Randolph and Attorney General John Randolph. Undoubtedly they talked about nonimportation.[30]

In the end, Washington backed the compromise agreement as "the best that the friends to the cause coud obtain here." He believed it would be more closely observed. Still, it dissatisfied him. Little wonder the inhabitants of other provinces with more stringent agreements should criticize the Virginia pact, he said. He wished it were "ten times as strict," thinking it "too much relaxed from the spirit with which a measure of this sort ought to be conducted. . . ."

If he considered the Virginia boycott too lenient, the pacts to the north might be too strict. Stringent nonimportation might "put to too severe a Tryal" the northerners' "Public Virtue," their willingness to sacrifice private convenience for the public good. They might be unable to "stand the Test much longer if their Importations are not equal to the Real Necessities of the People. . . ." Recent evidence suggested to Washington that imports had been too greatly restricted. The dissolution of the New York Association supported that conclusion, as did the "attempts (tho' unsuccessful as yet) in other places to admit a general Importation of goods, Tea only excepted."[31]

Militant though his own views were, he recognized that leaders must avoid getting too far ahead of those they led, must measure the distance between political goals and present realities. Successful leaders kept clearly in mind their principles and plans, while they assessed current circumstances and achieved what they could.

Returning home, Washington took the lead in signing up subscribers to the new Association. At the bottom of a printed copy of the agreement, he added in his own handwriting a paragraph specifically pledging Fairfax County signatories to abide by the terms. In his usual methodical manner, he had the broadsides circulated around the county. He also sat with George Mason and three other gentlemen on the local enforcement committee, probably serving as its chairman.

As a result of this systematic effort, some 333 inhabitants representing most areas of the county enrolled their names. Of perhaps greater significance, the Fairfax Associators comprised many of the leading gentlemen, including between seven and ten merchants from Alexandria, an overwhelming majority of the church vestrymen, the sheriff, the county court clerk, and fifteen of the seventeen justices of the county court. There were also many landowners, large and small. The men of property and influence in Fairfax gave the Association of 1770 at least their tacit support, making the county a leading center of resistance.[32]

Washington meant to follow the new agreement strictly. He placed an order for prohibited items on the condition that Parliament had "totally repeald" the act "Imposing a Duty . . . for the purpose of raising a Revenue in America. . . ." He would refuse "to receive any Articles contrary" to the boycott.

In that same letter, he issued the sort of complaint he had been filing in his commercial correspondence for over a decade now. His goods had gone to the wrong river, costing him additional expense. The items sent were incorrect, incomplete, or damaged, and they were overpriced. Though he grew little tobacco anymore, he still griped at getting a lower price than other planters obtained for leaf of no greater quality. These were common complaints among Virginia planters and a common subject of talk. They and other colonials were buying more and more English goods, eagerly joining in the consumer revolution that swept Britain at mid-century. But as in politics, they felt themselves abused by the representatives of the metropolitan culture and economy.[33]

Parliament kept the tax on tea and a few additional items to assert its authority but withdrew the other Townshend duties. As the ministry hoped, this undercut the colonial boycott. In the summer and fall of 1770, the northern nonimportation associations collapsed one after another—first New York, then Philadelphia, finally Boston. Though the Associators pledged still to refuse goods bearing revenue-raising duties, such a limited and desultory effort could have little impact in London. In December, George Mason reported that nonimportation to the South had fallen into "a very languid State." Most people seemed inclined to wait hopefully for a further conciliatory move from Parliament. But, he warned, should "the oppressive System of taxing us without our Consent be continued," the flame of resistance would break out again.

According to Mason, the associations had failed because they had been "form'd upon an erronious Principle." Effective nonimportation would require "one general Plan . . . exactly the same for all the Colonys . . . restraining only Articles of Luxury & Ostentation" together with any taxed goods, and encouraging the development of American manufacturing. "Such a Plan as this," Mason added intriguingly, "is now in Contemplation. . . ." Just who was considering this scheme he failed to specify.[34]

If importers in the rest of Virginia were ignoring the Association, Mason, Washington, and the other Fairfax committeemen intended to keep their county in line. So widespread were violations elsewhere that they requested Moderator Randolph to convene a general meeting to revise the nonimportation agreement once again. In mid-July 1771, Washington was in Williamsburg for a brief special Assembly session and probably attended the Virginia Association's general meeting. The gathering voted to dissolve the organization but to retain the boycott of tea, paper, glass, and painter's colors of foreign manufacture, all of which still bore revenue-raising duties. With that, organized commercial resistance in Virginia sputtered out.[35]

Five days later, Washington ordered goods from several English merchants. He announced the end of the Virginia nonimportation Association except against a small number of enumerated items. That remaining pledge he intended to keep. "You will please, therefore, to be careful that none of the glass, Paper, &c., contained in my Invoices, are of those kinds which are subject to the duty Imposed by Parliament for the purpose of raising a Revenue in America." Once again, as so often before, he registered lengthy complaints about the shipment, quality, and prices of the goods he received. A year later, he would consider suspending imports altogether and buying all his goods in Virginia.[36]

He ordered luxury items he had put off buying because of the nonimportation pact: eight pairs of boots and shoes, one dozen of the best cambric handkerchiefs with purple borders, a "Man's very best" bearskin hat, a topaz or some other handsome stone with the Washington coat of arms neatly engraved on it, a "Man's very best Riding Saddle," and other high-priced quality items. The Virginia gentleman was again buying costly and "fashionable" attire. He and his wife purchased many luxuries from across the ocean, clothes and furniture and fine foods and other fancy items. By adopting current London fashions, prominent Virginia families reinforced their claims to social leadership.[37]

Despite the passage of the Townshend Acts and the failure of the Crown to resolve American grievances satisfactorily, American colonials kept their faith in George III. Rather than blame their monarch for this new instance of oppression, they accused a corrupt Parliament dominated by a scheming ministry. When the king ignored their supplications, many concluded that his advisers and their "hirelings" had deceived him about American affairs, had depicted his subjects there as disloyal and rebellious. More than one provincial avowed that if only their sovereign knew the facts, he would applaud their virtue. Partial repeal of the Townshend duties in 1770 sustained the faith of moderates in the efficacy of petitions to the throne.[38]

In August 1770, to honor George III's supposed earlier role in repeal of the Stamp Act, leading inhabitants of New York City gathered at the bowling green to dedicate a statue of His Majesty. Made of lead and richly covered with gilt, it was the first equestrian statue of him in America. The notables joined his honor the lieutenant governor in drinking "their Majesties and other loyal Healths." But some New Yorkers paid homage to another advocate. At the instigation of the Sons of Liberty, the provincial Assembly had authorized a statue of William Pitt. The king was not the only possible champion of colonial rights.[39]

The former Colonel Washington had said he would willingly resort to arms to defend the traditional rights of Englishmen. In May 1772, he took out his old uniform from regimental days and put it on, not to fight, but to sit for his portrait. Young Charles Willson Peale had come over from Annapolis to record the one-time soldier's likeness.

The face in the painting seems rather too youthful for a man of forty. Some have suggested that this portrait was meant to recapture the wartime appearance of the chief defender of Virginia's frontiers against foreign invaders. Out of one pocket peeks a paper headed "Order of March." In the background swirls a river. Perhaps the viewer is prompted to recall that this is the hero of Braddock's massacre on the Monongahela.[40] Whatever reaction painter or sitter intended to evoke, surely donning that uniform and strapping on that sword stirred memories in the ex-soldier, memories of that earlier fight to safeguard English and Virginian rights and interests.

CHAPTER NINE

"A rising Empire"

Washington's political and commercial activities were aimed at greater self-determination for himself and his colony. He had switched from tobacco to wheat and other enterprises to reduce his debts, augment his wealth, and secure his economic independence. Land was another means to these ends.

In June 1767, he advised a deeply indebted neighbor: "[A]n enterprising Man with very little Money may lay the foundation of a Noble Estate in the New Settlemts." of the Ohio Valley. Look at "how the greatest Estates we have in this Colony were made; was it not by taking up and purchasing at very low rates the rich back Lands which were thought nothing of in those days, but are now the most valuable Lands we possess?" "[M]any good families" were selling their Tidewater properties to pay off crushing debts and "retiring into the Interior parts of the Country for the benefit of their Children." Moreover, "[s]ome of the best Gentlemen in this Country talk of doing so," gentlemen "who are not drove by necessity, but adopt the Scheme from principles of Gain."[1]

A gentleman freeholder seated on his plantation fortress and possessed of thousands of acres was thought to be insulated from any external power. Landed wealth would not only make Washington rich, it would guarantee his autonomy and his honor. During the late 1760s and early 1770s, he moved vigorously to acquire vast holdings in the West. Virginia's leading gentlemen made their fortunes speculating in land. He had grown up among some of the most skillful and successful.

In a province filled with energetic land-hunters, he became a central figure, a leader in the struggle for control of western lands. But as with his other endeavors, he kept butting up against Crown policies he considered discriminatory.[2]

Since his teens, he had been buying land, adding to the size of his plantations. Soon after retiring from military service, he had cast his eyes toward the rich soil of the Ohio Valley. To encourage recruitment, Governor Dinwiddie had issued a proclamation in February 1754 offering bounty lands to those who would enlist in the Virginia Regiment. As early as 1759, the retired colonel and some of his fellow officers petitioned for their shares of the 200,000 acres promised, but without success. They tried once more at the close of the war. In March 1763, the Board of Trade laid their memorial before the king, apparently again without result.[3]

In May 1763, Washington became a leading promoter of a scheme to acquire a vast expanse in the Great Dismal Swamp of southeastern Virginia. The plan was to drain it and convert it into farmland. The company included three members of the Executive Council: Robert Burwell, William Nelson, and Thomas Nelson, whose patronage Washington had sought at the outset of his military career.

Doubtless it was their powerful positions, as well as Washington's own membership in the Burgesses, that enabled this syndicate to get around two early legal obstacles. Royal instructions limited grants of Crown lands to a maximum of 1000 acres per individual. Washington and his nine partners requested and received an exclusive seven-year option on some 148,000 acres. To circumvent the restrictive imperial regulation, they added to their petition the names of 138 dummies, a means often used by Virginia land speculators to evade Crown policies they considered inconvenient or unjust.

In January 1764, the syndicate also engineered legislation that permitted them to pass through or to construct canals or causeways across any previously patented property in the Swamp without being subject to lawsuits by the owners. If an owner claimed damages and could reach no settlement with the company, a third party was to be called in to decide the matter.[4]

In June 1763, the land-hunter from Mount Vernon joined an even more grandiose enterprise known as the Mississippi Company. The nineteen speculators from Virginia and Maryland included his brother Jack and four Lee brothers: Richard Henry, Francis Lightfoot, William, and Thomas Ludwell. This group requested a twelve-year option on

2.5 million acres of land recently wrested from the French in the Ohio Valley. In return for an exemption from quitrents and taxes during the life of the option, they pledged to seat at least two hundred families on what would become some of the finest farmland in Ohio, Indiana, Illinois, Kentucky, and Tennessee. But before they had time to file their petition, the Crown drew a line reserving the country west of the Allegheny Mountains to the Indians "for the present."[5]

The royal Proclamation of 7 October 1763 blocked not only the scheme of the Mississippi Company adventurers, but also the bounty claims of the regimental veterans. After the war, colonial land speculators wanted to promote rapid settlement of the West, but with the expulsion of the French, the Crown had no need for American Britons to push the frontier any farther. Imperial officials thought colonization of the interior detrimental to the Empire as a whole.

Crown authorities had several aims. They wanted to establish a systematic and general Indian policy controlled by London rather than the various colonies. By protecting native property rights from white encroachment, they would maintain both peace and the military alliance that had won much of North America for Britain. This would also safeguard the lucrative trade in furs. White settlement would endanger these goals. New colonies in the interior would also make the colonial population harder to control. In addition, the greater distance from salt water would compel these settlers to manufacture articles they otherwise would buy from Britain.

While the ministry foreclosed settlement of the Ohio Valley and the Great Lakes, they opened eastern Canada and the Floridas to land grants. A thickly populated seacoast was more easily defended from foreign invasion. English-speaking colonists in the three provinces recently taken from the French would help guard against any uprising or subversion by the French Canadians. New colonies on the northern and southern coasts would mean new markets for British manufactured goods. They would also develop extractive industries vital to the Empire: in the North, fisheries, coal, timber, and naval stores; in the South, silk, wine, and tropical fruits. Crown ministers feared that inland colonies would lead to a divergence of interests. They failed to see that the policy itself and colonial opposition to it reflected interests that had already begun to diverge.

During the mid-1760s, Washington momentarily diverted his attention from the West while he concentrated on switching from tobacco to wheat. He fully intended, though, to expand his land holdings in order to make himself debt-free and independent. In September 1767, he launched an aggressive effort to acquire large tracts in the Ohio Valley.

To William Crawford, formerly a Virginia regimental captain and now an energetic frontiersman, he proposed a partnership. They would survey and patent large and fertile tracts near Pittsburgh and, eventually, farther down the river. The Royal Proclamation of 1763 still reserved the Ohio region to the Indians, but Washington called it merely "a temporary expedient to quiet [their] Minds. . . . Any person therefore who neglects the present oppertunity of hunting out good Lands and in some measure marking and distinguishing them for their own (in order to keep others from settling them) will never regain it. . . ." Crawford would seek out these good lands. Washington would secure them "so soon as there is a possibility of doing it" and would pay the expenses of surveying and patenting. They would divide up the properties in proportions agreeable to both. "[K]eep this whole matter a profound Secret," he urged Crawford. Partly, he wished to prevent censure "for the opinion I have given in respect to the King's Proclamation. . . ." But he also wanted to avoid alerting other speculators before he and Crawford had laid "a proper foundation for success."[6]

Late in 1768, the treaties of Fort Stanwix and Hard Labour reopened Ohio Valley lands to white settlement. In 1769, Washington claimed his portion of the 200,000 acres of bounty lands promised to veterans of the Virginia Regiment under Governor Dinwiddie's 1754 proclamation. This he considered a public debt owed those who had "toild, and bled for the Country." He wanted a large unoccupied area designated within which each veteran could select the best lands he could find. Governor Botetourt and the Council instead required the claimants to choose their proportionate shares from twenty separate tracts. As a result, Washington convened meetings of the veterans and got them to hire Crawford as a surveyor. He also traveled to the Great Kanawha River, a southern tributary of the Ohio below Pittsburgh, to supervise the surveys himself. It was he who allotted the bounty lands among the officers and soldiers.

Assigning himself a large share of rich bottom land along the Great Kanawha, he ignored a long-standing Virginia statute prohibiting riverfront tracts more than three times as long as they were deep. Some of his fellow veterans complained that he had given himself and his friend Dr. James Craik what Washington called "the cream of the Country." The land-hungry ex-colonel justified his conduct by arguing that without his initiative and enterprise none of the soldiers would have gotten their bounty lands. When one former officer wrote him in drunken indignation, mistakenly believing he had been denied his fair share, Washington shot back angrily. He would never "have taken the same language from you personally," he raged, "without letting you feel some marks of my resentiment. . . ." He only regretted "that I ever engag'd in behalf of so ungrateful and dirty a fellow as you are."[7]

A royal proclamation granted lands to officers who had served until their units were reduced, that is, until they were disbanded at the end of the war in 1763. Having retired in 1758, Washington failed to meet that criterion. Still, he somehow persuaded Governor Dunmore to give him a colonel's portion of 5000 acres of these 1763 bounty lands. The canny speculator knew full well the technical provisions of the proclamation. In January 1770, he asked his brother Charles to inquire discreetly among former officers in his neighborhood about the possibility of buying up their rights. Charles should buy only from those who had served until after the expedition against the Cherokees, and he should keep George's name out of the transactions. Here was yet another royal rule regulating colonial economic affairs that this Virginia land-hunter deliberately circumvented. He thought himself entitled to a large share of bounty lands because his soldierly service had helped win this territory for the British Crown. Once again, honor should have material as well as social rewards.

By personal claim and purchase of other veterans' rights under the two bounty proclamations of 1763 and 1754, Washington eventually acquired more than 35,000 acres in the Ohio Valley, some 40 percent of his estate at the time of his death.[8]

Washington's aggressive land-hunting was spurred by more than an appetite for personal wealth and independence. The farm families who settled the interior would, he expected, grow foodstuffs for export. This expansion of American-controlled commercial agriculture would further promote colonial self-determination.

The connection between his moneymaking schemes and this goal is most evident in his promotion of projects to develop the Potomac River Valley. As early as 1754, he had urged the possibility and importance of better water and land carriage along the upper Potomac. This would stimulate commerce and strengthen Virginia's stake in the Ohio Valley. In 1762, he offered his friend Thomas Johnson, Jr., observations on improving navigation at the Great Falls. For years, Johnson, who would eventually serve as Maryland's Revolutionary governor, spearheaded Potomac development.[9]

Beginning in 1769, Washington himself became an active and persistent promoter of plans to improve Potomac navigation. This coincided with the Crown's reopening of the West to settlement and his own efforts to secure bounty lands there. In December, he and fellow Burgess Richard Henry Lee drafted legislation to clear and make navigable the upper Potomac from Fort Cumberland down to the Great Falls. In April 1772, he sat on another Assembly committee to bring in a bill for a much enlarged plan to open navigation of the river from Fort Cumberland to Tidewater. Working with Virginians and Marylanders prominent in Potomac and western commerce and land speculation, he was one of the project's leading trustees.[10]

Washington knew that improved water transportation would boost the value of his western lands. It would cut the cost of shipping agricultural produce from them and manufactured goods to them. But he thought of more than personal profit-seeking. The navigation scheme also offered Virginians an escape from the restrictions of the tobacco trade. It would enable Ohio country farmers to produce foodstuffs marketable in Britain, Europe, and the West Indies. A promotional tract claimed that extending the navigable length of the Potomac would "greatly increase our Export of wheat gently lead our people off from Tobacco . . . [and] render a vast Extent of Back Country useful to Trade."[11] Washington's expansionist program promised him and his fellow colonials not only prosperity, but economic self-determination.

Beyond that, Washington pursued a vision of North American empire. His words shimmered with that idea. The navigation plan would make "Potomack the Channel of Commerce between Great Britain and that immense Territory Tract of Country *which is* unfolding to our view . . . ," funneling through it "the extensive and valuable Trade of a rising Empire. . . ." His expansionist dream ranged far ahead and wide in scope: ". . . I think the opening of the Potomack will at once fix the Trade of the Western Country" for Virginia and Maryland, "at least till it may be conduct'd through the Mississippi (by New Orleans). . . ."[12]

Some Virginians and Marylanders, particularly those unlikely to profit directly from the navigation plan, resisted it. Washington feared that "ill tim'd Parsimony and supiness" might forfeit the lucrative western commerce to Pennsylvania and New York. Decisive action would make the Potomac the chief avenue of trade to and from the great continental heartland. Inaction would forfeit this trade to enterprising men in the Middle Colonies. Though his vision foresaw an *American* empire, it would be an American empire in which Virginians played the leading role. Even in his nascent nationalism, he clung to some of his provincial bias.[13]

Fairfax County, and particularly the county seat, Alexandria, played a key role in Washington's expansionist scheme. After mid-century, the town emerged as the major commercial center in the Potomac River Valley. It dominated trade in grain and foodstuffs within the region and for foreign export. Washington and other local leaders boosted it as the great channel of trade to and from the Ohio country. Later, he would envision that function for the new Federal District across the river.

In August 1766, when George Johnston died, Washington replaced him as one of Alexandria's trustees. A few years later, he constructed a house for his convenience when there on business or pleasure. He also used his influence in the Assembly to promote the town's commercial interests. It was growing rapidly in commerce and population. In 1774, he introduced a bill to extend its boundaries. He and several merchants also collaborated on a legislative proposal that would give Fairfax and neighboring counties a special exemption from or reduction of Virginia's duties on imported rum. They wanted to augment the direct trade between the Potomac and the West Indies, circumventing middlemen in Philadelphia. Washington had a personal stake in the outcome. He planned to trade flour and herring for "the most Saleable kind of Rum and Sugars." In addition, fishing the Potomac had become a profitable enterprise for him and Alexandria. Burgess Washington therefore sought legislation to regulate inspection of herring.[14]

Washington and the merchants of Alexandria had hoped to make it the hub of commerce connecting the Potomac River Valley and the Ohio country with the Atlantic world. Unfortunately, those merchants lacked the capital to conduct the export trade on their own. They remained transshipment agents for entrepreneurs elsewhere who invested the necessary capital. The town never fulfilled its boosters' dreams.[15]

For several years, Washington and other speculators had heard rumors that the Crown would soon establish a new colony in the Ohio Valley. Creation of a government in the interior would increase the value of his holdings. Few white farm families would want to lease his lands there without civil and military authority to maintain order and to protect them from Indians resisting their encroachment. He never meant to sell his land to freehold farmers. Some of it he settled with black slaves and white indentured servants managed by white overseers. Most of it he planned to rent to tenant farmers on long-term leases. Tenancy was on the rise in Virginia's Northern Neck, and he was one of the region's substantial landlords. His expansionist vision foresaw, not a Jeffersonian freeholders' empire, but the spread of the traditional system of land tenure, labor relations, and racial and class hierarchy.[16]

Meanwhile, in London, influential men such as Lord Hillsborough, for several years secretary for the colonies, continued to oppose white settlement of the interior. In 1768, the ministry had relaxed the ban on land grants west of the Alleghenies, but proponents of the old policy used delaying tactics to prevent organization of a provincial government there. As in the past, they feared that an inland colony would provoke the Indians, disrupt the fur trade, and create a potentially rebellious political entity, while hurting rather than helping British commerce and manufacturing. They still favored colonization of the coasts as more advantageous politically, militarily, and economically. In April 1773, this viewpoint triumphed when the Privy Council once again forbade land grants or surveys beyond the Line of 1763 without special orders. At the end of 1773, establishment of a colony in the Ohio Valley, though approved, was still being put off.[17]

The Order in Council of April 1773 had no effect on Washington's bounty lands under Governor Dinwiddie's 1754 proclamation. Most of these he had already patented. But it did prevent him from making additional acquisitions by purchase. Still, he had one cause for hope: the order allowed grants under the royal bounty Proclamation of 1763. Basing their claims on that decree, he and other veterans sought to patent lands on the Ohio in the region claimed by Virginia. Virginia's Executive Council authorized this request. As before, Washington also looked to buy up the rights of other soldiers. He wanted to act quickly before another shift in policy threw up new roadblocks.[18]

But when Washington wrote Governor Dunmore about the matter, his Lordship sent a discouraging reply: "I do not mean to grant any patents on the Western waters, as I do not *think I* am *at present* impowered to do so." Since Dunmore had expressed this only as his opinion Washington decided to press the veterans' case further. The Privy Council, he pointed out, specifically permitted veterans to make claims under the 1763 bounty. He also reiterated his old contention about the 1763 Proclamation Line being only "a temporary expedient" to quiet the Indians. He and "a number of Officers" who had commanded Virginia troops depended on his Lordship to vindicate "their just rights." A delay by the governor would equal a refusal, as the western country had already begun "spreading over with Emigrants," who settled land without bothering to obtain legal title. Apparently in response, Dunmore allowed some surveys.[19]

On other fronts, Washington's dream of landed independence and American expansion kept clashing with the reality of imperial policy. The Mississippi Company lobbied unsuccessfully for nine years to get a whopping 2.5 million acres in the West. In January 1772, Washington finally wrote off his investment as a loss. Likewise, his efforts to satisfy his claims under the 1763 bounty by patenting tracts in West Florida proved fruitless. In the summer of 1773, an agent went land-hunting for him in the Gulf Coast country. According to the governor of West Florida, reported the agent, Lord Hillsborough believed the 1763 proclamation excluded provincial officers.[20]

This denial of what Washington considered his rightful claims reignited the anger he had felt as a colonial soldier slighted by the regular army. "I conceive the services of a Provincial Officer as worthy of regard as those of a regular one," he complained, "and [such regard] can only be withheld from him with injustice. . . ." Crown policies concerning western lands, imposition of revenue-raising duties, and his clashes with English merchants had all fed his sense of discrimination. His ventures in land speculation, farming, and trade reflected his growing conviction that the interests of the North American colonies and the mother country conflicted. This sense of grievance nurtured a new identity. "The Acct. of Lord Hilsboroughs Sentiments . . . ," he said, "I can view in no other light than as one, among many other proofs, of his Lordships malignant disposition towards us poor Americans. . . ."[21]

Hillsborough's views might, Washington feared, "set on foot an enquiry" which would suspend granting lands in Virginia under the 1763 bounty. He decided to act quickly before that opinion became official policy. He wanted to settle Palatine or, possibly, Irish tenants on his lands, as expeditiously as possible. Once seated, the Crown would find it hard to remove them or to take away Washington's property rights. Unfortunately, the scheme proved impractical, and Washington quickly abandoned it. He must continue to seek renters among Virginia's and Maryland's poor white planters. Meanwhile, he would have to rely on indentured servants, slaves, and transported convict laborers.[22]

The ministerial engineers tried in vain to dam up white emigrants. Settlers spilled over the Line of 1763 and flowed in swelling streams into the basin reserved for the Indians. Although men like Washington opposed the outright ban on land grants, they also resisted unauthorized squatting by frontiersmen. They favored orderly settlement. The supervision of duly constituted authority would keep the white population of the interior under government control and maintain their connections with the seaboard provinces. Colonial speculators, as much as the Crown, wanted to guard against a separation of interests between the coast and the hinterland. Controlled settlement would also serve the economic interests of the speculators.

Defying the imperial prohibition, white provincials pushed ahead and met natives ready to contest their encroachment. Friction between the frontiersmen and the Ohio Valley tribes broke out into war in the spring of 1774. Acquaintances and business associates reported the beginning of hostilities to Washington. They begged for immediate assistance from Williamsburg. Sixteen years after his service in the French and Indian War, the frontier folk still looked to the ex-soldier for protection. They depended on him and his influence in the capital, wrote one, "as you are a better Judge of our distrass than all Most aney other Jentleman. . . ." His response to their entreaties encouraged them to stand their ground.[23] Because of his past military exploits, his economic stake in the West, and his growing prominence in the House of Burgesses, they looked to Washington to advocate their defense.

The white-Indian conflict known as Dunmore's War showed again that frontier families settling beyond the reach of civil authority lived in jeopardy. It also demonstrated that having once put themselves in such danger, legally or not, white settlers expected the government to protect them. But just at this juncture the king's councillors in London announced a seemingly opposite policy.

The Quebec Act took the territory west of Pennsylvania, north of the Ohio River, and east of the Mississippi, including the Great Lakes, and made it a part of the Province of Quebec. The Crown still intended to set that area aside for the fur trade and the Indians. Although Washington's lands lay south of the river, any tenants working them would face a constant threat from roving bands of hunters and warriors, who might easily cross the Ohio from the Indian towns on its northern shore. Depredations by hunting parties, Indian and white, had already helped provoke Dunmore's War. The war and the Quebec Act added further obstacles in the path of Washington's plans to settle tenant farmers on his Ohio Valley lands.[24]

At that moment, events in Boston and London suddenly presented even greater threats to Washington's, and America's, interests and rights.

"Is . . . anything to be expected from petitioning?"

In the summer of 1774, George Washington became a central figure in Virginia politics. The crisis that followed the Boston Tea Party and the "Coercive" Acts provoked militant resistance throughout the colonies. In Fairfax County and then in the Virginia Convention at Williamsburg, he took a leading role in the movement of protest. His comments on these events reflect the influence on him of "Country Party" ideology.

When Parliament repealed most of the Townshend duties, it left revenue-raising imposts on a few items to uphold its constitutional authority to tax the colonies. The most significant of these levies was on tea. Various ministerial policies had also tried to undergird the chief dealer in that commodity, the East India Company. By mid-1773, the company, through its own and the government's mismanagement, staggered under a surplus of seventeen million pounds of tea. The North ministry came up with a solution useful to both the company and the administration.

Parliament granted the company the right to send tea directly to its own agents or to specified importers in the colonies. At the American port of entry, rather than at the English port of departure as previously, the threepenny-a-pound tax would fall due. By eliminating the commercial middlemen, the company could sell its tea to Americans at much cheaper rates—indeed, even with the tax, at prices that undercut all competition including smuggled Dutch tea. The ministry intended not only to reassert governmental authority, but to strengthen a source of revenue that in recent years had helped pay the salaries of colonial administrators. Evidently they hoped colonials would swallow the bitter pill of taxation if they could wash it down with drafts of inexpensive tea.

Colonial resistance had remained relatively quiescent for more than three years. These new measures reignited it. Late in 1773, protesters denounced the policy on both constitutional and commercial grounds. A legislature that included no American representatives had laid the levy, while the East India Company had been handed a virtual monopoly of the tea trade, an opportunity to drive colonial competitors out of business.

In New York and Philadelphia, opponents of the duty intimidated the company's agents into resigning their commissions. The "Committee for Tarring and Feathering" of the City of Brotherly Love warned Delaware River pilots against guiding the ship that would deliver the tea. Farther north, in Boston, the agents, two of them sons of Lieutenant Governor Thomas Hutchinson, refused to cave in to the demands of the militants. Sam Adams and his fellow agitators tried public scorn and threats of violence but without success. The tea ships arrived, only to swing at anchor for several weeks, unable to unload their cargoes. Finally, on the evening of 16 December 1773, to prevent government officials from seizing the tea and forcibly bringing it ashore, "Sons of Liberty" costumed as Mohawk Indians turned Boston Harbor into a giant teapot.

The mob action in Boston provoked the ministry and the overwhelming majority in Parliament to outrage. English public opinion was decidedly critical, even among friends of the colonial cause. In America, reaction to this destruction of property was also often negative. The administration took immediate steps to reassert Parliament's supremacy. They now believed that more than a constitutional principle was at stake. Agitators in the colonies, they concluded, sought nothing short of complete independence. They felt certain that such a separation would inevitably swing the American provinces into the orbit of France, spelling the end, not only of British dominion in North America, but of the entire British Empire. They must crush this incipient insurrection before it spread.

Late in March 1774, Parliament voted overwhelmingly in favor of the so-called Boston Port Bill: as of 1 June 1774, that port would remain closed to commerce until the town's inhabitants had made reparations to the East India Company. Other coercive measures would soon follow. As the ministry quickly discovered, they were trying to smother the flames of colonial dissent with dry straw.

From Boston, the cry for help went out and radiated along the network of correspondence committees that now linked the colonies and made resistance truly continental, truly American. News of the Boston Port Bill reached Williamsburg shortly after Washington arrived on 16 May 1774 for the meeting of the Assembly.[1]

Though he disapproved of the political vandalism in Boston, Washington considered the British ministry's response nothing short of "despotick."[2] He wanted to act vigorously to defend American rights but was unready to spurn those slower to move. He accepted the practical necessity of communicating and working with men who held differing, even opposing, views. As usual during visits to Williamsburg, he dined with the most powerful men in the colony, among them the current royal governor, Lord Dunmore; Speaker Peyton Randolph; Treasurer Robert Carter Nicholas; and the attorney general of Virginia, John Randolph, a man who would find himself isolated in the present crisis because of his conservatism.[3]

The night of 23 May, in the Chamber of the Executive Council, a group of militant Burgesses led by the magnetic orator Patrick Henry met in strictest secrecy. They included Thomas Jefferson, Francis Lightfoot Lee, and Richard Henry Lee. With them sat a private citizen in town on personal business, Washington's neighbor George Mason.

They reviewed the news of the last few days. Williamsburg buzzed with talk of the Boston Port Bill. The moment presented crisis and opportunity. What should they do? If the Burgesses publicly backed Boston now, Governor Dunmore would dissolve them immediately. They decided to have Richard Henry Lee draft a set of resolves, but the group would postpone introducing them until completion of the colony's business at the end of the session. Then let Dunmore dissolve as he willed. But the end of the session lay weeks away. The public was aroused now. They must act at once to reinforce the common outcry.

The conferees in the council room settled on a dramatic symbolic act. The Burgesses should set aside 1 June, the date on which armed British forces would shut up the port of Boston, as "a Day of Fasting, Humiliation, and Prayer." On that morning, the people's elected representatives would gather in their chamber and then proceed behind their speaker to the parish church. Prayers would be offered up and a suitable sermon preached. They would beg divine intervention to prevent the destruction of "our civil Rights, and the Evils of civil War; to give us one Heart and one Mind firmly to oppose, by all just and proper Means, every Injury to *American Rights*" and to inspire "the Minds of his Majesty and his Parliament . . . with Wisdom, Moderation, and Justice, to remove from the loyal People of *America* all Cause of Danger from a continued Pursuit of Measures pregnant with their Ruin." The House would encourage the entire colony to follow their example.[4]

Through this traditional ritual, British colonials would purge themselves of guilt in order to reaffirm their sense of special virtue and of divine chosenness. They repeatedly resorted to such ceremonies as a means of expressing and creating their evolving identity as Americans.

Shrewdly, Henry and his collaborators chose to have someone outside their circle propose the fast day. They selected Treasurer Robert Carter Nicholas, a man known for his political moderation and religious piety. The next day, 24 May 1774, Nicholas moved the resolution in the House. Overwhelming what little opposition arose, the Burgesses adopted the proposal and then went on to other matters.

They conducted public business as usual for the rest of that day, the next day, and through the afternoon of 26 May. Then, abruptly, Governor Dunmore summoned them into the Council Chamber, into the very room where Henry and his associates had, in Jefferson's words, "cooked up" the resolution. The governor now had that resolution in his hand. He told the Speaker and the Gentlemen of the House that its "Terms . . . reflect highly upon his Majesty and the Parliament of Great Britain; which makes it necessary for me to dissolve you; and you are dissolved accordingly."[5]

"This Dissolution was as sudden as unexpected. . . . ," said Washington. He had dined with Dunmore the evening before and breakfasted with him that morning. The governor had dropped no hint. It "is the very first time," observed Landon Carter ironically, that "Praying that His Majesty and his Parliament may be inspired from above with Wisdom, Justice, and moderation was ever thought derogatory to the honours of either of them, especially in an established Church, whose Liturgy proposes Collects for that very purpose and in words almost tantamount."

Reported Washington, "[T]here were other resolves of a much more spirited nature ready to be offered to the House wch. would have been unanimously adopted. . . ." These were being "withheld till the Important business of the Country could be gone through." He may not have known that Dunmore had heard rumor of those resolves. In fact, the governor had dismissed the Assembly, not because they had called the fast day, but to forestall the militants' planned next step.[6]

"As the case stands," complained Washington, "the assembly sat In 22 days for nothing. . . ." They had yet to pass any legislation. More than inconvenient, this was dangerous. War with the Indians now loomed on the frontier, but Virginia's militia law had expired. Dissolution of the Assembly had left the colony virtually defenseless. And another "matter of no small moment . . . a total stop is now put to our Courts of Justice. . . ." The statute setting the fee schedule for the court system had expired on 12 April, closing the courts to civil suits. This would stymie creditors acting to collect debts.[7]

The next morning, 27 May 1774, eighty-nine of the former Burgesses met at the Raleigh Tavern. Using Richard Henry Lee's draft resolutions as a basis, they addressed their "countrymen" on the "measures . . . best fitted to secure our dearest rights and liberty from destruction. . . : With much grief we find that our dutiful applications to Great Britain for security of our just, antient, and constitutional rights, have been not only disregarded, but that a determined system is formed and pressed for reducing the inhabitants of British America to slavery. . . ." The Virginia leaders urged a boycott of taxed tea and of all other commodities of the East India Company until Parliament redressed American grievances. They viewed an attack on one colony as an attack on all. They recommended an annual general congress of deputies from all the British American colonies. The late Burgesses concluded with a veiled threat that if Britain persisted in its course, the colonials would feel compelled to suspend Anglo-American trade totally.[8]

On Sunday, 29 May, Washington attended worship not once, but twice, a devotion to divine services unprecedented in his churchgoing. That same Sabbath, a courier clattered into town with dispatches from the corresponding committees of Annapolis, Philadelphia, and Boston.[9] On Monday morning, Moderator Peyton Randolph convened a meeting of the twenty-five former Burgesses still in Williamsburg.

Most important among the newly received papers was a letter from Samuel Adams. A meeting in Boston, he announced, had called upon all of the colonies to do what the Virginia Burgesses had just threatened: to cut off trade with Britain until Parliament repealed the Port Bill. Hearing this, most of those present agreed on the necessity of a new nonimportation association. They felt their fellow Virginians would concur in this. They disagreed, however, about stopping exports. In any case, they thought their numbers too few to commit the whole colony to any sort of boycott. They decided to call the members of the just-dissolved House to "a general Meeting" in Williamsburg on 1 August. These gentlemen should use the intervening two months as "an Opportunity of collecting the Sense of their respective Counties."

On Tuesday, 31 May, the twenty-five gathered again to sign the letter summoning the former Burgesses. They concluded their invitation on an urgent note: "Things seem to be hurrying to an alarming Crisis, and demand the speedy, united Councils of all those who have a Regard for the common Cause." [10]

On Wednesday, 1 June, in conformity with the resolves of the late House of Burgesses, Washington "Went to Church & fasted all day." In parish after parish throughout the province, Virginians set apart this "day of fasting, humiliation, and prayer" to seek God's protection and to assert their rights. One rector "exhort[ed] the people in his sermon to support their Liberties, concluding with the resolve for the fast, . . . in the room of God save the King he cried out God Preserve all the Just rights and Liberties of America." [11]

Washington ruminated on these events as he pursued a full schedule of business in the Williamsburg neighborhood and visited his wife's Bassett and Dandridge relatives in nearby New Kent County. Her brother Bartholomew Dandridge and brother-in-law Burwell Bassett had represented the county in the House and would soon be elected its deputies to the August Convention. Undoubtedly Washington discussed with them the crisis and possible measures of resistance. [12]

He seems to have expected that in the end Britain and her colonies would reconcile, for even as he joined the protest he asked his commercial agent in London about the possible market there for his wheat flour. He thought it likely that Americans would suspend trade with Britain. Had he expected the rupture to be lengthy, much less end in war, it is doubtful he would have bothered to make this inquiry. [13]

On 10 June, he reviewed recent events for his old friend George William Fairfax, who now lived in England. He "hopd, and expected" the upcoming Virginia Convention would adopt "vigorous measures . . . to obtain that justice which is denied to our Petitions and Remonstrances; . . . the ministry may rely on it that Americans will never be tax'd without their own consent[,] that the cause of Boston[,] the despotick Measures in respect to it I mean[,] now is and ever will be considerd as the cause of America (not that we approve their conduct in destroyg. the Tea) . . . we shall not suffer ourselves to be sacrificed by piece meals though god only knows what is to become of us. . . ." He thought "a general War" with the Indians "inevitable. . . ." Meanwhile "those from whom we have a right to seek protection are endeavouring by every piece of Art and despotism to fix the Shackles of Slavery upon us." The dissolution of the Assembly "has left us without the means of Defence except under the old Militia Invasion Laws which are by no means adequate to the exigency's of the Country. . . ." Nonetheless, he felt certain the governor would not call for new elections until he got orders from the ministry.

"[I]n short," said Washington, "since the first Settlemt. of this Colony the Minds of People in it never were more disturbd, or our Situation so critical as at present; arising as I have said before from an Invasion of our Rights and Priviledges by the Mother Country; and our lives and properties by the Savages. . . ." To add to the distress, frost and drought had damaged the wheat crop, the dismissal of the Burgesses had forced the courts to close, and "Circulating Cash" was in short supply.[14]

More and more this American colonial was coming to view the British ministry as an implacable enemy. He expected its agent in Virginia, Governor Dunmore, to leave the province without a legislature until he heard from London. To his surprise, Dunmore issued writs of election almost immediately. Washington would, of course, stand for office again.

Late in June, he set off for home, prepared to lead Fairfax County in supporting vigorous measures of resistance. On the way, he stopped overnight in Fredericksburg with his sister Betty's family. Probably he and his brother-in-law, Colonel Fielding Lewis, talked politics. The town had just appointed a committee of correspondence, with Lewis and Washington's brother Charles as members. Reaching Mount Vernon, he soon got political intelligence of developments in Maryland from Thomas Johnson, Jr., his associate in the Potomac navigation scheme.[15]

About this time, word arrived that the ministry was pressing Parliament for two more coercive measures. The first would alter the fundamental charter of government in Massachusetts. It would reduce the power of the lower House by giving the royal governor authority to appoint members of the Council and other officials. It would also sharply limit the authority of local officials. The second bill seemed equally dangerous: when Crown officers or citizens assisting them were accused of murdering persons engaged in allegedly illegal acts, the governor would have authority to send them out of the colony for trial if he thought they would be denied a fair trial in Massachusetts. The stated goal was to safeguard royal officials and loyal citizens defending the king's law and his government against agitators. To militants it seemed a scheme to protect official murderers. Outraged Americans saw these new bills as two more links in the shackles of slavery being forged by the British ministry. In May, Parliament had also passed the Quartering Act. This measure would help maintain order in Massachusetts by lodging soldiers in neighborhoods of unrest. Americans, imbued with the traditional British fear of standing armies, thought this an ominous adjunct to the other "Coercive" Acts.

On Sunday, 26 June 1774, Washington "Went up to Church" at Alexandria, rather than to the nearby Pohick Church where he still served as a vestryman. Probably he wanted to use this convenient gathering place to talk politics with influential members of the local gentry. Following the worship service, a knot of gentlemen collected in the churchyard. One of them, Colonel John West, the other incumbent Burgess from Fairfax County, confirmed that he had decided against running for reelection. Whom would they agree upon to succeed him? Washington suggested Bryan Fairfax, son of his old mentor Colonel William Fairfax. "Several gentlemen" responded that Fairfax had already refused because his more moderate approach to the crisis, he felt, put him out of step with the constituency.[16] They would have to defer choice of a candidate.

By now, Washington had taken his place as the foremost figure among the gentlemen who dominated politics in Fairfax County. This group, active in commerce and land speculation, exerted their influence beyond the boundaries of the county, up and down the Potomac River Valley. They decided who would represent Fairfax in the Assembly, apparently agreeing never to compete with one another for election. In the last two contests, Washington and West had run unopposed. During the present crisis, Washington wanted a colleague he felt he could count on. ". . . I think the country never stood more in need of men of abilities and liberal sentiments than now . . . ," he said.

With that in mind, the following Sunday, 3 July, Washington worshiped at Pohick Church, where he "entreated several gentlemen . . . to press Colonel Mason to take a poll. . . ." But George Mason, though influential in Virginia as a political thinker, personally abhorred politicking and preferred to stay out of office. Apparently the only other candidate available was Major Charles Broadwater. Washington thought him "a good man," but one who "might do as well in the discharge of his domestic concerns, as in the capacity of a legislator." Because of these misgivings, he still favored Mason or Fairfax and tried once more to persuade the latter gentleman. He warned, though, that he could "be of little assistance . . . because I early laid it down as a maxim not to propose myself, and solicit for a second." [17]

In espousing that principle, he affirmed the Whig gentleman's code of campaigning. To do otherwise would smack of promoting a faction. Of course, when political necessity required it, as it had with his colleague George Mercer in the 1761 Burgesses' election, Washington, like other gentlemen, felt the code could be relaxed. In 1774, he found no need for such pragmatism. Though Fairfax and Mason might refuse to run, the propertied gentlemen of the county would yet determine who succeeded West in the House.

When Washington tried to persuade his old friend Bryan Fairfax to stand for election, it became apparent that a gulf was opening between them. For the present, Fairfax opposed a commercial boycott. He doubted that many Virginians would keep it strictly. Such a failure would do more harm than good. He thought it "more proper to try what Effect a petition might have towards obtaining a repeal of the Duty." He "would willingly give the Parliament a fair Opportunity to do it, and therefore should be for a petition unaccompanied with any Threats or Claims (for we have already used them) and if such an Opportunity should be missed, we might be better able to judge of their real Intention towards us." But, he realized, few in Fairfax County shared his moderate opinions. [18]

Among those who had had their fill of moderate measures was the man to whom these words were addressed. Washington had adopted the "Country Party" view of a ministerial conspiracy to subvert the British constitution. During the past decade and a half, he had come to this political perspective at least partly through his reading.

Washington made works on history and politics a primary focus of that reading. According to one estimate, about one-fourth of the volumes in his library fell into those categories. [19] Most of the pamphlets dealt with contemporary political issues. The library of Martha Washington's first husband, Daniel Parke Custis, also had many volumes on these subjects. Washington brought this collection to Mount Vernon soon after his marriage. During the 1760s and 1770s, he had available to him many of the works that influenced the ideology of the American revolutionaries.

In his teens, he had begun to read an English history and *The Spectator* and had acquired a copy of *The Guardian*. The Custis library contained not only the latter two collections, but also *The Tatler*, *The*

Free Thinker, The Freeholder, John Trenchard and William Gordon's *The Independent Whig,* their enormously influential *Cato's Letters,* and all fourteen volumes of Henry St. John, Lord Viscount Bolingbroke's *The Craftsman.* The last-named periodical included the serialization of Bolingbroke's *Remarks on the History of England* and his *Dissertation Upon Parties.* Together these traced English constitutional and political development from 1640 down to the 1730s, in what Herbert Butterfield called the first "Whig" history. The Custis collection also had *Plutarch's Lives* in five volumes, a life of Oliver Cromwell, and many other works of ancient and modern history. Washington bought other books to educate his stepson Jack Custis. Among the titles of history and political thought was, perhaps most important, another "Whig" history of England, really almost a republican tract, that of "the celebrated" Mrs. Catharine Macaulay. Many books of both Custises, the father and the son, ended up in Washington's own library.[20] Although he never specifically mentioned reading these works, his political statements and his eventual incarnation of "Country Party" ideas indicate familiarity with such writings.

From the 1720s through the 1740s, the "Country Party" in Britain had as its ideological spokesmen a brilliant group of dissenting political thinkers and reformers. On the right, Bolingbroke led the radical Tories. On the left, Trenchard and Gordon spoke most effectively for the radical Whigs. "Country Party" thinking, more than any other intellectual influence, shaped the political outlook of the generation of Americans who fought the Revolution.[21]

These writers celebrated the glories of the English "constitution," that constellation of laws and customs, institutions and usage fashioned through centuries of historial experience, which they believed embodied the principles of "natural right." Britain's constitution, according to these ideologists, aimed most importantly at safeguarding the liberty of English subjects, both individuals and the people as a whole, against arbitrary rule by power-hungry monarchs and ministers.

In the early eighteenth century, in the generation of Trenchard and Gordon and Bolingbroke, a new sort of threat to the constitution arose. A financial and commercial revolution spawned a new class whose riches surged from speculation in paper stocks and bought for them social position and political influence. Establishment of a permanent funded national debt fueled the beginnings of Britain's transformation into the first industrial nation. The price of social change was heavy taxation of the agrarian classes.

Whig and Tory dissidents took alarm at the consequent displacement of the landed gentry. Men holding such property theoretically formed the foundation of the English constitutional system, their supposed economic independence guaranteeing their public virtue and thus the political independence of Parliament. Radical critics responded to the structural changes in English society in highly moralistic terms. They preached against the "corruption" of British politics and the decline of public virtue. In the policies and political machine of Robert Walpole they discerned, not a method to ensure political stability and to promote economic growth, but a scheme to extend ministerial "influence," aiming ultimately at the overthrow of the constitution.[22]

The "Country Party" attacks on the Walpole regime set the pattern of protest against subsequent ministries. Down through the American Revolution, English and American Radical Whigs detected a ceaseless ministerial conspiracy against liberty and the constitution. Administration, they charged, used the excuse of repeated international wars to load taxes on the people. By the mid-1760s, it had piled up a staggering national debt and drained Britain of its wealth. As a result, it allegedly had turned to taxing the colonies. The ministry ensured backing for its schemes, asserted the critics, by corrupting Parliament, buying seats, buying votes, dispensing patronage. Men whose support it could not purchase it tried to suppress.

Public corruption, it was believed, bred private vice. This was the era of Hogarth's "The Rake's Progress." Colonials visiting London expressed shock at the scale of immorality in every sphere. By the early 1770s, the British nation and Empire seemed headed for catastrophe and collapse. Political dissenters proclaimed that the ministry would stop at nothing to extend its power. America, they believed, was rapidly becoming the last refuge of British constitutional liberty.

The Radicals' analysis won widespread acceptance among American colonial leaders. It seemed to them to fit their political experience. It "explained" Crown authorities' arrogant disregard of provincial interests and provincial leaders. It located postwar imperial policies within a much larger pattern of constitutional subversion. Its idealization of the virtuous independence of the landed gentry meshed with the corporate self-image of the colonial elite, particularly in Virginia.

Washington's reply to Bryan Fairfax shows that he agreed with the radical political dissenters. Anger usually tangled his words and twisted his syntax, but now his rage came steady, straight, and strong.

He would "heartily" support "a humble and dutiful petition to the throne," he told his friend, "provided there was the most distant hope of success. But have we not tried this already? Have we not addressed the Lords, and remonstrated to the Commons? And to what end? Did they deign to look at our petitions? Does it not appear, as clear as the sun in its meridian brightness, that there is a regular, systematic plan formed to fix the right and practice of taxation upon us? Does not the uniform conduct of Parliament for some years past confirm this? Do not all the debates, especially those just brought to us, in the House of Commons on the side of government, expressly declare that America must be taxed in aid of the British funds, and that she has no longer resources within herself? Is there any thing to be expected from petitioning after this? Is not the attack upon the liberty and property of the people of Boston, before restitution of the loss to the India Company was demanded, a plain and self-evident proof of what they are aiming at? Do not the subsequent bills . . . for depriving the Massachusetts Bay of its charter, and for transporting offenders into other colonies or to Great Britain for trial, where it is impossible from the nature of the thing that justice can be obtained, convince us that the administration is determined to stick at nothing to carry its point? Ought we not, then, to put our virtue and fortitude to the severest test?"

He agreed with Fairfax that they should "attempt" no more than they could "execute," but he thought a nonimportation scheme more feasible than many believed. As to withholding exports, in effect refusing to pay debts owed British creditors, he had his "doubts." "[W]hilst we are accusing others of injustice, we should be just ourselves. . . ." He had gradually reduced what he owed and was now virtually debt-free. For other Virginians, the problem had become a major crisis. A credit boom in the late 1760s and early 1770s had enticed tobacco planters large and small to go deeper into debt. The sudden credit contraction of 1772, which was followed by a depression in the tobacco market, had hit them hard. Now in the summer of 1774, many planters discovered the connection between debts, merchants, and Crown ministers that Washington had long since discerned. "Country Party" ideology explained all of this to them as part of a conspiracy to undercut great planter autonomy and political leadership in order to complete the subversion of the English constitution. Washington agreed with the conspiracy theory but, for now, opposed a collective refusal to pay the considerable debt. "Nothing but the last extremity . . ." could justify such an action, he said. "Whether this is now come, is the question." [23]

CHAPTER ELEVEN

"There is no relief but in their distress"

As county meetings convened throughout Virginia, Washington's Fairfax made itself the model of militancy. On 5 July 1774, the inhabitants met in Alexandria, probably with Washington presiding. They voted a "subscription for the benefit and relief of . . . the industrious poor of the town of *Boston* . . . who, by a late cruel Act of Parliament, are deprived of their daily labour and bread. . . . [T]o keep up that manly spirit which has made them dear to every *American* though the envy of an arbitrary Parliament . . . ," the gathering pledged to send £273 sterling, 38 barrels of flour, and 150 bushels of wheat.[1]

The meeting also designated a committee to report back to the county two weeks hence with a set of resolutions that would guide Fairfax's representatives at Williamsburg in August. Washington stayed overnight at his house in Alexandria, probably to attend a meeting of the committee the following day. That group consisted of the leading gentlemen, in his words, the "first people" in the county, who chose him as their chairman. On 6 July, they drafted at least the outline of a set of resolves, apparently to be circulated for discussion before the next meeting of the county.[2]

On 14 July 1774, Washington again went up to Alexandria, where he and Major Charles Broadwater won election to the Assembly without opposition. In the customary Virginia manner, he "treated" the voters to refreshments and that night sponsored a ball.[3]

On Sunday, 17 July, George Mason, a member of the committee, came to Mount Vernon in the afternoon and stayed overnight. He and

Washington may then have put the Fairfax Resolves into their final form. On Monday, they rode up to Alexandria and met with the rest of the committee. After the gentlemen had made some minor alterations, they adjourned to the county courthouse, where at a general meeting of the freeholders and inhabitants, with Washington presiding, they presented the resolutions they had "adjudged advisable for this county to come to. . . ."[4]

Historians have often credited Mason with the sole, or at least the principal, authorship of the Fairfax Resolves. Certainly they bear the stamp of his style. That influential ideologist, the mentor of Virginia's revolutionaries, would surely have had a major voice in the deliberations of the committee. The group may have asked him to polish or even to flesh out the resolutions they had framed. Other scholars have suggested that Washington collaborated with Mason in writing them. But even if Mason alone, or Mason and Washington together, penned the words of these resolves, the ideas were those agreed upon by the whole committee on 6 July. The final results represented a consensus, not simply of these two leaders, but of the more vigorous proponents of American rights among the Fairfax County gentry. As in the past, Fairfax took a forward position in the resistance movement.[5]

As the gentlemen sat on the court bench, Washington was handed a lengthy letter from Bryan Fairfax. Expounding his misgivings about the tenor of the draft resolutions, Fairfax stated his belief that the colonies should send only a petition to the king, avoiding more extreme measures for the present. He excused himself from expressing these views in person, but private business kept him from the meeting, he said.[6]

Washington "hastily" looked the letter over and then "handed it round . . . the bench. . . . No person present seemed in the least disposed to adopt your sentiments," he told Fairfax later. "[T]here appeared a perfect satisfaction and acquiescence in the measures proposed. . . ." On second thought, there was one gentleman, "a Mr. Williamson, who was for adopting your advice literally," but no one supported him. The other gentlemen recommended against reading the letter to the entire meeting, as it was unlikely to make any converts, and some thought it "repugnant . . . to the very principle we were contending for. . . ." So Washington, as chairman, set it aside and went on to the business at hand.[7]

The Fairfax Resolves were far more thoughtful and complex than those of any other county. They offered a classic exposition of the "Country Party" theory of the English constitution and its corruption by designing politicians. The first settlers in America, they asserted, brought with them and passed to their descendants the privileges, immunities, and advantages of the constitution and government of England. Virginia's charter had confirmed these rights, but even if it had not, "the Laws of Nature and Nations" guaranteed them.

"[T]he most important and valuable Part of the British Constitution" was "the fundamental Principle," that the people would live only under those laws to which they had given their consent through their freely chosen representatives, representatives accountable to the people, sharing their burdens, and equally "affected by the Laws they enact[ed]." Without that provision, "the Government must of necessity degenerate" into despotism. Because geographical distance made American representation in Parliament impossible, only Virginia's Assembly could rightfully exercise legislative power.

But historically Parliament had "claimed and exercised the Power of regulating" colonial commerce, of restraining trade with foreign countries to protect British manufactures, and the colonies had accepted this policy. Why? The resolves offered a novel explanation: "[O]ur Ancestors submitted" to this arrangement "for the general Good of that great Body-politic of which we are a Part . . . ," even though it was "in some Degree repugnant to the Principles of the Constitution." For more than a century, that power had usually been exercised to the mutual benefit of the inhabitants of Great Britain and her colonies, "who during that long Period, always considered themselves as one and the same People. . . ." Americans had "Chearfully acquiesced," as long as internal policy and appropriations remained in the hands of the provincial legislatures.

Having established this constitutional and historical foundation, the resolves went on to the crisis of recent years. Parliament's claim to make "all such Laws as they think fit" to govern the people of the colonies "and to extort from us our Money with out our Consent" violated not only "the first Principles of the Constitution" and the colonial charters, but also "the natural Rights of Mankind." Enforcement of this claim would make the American legislatures only nominal and would reduce the people to slavery. The British ministry had "formed and pursued" "a premeditated Design and System . . . to introduce an arbitrary Government into his Majesty's American Dominions. . . ." To that end, they were "artfully prejudicing" the king and "inflaming the Minds" of the people of Britain, particularly by propagating the malevolent falsehood that the colonists intended to set up independent states.

The resolves next turned to measures of resistance. The inhabitants of Fairfax County would willingly contribute toward payment for the tea destroyed at Boston, but they also proposed a boycott of the East India Company "as the Tools and Instrument of Oppression." The county had already put itself among the most defiant of Virginia's localities by questioning Parliament's right to make any laws whatsoever for the colonies. It now stood among the most militant by proposing local extralegal committees to enforce a new nonimportation association. It also urged nonexportation if American grievances continued unredressed after 1 November 1775. Additionally, it called for a continental congress to "concert a general and uniform Plan" to defend American rights. The last proposal acted upon the idea that George Mason had said some people were considering back in December 1770.

Finally, the resolves recommended that the proposed congress "transmit an humble and dutiful" petition to the king, "asserting with decent Firmness our just and constitutional Rights and Privileg[es] . . . , declaring, in the strongest Terms, our Duty and Affection to his Majesty's Person, Family, [an]d Government," but warning him "to reflect, that from our Sovereign there can be but one Appeal." That appeal was the "last resort" Washington had considered five years earlier, the appeal to arms.[8]

Bryan Fairfax objected to much of this. He saw no evidence of a conspiracy to subvert American liberties, only sincere men honestly disagreeing and unfortunately misunderstanding one another. He preferred to urge a conciliatory attitude on both sides. He favored a petition. He opposed commercial compulsion. He thought the warning to the king a disturbing threat, better expunged. He found most objectionable the systematic denial of the authority of Parliament. This resolve, more than any other, would tend "to widen the Breach, and prevent a Reconciliation. . . ."[9]

These were Fairfax's objections, but he had stayed away, and Washington had chosen not to read his letter to the meeting. Of those present, only Mr. Williamson openly questioned the thrust of the resolves. Many others kept silent, telling themselves disagreement would be useless or feeling intimidated by the outspokenness of the militants who dominated the gathering.[10]

The meeting adopted the resolutions and appointed the newly elected Burgesses Washington and Broadwater to present them "as the Sense of the people of this County" at the August Convention in Williamsburg. It also ordered transmission of its proceedings to the printers at Williamsburg for publication.

In one additional way, Fairfax distinguished itself: the meeting appointed a committee of twenty-five "to Concert & Adopt such Measures as may be thought most expedient and Necessary." It would function as the kind of extralegal enforcement body proposed in the resolves. Most other counties waited until after the Convention to form such committees. The meeting named Washington as chair.[11]

Rind's *Virginia Gazette* published the fiery Fairfax Resolves on the eve of the Convention in Williamsburg. Almost simultaneously, hundreds of miles to the north, the *Boston Gazette* also printed them. The item began: "*AT A GENERAL Meeting of the Freeholders and Inhabitants of the County of* Fairfax, *on Monday, the 18th Day of July 1774, at the Court-house in the Town of* Alexandria, GEORGE WASHINGTON, *Esq, Chairman*. . . ."[12] George Washington? When had Bostonians last heard that name? It had been two decades since they had read of the courageous young provincial officer who had been the hero of Braddock's massacre. Now George Washington was emerging again as a leader in a new American struggle.

Two days after adoption of the Fairfax Resolves, Washington again displayed his adherence to Radical Whig ideas. More and more he and Bryan Fairfax disagreed, probably, he told his neighbor, because of "the different constructions we put upon the conduct and intention of the ministry. . . ." He saw no indication of a willingness in Parliament to repeal the recent coercive measures. He observed, or thought he observed, "that government is pursuing a regular plan at the expense of law and justice to overthrow our constitutional rights and liberties. . . ." How then could they expect any redress through humble and dutiful petitions contesting the right of Parliament to tax the colonies? They had already addressed the King, the Lords, and the Commons, "setting forth, that, as Englishmen, we could not be deprived of this essential and valuable part of a constitution." But to no avail.

The conduct of the Bostonians could never justify taking away Massachusetts's charter or exempting offenders from trial in the place where the offenses had been committed. Were not "all these things"—and now his indignation began rising higher—"self evident proofs of a fixed and uniform plan to tax us? If we want further proofs, do not all the debates in the H[o]use of Commons serve to confirm this? And has not General Gage's conduct since his arrival, (in stopping the address of his Council, and publishing a proclamation more becoming a Turkish bashaw, than an English governor, declaring it treason to associate in any manner by which the commerce of Great Britain is to be affected,) exhibited an unexampled testimony of the most despotic system of tyranny, that ever was practised in a free government? In short, what further proofs are wanted to satisfy one of the designs of the ministry, than their own acts, which are uniform and plainly tending to the same point . . . to fix the right of taxation? What hope then from petitioning . . . ? Shall we, after this, whine and cry for relief, when we have already tried it in vain? Or shall we supinely sit and see one province after another fall a prey to despotism?"

If he had any doubt that Parliament had no right to tax Americans without their consent, he would heartily agree to petitioning and petitioning only as "the proper method to apply for relief; because we should then be asking a favor, and not claiming a right. . . ." Washington believed, as the Fairfax Resolves asserted, that the right of a people to be taxed only by representatives of their own choosing found its basis in both "the law of nature and our constitution. . . . I think the Parliament of Great Britain hath no more right to put their hands into my pocket, without my consent, than I have to put my hands into yours for money. . . ." This view had already been urged on Parliament "in a firm, but decent manner, by all the colonies. . . ." Why petition them any more? "[W]hat reason is there to expect any thing from their justice?"

He was losing faith not only in Parliament, but in the king as well. "As to the resolution for addressing the throne," he said, he thought it useless and expected "nothing" from it. He would have refused to support it, "if the non-importation scheme was intended to be retarded by it . . . ," for he felt certain "that there is no relief but in their distress. . . ."

Washington had reached this conclusion five years earlier, in 1769. He had remarked then on the futility of petitions and had wanted to try economic pressure. In 1770, complaining of the weakness of Virginia's nonimportation pact, he had urged a more stringent scheme. Now, in 1774, he would press for rigorous restriction of imports.

"I think, at least I hope," he told Fairfax, "that there is public virtue enough left among us to deny ourselves every thing but the bare necessities of life to accomplish this end. This we have a right to do, and no power upon earth can compel us to do otherwise, till they have first reduced us to the most abject state of slavery that ever was designed for mankind." Undoubtedly stopping exports would effect the purpose more quickly, but "nothing but the last necessity" could justify the non-payment of debts owed Britain. Therefore, he had "doubts" about non-exportation. He wanted "to see the other method," nonimportation, tried first, because it was legal and would facilitate payment of the debts. Failing all that, there was "the last resort" he had faced up to half a decade before and that the Fairfax Resolves had threatened—the resort to arms.

He felt uneasy that he and his friend should "differ so widely in sentiment . . . in a matter of such great moment." He would distrust his own judgment, "if my nature did not recoil at the thought of submitting to measures, which I think subversive of every thing that I ought to hold dear and valuable, and did I not find, at the same time, that the voice of mankind is with me." By "the voice of mankind," Washington meant not popular opinion, but the distilled wisdom of collective historical experience. The right of American colonials to pay only those taxes voted by their elected representatives and, by implication, the right of resistance were natural rights. English historical experience had come to express and embody them in the institutions and laws known as the English "constitution," but they originated and inhered in human nature.[13] These beliefs were fundamentals of "Country Party" political thought.

Meanwhile, throughout Virginia, other county meetings adopted their own resolutions. Overwhelmingly they condemned the "Coercive" Acts and asserted the constitutional right of colonials to pay only those taxes levied by their elected representatives. Some, such as Albemarle County, explicitly denied the right of any external authority to legislate for Virginians. Chesterfield County boldly declared "that the sole Right of making Laws . . . and for raising and levying Taxes" was vested in the Assembly of Virginia and could never "be executed by any other Power, without Danger to our Liberties. . . ."

A great majority of localities called for a new nonimportation association. A surprisingly large number proposed immediate suspension of all trade, but the more influential counties shared Washington's view that discontinuing exports while the colonies were deeply in debt would be an act of injustice. Albemarle, where Thomas Jefferson drafted the resolves, joined Fairfax in calling for an end to exports in the fall of 1775 should other measures prove unavailing. To advance economic self-sufficiency, some meetings urged promotion of domestic manufacturing. A small number, like Fairfax, immediately established local enforcement committees.

Many Virginians were coming to feel a sense of common cause and common identity with the inhabitants of the other colonies. More than a dozen counties called for or expected a continental congress to spearhead united action. Still, they considered themselves loyal subjects of the British Crown. The resolutions of most counties refuted the charge that colonials contesting parliamentary authority intended to establish independent states. They also professed their unswerving allegiance to their monarch.

As the freeholders and inhabitants of Caroline put it: "That the Design of our Meeting may not be misinterpreted, we think it proper to declare, what would otherwise be unnecessary, that we will preserve all due Obedience and Fidelity to the Royal Person and Government of his sacred Majesty King George III." Following the meetings in Princess Anne, Richmond, and Westmoreland, patriotic toasts were drunk avowing loyalty to George III and a desire for reconciliation. The company in Westmoreland, Richard Henry Lee's home county, drank: "God bless the King; may he long reign the King of a free and happy people"; to "The Queen and the Royal Family"; and to "Union of Great Britain and the Colonies."

These Virginians, like many in other colonies, still blamed their troubles on conniving, power-hungry ministers. Their suspicions stopped short of their monarch. But in other quarters, the king was obviously being watched closely. More than half a dozen meetings, among them Jefferson's Albemarle, omitted mention of the monarch. They withheld the traditional pledges of loyalty, but as yet avoided indicting George III himself. The freeholders of Patrick Henry's Hanover asserted, "A steady Loyalty to the Kings of England has ever distinguished our Country," but they warned, "God grant we may never see the Time when that Loyalty shall be found incompatible with the Rights of Freemen." Only Washington's Fairfax plainly warned George III of the violent consequences if he betrayed America's duty and affection to him and his government.[14]

On 23 July 1774, Thomas Johnson, Jr., spent the day at Mount Vernon. He came with William Paca, another leading member of the Maryland Committee of Correspondence. Both would become delegates to the approaching Continental Congress in Philadelphia. The next day, a Sunday, Washington worshiped in Alexandria. His churchgoing was usually sporadic, but in recent weeks he had attended frequently. The parish churchyard, a convenient gathering place where planters talked business, had become a forum for politics. On Thursday,

Washington set out for the Convention in Williamsburg. He spent that night and part of the next day in Fredericksburg with Fielding Lewis and on Saturday reached Burwell Bassett's, staying there all day Sunday. Undoubtedly he talked politics with these brothers-in-law and fellow Burgesses. He arrived in Williamsburg on Monday.[15]

The delegates convened in the Capitol. It was the fullest representation at any colony-wide meeting Washington and others could remember. The Convention immediately and unanimously agreed on the necessity for "a general congress of deputies from all the Colonies," to meet as soon as possible. They also debated a program of action.[16] By the end of the week, they had hammered out a plan closely following the Fairfax Resolves presented by Washington.

The Convention established a new nonimportation association to begin 1 November 1774. It also sought to encourage domestic manufacturing and, thereby, economic self-sufficiency. It warned that if American grievances remained unredressed after 10 August 1775, exports to Britain would be cut off. It deferred the weapon of nonexportation out of a sense of justice to their British creditors and to avoid injuring Virginians who had already invested in the current year's tobacco crop.

The delegates reiterated standard colonial affirmations of affection and allegiance to the king and a desire for continued connection with Great Britain. Significantly missing was a request that the Continental Congress beseech the throne for redress. Apparently a majority of the deputies had finally come to Washington's long-held opinion that petitions were futile, that only commercial coercion would get results.[17] Most important, the new association would be enforced by local extralegal committees, as the Fairfax Resolves proposed.

Perhaps because of the influence of those resolves in shaping the new association, Washington emerged as a central leader in the current crisis. In recent years, he had become one of the more important members of the Assembly and a powerful commercial and political leader in the Chesapeake region and the newly settling West. His active support of economic resistance had established him as a firm asserter of colonial rights, moderate in tone, but resolute in conviction and action. On Friday, 5 August, the deputies elected him one of Virginia's seven delegates to the Continental Congress. He stood third in the poll, winning ninety-eight votes, nine more than the fiery orator Patrick Henry and only a few less than the front-runners, Speaker Peyton Randolph and Richard Henry Lee.[18]

Washington reported some of the Convention's results to Thomas

Johnson, Jr. In preparation for the Congress in Philadelphia, he urged his fellow delegates-elect Randolph and Lee to collect data on Virginia's annual exports and imports and "got an account" from George Wythe, Clerk of the House of Burgesses, of the province's "number of taxables." Before leaving Williamsburg, he also bought the published version of a set of resolutions drafted by Thomas Jefferson for the Convention's consideration. The pamphlet was entitled "A Summary View of the Rights of British America." [19]

Jefferson's "Summary View" took a long and radical step forward in American attitudes. It declared Parliament "the legislature of one part of the empire" only, one legislature among several. In effect, it propounded a theory of a British commonwealth of nations, each self-governing but sharing a monarch. The king it described as the "chief magistrate of the British empire," as "no more than the chief officer of the people, appointed by the laws, and circumscribed with definite powers, to assist in working the great machine of government . . . and consequently subject to their superintendance."

Going beyond protests against the recent "Coercive" Acts, Jefferson traced a history of systematic violation of American rights, rights grounded in nature as well as the English constitution, violations practiced by British kings as well as Parliament. They had repeatedly blocked British America from freely trading with the world, restricted colonial manufacturing, required Americans to buy British goods. They had extorted taxes, disallowed laws, and dissolved legislatures, for long periods depriving colonials of the instruments of self-government.

During previous reigns, these violations "were less alarming, because repeated at more distant intervals. . . ." But the reign of his present majesty had marked itself by a "rapid and bold succession of injuries. . . . Single acts of tyranny may be ascribed to the accidental opinion of a day," wrote Jefferson, "but a series of oppressions, begun at a distinguished period, and pursued unalterably thro' every change of ministers, too plainly prove a deliberate, systematical plan of reducing us to slavery." To put down resistance to his "arbitrary measures," the current king had sent "large bodies of armed forces," outside troops beyond control of the civil powers of the provinces. Jefferson concluded with sharp and warning words to the king: "[K]ings are the servants, not the proprietors of the people. Open your breast Sire, to liberal and expanded thought. Let not the name of George the third be a blot in the page of history." [20]

The "Summary View" was a rehearsal for the Declaration of Independence two years later. In mid-1774, its attitude toward the king was still a minority opinion. The members of the Convention read Jefferson's draft but avoided using it as a model for instructing the congressional delegates.[21] It went too far for the moderate majority.

Most colonials continued to fix the blame on scheming ministers and to argue that in defending their own rights they supported the constitutional prerogatives of the Crown. Tory contemporaries and many historians have argued that American provincials could not simultaneously deny parliamentary sovereignty and pledge allegiance to the king. But the militants saw nothing inconsistent in their position. A group of New Yorkers recognized no contradiction in having a band play "God Save the King" when they bid farewell to Isaac Low as he departed for the First Congress. Nor did they later sense any hypocrisy in flying from their liberty pole a flag proclaiming on one side "The Congress and Liberty" and on the other "The King."[22]

Meanwhile, Josiah Quincy, Jr., of Massachusetts said what no other provincial polemicist thought, or at least dared to write. His *Observations on the . . . Boston Port Bill* charged the king as a co-conspirator with his ministers. A "Father of his Country," raged Quincy, would have prevented the injustices rather than punishing Massachusetts for its protests. Customarily Britons referred to the reigning monarch as "the wisest and best of kings," but the bitterly disillusioned Quincy rejected "that lying appelation." Despite everything, on a visit to London in November, he succumbed to the sight of George III in all his royal splendor presiding over the rituals to open the new parliamentary session. British colonials did more than simply submit to monarchical rule. They affirmed kingship as an essential part of the English constitution. They venerated their sovereigns. They put their faith in the righteousness and benevolence of their king.

Historians can reconstruct eighteenth-century British ideas of the role of the Crown in the English constitutional system. It is far more difficult to reimagine the moral and emotional power of those beliefs, to comprehend their hold on the hearts and minds of American provincials. Interwoven with new ideas of limited monarchy ran an older skein of veneration of kingly rule. Colonials declared their devotion to the king and kingship in public proclamations, political petitions, fast and thanksgiving and election day sermons, even in their almanacs. The birthday of the king was one of the few public holidays usually observed throughout the Empire. Colonial newspaper editors reported fully to their readers the doings of the king and the royal family. The colonists professed their loyalty, not only to the institution of the Crown, but to the ruler who wore the diadem. Over the British nation reigned a monarch whom his subjects everywhere loyally, even affectionately, regarded in traditional patriarchal terms as the "Father of his Country."[23]

But a spirit of pessimism began to grow in the summer of 1774. That pessimism was evident in the sober American observances of the king's birthday and in the refusal of Boston, Philadelphia, and Charleston to celebrate that occasion at all. More and more colonials wondered how a genuinely public-minded monarch could be so completely deluded by his counselors as to acquiesce in their actions. Josiah Quincy might stand alone in his denunciation of the king as co-conspirator, but other American militants, men again like Jefferson, as yet unready to go that far, began to declare that their loyalty had limits. They would refuse to submit unconditionally to a monarch controlled by his ministers. The Fairfax Resolves spoke for this point of view.[24]

Washington undertook to enforce the new nonimportation pact in Fairfax County even as he prepared to leave for the Continental Congress. In late August, leading local merchants, all of them members of the County Committee, and other influential citizens of Alexandria stopped at Mount Vernon for visits of a day or two. Other guests included notables from across the river in Maryland and one of the Moylan brothers, merchants of Philadelphia.[25]

There was one other task to be taken care of before the trip to Philadelphia. Bryan Fairfax had written yet another long and troubled letter. He complained half-apologetically about Washington's suppression of his letter at the county meeting in July. Others who shared his disquiet had felt intimidated into silence, he said.

In a worried ramble, Fairfax reviewed historical and legal precedents and suggested that those who now denied Parliament's right to make laws for the colony, men like George Mason and Richard Henry Lee, were contradicting their past positions. But perhaps he was wrong. Perhaps he was mistaken about the intentions of the British ministry. He had been fretting anxiously that his neighbors thought his views at odds with the principles for which colonials were contending. He apologized for his long letter. He virtually begged his friend to help him settle his uneasy mind. He felt certain "that no Man in the Colony wishes it's Prosperity more, would go to Greater Lengths to serve it, nor is at the same time a better Subject to the Crown."[26]

If divided loyalties stymied Fairfax, his neighbor at Mount Vernon suffered no such conflict. Besides, Washington's leadership in the resistance movement left him little time to try to change his friend's political opinions. By way of excuse, he said he had nothing to add to the discussion in the current newspapers. He offered only a terse general restatement of his "Country Party" political convictions, grounding his actions in the same combination of natural and constitutional rights he had previously affirmed.

"[A]n innate spirit of freedom first told me, that the measures, which administration hath for some time been, and now are most violently pursuing, are repugnant to every principle of natural justice; whilst much abler heads than my own hath fully convinced me, that it is not only repugnant to natural right, but subversive of the laws and constitution of Great Britain itself, in establishment of which some of the best blood in the kingdom hath been spilt."

He felt satisfied that the British Parliament no longer acted according to "the principles of justice" but were following a deliberate plan to trample "upon the valuable rights of Americans. . . . [I]s it a time to trifle, or risk our cause upon petitions, which with difficulty obtain access, and afterwards are thrown by with the utmost contempt? Or should we, because heretofore unsuspicious of design, and then unwilling to enter into disputes with the mother country, go on to bear more, and forbear to enumerate our just causes of complaint? For my own part, I shall not undertake to say where the line between Great Britain and the colonies should be drawn; but I am clearly of opinion, that one ought to be drawn, and our rights clearly ascertained. I could wish, I own, that the dispute had been left to posterity to determine, but the crisis is arrived when we must assert our rights, or submit to every imposition, that can be heaped upon us, till custom and use shall make us as tame and abject slaves, as the blacks we rule over with such arbitrary sway." Only "unanimity" and "firmness" among the colonies could prevent their subjugation.[27]

At this point, Washington's thinking was fluid. The relationship between Great Britain and America must be redefined. Its form he left open, but colonial rights must be guaranteed. Calling Virginia's Assembly its "Parliament," he disavowed the right of the British Parliament "to tax us . . . unrepresented as we are. . . ." Probably he favored a restructuring of the Empire in a manner similar to that implied in Jefferson's "Summary View," a confederation of self-governing states affiliated by allegiance to a common monarch. As yet, he was unready for a complete break, lamenting "the unhappy difference which at this time subsists betw'n great Britain and her Colonies. . . ."[28]

Edmund Pendleton and Patrick Henry arrived at Mount Vernon on Tuesday, 30 August, to accompany their fellow delegate to the Congress in Philadelphia. That evening, George Mason and Thomas Triplet, both members of the Fairfax County Committee, also came and stayed the night. On Wednesday, the five men talked until midday. Then Washington, Pendleton, and Henry rode north.[29] George Washington had become one of Virginia's most influential leaders. Soon the entire continent would be casting their eyes in his direction.

CHAPTER TWELVE

"To excite others by our Example"

In Philadelphia, there was more talk of politics. John Adams might complain that the excess of debating and speech-making prolonged the proceedings of the Congress. He knew, though, that the real business of the delegates was talk out-of-doors, talk over dinners and at informal gatherings, talk to get acquainted and to exchange views, to ascertain the political climate and interests in the various provinces, to assess one another's abilities and opinions, and to form connections. For two months, colonial leaders talked and listened and learned.[1]

Philadelphia was a classroom in continental politics. The delegates came to school, self-consciously studying to overcome provincialism. They believed that for the cause of the colonies to prevail, they must stand together. They were formulating more than a unified political program. They were helping to fashion a common identity. That identity first found expression in the colloquial term that soon came to designate the combined American provinces. People began to speak of "the Continent."[2]

With a kind of wary enthusiasm, the delegates circled round, measuring one another's militancy. The New Englanders in particular filled their diaries and letters with assessments of their new political acquaintances. Already they were finding many of the Pennsylvanians, Joseph Galloway chief among them, rather too cautious and conservative. And some of those men would soon become loyalists or at least neutralists. The Virginians were another matter. Adams excitedly called them "the most spirited and consistent of any." Delaware's Caesar

Rodney said that the Massachusetts men had a reputation for violence, but alongside the Virginians, South Carolinians, and Rhode Islanders, they were moderates. Thomas Lynch of South Carolina found a vigorous spirit of resistance flourishing virtually everywhere.[3]

Washington too spent these weeks schooling himself in the politics of "the Continent." He dined with the "Farmer" John Dickinson and at the home of another Pennsylvania delegate, Thomas Mifflin, a Philadelphia merchant who made his house a meeting place for members of the Congress. He got to know the young lawyer Joseph Reed, active in the resistance movement and soon to serve on Philadelphia's Committee of Correspondence. Reed and Mifflin would become two of Washington's aides when he took command of the Continental Army the following spring. He was also a guest in the homes of men prominent in Philadelphia's political and commercial establishment, and on various occasions he dined with delegates from Maryland, Massachusetts, and New York. Although he served on the vestry of his local parish, he was far from a regular churchgoer. Yet intriguingly, in Philadelphia, he attended services at Presbyterian, Quaker, Roman Catholic, and two Anglican churches.[4]

If George Washington was carefully studying the people he met, he was also presenting himself for their consideration. Observers found impressive the tall, youthful Virginian's physical presence. They spoke of his "easy Soldierlike Air, & gesture" and his "manly Gait." He displayed these qualities at the ball given by the Pennsylvania Assembly in honor of the congressional delegates.

People were struck too by less tangible traits. A visiting Rhode Islander described the colonel as "a man noted as well for his good Sense, as his Bravery." A fellow Virginian said: "He is a modest man, but sensible & speaks little—in action cool, like a Bishop at his prayers." He was "a tolerable speaker in public," according to one New England delegate, "who speaks very modestly and in cool but determined style and accent."[5] John Adams had bewailed the egotistical speechifying of too many delegates. Such "patriots" might thunder and bluster against ministerial tyranny. Washington would speak only when he had something to say and then without bombast. Whiggish political essayists had repeatedly warned the people against fiery and flamboyant demagogues. Washington's personal and rhetorical modesty, his determined good sense, fit the Whig model of leadership.

That ideal also demanded a commitment to act, a willingness to risk one's self, one's life. Observers now remembered the colonel as "Virginia's Hero" in the late war. They recalled that he was "in the first Action in 1753 & 1754 on the Ohio, & in 1755, was with Braddock, & was the means of saving the remains of that unfortunate Army."

There was no doubt of Washington's courage, nor, commentators felt, of his commitment to the colonial cause. Hearsay had it that on learning of the bill closing the port of Boston he had made a "most eloquent Speech" pledging to raise and arm and lead one thousand men at his own expense. "His Fortune," went the exaggerated report, "is said to be equall to such an Undertaking." According to another rumor, those volunteers were even now ready to march to Boston with that "brave and experienced Officer" at their head. Yet another tale had Washington exclaiming "he wished to God! the Liberties of America were to be determined by a single Combat between himself" and King George.[6]

Even while these stories revived the public memory of Washington as an American hero and began the creation of a new legend, a former comrade from the Virginia Regiment, apparently unaware of the colonel's reputed militancy, wrote to warn him about the Boston radicals. Robert Mackenzie had served as a captain under Washington and was now a regular lieutenant with the British forces dispatched to pacify the Massachusetts Bay.

The "fixed Aim" of the populace, said Mackenzie, was "total Independance. . . ." He thought it necessary "that abler Heads and better Hearts shd. draw a Line for their Guidance," in other words, that more responsible leaders should thwart the agitators. "[T]he rebellious and numerous Meetings of Men in Arms, their scandalous and ungenerous Attacks upon the best Characters in the Province. . . , and their repeated but feeble Threats to dispossess the Troops have furnished sufficient Reasons to Genl. Gage to put the Town in a formidable State of Defence. . . ."[7]

Mackenzie's letter arrived in the midst of the Congress. Before Washington could reply, he had much political business to look after, had many chances to talk with and observe the very leaders Mackenzie warned against. He and Richard Henry Lee spent a good part of one day consulting with the Massachusetts men, one of those occasions when Lee cemented his political connection with John and Samuel Adams.[8] None of these contacts convinced Washington of Mackenzie's assertions. They only intensified his own conviction of a conspiracy against American liberty. They confirmed him in the "Country Party" view of the despotic direction of the British government.

"... I conceive, when you condemn the conduct of the Massachusetts people, you reason from effects, not causes," he told Mackenzie, "otherwise you would not wonder at a people, who are every day receiving fresh proofs of a systematic assertion of an arbitrary power, deeply planned to overturn the laws and constitution of their country, and to violate the most essential and valuable rights of mankind, being irritated, and with difficulty restrained from acts of the greatest violence and intemperance. For my own part, I confess to you candidly, that I view things in a very different point of light to the one in which you seem to consider them; and though you are led to believe by venal men, ... who, for honorary or pecuniary gratifications, will lend their aid to overturn the constitution, and introduce a system of arbitrary government, although you are taught, I say, by discoursing with such men, to believe, that the people of Massachusetts are rebellious, setting up for independency, ... give me leave, my good friend, to tell you, that you are abused, grossly abused. ..."

Such an opinion he could "advance with a degree of confidence and boldness, which may claim your belief, having better opportunities of knowing the real sentiments of the people you are among, from the leaders of them, in opposition to the present measures of the administration, than you have from those whose business it is, not to disclose truths, but to misrepresent facts in order to justify as much as possible to the world their own conduct. ..."

"... I think I can announce it as a fact, that it is not the wish or interest of that government, or any other upon this continent, separately or collectively, to set up for independencey. ..." "I am as well satisfied as I can be of my existence that no such thing is desired by any thinking man in all North America; on the contrary, that it is the ardent wish of the warmest advocates for liberty, that peace and tranquility, upon constitutional grounds, may be restored, and the horrors of civil discord prevented."

"[B]ut this you may at the same time rely on, that none of [the colonies] will ever submit to the loss of those valuable rights and privileges, which are essential to the happiness of every free state, and without which, life, liberty, and property are rendered totally insecure." "[A]nd again give me leave to add as my opinion, that more blood will be spilt on this occasion, if the ministry are determined to push matters to extremity, than history has ever yet furnished instances of in the annals of North America, and such a vital wound given to the peace of this great country, as time itself cannot cure, or eradicate the remembrance of." [9]

In this as in previous such political statements, Washington spoke in a distanced voice. He failed to identify himself as one of "the warmest advocates for liberty." Once again he assumed the stance of an objective observer rendering opinions on events. He couched a radical analysis of the situation in moderating phrases: "I conceive," "I think I can announce it as a fact," "Give me leave to add as my opinion. . . ." In this letter, we catch the tone of the man his fellow delegates met, modest and sensible, cool but determined.

Yet stripped of its softening phrases, here is a bold assertion of a vast and vicious conspiracy against American rights. One major aim of that conspiracy, American Radical Whigs believed, was to undercut the power of the indigenous colonial governing class by displacing it with a caste of Crown-controlled officials.

The colonies' appointed executive councils predominantly comprised men from the wealthiest and most prominent colonial families and, more important, those most heavily involved in imperial commerce. They tended, therefore, to share the imperial point of view. The Crown also named a roster of other high officers, for instance, province-wide judges and customs collectors. More and more, it seemed, these positions had become sinecures for placemen. Some appointees were political hacks, some professional bureaucrats. Many were born in England or Scotland or at least a colony other than the one where they held office. Some well-connected individuals, such as Thomas Hutchinson of Massachusetts, held several offices, boosting both their income and their influence. Whether native-born or "foreign," these higher officials typically adopted the imperial outlook. As the political crisis intensified, they found themselves increasingly at odds with provincially oriented lower House leaders.

Domination of higher colonial offices by Crown allies and placemen stymied advancement by ambitious American political leaders. Those without connections in the imperial establishment found themselves shut out of the top ranks of government. Now in Philadelphia, Washington met such men, recognized leaders in their provincial assemblies, often successful in local commerce as well as politics, but whose rise to the upper levels of authority had been thwarted. Throughout the colonies had emerged a pattern of blocked careers. Many of the most talented and ambitious members of Washington's generation had been cut off from the highest echelons of power.[10]

To win appointment, individuals without wealth or "interest" must court powerful men. Robert Mackenzie reported having seen in London

George Mercer, Washington's aide in the regiment and for a time his fellow Burgess from Frederick County. In 1765, Mercer had mistakenly accepted appointment as distributor of stamps in Virginia under the Stamp Act and had incurred public calumny. Lately he had been in England seeking another government position with which to repair his broken fortune. "I wish you had mentioned his employment, poor Mercer!" Washington said. "I often hear from him; much cause has he, I fear, to lament his having fallen into the accursed state of attendance and dependance."[11]

"Country" ideology made sense of this welter of baffled individual striving. It discovered political causes behind personal vexations. Native-born gentlemen of property, preferably landed property, were the legitimate and best qualified rulers. Rooted in local communities and closely in touch with local needs, they would wield power most effectively and least dangerously.

A generation earlier the Walpole ministry allegedly had sought to subvert the "constitution" by breaking the power of England's politically independent landed gentlemen. It maneuvered to supplant their parliamentary representatives with cohorts of placemen bought with Crown patronage to favor Crown policies. In the post-1763 era, the British ministry, having supposedly accomplished the corruption of the political nation at home, reputedly extended its conspiracy against constitutional liberty to the colonies. Completion of their design required displacing the provincial landed gentry from political leadership. Hence, the hordes of "foreign" placemen and the favoritism toward colonials with imperial connections.

Washington himself had once agonized in the condition of "attendance and dependance," soliciting the "interest" of governors Dinwiddie and Shirley, generals Braddock and Forbes, and Lord Loudoun. Imperial officials and regular officers had often ignored his expertise about provincial conditions and, he believed, had refused to reward him with the royal commission he merited. The victim of prejudice against provincials, he had given up his quest to push his "fortune in the Military way." As a Burgess and in his business enterprises, he had repeatedly grappled with the seemingly willful obtuseness of imperial policymakers toward colonial affairs. From his perspective, Crown officials flouted colonial experts in making government policy as they had in military planning. The "Country" analysis explained this to him as much more than anticolonial discrimination. It was part of a systematic plan to destroy the power of colonial leaders in order, ultimately, to destroy colonial liberty.

Years earlier, thwarted aspirations had caused Washington to begin to question the equity of the British political system. Other ambitious young colonials in similar situations had felt similar doubts. As events moved along, they too had begun to wonder if any justice was to be found within the Empire. Washington had said in 1769 that no man should hesitate to take up arms in defense of constitutional liberty. Now in Philadelphia, he had taken the pulse of the continent and learned that many others were ready, like him, to do battle if necessary. And so his letter to Mackenzie coupled its assertion of a conspiracy against American rights with an ominous, not to say prophetic, warning that colonials, though preferring reconciliation to independence, would willingly fight a bloody war.

Within or without the Empire, provincial society would remain much the same. George Washington sought no leveling of classes. The hierarchical order worked to his satisfaction. Landed gentlemen, the proper leaders of their communities and colonies, should continue to hold the reins of power. For the most part, he thought, that system ensured government by men of ability and honor, men like himself. More and more, his business and political endeavors had aimed at economic and political self-determination for him and his country. Originally he had defined that power narrowly, but increasingly he had been favoring greater autonomy under indigenous colonial leadership within the Empire. As yet he was unready to seek a complete separation.

British Americans should govern themselves, while retaining their allegiance to the Crown and their connection with the Empire. Fundamentally that is what the Congress said in its various official statements; that is what colonials had been saying for some time. But the definition of such self-government, the nature of the relationship of colonies to mother country, that had been changing. The meaning of self-government had been expanding. The ties desired with Great Britain were becoming more tenuous.

Just how much the thinking of some colonials had changed became apparent in the response to a plan of union between Britain and the colonies proposed by Joseph Galloway. Galloway, Speaker of the Pennsylvania Assembly, had firmly advocated American rights, as had many other moderates. Yet he and they just as firmly asserted that colonial rights must be, could only be, preserved through a connection with Great Britain.

As a starting point for negotiations to end the crisis, Galloway offered a plan that would partially redistribute power within the Empire. Each colony, operating under its present constitution, would govern its internal affairs, while a Grand Council, a triennial American legislature, would oversee "the general affairs of America." A Crown-appointed president-general would administer this continent-wide government and must give his assent to all acts of its Grand Council. Either Parliament or the Council might originate legislation affecting relations between two or more colonies and between all of the colonies and Great Britain. All such legislation must pass both legislatures; in other words, each had a veto on the acts of the other. This would give Americans a far greater voice in imperial policy-making, but, as Galloway described it, the Grand Council would nonetheless sit as a subordinate branch of the British legislature.

The moderates in Congress favored the plan; the militants immediately opposed. The former asserted the necessity of a supreme legislative head. The latter charged that this would diminish the authority of the provincial legislatures. Galloway might answer that his council would give each colony a voice in regulating general affairs, but to no avail. In the sequel, the Continental Congress would struggle through eight years of war and four years of turbulent peace trying to resolve the dilemma of state versus central authority and of the distribution of power among these entities.

The militants also objected that the American legislature would fall prey to the sort of corrupting ministerial influence that had killed Parliament's independence. This criticism touched something deeper than a fear of bribery. Those for whom the radicals in Congress spoke feared the moral contamination of a British nation they saw as decadent. From London, Benjamin Franklin opposed Galloway's plan on just those grounds: "When I consider the extreme corruption prevalent among all orders of men in this old rotten state, and the glorious public virtue so predominant in our rising country I cannot but apprehend more mischief than benefit from a closer union." [12]

Those who wanted to weaken connections with Britain were now in the ascendant. The militants wiped even the mention of Galloway's plan of union from the records of Congress. Still, if they wanted looser ties to the mother country, few favored outright severance. Perhaps Sam Adams had gone that far. Possibly even his cousin John. Not many more, despite ministerial propaganda to the contrary. Sam Adams, canny politician, astute revolutionary that he was, knew this. From Philadelphia, he reported to a political confederate back home that the other provinces would fully support Massachusetts in defending itself, but for now he doubted they would sanction establishment of any revolutionary republican regime. [13]

Between the Adamses and Galloway, closer to the Adamses, milled the majority of the delegates. The acts of the Congress reflected their views. The Declaration of Rights plainly reiterated the exclusive prerogative of the provincial legislatures to make laws for the colonies, subject only to the veto of the Crown according to established practice. They agreed that Parliament should have the power to regulate imperial commerce, but conspicuously failed to base this authority on constitutional right. Also of significance, the Declaration asserted that only with the consent of the legislature of a given colony could the Crown legally station a standing military force there in time of peace. The statement additionally maintained that political reconciliation depended at a minimum on repeal of the "Coercive" Acts.

In a petition to George III, Congress laid the blame for their grievances, not at the foot of the throne, but at the feet of scheming ministers who blocked supplications to the sovereign. Refusing as yet to implicate their king in ministerial crimes, they pledged their loyalty and called upon him as "the loving father of your whole people" to protect his colonial subjects.

Most important, the delegates created a Continental Association of nonimportation, nonconsumption, and nonexportation. They modeled it on the newly formed Virginia Association, derived in turn from the Fairfax Resolves. The prime feature of the pact, again originating in Fairfax County, was the establishment of local extralegal enforcement committees, in effect, quasi-governmental entities.[14] By this means, the militants legitimated the creation of instruments with which to intimidate their opponents. Through the committees they also could form military forces to conduct armed resistance should that become necessary.

Having adopted these measures and agreeing to convene again in the spring of 1775 to reassess the situation, the delegates adjourned. Just before he left Philadelphia, Washington bought "sundry pamphlets," among them copies of "The Association." He intended to see the Continental agreement vigorously supported in Virginia.[15]

Washington had played no conspicuous public part in the Congress. Penmen and orators had drafted the major documents. Still, he had contributed to the deliberations and had gotten a concentrated education in the affairs of "the Continent" and of each colony. Most important, representatives of the various provinces had met him, had begun to talk about him.

Months earlier he had rejected petitions to the king and Parliament as useless, favoring economic coercion as the only effective weapon. Now he was preparing to fight. During his absence from home, a number of gentlemen and freeholders of Fairfax County had met, with George Mason in the chair, to form an independent company of one hundred volunteer soldiers. Undoubtedly Mason and Washington had discussed the matter before his departure for Philadelphia. Given the urgency of the situation, they evidently had agreed that Mason should draft articles for such an association and convene the initial meeting. The subscribers acted, they said in Mason's words, because of the "extreme Danger" from "the Indian Enemy in our Country" and the threatened "Destruction of our Civil-rights & Liberty. . . ."[16]

A committee of three merchant-members wrote Washington in Philadelphia asking him to obtain for the company a pair of colors, two drums, two fifes, and two halberts. It was perhaps significant that they left it to him "to determine whether it may be proper or necessary to vary from the usual Colours that are carried by the Regulars or Militia." He ordered these accoutrements and for himself purchased a sword chain and ordered a sash, gorget, and epaulettes.[17]

By establishing its extralegal military force, the first independent company in Virginia, Fairfax once again put itself in the forefront of resistance. Contrary to some historians' assertions, the Virginia Convention of August 1774 had not authorized formation of such militia companies. Fairfax was acting on its own. The subscribers entered into the militia association, they declared, "being sensible of the Expediency of putting the Militia of this Colony upon a more respectable Footing, & *hoping to excite others by our Example* [emphasis added]. . . ." Clearly they intended to have an effect beyond the bounds of their community. Their action did not go unnoticed. In the midst of the deliberations of the Continental Congress, the *Pennsylvania Gazette* reported this important news from Fairfax County, Virginia.[18]

CHAPTER THIRTEEN

"Can a virtuous Man hesitate in his choice?"

Back home in Virginia, Colonel Washington helped outfit the independent companies springing up there. He soon accepted command of the Prince William County Company. During the next few months he agreed to head those from Fauquier, Richmond, Spotsylvania, and, of course, Fairfax. He also aided the Caroline and possibly the Loudoun County committees in getting gunpowder. From Philadelphia, he ordered military exercise books, muskets, bayonets, and other military equipment. Martial appearance was as important as martial discipline, so he ordered silk sashes, gorgets, and shoulder knots for the officers, prescribing the items in great detail. The military preparations in Fairfax County were noted and admired outside Virginia.[1]

Throughout that winter of 1774–5, a steady stream of visitors came to Mount Vernon to discuss politics and defensive arrangements. For six days in late December and early January, Colonel Washington conferred with the flamboyant Charles Lee. Lee had served with him on Braddock's expedition, retired as a half-pay major at the close of the Seven Years' War, become a major general in the service of the king of Poland, and returned to America in 1773. Recently, traveling up and down the seaboard and lobbying the delegates to the First Congress, he had argued assiduously that Americans, properly trained, could stand up to British regulars. He had just helped Maryland muster its militia. Now he was preparing for publication a plan to organize American forces.[2]

Meanwhile, Washington supervised enforcement of the Continental

Association by the Fairfax County Committee and oversaw that committee's reelection and reorganization. From time to time, he also reviewed and drilled the Fairfax and other independent militia companies.[3]

Soldiers shoot bullets, bullets cost money. Where would that money come from? Washington, George Mason, and a few other leaders decided in mid-January 1775 to assess every tithable inhabitant in Fairfax County three shillings. The sheriff or some other designated persons would collect the funds and turn them over to the committee to purchase ammunition. Washington and the others justified this levy by asserting that procurement of ammunition would "be for the common benefit, protection, and defence of the inhabitants. . . ." The committee would keep a list of all who refused to pay. Washington and Mason undertook to advance the necessary funds personally, collect the "contributions," and buy the ammunition and gunpowder.[4]

Governor Dunmore was probably referring to Fairfax when he reported that "One County has already laid a capital tax of 3s."[5] Dunmore had it right. Washington and Mason might try to disguise what they were doing by having the committee say it "recommended" payment of the levy. Their suggestion that the sheriff collect the money and their proposal to keep a list of the recalcitrant made clear that these were no voluntary contributions.

Simultaneously, the Fairfax Committee began to reorganize and expand its independent militia force. Borrowing from the program recently implemented by the Maryland Provincial Committee, it "recommended" that the adult male inhabitants of the county form themselves into 68-member companies. It had Mason draw up a plan for enrolling volunteers into these companies. The original Fairfax militia association had comprised 100 gentlemen and other freeholders. The county leaders "intended" the new association "to consist of all the able-bodied Freemen from eighteen to fifty Years of Age. . . ."[6]

This militia plan and the "tax" to support it once more made Fairfax the most militant of Virginia's counties. Both had originated with Washington and Mason. Probably again "hoping to excite others by our Example," they led their community to set the pace by forming what was, in effect, the beginnings of a parallel government. As before, the decisions in Fairfax drew attention outside Virginia.[7]

Washington and Mason used the Maryland Provincial Committee's rationale for this revolutionary act, an explanation combining traditional ideology with trenchant irony: "Resolved . . . ,That a well regulated militia, composed of gentlemen, freeholders, and other freemen, is the natural strength and only stable security of a free government, and that such militia will relieve our mother country from any expence in our protection and defence; will obviate the pretence of any necessity for taxing us on that account, and render it unnecessary to keep any standing Army (ever dangerous to liberty) in this province." [8]

People were thus arming not only in Virginia and Maryland, but in New England and the Middle Colonies as well. It seemed that everywhere men were drilling to master the military exercise. One Philadelphia gentleman, intoxicated with enthusiasm for arms, wrote to a member of Parliament, "[W]e begin to think the whole force of *Great Britain* could not subdue us." Maryland's Samuel Chase quoted Colonel Washington as praising the "noble Ardour" prevailing in Virginia. According to Chase, Washington had reported that "Men are forming themselves into independent Companies, chusing their officers, arming, Equipping, & training for the worst Event. The last Appeal!" [9]

British propagandists blamed this martial fervor on a handful of agitators, on the peripatetic Charles Lee in particular. He had offered, it was said, to head a continental army. Lee himself denied all of this to Edmund Burke: "To think myself qualified for the most important charge that ever was committed to mortal man, is the last stage of presumption. Nor do I think the Americans would, or ought to confide in a man (let his qualifications be ever so great) who has no property amongst them." He failed to mention that they were also put off by his rhetorical extremism and especially by his open assaults on George III. [10]

Americans, said a Pennsylvanian, would "prefer men born among them for commanders, to the most experienced foreign officers. Moreover the colonies are not so wrapped up in Gen. Lee's military accomplishments as to give him the preference to Col. Putnam and Col. Washington,—men whose military talents and achievements have placed them at the head of American heroes. There are several hundred thousand Americans who would face any danger with these illustrious heroes to lead them." [11]

An anonymous Virginian versifier, setting new words to a popular song, named his colony's choice to lead: "In spite of Gage's flaming sword, / Or Carleton's Canadian troop, / Brave Washington shall give the word, / And we'll make them howl and whoop." Early in 1775, people elsewhere were also talking about the colonel. From England, a friend wrote him of reports "in London, that you are Training the People of Virginia to the Use of Arms. . . ." [12]

Washington followed these developments closely, gathered political intelligence, kept his finger on the pulse of public opinion. He tracked emerging events through private letters, the public press, and the most recent pamphlets. He read publications by everyone from the radical Charles Lee to the Tory Samuel Seabury.[13]

"[T]hings wear a disagreeable aspect," he said in February, "and the minds of men are exceedingly disturbed at the measures of the British government." In a speech to the new Parliament, the king had pledged to put down lawlessness in America. He had ignored the petition of the Continental Congress. George Mason had "little Hopes of a speedy Redress of Grievances . . . on the Contrary we may expe[c]t to see coercive & vindictive Measures still pursued. It seems as if the King either had not receiv'd or was determined to take no Notice of the Proceedings of the Congress." Washington agreed. "The King's Speech and Address of both Houses, prognosticate nothing favorable to us. . . ." Still, subsequent events and information gave him "reason to believe" the ministry had begun to see that their "forcible measures" would fail. "A little time must now unfold the mystery, as matters are drawing to a point."[14]

The original Fairfax Independent Militia Association, organized the previous September, had pledged to defend "the legal prerogatives of our Sovereign King George the third, and the just Rights & Privileges of our Country, our Posterity & ourselves upon the Principles of the British Constitution." Now in February 1775, in consultation with Washington, Mason drafted the new militia plan. Altering the association's stated purpose, he omitted mention of the king.[15]

If he and Washington increasingly doubted the willingness of the monarch and his ministers to redress colonial grievances, many other Americans still clung to faith in their king, still blamed his advisers for deceiving him. In March, the Richmond County Independent Company begged "leave to inform [Colonel Washington] that they have unanimously chosen him their Commander, should they be obliged to have recourse to Arms to defend their King and Country. . . ."[16]

Speaker Peyton Randolph had called for the Virginia Convention, the extralegal counterpart to the House of Burgesses, to meet at Richmond in March 1775. The election of Convention delegates offers an illustration of the way in which revolutionary county committees were taking control of public affairs by appropriating the aura of legitimacy attached to the constituted government. Early in February, Washington asked Mason's advice regarding selection of Fairfax's delegates. It seemed to Mason "that the Burgesses for the County are our proper Representatives upon this Occasion; and that the best method to remove all

Doubt or Objection, as well as to save Trouble, will be for the County Committee to meet & make an Entry & Declaration of this, as their Opinion." On 20 February, Fairfax County voters elected their Burgesses, Washington and Charles Broadwater, to represent them in Richmond.[17]

The Convention proceedings pointed up Washington's increasing importance in the resistance. Virginia militancy was mounting. A meeting in Augusta County "entirely agree[d] in opinion with the gentlemen of Fairfax county, that a well regulated militia is the natural strength, and stable security, of a free government. . . ." They instructed their delegates to press for officers and men in each county to follow Fairfax's example by mastering the military exercise.[18]

On the Convention's fourth day, Patrick Henry too addressed the need for more systematic military preparations. Borrowing the rationale used in Maryland and Fairfax, he moved "that this Colony be immediately put into a posture of Defence. . . ." More moderate voices wanted this stated only "*as the Opinion of this Convention*," but the radicals won the day. A committee which included Colonel Washington would prepare "a Plan for embodying, arming and disciplining . . . a Number of Men" sufficient to defend the province.[19]

The committee's report and the program the Convention adopted also drew upon the Maryland and Fairfax County plans. The report offered a scheme for organizing military companies and proposed that local committees "collect from their Constituents" money to buy such items as gunpowder and lead. It also "earnestly recommended to each Individual to pay" the amounts "the respective Committees . . . judged requisite." This sounded like voluntary compliance, but cautious delegates knew better. The three-shilling levy in Fairfax demonstrated, if demonstration were needed, that the squeeze of public stigma could easily turn a voluntary contribution into a virtual tax.

The proposal sparked a lively debate over constitutional as well as practical questions, questions of taxation and representation. Fearing the portent of the proposal, one delegate wanted to know, "How will it appear to his Majesty?" In the end, the militants swept along the doubters, and the measure passed unanimously.[20]

Washington sat on a second committee "to prepare a Plan for the Encouragement of Arts & Manufactures in this Colony." The description was perhaps disingenuous. Its real responsibility was to report methods of fashioning the tools of war. Beyond military measures, Washington wished to see domestic industries developed in America.

He was already in touch with men interested in promoting indigo, the growing of cotton, manufacture of cotton cloth, and the production of linen from hemp.[21]

The Convention had one other important question: election of delegates to the Second Continental Congress at Philadelphia in May. The same seven men who had represented Virginia the previous autumn were chosen again. Speaker Peyton Randolph, of course, once more topped the poll as he had at the Williamsburg Convention of August 1774. In that vote, Richard Henry Lee had stood second, followed by Washington and Patrick Henry. But now in Richmond, Colonel Washington ranked just behind Mr. Speaker, with Henry third and Lee fourth. As the political crisis deepened, Virginians were looking for leadership from their foremost soldier.[22]

On that same day, Washington wrote his brother Jack praising Jack's part in the formation of Stafford County's independent company. He himself had promised to review the Richmond Company next summer, "they having made me a tender of the Command of it. . . ." At that time, "I could review yours and shall very cheerfully accept the honr. of Commanding it if occasion requires . . . , as it is my full intention to devote my Life and Fortune in the cause we are engagd in, if need be. . . ."[23]

The Convention wound up, and Colonel Washington rode for home. He had hoped to visit his Ohio lands that spring to inspect the work of white indentured servants and black slaves building cabins and planting crops.[24] Pressing public responsibilities now made that trip impossible.

The war with the Ohio Valley Indians known as Dunmore's War had come to an end. The major engagement, the Battle of Point Pleasant, had taken place in October 1774, at the mouth of the Great Kanawha River, not far from the main tract of land Washington had claimed under Governor Dinwiddie's 1754 bounty proclamation. Farther east, at the mouth of the Hockhocking, troops under Governor Dunmore built a small stockade on another piece of land owned by Washington. William Crawford, once a captain in the Virginia Regiment and more recently Washington's partner in land-hunting, had surveyed these claims. Now a major, he commanded a company of some five hundred men. Setting out on the expedition against the Indians, he promised Washington he would resurvey one particular tract to obtain a more accurate measurement. As if to symbolize the reasons for this war, he marched off armed with both weapons and surveying instruments.[25]

During the winter and spring, white settlers and his fellow Burgesses continued to seek out the former frontier colonel's expertise. The Ohio

Indians were discontented with the peace treaty negotiated by Governor Dunmore. To end several months' delay the House eventually appointed six commissioners to implement it. They named Washington as chair, but by that time he had accepted another commission in Philadelphia.[26]

Meanwhile, peace with the Indians permitted Washington to resume settling his western lands. The servants and slaves he had sent out under white overseers could again bend to the task of "improving" his vast acres. But on his way back from Richmond, he heard an alarming rumor: Governor Dunmore might nullify all of the patents granted under the 1754 proclamation, on the ground that William Crawford had never been legally qualified as a surveyor. The entire 200,000 acres, including some 23,000 registered to Washington, would then have to be resurveyed. He and the other veterans might have to hunt out new lands to replace those patented to them since December 1773. Washington wrote Dunmore to substantiate the report. The royal governor confirmed it in a curt note.[27]

Fortunately, the matter was quickly resolved, but it pointed up again the need to safeguard the rights of veterans who had defended Virginia and the Empire. In 1778, in the midst of war, Virginia's revolutionary legislature would validate the claims of the state's veterans from the French and Indian War under both Dinwiddie's 1754 proclamation and the Royal Proclamation of 1763. They would pass this legislation at the instigation of General George Washington.[28]

Even while he queried Governor Dunmore about this sudden reversal, he continued to lead military planning. Throughout April and into the first week of May 1775, more visitors came to Mount Vernon to take counsel with the colonel: merchants from Alexandria, lawyers from across the river in Maryland, young men zealous to assert American rights and looking for leadership. Eighteen-year-old Harry Lee came. Before long he would be called "Light Horse" Harry, a daring and resourceful cavalry commander. General Charles Lee returned to confer for another five days. Major Horatio Gates, who had served as a captain in Braddock's army with Washington and Lee, also spent two days.[29]

There was still much work to be done outfitting Virginia's independent companies. Several times Washington went up to Alexandria to drill the force mustering from Fairfax. He also traveled to town to chair the meetings of the County Committee and to win reelection as a delegate to the Virginia Convention.[30]

Without mentioning his own active role, he described events to his old friend in London, George Mercer. Many counties had raised "[a] great number of very good companies" even before the Convention's recommendations; these "are now in excellent training. . . ." The people wished "for nothing, more ardently, than a happy and lasting reconciliation with the parent State," he said, but they would never "purchase it at the expence of their liberty, and the sacred compacts of Government."[31] By now, this had become a standard refrain of colonial militants: Assure that Americans preferred reconciliation. Warn that they would never yield their rights. Announce their preparations and willingness to fight if necessary.

Fairfax had been the first county to raise an independent militia company. Now that company made an important change in its organization. In February, George Mason had proposed and the company had voted to elect the officers annually.[32] Radical Whigs had long advocated annual election of legislators. Coupled with it usually went a plan for rotation in office: no officeholder could serve two successive terms. These reforms were intended to make those who exercised governing power accountable to their constituents frequently. Annual election and rotation would also keep them in closer touch with the needs and concerns of those they ruled. In addition, they would prevent the entrenchment in power of selfishly ambitious individuals and of "parties," political factions pursuing private interests rather than the public good.

Many, though by no means all, of the militant defenders of American rights favored these electoral reforms. But even some strong supporters of the colonial cause thought such changes would undermine established authority, weaken the position of the rightful governing class, cause a leveling of social ranks. The Richmond Convention relied on Mason's militia plan in its program of defensive preparation, but ignored his proposal for the annual election of officers.[33]

In mid-April 1775, possibly on the fifteenth, the members of the Fairfax Independent Company gathered at Alexandria to discuss the rules and basis of their organization.[34] Some members wanted to make only inhabitants of the town eligible for election as officers. Others, undoubtedly residents of other parts of the county, disagreed. This seemingly parochial dispute stirred a lengthy debate about the political philosophy underlying colonial resistance.

One man moved that the company should not only elect, but also rotate, its officers annually. They would serve one year and then return to the ranks for the following year before becoming eligible for reelection. He made one exception to this rule: the commander of the company, Colonel George Washington, would be permitted to hold his rank indefinitely. George Mason rose in support of the motion. His eloquent remarks distilled the principles of revolutionary ideology. They also pointed up the connection between those beliefs and Washington's emerging historical role.

Mason invoked the authority of "the deepest politician who ever put pen to paper," Niccolò Machiavelli, whose *Discourses* had framed republican political thought for three centuries. The great Florentine theorist had "wisely observed," said Mason, "that no institution can be long preserved, but by frequent recurrence to those maxims on which it was formed." This led him into some reflections regarding "the principles on which" the militia association "was first instituted. . . ."

"This company is essentially different from a common collection of mercenary soldiers," Mason said. They had formed it for the public good, to defend their country, to preserve their ancestral and constitutional rights, "to rouse the attention of the public, to introduce the use of arms and discipline, to infuse a martial spirit of emulation, and to provide a fund of officers. . . ."

"Every power," he continued, "every authority vested in particular men is, or ought to be, ultimately directed to" the sole end of serving the general good. "[W]henever any power or authority whatever extends further, or is of longer duration than is in its nature necessary for these purposes, it may be called government, but it is in fact oppression. . . . [W]hen we reflect upon the insidious arts of wicked and designing men, the various and plausible pretences for continuing and increasing authority, the incautious nature of the many, and the inordinate lust of power in the few, we shall no longer be surprised that freeborn man hath been enslaved, and that those very means which were contrived for his preservation have been perverted to his ruin. . . ."

The most successful means ever devised "[t]o prevent these fatal effects," asserted Mason, was frequent elections. "Whenever this is neglected or evaded . . . or whenever any military establishment or authority is not, by some certain mode of rotation, dissolved into and blended with that mass from which it was taken, inevitable destruction to the state follows. . . ."

The constitution of "our mother country," he warned, showed "strong symptoms of decay. It is our duty by every means in our power to prevent the like here." To give officers of the Fairfax Company "power for life, or for an unlimited time" would establish a precedent that might "prove fatal." The proposed regulation would "prevent the abuse of authority, and the insolence of office on the one hand, and create a proper spirit of emulation on the other; and by an annual rotation, will in a few years breed a number of officers." But, he concluded, "the exception made in favor of the gentleman who by the unanimous vote of the company now commands it, is a very proper one, justly due to his public merit and experience; it is peculiarly suited to our circumstances, and was dictated, not by compliment, but conviction."[35]

Mason's remarks touched upon several themes central to Washington's subsequent career. Most obvious was the fear of military despotism. Ambitious leaders and successful and popular military commanders would want to increase their powers and would tend to abuse them. Because the appetite for power was insatiable, no man should be given even a portion of it for an unlimited time. Annual elections and rotation of officers would prevent power-hungry men from entrenching themselves. Because individual virtue was unreliable, institutional mechanisms must be employed to forestall public vice and inculcate public virtue. In addition, reliance on a militia of citizen-soldiers would promote public spirit and muster martial virtues.

Fear that a victorious and popular general could make himself a military dictator was to shape Washington's conduct. Fear of a standing professional army and faith in a people's militia was to plague the commander-in-chief throughout the coming war as he tried to train and field an effective fighting force.

In one sense, Mason's view of the state of liberty in the world was dark and pessimistic. Corruption seemed to have overtaken the mother country. Colonials must strive to prevent the decay from infecting America. But, to alter the metaphor, if the flame of liberty flickered in England and had gone out elsewhere, it burned brightly in America. Mason and many others thought of its presence as a "sacred deposit." It came to them as a trust and a calling that they could fulfill only by pristine devotion to the stated principles of liberty. Thus, he could assert that if the Fairfax Company invested their officers "with a power for life, or for an unlimited time, we are acting diametrically contrary to the principles of that liberty for which we profess to contend."

Yet even as he issued this warning, Mason joined with the others in making an "exception . . . in favor of" the company's unanimously chosen commander, George Washington. This action was "proper" because of "his public merit and experience" and was "peculiarly suited to our circumstances." The situation of the company required the expertise of a seasoned soldier, Mason seemed to be saying, and Washington's proven public-spirited character guaranteed against abuse of power. Unlike other men, his virtue *was* reliable. Furthermore, his "public merit" would serve as a model for the young officers who would follow his lead. His own public-mindedness would ensure its vigor in those who looked up to him. This exception, Mason assured, "was dictated, not by compliment, but conviction." It was no servile flattery, but sincere acknowledgment of Washington's superior virtues and qualities.[36]

In late April 1775, as the Fairfax Company drilled, alarming news came from two directions at once. To the south, in Williamsburg on 21 April, a British naval officer and fifteen marines, under Governor Dunmore's orders, had entered the public magazine and carried off all the gunpowder. Angry townsfolk had started to march on the Palace, but Speaker Randolph and others had temporarily defused the situation by quieting the crowd and addressing the governor. Dunmore's pledge to return the powder should the security of the town or colony require it satisfied no one.

The Spotsylvania Independent Company called upon nearby county companies to meet them at Fredericksburg on 29 April, prepared to march on Williamsburg. The officers also notified Colonel Washington. The Prince William and Albemarle contingents, their commanders announced, awaited his orders. Apparently they expected him to lead the march on the capital.[37]

Almost simultaneously, express riders from the north reported that on 19 April, British infantry had clashed with military volunteers at the village of Lexington, Massachusetts. They had killed eight and wounded ten. There had been another encounter later that day at nearby Concord. Provincial riflemen had then harassed the retreating British all the way back to Boston. Colonials now had the occupied town virtually under siege. The British provocation and the American response might be the outbreak of hostilities for which militant colonials had been preparing.

Hundreds of armed men thronged at Fredericksburg on 29 April, but Colonel Washington remained at Mount Vernon preparing to set out for the Congress the following week. He, Speaker Randolph, and other leaders urged the mobilizing militiamen to return home. The governor had privately promised to return the powder. Clearly they believed this was not the issue upon which to base armed resistance. Hotheads might talk of defending Virginia's honor. A week later Patrick Henry would head a band that compelled the governor to pay for the appropriated powder. Washington knew the onus must be put on imperial authority. The aggressive British actions at Lexington and Concord offered a better justification for colonial military action. "[A]fter a Long debate," Alexander Spotswood, a Spotsylvania Company officer, informed Washington, "it was at last agreed we Shd. not March to Williamsburg[.]"[38]

Spotswood was one of those young men eager to serve his country by fighting "in the Glorious cause of liberty, at the Risk of my life & fortune. . . ." He and others expected the first item before Congress would be establishment of regular armies throughout the continent. No one doubted, he said, that Washington would then "have the Command of the Whole forces in this Collony. . . ." He hoped the colonel would consider him worthy of a commission.[39]

Washington discussed these developments with visitors to Mount Vernon, including Horatio Gates and several fellow Burgesses. On 4 May, he and Richard Henry Lee took the road for Philadelphia, traveling in Washington's "chariot" with its coachmen and postilion. The colonel brought along his military uniform and may have worn it on the journey. In Baltimore, he was asked to review the local troops. That city had already established four companies and was raising three more.[40]

Delegates traveling from north and south found the martial ardor of Maryland matched elsewhere. The whole continent burned with what Charles Royster has called the "rage militaire." In Philadelphia, even some Quakers had formed militia companies. The City of Brotherly Love had become a city of citizen-soldiers drilling daily to master the military exercise. It was said that the hitherto backward New Yorkers were now raising troops. The North Carolina delegates exhorted the people back home to form companies in every county.

Silas Deane of Connecticut instructed his wife to "secure my Gunn, and let No one have it. . . . I choose not to be taken, Unarmed." The scholarly John Adams exclaimed to his wife, "Oh that I was a Soldier! I will be. I am reading military Books. Every Body must and will, and shall be a soldier."[41]

In New York and Pennsylvania, said one southerner, "a Tory dare not open his mouth. . . ." Radicals now stigmatized men like Joseph Galloway as "apostate" for advocating another petition to the king. He had resigned from Pennsylvania's congressional delegation. Reportedly, someone had sent him a box containing a halter and a note that read, "[A]ll the Satisfaction you can now give your injured Country is to make a proper use of this and rid the World of a Damned Scoundrell."[42]

Samuel Curwen of Massachusetts considered himself "a moderate" but had been branded a Tory. Deciding "to seek some secure asylum," if possible in America, he took ship for Philadelphia. Within two days, he realized that residence in the town "would be unpleasant if allowed at all, when it shall be known that I am what is called an addresser," one condemned for favoring further petitions to the Crown and Parliament. He spent an evening at the home of Joseph Reed, where he met three Virginia delegates, including George Washington. The conversation centered "chiefly" on how to block the Delaware River to keep Royal Navy ships from coming up to the city. "I could not perceive the least disposition to accommodate matters or even risk." Four days later, Curwen left for London.[43]

Washington himself was becoming more militant, less tolerant of those who held back. Word had come that the Crown planned to send troops to occupy New York. That colony, he reported, was now "said, not only to be hearty, but zealous in the cause. . . ." He hoped "it may be so but, as I never entertaind a very high opinion of your sudden Repentances, I will suspend my opinion till the arrival of the Troops there."[44]

In late May 1775, he remained unready openly to count the king a co-conspirator with his ministers, but he *was* willing to hint at such a charge. He deliberately labeled the British forces involved at Lexington and Concord as the "Ministerial troops . . . for we do not," he told a friend in England, "nor cannot yet prevail upon ourselves to call them the King's Troops. . . ."[45]

He also was touting the prowess and fighting spirit of American soldiers. He had collected accounts of the skirmishes of 15 April in Massachusetts, he said. "[S]tripped of all colouring," the plain fact was that only the regulars' hasty retreat had saved them from surrender or destruction. Lord Sandwich had disparaged the courage and military capacity of colonials. Perhaps this would convince him and others "that the Americans will fight for their Liberties and property, however pusilanimous, in his Lordship's Eye, they may appear in other respects."

"Unhappy it is though to reflect," lamented Washington, "that a Brother's Sword has been sheathed in a Brother's breast, and that, the once happy and peaceful plains of America are either to be drenched with Blood, or Inhabited by Slaves. Sad alternative! But can a virtuous Man hesitate in his choice?"[46]

CHAPTER FOURTEEN

"Partiallity . . . assisted by a political motive"

George Washington's chief biographers have depicted him as a sort of compromise candidate for command of the Continental Army. Many people preferred other men for the job: Artemas Ward, the New Englander already in charge at Boston, or Charles Lee, the experienced English professional soldier. Opposition to Washington arose not only from New England, but even from Virginia. In the end, Congress settled on him to compose sectional rivalry. These historians also suggest that though Washington had some hints Congress might seek his services, the appointment came as something of a surprise. Deeply troubled by his own sense of inadequacy, but prompted by a conviction of patriotic duty, he reluctantly accepted the trust.[1]

These interpretations rely heavily on John Adams's account of the appointment in his autobiography. Written some three decades later, that recollection is in significant respects faulty and unreliable.[2] A fresh look at the contemporary evidence supports a different interpretation.

The Congress never seriously considered anyone but Washington for the command. He himself not only anticipated the impending call, but made his availability apparent. Despite his expressed misgivings, he wanted the appointment, because of his fervent commitment to the colonial cause and in order to satisfy his unquenched yearning for public honor. The reasons the delegates turned to Washington also require reexamination. He himself said it was because of the "partiallity of the Congress . . . assisted by a political motive. . . ."[3] That "partiallity" and that "political motive" can be fully understood only within the ideological context of the Revolution.

Meeting in secret on 11 May 1775, its second day in session, the Congress came to grips with the stark situation. Colonial agents in London reported that the king had rejected the petition of the previous fall, that other attempts at reconciliation had failed, and that more troops were on the way. The Massachusetts delegation submitted a sheaf of statements documenting the clashes at Lexington and Concord. They also announced the votes of their Provincial Congress to raise more than 13,000 troops and to call upon the other New England colonies to enlist proportionate numbers. Massachusetts now sought the military support of the Continental Congress.[4]

From the outset, the delegates were compelled to consider military measures on a continental scale. That implied creation of a Continental army and appointment of continental generals. A tangle of knotty problems must be untied. In both organization and appointments, they must try to harmonize the sometimes competing, often legitimate, occasionally narrow and exasperating concerns and interests of various provinces and personalities. Some men from the Middle and Southern Colonies feared the New Englanders might use a veteran army to back up their pretensions to geographical expansion. At the same time, conciliationists dragged their feet on military measures, calling for yet another petition to the throne. "Our unweildy Body moves very Slow," said John Adams.[5]

Despite these obstacles, over the next few weeks, Adams and others felt increasingly sure Congress would establish an American Continental army. Militants would concede to conciliationists one more address to the king, but the momentum was on the side of military measures.

Washington immediately took the leading role in military planning. On 15 May, the fifth day of the session, he was made chair of a committee to counsel New York on defensive preparations. Redcoat reinforcements were expected there. The New Yorkers had asked what they should do. Stay vigilant but peaceable, Washington's committee advised, unless the British take hostile action. Then resist.

These recommendations set off a lengthy discussion in the Committee of the Whole about general matters of defense and reconciliation. The result, adopted on 25 and 26 May, was a compromise between the moderates and the militants: Congress coupled its military counsel to New York with another petition to the king. Still, simply by giving the advice, it had taken an important step toward assuming the direction of military affairs. It urged New York to raise three thousand troops, give them bounties and pay no higher than those offered in New England, and enlist them until 31 December, unless Congress ordered their discharge sooner.[6]

A second committee was quickly constituted, with Washington at its head, to draft plans for an intercolonial system to supply "Ammunition and military stores." Among other proposals, it recommended that the New England towns send gunpowder to "the American Army" before Boston. Congress momentarily postponed action on that report while it took up another request from Massachusetts. Because "the Army now collecting from different Colonies is for the general defence of the rights of *America*," the Provincial Congress "beg[ged] leave to suggest" that the Continental Congress consider "taking the regulation and general direction of it. . . ."[7]

The consensus toward which Congress had been laboring for three and a half weeks crystallized by 3 June. On that day, it voted to borrow £6000 to buy gunpowder "for the Continental Army" and appointed another committee "to bring in an estimate of the money necessary" for a twelve months' military campaign. Again, it called upon Washington to take the chair.[8]

On Wednesday, 14 June, it took the final step. It authorized recruitment of ten companies of riflemen, six from Pennsylvania and two each from Maryland and Virginia. They would march to Boston and be enlisted "in the American continental army . . . under the command of the chief Officer in that army." Washington headed a fourth committee to draft rules and regulations governing these and all troops raised by the Continent.[9]

Washington's chairmanship of these committees gave leading delegates from nearly every colony opportunity to work with him. Looking to him for soldierly leadership, they listened to his expert advice and took the measure of the man. "Coll. Washington appears at Congress in his Uniform," reported Adams, "and, by his great Experience and Abilities in military Matters, is of much service to Us."[10]

As the delegates undertook to create a Continental army during these weeks, they necessarily were considering whom to elect as its commander-in-chief. George Washington seemed the obvious choice. In and out of Congress, people had been talking about him for some time. His chairmanship of the various military committees had demonstrated to the members his military expertise and, more important, his public character.

By 14 June at the latest, the day they confirmed their decision to establish a Continental force, a consensus had jelled among them in favor of his election. On that date, one of the Virginia members announced: "Col. *Washington* has been pressed to take the supreme command of the American Troops encamped at Roxbury, and I believe will accept the appointment though with much reluctance, he being deeply impressed with the importance of that honourable trust, and diffident of his own (superiour) abilities." [11]

On Thursday, 15 June, as their last item of business, the delegates unanimously elected Washington "to command all the continental forces, raised, or to be raised, for the defence of American liberty. . . ." As the first item on Friday morning, the president of the Congress, "from the chair informed Geo: Washington Esqr." of this decision "and desired his acceptance of it. Whereupon Colonel Washington, standing in his place," delivered a short and simple but much noted speech. [12]

Washington's biographers have contended that he was the second choice of many of the delegates. Douglas Southall Freeman believed "perhaps a majority of the New Englanders favored" Artemas Ward, current commander of the Massachusetts troops. [13]

To the contrary, the contemporary sources indicate limited support for Ward in Congress and deep dissatisfaction with him in Massachusetts. Key provincial leaders thought him honest but incompetent. On 7 May, James Warren of the Massachusetts Provincial Congress complained to John Adams of the "shifting, fluctuating state" of the army. He felt it needed "a more Experienced direction. I could for myself wish to see your Friends Washington and L[ee] at the Head of it and yet dare not propose it tho' I have it in Contemplation. I hope that matter will be Considered with more propriety in your Body than ours." On 4 June, Elbridge Gerry wrote to the entire Massachusetts congressional delegation on behalf of himself and Dr. Joseph Warren, president of the Provincial Congress. He too reported the need of "a regular general to assist us in disciplining the army. . . ." He and Dr. Warren favored Washington for the chief command, he said. [14]

Both James Warren and Elbridge Gerry wrote again on 20 June. Matters had become more critical. They roundly condemned General Ward's military incapacity. Massachusetts's internal politics prevented his replacement from within the Provincial Congress, they said, but the

Continental Congress could supersede him with Washington when they incorporated the New England forces into a Continental army. They were unaware that Congress had already taken that step five days earlier. Historians may have ignored these last two letters because, coming after Washington's appointment, they obviously had no influence on the decision. But they only made more explicit what was clear in the earlier letters: The top leaders in Massachusetts thought Artemas Ward wholly inadequate for the command. They wanted him replaced with Washington. New England delegates to Congress including John Adams, Samuel Adams, and Silas Deane heard and responded to their concern.[15]

Still, some members of Congress did resist replacing Ward with Washington. John Adams recollected years later that the delegates opposed to appointing Washington had argued that the army was made up of New Englanders who had a general of their own with whom they were satisfied. More important, they asserted that those troops "had proved themselves able to imprison the British Army in Boston, which was all they [the opponents of Washington's appointment] expected or desired at that time." Edmund Pendleton of Virginia and Roger Sherman of Connecticut "were very explicit in declaring this Opinion. . . ." Pendleton in particular "was very clear and full against" Washington's election. Thomas Cushing of Massachusetts "more faintly" opposed it, fearing discontent in the New England army. Robert Treat Paine, also of Massachusetts, spoke highly of General Ward, his friend and college classmate, "but gave no Opinion upon the question" of replacing him with Washington. This weak opposition, Adams recalled, quickly collapsed.[16]

Although no contemporary evidence corroborates Adams's memory of any of this, it seems probable that resistance to Washington's appointment did arise. It came not from New Englanders, but from moderates. All of the men mentioned by Adams belonged to that camp. Their advocacy of Ward most likely was a tactic playing upon provincial prejudices to achieve their real aim. They tried to use sectional suspicions to limit continental involvement, to dampen the enthusiasm for warlike measures. For the present, "all they expected or desired" was "to imprison the British Army in Boston." They wanted no wider war.

Washington's biographers have concluded that Charles Lee was an even more popular competitor for the chief command. Supposedly Gerry and Dr. Joseph Warren favored Lee because of his considerable professional military experience. According to Freeman, if his birth outside America excluded Lee from consideration, Gerry and Warren would favor "the beloved Colonel Washington" as a suitable second choice.[17]

This conclusion results from a misreading of Gerry's letter of 4 June to the Massachusetts delegates. "[A]lthough the pride of our people would prevent their submitting to be led by *any* general [emphasis added] not an American," he wrote, "yet I cannot but think that general Lee might be so established as to render great service by his presence and councils with our officers." The problem was not that Lee's foreign birth precluded him from the supreme command. Gerry thought it would make him publicly unacceptable for any general commission.

Gerry declared plainly that he wanted Washington as commander-in-chief. "I should heartily rejoice to see this way the beloved Colonel Washington, and do not doubt the New-England generals would acquiesce in showing to our sister colony Virginia, the respect, which she has before experienced from the continent, in making him generalissimo." Provincial pride did not exclude a fellow American. Dr. Warren agreed with him in all of this, Gerry noted emphatically.[18]

On 20 June, Gerry stated even more clearly that Lee's foreign nativity was an obstacle to granting him any general commission. "General Lee must be provided for and heartily engaged in the service *without being Commissioned at present* [emphasis added]," he advised. "He is a stranger and cannot have the Confidence of a Jealous people when strugling for their Liberty. He will soon become familiar and be courted into office, I revere him as an Officer and wish he had been born an American." Congress had, in fact, just days before, appointed Lee a major general, but his foreign birth had indeed been a stumbling block.[19]

John Adams agreed that the difficulties in getting Lee appointed a general were "the natural prejudices, and virtuous attachment of our countrymen to their own officers. . . ." These attitudes were apparently the chief obstacles not only in Massachusetts, but in Congress as well. The cousins Adams might feel sure that Lee, though "not born an American," had "heartily espousd the Cause of America. . . ." Others still had deep misgivings about the man.[20]

This "jealousy" about Lee's nativity was something more than mere parochial prejudice. It had an ideological basis. In the eighteenth century, "jealousy" had as one of its meanings, a meaning now largely abandoned, "Solicitude or anxiety for the preservation or well-being of something; vigilance in guarding a possession from loss or damage."[21] Jealousy in that sense was a positive attribute and specifically a public virtue. It was thought safest to entrust power to men with deep roots in the country, men with a stake in society, men with property and connections. Such individuals would govern most wisely and use power least dangerously. They would rule well because they arose from among the people they ruled and because, returning to live among those people, they would feel the effects of their decisions while in power.

Whig "jealousy" had in part spurred the charge of a ministerial conspiracy to supplant native colonial leaders, men of independent property, with Crown sycophants and particularly with "foreign" placemen. Charles Lee himself had asserted back in December that his birth outside America and his lack of property in the country would prevent Americans from confiding command of their armies to him. That ideological premise was now being applied to the appointment of Continental generals.[22]

The delegates had other reasons for their misgivings about Lee. Probably they feared less the depth of his commitment to the cause than the fierceness of his engagement, the extremism of his opinions. Repeatedly and openly he had spoken against monarchy and denounced George III as a tyrant. Few Americans were ready as yet to advocate such views. And, at a time when American leaders were straining to keep the continent united, Lee had urged punitive action against the conciliationist legislators of New York. Further complicating his appointment, he was reluctant to accept a commission as a major general until Congress indemnified him from the loss of property.[23] This financial demand contrasted sharply with Washington's refusal of pay.

There was also the matter of Lee's personal eccentricity. He was, in John Adams's words, "a queer Creature," a man who said he preferred the company of his dogs to that of human beings. Adams might willingly overlook Lee's "Oddity," might "forgive a Thousand Whims for the Sake of the Soldier and the Scholar." Others were less complaisant.[24]

The Adamses argued that Lee's presence would enhance the reputation of the American army, would strengthen its credibility with the ministerial generals occupying Boston, would encourage British officers of merit to come over to the American side. Most important, the newborn army needed generals of ability and experience. In the end, recognition of that necessity, bolstered probably decisively by Washington's personal request to have Lee with him, carried through Congress his appointment as the second major general. Still, it had taken a "scuffle," as John Adams put it, to choose the general officers and particularly to get Charles Lee included among them. Given that difficulty, it is hardly imaginable that anyone seriously considered Lee for the chief command.[25]

If "jealousy" of Charles Lee as a "stranger" provoked resistance to enrolling him as a major general, "jealousy" of a different sort helped swing the top command to George Washington. The southerners, that is, the non–New Englanders, in Congress feared that a veteran New England army headed by a New England general might expel the British and then turn to conquer the rest of the continent. Looking back, John Adams could not determine "[w]hether this Jealousy was sincere, or whether it was mere pride and a haughty Ambition, of furnishing a Southern General to command the northern Army." The notion of "sincere Jealousy" seems odd until we recall again that in the eighteenth century jealousy meant vigilance in guarding something of value. If the non–New Englanders were jealous in this sense, Adams was saying in retrospect, they had been expressing a legitimate concern. It was supported by the authority of political ideology and historical experience. It was wariness against the insatiable appetite of men for power and the danger of military despotism.[26]

As loyalists like Joseph Galloway dropped off or were forced out, it became yet more necessary to avoid intercolonial rivalry, to pursue unified action, to maintain a working consensus within the revolutionary party.[27] In addition, their political ideology taught them to seek unity. The fraternal and familial and communal language of their religious heritage and of the "Country Party" tradition called upon them to strengthen their common bonds, to seek the common good, to resist divisiveness.

The New Englanders in particular worked earnestly to prevent intercolonial "jealousy" from undermining the unity of the cause. Washington's "appointment," asserted Eliphalet Dyer of Connecticut, "will tend to keep up the Union & more strongly Cement the Southern with the Northern Colonies...." John Adams and others agreed.[28] From the outset, Americans looked to George Washington for unifying leadership. He would quickly become the center of their union and would remain so for the rest of his career and even beyond his own lifetime. The "political motive" that, according to Washington, prompted his appointment was the effort not only to overcome provincial rivalry and sectional "jealousy," but also to promote and maintain continental unity.

The call to command the army came as no surprise to Washington. His name had been discussed at least since December. Anticipating the appointment even before he left Mount Vernon in early May, he had intended to have a will drafted. The press of preparations had post-poned that task. After arriving in Philadelphia, he asked his personal attorney and fellow Virginian Edmund Pendleton to prepare one. En route to Philadelphia, the request to review Baltimore's volunteer com-panies had indicated that people outside Virginia were looking to him for military leadership.[29]

As the delegates began discussing the possible establishment of an American Continental army, it became even more obvious to him that he was the preferred candidate for the command. Just one week into the session, he advised the Fairfax County Committee to select a sub-stitute delegate should the Virginia Convention meet during his ab-sence. Not only did he see the impending appointment, he assumed his wife was aware of it as well. "You might, and I suppose did perceive, from the Tenor of my letters," he wrote her after his election, "that I was apprehensive I could not avoid this appointment, as I did not even pretend ⟨t⟩o intimate when I should return."[30]

Washington's response to his selection was complex emotionally and politically. "[F]ar from seeking this appointment," he declared, "I have used every endeavour in my power to avoid it. . . ." Partly he felt con-cern for his wife. "I shall feel no pain from the Toil, or the danger of the Campaign," he told her. "My unhappiness will flow, from the un-easiness I know you will feel at being left alone."[31]

Even more, he feared that his abilities and military experience might prove unequal "to the extensive & important Trust. . . ." He had good reason for that apprehension. Previously he had commanded only a provincial regiment, no more than a few hundred men. Briefly he had led a division under General Forbes. This gave him greater experience than any other provincial officer, undoubtedly increasing the confidence of Congress in him. Still, he thought his preparation insufficient. He had faced vexing problems of recruitment and supply, but on a small scale. Now he was to organize and lead an army to defend an entire continent, an army still mostly on paper. He was to mold a fighting force that must go up against what many considered the most formidable army in the world. Britain, he had concluded, was determined to force Americans into a full-scale war, and he was to be entrusted with directing the de-fense of American liberty. Little wonder, then, that he fretted about his capacity for the command.[32]

Outweighing these anxieties was an issue of honor. Washington had strained all his life to register his claims to social merit, to win valida-tion by his society and especially by its leading members as an honorable gentleman, a man who embodied their material and moral aspirations. Throughout his life, he also feared the downfall of his reputation. Calumny had been heaped on General Braddock after the massacre on the Monongahela. At the time, Washington had commented that such censure "often falls very wrongfully." If he himself failed now in the Continental command, he said, "the cause will suffer, & more than probable my character along with it, as reputation derives it[s] principal support from success. . . ."[33]

But he could not refuse the appointment "without exposing my Character to such censures as would have reflected dishonour upon myself, and given pain to my friends—this, I am sure," he told his wife, "could not, and ought not to be pleasing to you, & must have lessend me considerably in my own esteem." And so he was about to put at risk that which he valued most, his good name. "I am Imbarked on a wide Ocean, boundless in its prospect & from whence, perhaps, no safe harbour is to be found."[34]

Washington was neither religiously fervent nor theologically learned. His creed espoused no more than a single doctrine—not really a doctrine at all, rather, a deep-seated conviction. An unseen but beneficent power directed the universe and human affairs. Usually he referred to it as Providence or Heaven. At times, he called that power God, at times Destiny. Long ago he had expressed the belief "that there is a Destiny which has the control of our actions, not to be resisted by the strongest efforts of Human Nature." He believed he felt that force operating in his life more momentously than at any time before. "[I]t has been a kind of destiny that has thrown me upon this Service . . . ," he said. Therefore he hoped "that my undertaking of it, is designd to answer some good purpose." He could only "rely . . . confidently, on that Providence which has heretofore preservd & been bountiful to me. . . ."[35]

If he felt the pull of Destiny or Providence, Washington also very much wanted the call. For more than two decades now, a sense of grievance had been growing inside him, a feeling of outrage at anticolonial discrimination. For the past decade, he had fought that prejudice politically and had labored to obtain a measure of political and economic self-determination for himself and the colonies within the British imperial system. Finally, he had come to see the pattern of biased arrangements as part of a larger conspiracy against English constitutional liberty. Unwilling any longer to accept a subordinate status within the Empire and refusing to yield to what he believed would be political enslavement, he had declared his readiness to defend American rights by force of arms. For the last twelve months, he had energetically engaged in military measures, had declared his "full intention to devote my Life and Fortune in the cause . . . if need be. . . ."[36]

Though he had misgivings about the appointment and had done nothing directly to solicit it, he had made plain his availability. Most tangibly, he had announced his readiness to serve by coming to the daily sessions of Congress in military uniform. His rekindling dream of military glory, his political commitments, and his continued striving for public recognition, all now coincided and opened onto the more expansive vista of a greater honor. The yearning for esteem became a quest for historical immortality. The desire for distinction became the spur of fame.

CHAPTER FIFTEEN

"Something charming . . . in the conduct of Washington"

Congress selected him to command the Continental Army, said Washington, because of "partiallity . . . assisted by a political motive."[1] The "political motive" was undoubtedly the intent to allay regional "jealousy" and to promote continental unity. But what had made the Congress partial to him? To understand their response, we must refer again to the ideological basis of the American Revolution. At the time of his appointment, Washington carefully shaped his public performance to match "Country Party" beliefs and ideals, that cluster of political values he shared with his fellow revolutionaries.

One of the central concerns of "Country" thought was the danger of political power. Basic to the ideology and psychology of the American Revolution was a fear of power, almost an obsession with it as expansive and corrupting and ultimately oppressive. Much of the "Country Party" analysis described the etiology of power, the ways in which it swelled, if unbridled, and then subverted public liberty and personal autonomy. To check such dangers, the reformers proposed institutional constraints: written constitutions, the separation of powers, legal restrictions on the authority of offices and officeholders, civilian control of the military.

Ultimately these legal mechanisms would fail, dissenting writers warned, if the character of a people and of their rulers was deficient in the "spirit of liberty." But if governmental power were limited, what would guarantee public order and safety? The answer again was the character of the people and of their rulers. The obverse side of the preoccupation with placing limits on power was the concern to promote public virtue.

"Country Party" exponents offered more than a description of the pathology of power and prescriptions for institutional reform. They proposed a set of standards to guide conduct in the public realm. They held up a yardstick against which to measure political and military leadership. As they outlined the steps by which insatiable power always encroached upon helpless liberty, British and American essayists delineated the character and conduct of two kinds of political figures. Repeatedly they set forth the traits by which to distinguish the true patriot from the false.

While the pseudo-patriot pretended devotion to the public good, in reality he governed for himself rather than for the people. Dominated by a lust for lawless authority, he connived to augment his power, to make it independent of the people from whom he derived it and for whose sake he had received it. He multiplied offices and filled them with corrupt and incompetent supporters who served at his will to do his bidding. He sought to make the people's legislative representatives his servile dependents. He stirred dissension and fomented factions to create new opportunities for extending his power further.

Most dangerously, he built a standing army in time of peace to enforce his aims and to intimidate the people from asserting their rights. History abounded with demagogues who used mercenary armies to destroy the liberty of their homelands. Time and again popular military heroes, Caesars and Cromwells, had freed their countries from dangers foreign and domestic only to use the acclamation of their fellow citizens and the devotion of their troops to make themselves dictators. An alert people must watch vigilantly for these danger signals of designs against their freedom.

Because power perpetually threatened liberty, the dissenting political writers gave their greatest attention to pretended patriots ambitious for themselves. But much of the rhetorical and moral force of these warnings resulted from their contrast with the ideal of the public-minded man devoted to the welfare of his country.

The true patriot never solicited office. He always had office thrust upon him by circumstances and by the call of his fellow citizens. The true patriot never pursued office because he had no need to. He was a man of independent wealth and independent outlook, who could neither be bought nor "meanly influenced." He was self-evidently a lover of virtue, who inculcated it in others "by precept and example." Never encouraging dissension, he always sought unity and harmony in the community. Never placing himself above the law, he always remembered that the people had entrusted him with power to serve them rather than himself. Again the essayists drew examples from the pages of history, Brutus and Cincinnatus and Timoleon and others.[2]

Towering among these models of virtue and patriotism stood the figure of Cato. John Trenchard and Thomas Gordon's serial essays, *Cato's Letters*, achieved extraordinary and widespread influence, while Joseph Addison's play *The Tragedy of Cato* won universal popularity. Together these works "fused with . . . the colonists' selectively Whiggish reading of the Roman historians" to form what Bernard Bailyn has called a "'Catonic' image, central to the political theory of the time, in which the career of the half-mythological Roman and the words of the two London journalists merged indistinguishably."[3]

Addison's tragedy embodied the ideals propounded by Trenchard and Gordon and other Radical Whig writers throughout the eighteenth century. This rather stiff play presents its hero almost as a schematic outline of the Whig ideal of public-minded conduct. Cato flawlessly exemplifies patriotic virtue, especially in his readiness to sacrifice himself and his sons at his country's call. "Thy life is not thy own, when Rome demands it," he proclaims. Viewing the "glorious wounds" of his fallen son, he laments only "that we can die but once to serve our country." For Rome's sake, he would willingly sacrifice all but his virtue. Addison contrasts Cato's selfless patriotism with Julius Caesar's ambition for lawless domination. He also counterposes it to the scheming of false patriots who stir up factions, hire foreign mercenaries, and, to promote their own interests, sell out their nation to a dictator.

Cato's balanced temperament distinguishes him from those of phlegmatic humor whose diffidence inhibits them when they should act and from those of violent emotions whose excessive zeal carries them to rash extremes. He epitomizes the virtues of temperateness and prudence. He has gained complete mastery over his passions without crushing them. He displays the noble, courageous, and virtuous sentiments of the true lover of his country. No wonder, then, that the young Numidian prince Juba adopts Cato as the pattern to follow in shaping his own character and conduct.[4]

The Tragedy of Cato was the most popular and influential play in the American colonies throughout the eighteenth century. Washington himself became intimately familiar with it.[5] Still, we misunderstand its significance in the minds of Americans and of Washington if we see it as the primary inspiration for his conduct. That age loved Addison's tragedy because it embodied their ideals of patriotism, selflessness, and emotional self-mastery and their beliefs about power, ambition, and tyranny. They reiterated those beliefs and ideals in essay after sermon after speech after pamphlet. Washington and his contemporaries quoted *Cato* because Addison's epigrams concisely expressed political and moral axioms drilled into their minds by three generations of preceptors. George Washington shaped his conduct to the pattern, not merely of Cato, but of the Catonic image.

At the beginning of the Revolutionary War, the general paraphrased *Cato* to one young colonel: "In such a Cause every Post is honourable in which a Man can serve his Country." Three months later he praised that same officer for his leadership in the heroic expedition against Quebec, once more paraphrasing Addison's hero: "It is not in the power of any Man to command success," he said, "but you have done more—you have deserved it." That gallant and capable commander was an ambitious young man who apparently never took to heart the example of Cato. His name was Benedict Arnold. Meanwhile George Washington exerted himself to embody the Whig ideal of true patriotism.[6]

Washington's response to his election as commander-in-chief reflected these beliefs. His statements that his abilities were unequal to the task and that he had done nothing to solicit the appointment were more than an expression of personal feelings. He intended to make a declaration to the public. He expressed these thoughts not only to his politically active brother Jack and to his brother-in-law and fellow Burgess, Burwell Bassett. More important, he put them in a public letter to the officers of the independent militia companies in Virginia whose command he had undertaken.

"I am now about to bid adieu to the Companies under your respective commands, at least for a while," he told them. "I have launched into a wide & extensive field, too boundless for my abilities, & far, very far, beyond my experience—I am called by the unanimous voice of the Colonies to the command of the Continental army: an honour I did not aspire to—an honor I was sollicitous to avoid upon full conviction of my inadequacy to the importance of the service; the partiallity of the Congress however, assisted by a political motive, rendered my reasons unavailing & I shall, to morrow, set out for the camp near Boston." Newspapers in Williamsburg, Philadelphia, and Boston published this letter. They followed it with six lines of verse which began, "Go, Gallant Washington. . . ."[7]

Washington's congressional colleagues did not share his misgivings about his talents and experience. Rather, his humble appraisal of his own abilities seems to have helped convince them not only that he had greater capacities than he recognized, but that he could safely be entrusted with extensive power. His "great modesty" particularly impressed them. "[I]f any thing," said one delegate, he was "too modest." When John Adams proposed him for the command and began to list his attributes, remembered Adams long after, "Mr. Washington, who happened to sit near the Door, as soon as he heard me allude to him, from his Usual Modesty darted into the Library Room." Another New Englander called him "no harum Starum ranting Swearing fellow but Sober, steady, & Calm." "He is no lover of parade," Silas Deane told his wife, "so do not put yourself into distress" if the general should stop there on his way to Boston.[8]

Though modest, Washington was far from timid. Congressional delegates described him as the "heroic" and "brave" General Washington. He was "said To be as fixed and resolute in having his Orders on all Occasions executed as he is cool & deliberate in giving them."[9] "Modest," "sober," "resolute." Washington presented himself as the very opposite of the rabble-rousing demagogue.

His words and actions neatly fitted and expressed the values of his generation in other ways as well. According to "Country Party" ideology, the public-minded man never sought office; his country always called him to it. Washington repeatedly declared that he had not solicited the appointment. "[I]t was by no means a thing of my own seeking, or proceeding from any hint of my friends." "I have been," he said, "called upon by the unanimous Voice of the Colonies to take the Command of the Continental Army." Following the victory over the British at Boston in March 1776, he responded to public praise by asserting again that the commission had come to him unsought: "When the councils of the British nation had formed a plan for enslaving America . . . I esteemed it my duty to take a part in the contest, and more especially on account of my being called thereto by the unsolicited suffrages of the representatives of a free people. . . ."[10]

Venal politicians sought office for pecuniary gain. The public-minded man would have no need to pursue office, because he would be a man of independent means. His economic self-sufficiency would guarantee his political independence. Proposing Washington's name for the generalship, John Adams pointed out that in addition to his "great Talents and excellent universal Character," his "independent fortune . . . would command the Approbation of all America, and unite the cordial Exertions of all the Colonies. . . ." A few days earlier, the New York Provincial Congress had stressed the importance of choosing men of wealth as Continental generals. Property, they believed, helped guarantee that a man would perform public duties faithfully and yield power readily when the general weal required it. This notion illuminates the significance of the rumor during the First Congress the previous fall that Washington was rich enough to raise, arm, and lead one thousand men at his own expense.[11]

Washington spoke to precisely this conviction and concern in his address to Congress accepting the appointment. "As to pay," he said, "I beg leave to Assure the Congress that as no pecuniary consideration could have tempted me to have accepted this Arduous emploiment at the expence of my domestk ease & happi⟨ness⟩ I do not wish to make any proffit from it: I will keep an exact Account of my expences; those I doubt not they will discharge & that is all I desire." This quiet symbolic gesture, one of the most important acts of Washington's entire career, deeply impressed his audience. It was a major step in the establishment of his fame.[12]

Ideally the public-minded man served his country, not only without thought of personal gain, but without regard to personal risk. He sought no profit, he avoided no loss. It was an antique ethic of self-sacrifice. "There is something charming to me in the conduct of Washington," said John Adams. "A gentleman of one of the first fortunes upon the continent, leaving his delicious retirement, his family and friends, sacrificing his ease, and hazarding all in the cause of his country! His views are noble and disinterested. He declared when he accepted the mighty trust, that he would lay before us an exact account of his expenses, and not accept a shilling for pay."[13]

For some, he had already become a model worthy of emulation. Silas Deane of Connecticut called him "his Countrys Freind—who sacrificing private Fortune independant Ease, and every domestic pleasure, sets off at his Countrys call, To exert himself in her defence without so much as returning to bid adieu to a Fond partner & Family. Let Our youth look up to This Man as a pattern to form themselves by, who Unites the bravery of the Soldier, with the most consummate Modesty & Virtue."[14]

Washington's independent fortune and his refusal of a salary seemed to guarantee his disinterested commitment to the cause. More than that, they proved his fitness to lead an army of citizen-soldiers. In contrast,

American republicans disdained British officers and soldiers as mercenary hirelings. Benjamin Franklin expressed the common opinion of the
superiority of armed citizens to professional soldiers. The fainthearted
would recover their "Spirits," he assured, "when they find by Experience how inefficient merely mercenary the regular Troops are, when
oppos'd to Freeholders & Freemen, fighting for their Liberties & Properties. A Country of such People was never yet conquer'd, (unless
through their own Divisions) by any absolute Monarch and his Mercenaries. But such States have often conquer'd Monarchies, and led
mighty Princes captive in Triumph." [15]

It also gratified provincials to find metropolitan observers acknowl-
edging the disinterested virtue, indeed the moral superiority, of the
American commander. American newspapers reprinted a paragraph
from a London paper: "General Washington who was lately appointed
Generalissimo over the provincials, has refused any salary, and is to
attend to the hazardous duty alloted him from principle only. A most
noble example, and worthy of imitation in Great Britain, particularly at
this time; for if there were a few disinterested patriots, like Washington,
the supplies of the Mother Country would soon lessen the national
debt, without any requisition from the Colonies." [16]

In March 1776, the legislators of Massachusetts declared: "[Y]our
nobly declining to accept the pecuniary emoluments annexed to this
high office, fully evidenced to us that a warm regard to the sacred rights
of humanity, and sincere love to your country, solely influenced you in
the acceptance of this important trust." The Continental Congress likewise lauded his greatness of mind in rejecting any compensation but the
pleasure of promoting his country's happiness. The American patriot
put the kings of Europe to shame, Tom Paine later proclaimed. While
they drew from their subjects' labors "a prodigality of pay" they did
not deserve, Washington rendered every service without pecuniary reward. Again and again his contemporaries praised him for abandoning
private affluence and comfort to serve the public good. His independent
fortune, they repeatedly asserted, made possible his disinterested commitment to the cause and to his country. His refusal of pay proved his
patriotism.[17]

The revolutionary generation of Americans warned themselves
against the dangers of professional soldiers and professional armies. As
a provincial officer, Washington had thought these fears exaggerated.
The seeming inability of lawmakers to understand military requirements had galled him. Though he had enforced strict discipline to keep

his troops from mistreating civilians, he had shown no special sensitivity to the widespread fear of military abuses of power. Sixteen years as a Burgess and two stints as a congressional delegate had instructed him in these issues. They had educated him about the legislative process and the legislative mind, had taught him how to negotiate and accommodate and compromise, how to work with elected leaders.

Equally important, he had gotten closely in touch with an ideological tradition that cautioned against standing professional armies, celebrated reliance on militias of citizen-soldiers, and demanded strict subordination of the military to civilian authority. The "Country Party" writings that shaped his view of the constitutional and political crisis carried vigorous preachments about these matters. That ideology once again made sense of colonial experience. During each of the imperial wars, Crown authorities had subordinated provincial interests and provincial leaders to British policies and officers. Long-term developments in the British professional army and events in recent years, particularly the Quartering Act of 1774 and the occupation of Boston, seemed to bear out the warnings: imperial officials were deliberately subverting the British heritage of civil control of the military.[18] Americans looked to their new General Washington to combat this ominous trend.

Even before his appointment as commander-in-chief and probably helping to bring it about, Washington deliberately displayed himself as a citizen-soldier. He appeared daily at the sessions of Congress in uniform. That uniform, one of his own design,[19] brought to mind his previous defense of colonial rights and his willingness to fight for them again. He presented himself, not as a professional soldier, but as a gentleman commander of militia volunteers, the Fairfax Independent Company. The outfit itself expressed the Anglo-American belief that civic virtue was most fully reflected when a freeman became a warrior.

Throughout the war, the fear of military power, of a professional standing army, undermined support and supply of the Continental forces. Many also feared that a military leader of Washington's astounding popularity, backed by an army devoted to him, could easily make himself dictator of America. The New York Provincial Congress expressed that anxiety indirectly in an address to the general less than two weeks after his appointment. While they praised his ability and virtue, they proclaimed "the fullest Assurances"—or perhaps it was their fretful hopes—"that whenever this important Contest shall be decided . . . You will chearfully resign the important Deposit committed into Your Hands, and reassume the Character of our worthiest Citizen."[20]

Here was another public occasion for an important political gesture on Washington's part. His reply was carefully tailored to allay the fear of military despotism. It set the tone for all his future military service. Speaking for himself and his colleagues, he said: "When we assumed the Soldier, we did not lay aside the Citizen, & we shall most sincerely rejoice with you in that happy Hour, when the Establishment of American Liberty . . . shall enable us to return to our private Stations in the bosom of a free, peaceful, & happy Country."[21]

The members of New York's revolutionary legislature ordered publication of their address and Washington's reply. Newspapers up and down the seaboard printed them. At the moment he assumed the role of primary leader in the Revolution, he spoke once again to the deepest concerns and fears of those who looked up to him. Landon Carter, one of his mentors as a young man, wrote to render him the fulsome praise he had always sought: "Go on, my Dear Sir, and impress on every memory, 'the man who resolved never to forget the Citizen in the General.'" And indeed, Washington strove and succeeded in stamping that impression on most memories.[22]

From the very first, the commander's communications with Congress and government officials at all levels strained to demonstrate his submission to civilian authority. He deliberately adopted a deferential manner. He intended to make his strict subordination to civilian authority conspicuous. He meant to dispel any fears that he might use the army for purposes other than the defense of American liberty. He did not want to stretch his powers, he assured. He only hoped to advance the public weal. His strict government of the army, his discipline of the soldiers, his punishment of fraud, his orders against plundering, his command that Continental officers cooperate with and assist civil magistrates, all aimed at quieting the fear that the Continental Army would become yet another lawless oppressive horde and he a military dictator.[23]

General Washington's regulation of his troops won widespread publicity and praise. The disciplined, law-abiding republican army under his command was contrasted with the lawless mercenaries said to make up Britain's professional force. His orders requiring respect of civil magistrates and civilian inhabitants were reprinted in newspapers far from the scene of action.[24]

The Massachusetts legislators indicated the importance to his contemporaries of this feature of his conduct. Following the victory at Boston in March 1776, they praised his "mild, yet strict Government of the

Army [and] your attention to the Civil Constitution of this Colony. . . ."
His reply showed his awareness of the way in which his scrupulous subordination was contributing to the establishment of his fame: "Your
acknowledgment of my attention to the civil constitution of this colony
. . . demands my grateful thanks. A regard to every Provincial institution, where not incompatible with the common interest, I hold a principle of duty and of policy, and it shall ever form a part of my
conduct."[25]

Legislators and orators and writers extolled Washington's public-
minded actions. The Marquis de Chastellux, the French soldier-intellec-
tual, remarked in 1780 that throughout the war the general had obeyed
Congress. Americans, he said, knew "how to appreciate all the merit
contained in this simple fact." At the end of the war, one such American
who had greatly influenced Washington's political development, his
neighbor and colleague George Mason, praised the commander's "strict
Attention to the authority of the Civil-Power." That line of conduct,
noted Mason, had endeared him to his fellow citizens. Thomas Jefferson
summed up the matter for his generation, stating the reason they had
placed Washington among those who "merited . . . an everlasting remembrance. . . . [H]is was the singular destiny and merit," said Jefferson, ". . . of scrupulously obeying the laws through the whole of his
career, civil and military, of which the history of the world furnishes no
other example."[26]

Washington's generation also particularly admired his mastery of his
emotions. As a frontier regimental commander, he had filled his letters
with complaints and criticisms. Throughout the 1760s and early 1770s,
he had complained frequently to the English commercial agents with
whom he did business. On one occasion, he fired off a lengthy and
angry letter to two wheat merchants in Alexandria. Another time, he
roared at a former regimental officer who had accused him of bad faith.
Other recipients of his letters found themselves inundated by eruptions
of Washingtonian wrath. Occasionally he still exploded with violent
anger toward what he considered ill-treatment, incompetency, or betrayal. But during the Revolution and after, he tried to confide such
expressions only to trusted friends. As he had matured, he had placed
his temper and all his other emotions under stricter control.[27]

Washington's contemporaries noted his struggle to master his emotions. Gilbert Stuart, who painted his portrait more than once, thought
his features indicated the strongest and most ungovernable passions.
Had he lived among savage tribes, Stuart believed, he would have been

the fiercest of men. Said Jefferson: "His temper was naturally irritable and high toned; but reflection and resolution had obtained a firm and habitual ascendency over it. If ever, however, it broke its bonds, he was most tremendous in his wrath." Henrietta Liston, wife of the first British minister to the United States, came to know Washington well. "[H]e acquired a uniform command over his passions on publick occasions," she reported, "but in private & particularly with his Servants, its violence sometimes broke out."[28]

In public, Washington became more and more circumspect, not only in expressing anger, but in revealing any of his emotions. He himself indicated this at the time of his retirement from the presidency. Lady Liston remarked to him "that his countenance indicated the pleasure to which he looked forward. You are wrong[,] replied he, my countenance never yet betrayed my feelings. . . ." During the Revolution and after, he increasingly guarded his true thoughts and feelings. His self-protectiveness, like his self-control, was studied.[29]

Washington's contemporaries witnessed and esteemed in him a self-mastery they could only term Catonic. Gouverneur Morris expressed the general reaction: "[F]ew men of such steady, persevering industry ever existed, and perhaps no one who so completely commanded himself. Thousands have learned to restrain their passions, though few among them had to contend with passions so violent. But the self-command to which I allude was of higher grade. He could, at the dictate of reason, control his will and command himself to act."[30]

To a generation that feared the social and political danger of uncontrolled human passions, it was vital that individuals keep their emotions under the "dictate of reason." To a people swirling in the turbulence of nation-founding, it seemed essential that their principal leader should be able both to restrain his own passions and to model self-mastery to every citizen of the Republic. If the future of free government in America depended upon the virtue of the people, they needed an exemplar of virtuous self-control to pattern themselves on. A society that incited its members to compete strenuously with one another for material success and social distinction found it necessary to instill in them internal restraints that would protect the community from disintegration.

George Washington also vividly impressed his contemporary audience because he looked the part he played. His appearance and manner seemed to express his character, personal and public, just as that culture said it should. His bearing bespoke authority, his demeanor inspired confidence. Those who met him described his physical carriage and personal presence as graceful, dignified, majestic. "His person," said Jefferson, "was fine, his stature exactly what one would wish, his deportment easy, erect and noble. . . ."[31]

"I was struck with General Washington," Abigail Adams told John when she first met him. "You had prepared me to entertain a favorable opinion of him, but I thought the one half was not told me. Dignity with ease, and complacency [by which she meant complaisance or affability], the Gentleman and Soldier look agreably blended in him. Modesty marks every line and feture of his face. Those lines of Dryden instantly occurd to me

> 'Mark his Majestick fabrick! he's a temple
> Sacred by birth, and built by hands divine
> His Souls the deity that lodges there.
> Nor is the pile unworthy of the God.'"

Remarked Benjamin Rush at the beginning of the war: "[H]e has so much martial dignity in his deportment that you would distinguish him to be a general and a soldier from among ten thousand people. There is not a king in Europe that would not look like a valet de chambre by his side."[32]

The impression Washington made was no accident. He had consciously cultivated a style of presenting himself. Jefferson would later also describe him as "the best horseman of his age, and the most graceful figure that could be seen on horseback." And so the newly appointed commander-in-chief dramatically departed Philadelphia escorted by officers of the militia, members of the Philadelphia Light Horse, the entire Massachusetts delegation, and other members of Congress, as a band played, while he himself rode on a charger. Only some miles later did he dismount and continue his journey in a carriage drawn by two white horses. Knowing that attire added to his image, he chose his dress carefully. For his entrance into New York City, he donned a plumed hat and a purple sash. Again he mounted horse to ride in the enthusiastic parade that ushered him into the city.[33]

During the war, he painstakingly prescribed the uniforms of his officers and soldiers to engender respect for the Continental Army and bolster public and military morale. As commander and as president, he meticulously matched what he wore to the role he played. The effect he achieved resulted from his studied preparation for his public performance. More and more he saw himself as "a figure upon the stage," playing the primary role in a great historical drama.[34]

In an age when public figures frequently struck dramatic poses, George Washington was a consummate actor. His skill is all the more notable because he was never a poseur. He never lapsed into the histrionic. Others, particularly those with greater oratorical gifts, might overplay their parts. He kept his performance understated and subtle. This was a major element of his appeal. It showed he had carefully read his audience. They feared bold, flamboyant, charismatic figures who might manipulate the passions of the people, might stir them up and lead them into turbulence and anarchy. The danger was that all this would end in dictatorship. Washington's restrained performance allayed such fears. His great skill was that on important public occasions he successfully avoided the melodramatic without loss of effect. Repeatedly at such moments, moments like his acceptance of the Continental command and his response to the New York Provincial Congress, he chose the right pose, the right gesture, the right words.

The announcement of Washington's appointment, his journey from Philadelphia to Boston, and his first weeks in the command, all fixed attention on him. With that movement he stepped, as it were, from among the crowd of supporting players into the central role of the revolutionary drama. For the next quarter of a century, his audience would keep their eyes fixed on him almost continuously.

CHAPTER SIXTEEN

"God Save Great Washington! God Damn the King!"

American provincials genuinely believed in both their king and kingly rule. Many affirmed a particular ideal and theory of constitutional monarchy grounded in "Country Party" ideology. They clung to these beliefs tenaciously and to the very end. When they concluded that George III had betrayed both their trust and their ideals, they fiercely rejected him and repudiated the institution of kingship.[1] But this is only part of the story. This radical shift in the consciousness of many Americans can only be understood by considering the transfer of praise and affection from George III to George Washington. The fall of the king and the rise of the general were complementary historical events.

Colonials shared a deeply held faith in royal rule. Equally important, for the past generation, a specific ideology of British kingship had shaped their expectations and perceptions of their monarchs. They found it in the writings of Henry St. John, Viscount Bolingbroke, leader of the "Country Party's" Radical Tory wing. In the North American colonies, Bolingbroke long enjoyed an influence on a par with that of the Radical Whigs. He agreed with them on the necessity of institutional reforms (annual elections and rotation in office, abolition of the standing army and renewed reliance on local militia forces), but he had less and less faith that such measures could turn back the tide of civic corruption. For him, political salvation lay in a renovation of the British "constitution," a renewal of the fundamental principles and values of the society, a revival of the "spirit of liberty."[2]

Bolingbroke found the solution to this distressing dilemma in *The*

Discourses of Machiavelli. The great Florentine political theorist had observed, "[A]s a general rule . . . it never or rarely happens that a republic or monarchy is well-constituted or its institutions entirely reformed, unless it is done by only one individual." Here Machiavelli drew a parallel between the founding of a new state and the reforming of a corrupt one. Both events occurred in the moments of greatest political and moral fluidity in the life of a commonwealth. The institutions of society and the "manners" of the people, the constitutive elements of a polity, either had yet to be established or had so degenerated that they must be reestablished. In the life of any nation, these two occasions bristled with the greatest dangers. The most probable means of successful passage through them, according to Machiavelli, lay in reliance on a great man acting alone.[3]

Even before Bolingbroke, British political commentators had quoted Machiavelli's dictum and had prayed for the advent of a ministerial or monarchical savior. It remained for him, though, to give the concept its most powerful formulation. He called it "The Idea of a Patriot King."[4]

Amid the selfish pursuit of private interests, only a Patriot King, "the most uncommon of all phaenomena in the physical or moral world," could "restore the virtue and public spirit essential to the preservation of liberty and national prosperity." Only he could enforce the measures necessary to save the nation. He would dismiss avaricious power-abusing politicians and replace them with men of true ability, true patriotism, and true ambition, that is, ambition for lasting fame. He would reduce the standing army because it endangered national liberty. Knowing that "[t]he good of the people is the ultimate and true end of government," he would consider himself subject to the constitution and the laws and would exercise his power as a trust from his people. Above all, he would "espouse no party, but . . . govern like the common father of his people. . . ."

Bolingbroke's view of society had no place for legitimately competing interest groups, let alone class conflict. The hierarchical ranks of his ideal agrarian social order formed an organic unity. For him, "[t]he true image of a free people, governed by a Patriot King, is that of a patriarchal family, where the head and all the members are united by one common interest, and animated by one common spirit. . . . Instead of abetting the divisions of his people, he will endeavour to unite them, and to be himself the centre of their union. . . ." Here Bolingbroke expressed one of the chief concerns of "Country Party" political thought: a society that encouraged individual liberty was always in danger of divisions caused by private ambitions and competing interests. Paradoxically, as William Liddle has pointed out, the liberty of a free people, according to Bolingbroke, "might ultimately depend upon the character of their prince...."[5]

A Patriot King could be trusted with great powers because the people would recognize in him a prince virtuous in character and public-minded, devoted to their welfare and their liberty, ambitious for their good and not his own aggrandizement. Unlike tyrants, he in his wisdom would recognize that the greatest security of his reign lay in winning the affection of his subjects. "Nothing less than the hearts of his people will content such a prince," wrote Bolingbroke, "nor will he think his throne established, till it is established there."[6]

Following publication of Bolingbroke's essay in 1749, the "idea of a Patriot King" almost immediately became a standard term and concept in Anglo-American political discourse. Colonials adopted it quickly and enthusiastically. Bolingbroke's patriarchal agrarianism had particular appeal in the southern provinces where the great planters held sway. The "Country Party" critique underlay the colonial view of British imperial politics. It "explained" their treatment at the hands of Crown officials. They began to look for a patriot prince to implement the program of the Opposition and to safeguard the interests and rights of the colonies.[7]

When George III ascended the throne, British Americans hailed him as the awaited Patriot King. Many would have agreed with young John Adams that his first official acts had avowed "sentiments worthy of a King—a Patriot King." Colonials convinced themselves that the inauguration of the new reign marked the implementation of the "Country Party" program.[8]

Mistakenly crediting George with a central role in repeal of the Stamp Act, they again assumed his allegiance to "Country Party" ideals. When a group of Bostonians gathered to celebrate the first anniversary of their riotous intimidation of the Stamp officer, they offered a toast: "*May the British Empire be always happy in a patriot King of the House of Brunswick.*"[9] Colonials likewise blamed the Townshend duties not on George, but on Parliament and the ministry. And again, repeal reassured them of the efficacy of supplicating their king.

This patient trust in the ultimate goodness and justice of their sovereign contrasted sharply with the antimonarchical actions of the contemporaneous Wilkes and Liberty movement in England. Colonials might agree with Wilkite criticisms of the administration, might support the reforms demanded by these English radicals, but generally they felt shock and dismay at their mob violence and at the great disrespect for the king. From 1767 to 1773, nearly every antimonarchical polemic published in the colonies originated in England. Moreover, no significant inclusion of the king in charges against the ministry appeared in America during that period.[10]

Yet George III had failed to heed the cries of his colonial subjects. He received but ignored American petitions, and colonial newspapers reported his cold reaction to addresses from English supporters of America. In the early 1770s, some Americans began to ask how "the best of Kings" could be so completely deluded by his advisers. Probably a majority of colonials still clung to the illusion of royal innocence, still expected George III yet to prove himself a "Patriot King." That phrase fell into disuse during these years as provincial writers and preachers applied it less often to their sovereign. But the idea, if not the phrase, remained in force. Colonials held to the hope that their monarch would match their expectations.[11]

From the summer of 1774 through the early fall of 1775, and even despite the bloodshed at Lexington and Concord, most Americans apparently clutched at the hope that their king would have a change of heart. The Continental Congress still publicly pinned the blame on the British ministry. Even militants like Washington avoided implicating the monarch, by carefully labeling British army forces as the "Ministerial Troops." He spoke for many when he said, "[W]e do not, nor cannot yet prevail upon ourselves to call them the King's Troops." Some polemicists warned George III that by his actions he might "un-king" himself. A few called him tyrant already. But the surprising fact is that down to the end of 1775 so little colonial propaganda attacked the king.[12]

Washington's actions between mid-1775 and mid-1776 helped move his fellow Americans toward independence and repudiation of the king.[13] During the past two decades, his experiences as a provincial soldier, planter, and politician had kept throwing him right into the middle of the imperial-colonial controversy. Slowly his sense of himself had been changing. He had once put Virginia's interests first, giving short shrift to the needs of the other provinces or the Empire. More and more, he thought of himself as an American, thought in terms of the community of interest of the American colonies. During the past year, his contacts with congressional delegates from those various provinces had encouraged him to adopt a continental perspective. His new commission to command, indeed to create, a Continental army seemed to require precisely that outlook.

From the first, the necessities of the command, his evolving nationalist identity, and the ideological injunction to seek unity urged General Washington to try to abolish provincial distinctions within the army. To that end, he wanted the soldiers in uniform clothing. He avoided even the appearance of "partiality" toward fellow Virginians. He wanted appointment of officers shifted from the provincial governments to the Continental Congress. He wanted those appointments made according to merit and not nativity. This more just arrangement, he felt, would give an equal chance to the committed, ambitious, and talented young men of every province, would promote the most capable officers, and would unify the cause. The policy conflicted with the old idea that public virtue and zeal for the cause originated from rootedness in a more local community. He failed to overcome the tenacious grip of state control, but the attempt evinced an incipient nationalism which his military service would intensify.[14]

Washington's language also reflected this developing nationalism. He used the word *country* in two senses. As in the past, he employed it when referring to the individual provinces. He recognized that provincial connections engendered emotional attachments and incurred public obligations. Almost simultaneously he began to speak somewhat self-consciously, but nonetheless deliberately, of "the Cause of our Common Country." He lamented complaints in New England about Congress's arrangement of the appointment of general officers. ". . . I should hope every Post would be deemed honourable which gave a Man Opportunity to serve his Country," he said, paraphrasing Addison's *Cato*. Already in mid-July 1775, he was thus asserting that individuals had patriotic responsibilities beyond their own colonies, to America as a whole.

Trying to persuade a disgruntled brigadier general from Massachusetts to keep his commission, he argued that the man owed his service not only to "your bleeding Country," Massachusetts, but also to the United Colonies collectively. The "other Colonies have also their Claims upon you, not only as a Native of America," but because they had made common cause with his home province. The outcome of the contest, the future well-being of the whole continent, must affect him "as a Member of the great American Body. . . ." Within a few months, Washington was clearly asserting that Americans had a duty to defend their "country," America.[15]

The American Revolution was more than a war of weapons. It was a war of words and of ideas. A month after assuming the command, General Washington launched a propaganda barrage, another public gesture of symbolic significance. Reportedly American officers held prisoner at Boston had been tossed into a jail for common criminals. According to intelligence, the British had also mistreated the wounded and ill and ignored the rank of officers. Commanding the besieged British forces was Lieutenant General Thomas Gage, Washington's old comrade from the Braddock expedition. He wrote Gage protesting these abuses and calling upon him to respect "the Rights of Humanity, & Claims of Rank. . . ." He threatened retaliation against British officers in American hands. He warned that the British misconduct would tend "to widen that unhappy Breach, which you, *and those Ministers under whom you act*, have repeatedly declared you wish'd to see forever closed [emphasis added]." Clearly, in this public letter, Washington meant to maintain the distinction between the ministry and the king.[16]

But Gage refused to have it so. His reply pounded home the point that the revolutionaries were guilty of rebellion against Britain's royal ruler. He admitted he was disregarding the rank of American officers, "for I Acknowledge no Rank that is not derived from the King." Nonetheless, the prisoners had received humane treatment, although as traitors they were "destined to the Cord. . . ." He leveled a charge of his own: numbers of the "King's faithfull Subjects" were being coerced into taking "Arms against their King and Country." Washington, he declared, acted under "usurped Authority," while he "acted under the King," despite the rebel general's "insinuations in regard to Ministers. . . ." His Majesty and his advisers wished to see the "unhappy Breach forever closed" between mother country and colonies, but "those who long since projected the present Crisis, and influence the Councils of America, have views very distant from Accomodation. . . . [T]o God who knows all hearts," proclaimed Gage, "be the appeal. . . ."[17]

Washington concluded the exchange with a double-barreled blast which is a small classic of political propaganda. "Whether British, or American Mercy, Fortitude, & Patience are most preeminent . . . ," he rejoined, "whether our virtuous Citizens whom the Hand of Tyranny has forced into Arms, to defend their Wives, their Children, & their Property; or the mercenary Instruments of lawless Domination, Avarice, and Revenge best deserve the Appellation of Rebels, and the Punishment of that Cord, which your affected Clemency has forborne to inflict ... were altogether foreign to my Subject. I purposely avoided all political Disquisition; nor shall I now avail myself of those Advantages, which the sacred Cause of my Country, of Liberty, and human Nature give me over you. Much less shall I stoop to Retort & Invective."

He repudiated the charge that loyalists were being coerced. "[T]hose execrable Parricides, whose Counsels & Aid have deluged their Country with Blood, have been protected from the Fury of a justly enraged Poeple. Far from compelling, or even permitting their Assistance, I am embarassed with the Numbers who crowd to our Camp animated with the purest Principles of Virtue, & Love of their Country."

The American commander might disavow coercion of Tories, but he was drawing lines of loyalty, forcing people to choose sides. Still, he as yet avoided calling upon them to repudiate their king, avoided implicating the monarch in tyranny, avoided even mentioning him directly.

"You affect, Sir, to despise all Rank not derived from the same Source with your own. I cannot conceive any more honourable, than that which flows from the uncorrupted Choice of a brave and free People—The purest Source & original Fountain of all Power." Washington might sidestep the complicity of the king for the moment, but already in this succinct Whig-republican statement, he was setting the stage for a shift of allegiance.

Both sides claimed God as an ally. "May that God to whom you then appealed, judge between America & you!" declared Washington. "Under his Providence, those who influence the Councils of America, and all the other Inhabitants of the united Colonies, at the Hazard of their Lives, are resolved to hand down to Posterity those just & invaluable Privileges which they received from their Ancestors.

"I shall now, Sir, close my Correspondence with you, perhaps forever. If your Officers who are our Prisoners receive a Treatment from me, different from what I wish'd to shew them, they & you, will remember the Occasion of it." [18]

Washington sent copies of this correspondence to the Congress in Philadelphia. A letter reporting the exchange and written by someone in the camp at Cambridge first got it into the press. Congress also ordered the letters between the generals published. Newspapers up and down the continent printed them, to the satisfaction of readers such as Benjamin Rush, who praised Washington's "manly behavior." Already he was becoming the chief spokesman of the revolutionary cause. [19]

Washington realized earlier than most that the issue would be settled by force of arms and that the war would be protracted. This, he recognized in the fall of 1775, required the reenlistment and reorganization of his entire army. In October, a congressional committee huddled with him at Cambridge to hear his recommendations. The alterations he proposed would move the United Colonies much farther down the road toward independence. Congress adopted every one. The army would be augmented. Courts-martial would have authority to enforce stricter discipline by imposing stiffer punishments. Captured British spies would face the death penalty. Mutiny and sedition by officers and soldiers in the Continental Army would now also be tried as capital crimes. These last two acts, voted by Congress in the first week of November, were implicitly acts of sovereignty by an independent nation. They had originated with the commander-in-chief.[20]

Meanwhile moderates still clung to the hope that their king would bring about a reconciliation, but George III refused to accommodate their dreams. Instead, step by step, he shattered them. Word came that in early April he had received the petition of London officials protesting the administration's colonial policy. He was surprised, he said, that they would encourage "the rebellious opposition" in his North American colonies. In mid-September, reports arrived of his pledge to a second group of London petitioners to uphold "constitutional authority" as long as "a part of my American Subjects" continued to oppose it. The first week of November, Americans received his "Proclamation for suppressing Rebellion and Sedition," issued on 23 August. Congress tried to counter this royal accusation and continued to differentiate the sovereign from his advisers. "We will not, for our part," they declared, "lose the distinction between the King and his Ministers." Despite this official assertion of faith in their monarch, the delegates were shaken by his proclamation.[21]

The next week's news brought Congress two more jolts. The king would make no reply to their latest petition; the British army in the colonies would be reinforced. These actions cut the ground from under advocates of petitioning and reconciliation. Blow by blow, George III himself battered Americans' Bolingbrokean delusions about him. For many, the knockout punch landed in January 1776. On 26 October, addressing Parliament, the king had accused colonial militants of open revolt "for the purpose of establishing an independent empire." He had vowed to put down this rebellion and announced his enlistment of Hanoverian and other foreign mercenaries to assist in the task.[22]

Washington later said he had given up any hope of accommodation when he learned in November 1775 of the King's proclamation for suppressing rebellion. In point of fact, even before that fateful news he had been backing policies aimed at independence. Now that the king himself had shaken the faith of conciliationist colonials, the rebel general aimed at independence more directly, more vigorously. In November, he urged the arrest and suppression of Tories in New England. In December, he advocated a test act compelling everyone to declare their allegiance. He also began to disparage the monarch openly. Sarcastically he referred to George III as "the best of Kings."[23]

George Washington's views of the conflict with Britain had long ranged ahead of other Americans' opinions. During the preceding decade of controversy, colonial attitudes toward Parliament had changed dramatically, and the generations-long ties to the mother country had weakened. Meanwhile, the view most colonials held of George III had remained almost transfixed by reverence for the traditional patriarchal conception of monarchy and by the idea of a Patriot King. A revolution in American consciousness had been gathering momentum since the spring of 1774. This transformation of attitudes expressed itself primarily toward the king, but it involved a repudiation of kingship and of the British nation as well. For many Americans, it meant disillusionment with an old faith and adoption of a new one. George III had violated their trust in him. He had proved himself a tyrant rather than a Patriot King.

Through the end of 1775, most of the published renunciations of loyalty to the king showed surprising restraint. It was as though, having confronted their delusion and admitted it to themselves, people feared to say aloud the full depth of their pain and anger. It seemed that the repudiated vision still held some power of enchantment. The king's speeches and acts in the last months of 1775 sent a shudder through that vision. Then in January, Thomas Paine touched the point of his pen to it and broke the spell.

Paine spoke and a host of others found their voices to denounce George III. *Common Sense* attacked the institution of monarchy head-on. Other advocates of independence excoriated the monarch himself. They had discovered in him not a Patriot King but a "Royal Criminal," "the whining King of Great Britain," the "cruelest Sovereign *tyrant* of this age." All of the charges colonial militants had hurled at the ministry they now loaded on the king. From the beginning of his reign, he had aimed at arbitrary power. He was "the author of all the measures carried on against America." "King George the Third," proclaimed the freeholders of Charlotte County, Virginia, "under the character of a parent, persists in behaving as a tyrant."[24]

General Washington praised "the sound doctrine and unanswerable reasoning" of *Common Sense*. It was "working a powerful change . . . in the minds of many men . . . ," he said. He expected it to promote the cause of independence. As Paine's pamphlet began to have its effect, Washington urged his allies in Congress against negotiations. He favored a declaration of independence. He denounced the king's most recent measures to deprive "us of our Constitutional Rights and Liberties." "[T]he Name of Majesty," he declared, ". . . ought to promote the happiness of his People and not their Oppression." He began to call the enemy forces not the "ministerial troops," but the "king's troops."[25]

Americans, Washington knew, would ". . . from their form of government, and steady attachment heretofore to royalty . . . come reluctantly into the idea of independence, but time and persecution bring many wonderful things to pass. . . ." He recognized that for most of them the issue of independence revolved around their adherence to monarchical government and the king and their attachment to the English nation. Perhaps he himself had adopted the idea earlier and easier partly because he had long ago concluded that the British ministry would never have pursued their oppressive policies without "the firmest perswasion that the People were with them."[26]

As Washington's nationalism intensified in the early months of 1776, he began to require that people choose sides. In January, he directed General Lee to disarm Tories in New York. In the spring, he supported more stringent measures to suppress loyalism. He wanted loyalist leaders arrested. He wanted persons disaffected from the revolution restrained and punished. More than pragmatic policy, these views reflected his own zealous engagement. To him, Tories were traitors to their country, "abominable pests of Society" who should be rooted out.[27]

The revolution in American attitudes toward the king accelerated during these months. In one colony after another, radicals pressed the issue of independence by urging the revolutionary governments to ground their authority in the people rather than the Crown. On 15 May, Congress called for the suppression of all provincial governments deriving their authority from the king. In midsummer, the delegates of the self-emancipating American states declared the independence of their sovereignties. Justifying the separation, they listed the crimes, not of the Parliament or of the ministry, but of King George III.

"A Prince," they said, "whose character is ... marked by every act which may define a Tyrant, is unfit to be the ruler of a free people." [28]

Publication of the Declaration of Independence ignited an instantaneous reaction. In New York, Boston, Worcester, and Providence, crowds gathered at courthouses, provincial capitol buildings, churches, and taverns to tear down the king's coat-of-arms. Boston mobs burned shop signs bearing crowns and royal lions. Citizens of Savannah conducted a mock funeral for the "late" unlamented monarch, drawing "a greater number of people than ever appeared on any occasion before in this province." Irate New Yorkers pulled down the gilded equestrian statue of George erected to honor him following repeal of the Townshend Acts. They beheaded it and broke it into pieces. Its two tons of lead were made into bullets to fight the king's "Red Coated & Torie Subjects." [29]

These furious outbursts were more than the propaganda maneuvers of political agitators. They expressed a traumatic transformation of belief. They represented the explosion of a dream. Bolingbroke's vision of a Patriot King had eloquently fused the traditional belief in paternalistic monarchy with the political program and principles of "Country Party" ideology. Colonials had convinced themselves that George III could and would fulfill their expectations. Only at the very end did most conclude that he was neither the Common Father of his People nor the awaited Patriot King. They felt he had betrayed their trust in his paternal rule, had flouted the political principles they had expected him to follow. This double wound, psychic and political, accounts for their rage.

They now decided that not the ministry but the king himself was the fountainhead of tyrannical ambition. It had become necessary, not simply to insulate America from the encroachment of Parliament, but to sever all connections with the Empire before the contagion of corruption emanating from the Crown and contaminating the nation fatally infected American public virtue. In their righteous indignation, they rid themselves of kingship and all hereditary rule, rejecting even limited constitutional monarchy. Instead they established republican governments, announcing to the world and warning themselves that the success of this new system would rest on their own virtue.[30]

When revolutionary Americans expelled George III from their hearts, they immediately adopted a native hero and leader. Curtis Nettels marked the victory at Boston in March 1776 as "the event which first placed [Washington] upon the pedestal" of fame. But even before that triumph, Americans had begun to celebrate his character. Soon after his appointment as commander-in-chief, Douglas Southall Freeman noted with surprise, observers began to describe him in the exalted terms they would use for the rest of his career.[31] In the very months when they repudiated one George, they embraced another.

Until his appointment as Continental commander-in-chief, George Washington had played a secondary role in the revolutionary drama. Now he moved to the center of the stage. Up and down the Atlantic seaboard, the attentive audience fixed their eyes upon him. Newspapers announced his appointment, then followed his journey to the American camp at Cambridge, Massachusetts. His progress northward, he told Richard Henry Lee, was "a good deal retarded, principally by the desire the different Townships through which I traveld express'd of shewing respect to the Genl of your armies. . . ." Already he was beginning to speak of his public self in the third person, indicating his deliberate performance of that part.[32]

Everywhere, it seemed, local officials wanted to greet him and companies of light horse came out to escort his entourage. A cavalcade ushered him into New York City, reported the gazettes, with "a greater number of the principal inhabitants of this City than ever appeared here on any occasion before." There, as indeed all along his route, Washington moved, in the words of one Tory, "amidst the repeated shouts and huzzas of the seditious and rebellious multitude. . . ." New Englanders began applauding his appointment and proclaiming their confidence in him even before he arrived.[33]

Writers again recalled Washington's heroism at Braddock's defeat and added to his legend. According to one newspaper report, Sir Jeffery Amherst had pledged, if given only five thousand English regulars, to march from one end of the North American continent to the other. Hearing this, Colonel Washington supposedly replied that with one thousand Virginians he would engage to stop Amherst's march. "It is the fashion at St. James' to despise the Americans, to call them cowards, poltroons, &c. . . . The very able, spirited, and prudent conduct of this gallant officer when he covered and preserved the remains of the English army after one of their defeats last war in North America, has endeared him to every brave man, and stamped him with the name of being a most noble officer."[34]

Significantly for Americans, this story originated in Britain. More important, the recollection of Braddock's massacre reminded them that twenty years earlier, the provincial Colonel Washington had proved the superiority of American citizen-soldiers over British regulars. According to the apocryphal boast, he thought one American fighter the equal of five British.

As if to make his pledge fact, the Fairfax Independent Company declared their readiness "to join the Troops at Cambridge, or to march" anywhere else the general commanded. They addressed him as "their patron, friend & worthy citizen." Soon several companies of Virginia riflemen were heading north. They were "All chosen riflemen," affirmed a correspondent of Purdie's *Virginia Gazette*, "eager to hazard their lives in their country's cause, and to follow the fortunes of their beloved Washington!" [35]

Remembrance of Washington's earlier heroism caused some to recall the theological gloss on Braddock's defeat by the noted preacher Samuel Davies. In 1755, Davies had proclaimed America's divinely ordained mission to model civil and religious liberty to the world. Fulfillment of that errand, colonial revolutionaries now believed, made necessary an appeal to Heaven, an appeal to arms. Davies's wish had been that Providence had "preserved" the young Colonel Washington "*for some* important *service to his country*." At the urging of Benjamin Rush, *Dunlap's Pennsylvania Packet* now reprinted those words, hoping they would "*prove* prophetic *of the success of the* COMMANDER IN CHIEF *of the American Army*." [36]

In "American Liberty," young Philip Freneau reminded his audience that Washington had "fought at wild Ohio's flood, / . . . When Braddock's fall disgrac'd the mighty day. . . ." He also predicted the destruction of Britain as Heaven's vengeance for its crimes. But before that day of wrath, "A monarch first of vulgar soul should rise, / . . . Whose heart should glow with not one gen'rous thought, / Born to oppress, to propagate and rot. . . ." [37]

The martial enthusiasm of the moment carried Washington into Cambridge. He is "much beloved and admired . . . ," said one observer; "his appointment to the Chief Command has the general suffrage of all ranks of people here. . . ." Military discipline and skill among the troops improved markedly. Part of the praise was due to his strict enforcement of order and revolutionary virtue among his troops. Immediately he began to make them into a model republican army. Washington, a friend told John Adams, "has in a manner inspired Officers and Soldiers with a taste for Discipline and they go into it readily, as they all venerate and love the General." "Gen. W. is the Delight of the Army," Ezra Stiles told his diary. Said Hannah Winthrop to Mercy Warren, "Must not we expect Success under the direction of so much goodness."[38]

Americans looked to Washington as their champion. Phillis Wheatley, "the African Poetess," a young black woman of Providence, Rhode Island, addressed lines of verse to his Excellency: "[F]irst in place and honours . . . Fam'd for thy valour, for thy virtues more, / Hear every tongue thy guardian aid implore!" James Warren thought him "certainly the best Man for the place he is in. . . ."[39]

Writers began to dedicate their works to him. A brigantine was christened with his name. Eventually, the Continental Navy and the navies and privateers of individual states would include a frigate, two galleys, another brigantine, a schooner, five sloops, and four other ships named "Washington," and a vessel called the "Lady Washington." Also, a custom started that summer and fall that became almost a mania. In Boston, Dorchester, and Andover, Massachusetts, in Williamsburg, Virginia, and in Newcastle, Delaware, leading families baptized male offspring with the name George Washington.[40]

In mid-November, Martha Washington left Mount Vernon with a small entourage to join her husband at Cambridge. The attention she received from dignified personages along the route amazed her. At Philadelphia, military escorts accompanied her arrival and departure. She came and left "in as great pomp as if I had been a very great somebody." At Elizabethtown, New Jersey, the local light horse contingent and most of the principal gentlemen honored her passage. When she reached Newark, the bells were set to ringing while Colonel Allan's company of minutemen mounted guard. Massachusetts gave her a welcome described by one observer as befitting "the Lady of His Excellency General Washington." In January 1776, a family in Dunstable, Massachusetts, gave that Lady's name to an infant daughter. At her baptism, the child "was dressed in blue and buff, with a sprig of evergreen on its head, emblematick of his Excellency's glory in the provincials affection."[41]

Americans had already been christening infant children in honor of their new champion. Early in 1776, they began naming places after him as well. In March, freeholders and other inhabitants of the District of Stoughtonham, Massachusetts, incorporated as a township. "[T]o perpetuate the Memory of His Excellency George Washington Esquire General in Chief of the Army of the United Colonies," they called the town Washington. This apparently was the first geographical place named for him. In the spring, on New York's Manhattan Island, Mount

Washington, now known as Washington Heights, received its name. By the end of 1776, revolutionary state legislatures had established the "Washington District" in North Carolina, the Town of Washington in New Hampshire, and Washington counties in Maryland and Virginia.[42]

Americans were celebrating Washington as a way of celebrating themselves. The people of Britain were corrupt, tamed by the standing army of a tyrant king. But that army was no match for citizen-soldiers led by a citizen-general. Among the "Remarkable EVENTS *in the Year 1775,*" the *Pennsylvania Packet* numbered the following occurrence: "An Army of Americans commanded by a VIRGINIA FARMER, blocked up 10,000 British troops, commanded by three of the ablest Generals in the British service." Peter Thacher, the Boston Massacre orator for 1776, contrasted the universal dissipation of Britons with the freedom-loving hardiness of Americans, the cowardice and vice of British army officers with the bravery and humanity of America's generals. "When I name a Washington," proclaimed Thacher, "my audience will feel the justice of the remark, and acquit me of the charge of flattery."[43]

The expulsion of the British from Boston in mid-March 1776 set off yet more celebration of Washington as soldier and patriot. After "the Ministerial butchering, murdering and plundering banditti of Lord North's mercenaries" retreated, ran a newspaper account, the town was "enter'd by the victorious Troops of the Thirteen United Colonies of North America, commanded by that truly magnanimous General WASHINGTON. . . ." The press extolled "the wisdom, firmness, intrepidity and military abilities of our amiable and beloved General. . . ." Newspapers reported ceremonies honoring him, printed the addresses of the Massachusetts revolutionary legislature and the Boston Selectmen, and published the honorary degree conferred on him by Harvard College.[44]

The praise emphasized his fulfillment of "Country Party" standards: his refusal of pay, his respect for civilian authority, his strict governance of the army, his disinterested patriotism. Having watched his conduct closely for nine months now, these observers concluded that George Washington matched their ideals of public-minded leadership.

The victory also prompted poetic praise. Phillis Wheatley's metrical address of the previous fall was now published in Pennsylvania and Virginia. Another New Englander set down some ". . . Remarks on the Present War," proclaiming that Washington had "let proud tyrants know, / How far their bounds should go / And then his bombs did throw / Into their den." Farther south, "A Virginian" called upon his fellow Americans: "[A]wake, awake! / Your liberty your all's at stake. . . . Deaf to your cries, the royal ear / Quite stopt, will no remonstrance hear; / . . . Prepare for war, it is no crime, / It's virtue, and it is high time. / . . . Great Washington prepares the way / Nor can he doubt to win the day."[45]

On the very eve of independence, the discovery of a plot which included plans to assassinate Washington sent shock waves through the continent. The conspirators included the loyalist mayor of New York City and several soldiers in the general's personal guard. They had planned to kill him, his staff officers, and the other generals, blow up the magazines, spike the cannon defending the town, and open the way for the invading British army.[46]

Ironically, in its failure, this plot which had meant to deal the revolt a shattering blow instead strengthened the hand of the revolutionaries. It convinced nationalists of the perfidy of Britain and provoked calls for hard handling of loyalists. It confirmed the conviction that God favored the rebels. And it encouraged revolutionaries to see George Washington as the center and embodiment of their cause. Officers and soldiers of several New England regiments felt a "strong Impulse of Duty & affection," they told Washington, "to engage *to live or die by you,* whom our common enemies have marked out as one of the principal obstacles which retard their progress toward despotism. . . . We assure your excellency of our firm attachment to the rights of our Country and the person of our General. . . ."[47]

The British soon tried a less lethal maneuver that again implicitly recognized Washington's central importance. General Howe sought to open peace negotiations with him, but Washington refused to allow this wedge between himself and the Congress. Once more he made clear his strict submission to civil authority.

The incident had even greater symbolic significance. Howe's first letter was addressed to "George Washington, Esq." The American commander-in-chief rejected it because it failed to acknowledge his official status. A second letter came for "George Washington, Esq., &c. &c. &c." Again the rebel general refused it. At last, no less a person than Howe's Adjutant sought an interview with "His Excellency" General Washington. Lord Howe had intended no affront, assured Colonel James Patterson. He held General Washington's "person and character in the highest esteem. . . ." The "&c. &c. &c. implied everything that ought to follow." He then laid the identical letter on the table in front of Washington, who again declined accepting it. "[I]t was true," rejoined the American, "the &c. &c. &c. implied every thing, and they also implied any thing. . . ."

Patterson declared that Lord Howe and General Howe had come with "great powers" to effect "an accommodation." Washington replied, according to American accounts, that apparently they had only the power "to grant pardons; that those who had committed no fault wanted no pardon, that we were only defending what we deemed our indisputable right." They talked at some length about treatment of prisoners. Again the American seemed to have the Englishman on the defensive, constantly apologizing, justifying, hoping the general would not blame the entire British army or nation for a few misbehaving individuals. "There was a pleasing confusion on him the whole time," reported an American general; "indeed I do not wonder at it, as he was before one of the greatest men of the age. . . ."

This event needed no embroidering by later legend-makers, for this was George Washington in his element. He was no orator who could sway crowds. He was at his best in personal political or diplomatic encounters like this one. His political instincts and experience, his acute awareness of social roles, his studied self-presentation, and (contrary to the later mistaken impression of him as cold and haughty) his charm and wit told him on such occasions precisely what to say and do.

Washington's besting of Patterson of course delighted revolutionaries. Congress "highly approve[d]" of his conduct in upholding the "Dignity" of his station and ordered all American commanders to follow his example. In fact, he had done more. He had forced the enemy tacitly to acknowledge the dignity and sovereignty of the fledgling nation and the legitimacy of the revolutionary cause. And again he had acted as the leading spokesman and symbol of both.[48]

From the time of his appointment, the partisans of revolution had been making Washington the central symbol of the republican cause. Since the beginning of 1776, they had been deliberately substituting him for King George III. In January, fired by martial and patriotic fervor, they started to sing. They sang of their young nation striding vigorously into the world and thrusting aside the corrupt and tottering parent state. They sang a vision of national greatness, power, and wealth. They sang of "War and Washington!"

> Vain Britons, boast no longer with proud indignity,
> By land your conquering legions, your matchless strength at sea,

Since we, your braver sons insensed, our swords have girded on.
Huzza, huzza, huzza, huzza, for war and Washington.

. . . .

Great Heaven! is this the nation whose thundering arms were hurled,
Through Europe, Afric, India? whose navy ruled a world?
The lustre of your former deeds, whole ages of renown,
Lost in a moment, or transferred to us and Washington!

Yet think not thirst of glory unsheaths our vengeful swords
To rend your bands asunder, or cast away your cords,
'T is heaven-born freedom fires us all, and strengthens each brave son,
From him who humbly guides the plough, to god-like Washington.

For this, oh could our wishes your ancient rage inspire,
Your armies should be doubled, in numbers, force, and fire.
Then might the glorious conflict prove which best deserved the boon,
America or Albion, a George or Washington!

Fired with the great idea, our Fathers' shades would rise,
To view the stern contention, the gods desert their skies;
And Wolfe, 'midst hosts of heroes, superior bending down,
Cry out with eager transport, God save great Washington!

. . . .

Proud France should view with terror, and haughty Spain revere,
While every warlike nation would court alliance here;
And George, his minions trembling round, dismounting from his throne
Pay homage to America and glorious Washington![49]

Americans would continue to sing of their leader. The barefoot soldier at Valley Forge, said an army doctor, "labours thro' the Mud & Cold with a Song in his mouth extolling War & Washington. . . ." A British officer held prisoner of war griped of "the noise of the American soldiers" guarding him, "who vociferate their songs so loud that the whole house rings with War and Washington, a favourite ballad." A New Jersey family scandalized Baroness von Riedesel, the wife of a Hessian general, by rewriting the words of a familiar anthem. "God save great Washington!" they chorused, "God damn the King!"[50]

CHAPTER SEVENTEEN

"The hearts of his countrymen"

Despite the Declaration of American Independence from Great Britain, despite the rejection of royalism in favor of republicanism, the "revolution" was incomplete in midsummer 1776. It took eight years of civil war to decide America's relationship to George III and to the British Crown and Empire. In July 1776, probably less than a majority of Americans had undergone the transformation of consciousness. A sizable and influential minority identified themselves defiantly as loyalists. Between the loyalists and the revolutionaries milled the people whom John Shy has called "the great middle group of Americans," probably a majority of the population. "[D]ubious, afraid, uncertain, indecisive," they felt "nothing at stake . . . could justify involving themselves and their families in extreme hazard and suffering." At least in the early years of the war, they were "suggestible, manipulable, potentially loyal subjects of the crown."[1] The opposing sides contended for the hearts and minds of that great middle group, the undecided and uncertain majority.

Both sides resorted to intimidation and physical coercion. In the long run, it is probable, as Shy asserts, that the violent excesses of the British troops, the German mercenaries, and particularly the American Tory militiamen did much to alienate the people in the middle, to push them toward the side of republican independence.[2]

The opposing forces also wielded ideological weapons, instruments of persuasion rather than coercion. Each resorted to the arsenal of ideas to bolster their own supporters, to discredit the enemy, and to win over the uncommitted. The royalists had the advantage of traditional faith in Britain's constitutional monarchy and mixed government and fear of the supposed instability of republicanism. The rebels could rely on widespread adherence in America to "Country Party" ideology. Both sides also appealed to patriotic sentiments, the former to generations-long ties with the mother country, the latter to nascent American nationalism.

The royalist side had one more asset. Ironically, it was King George III himself. Despite all the rhetoric declaiming that monarchs must submit to the laws and that the people had a right to overthrow tyrants, even the most militant colonists had maintained their adherence to their sovereign until the very end. The more moderate, the undecided, broke the bands of allegiance with even greater difficulty. Traditional convictions held on tenaciously. Tory and British propagandists exploited the psychological and moral force of old beliefs, ideas of the wickedness of rebellion, of the necessity of obedience to and reverence for kings, of the sovereign as the center of the nation, of faith in the goodness and character of George III, of reliance on him as the protector and Father of his People.[3]

Perhaps the strongest evidence of the continuing power of monarchical sentiments was the repeated assaults throughout the war on George Rex and kingship by "patriot" propagandists. These polemicists knew the strength of the old attachments, knew they could defeat the cause and reverse the revolution. Yet, even after the battle of Yorktown had settled the military and, more important, the political conflict, writers and poets continued to villify the king. They called him a tyrant, a "monster in human form." They likened him to Charles I and compared him to Cain. This was not only propaganda aimed at stamping out belief in monarchy and smashing faith in George III. It throbbed with the wound of betrayal felt by those who once had trusted in the king. In Boston in 1780, "A Soldier" excoriated the British monarch. "Your name darkens the moral sky and stinks in the nostrils of the world," he raged. "America is not so much interested in your death as Britain; but for the good of mankind, we wish to see you publicly executed, as a just reward for your tyranny and murders, and for an example to all tyrants." Exclaimed a Philadelphia verse-maker in 1778: "[O]ne prayer is left, which dreads no proud reply, / That He who made you breathe, would bid you die."[4]

Throughout the war, polemicists attacking George III sought to replace him with George Washington. The American hero was more than a propaganda weapon to win over the undecided in this psychological and ideological warfare. His image expressed an essential part of the republican nationalist faith of many, probably most, of the members of the revolutionary party. For them, he was the unifying symbol of the cause and the focal point of the new nation. Rebel propaganda explicitly contrasted the two Georges.

Poets celebrating American independence substituted the general for the king. In August 1776, "W.P." of Buckingham County, Virginia, exhorted: "Crush all the tyrant's crew, / Dogs that our lives pursue; / WASHINGTON them subdue / Conquer them all. . . . That George is now no more / King of this fertile shore, / From whence he drew his store, / Completes our joy. . . . GOD save great WASHINGTON, / Virginia's warlike son, / And make him brave."[5]

In February 1777, a few weeks after Washington's victories at Trenton and Princeton, Francis Hopkinson published a new political "Catechism." It denounced King George as a despot and asked, "Who is the best man living?" "His Excellency, General Washington," was the answer. He had left "a peaceful habitation and an affluent fortune" to defend his country. His private life warmed the hearts of all around him. His public conduct commanded "universal respect and admiration." "If there are spots in his character, they are like the spots in the sun, only discernible by the magnifying powers of a telescope. Had he lived in the days of idolatry, he had been worshipped as a god. One age cannot do justice to his merit, but the united voices of a grateful posterity shall pay a cheering tribute of undissembled praise to the great asserter of their country's freedom."[6]

Washington's role as the unifying symbol of the new republic led to quasi-"monarchical" veneration of him. Royalist language and customs became American nationalist and republican symbols. In January 1776, revolutionary propagandists began to denounce George III as an "unnatural father." Simultaneously, a private correspondent, anticipating the appelation that would become most closely associated with Washington's name, addressed the general as "our political Father and head of a Great People." Two years later, the *Lancaster Almanack* first publicly called him "the Father of His Country." American almanacs for 1777 almost uniformly deleted mention of George III's birthday and other royal holidays, although only one listed the anniversary of Independence. Army officers celebrated Washington's birthday at Valley Forge in February 1778. In 1779, civilians began to observe the occasion. Within a few years, the Twenty-second of February had become an important patriotic holiday. In the early nineteenth century, it would be second only to the Fourth of July.[7]

Revolutionary polemicists assigned Washington the leading role in the struggle against the tyrant George. "When urg'd by thirst of arbitrary sway / And over-weaning pride, a ruthless king / Grim spurn'd us ... / And in the tyrant all the father lost; / ... Then with one voice thy country call'd thee forth, / Thee, WASHINGTON she call'd:—With modest blush, / But soul undaunted, thou the call obey'd, / To lead her armies in the martial field." Hortentius (the pseudonymous Governor William Livingston of New Jersey) and other writers agreed: Washington's example had inspired others to resist tyranny. His virtue and valor had drawn Americans to fight by his side.[8]

Writers who exhorted the people to support the army often seemed to equate commitment to the cause with loyalty to Washington. Again and again throughout the war, they declared victory within the grasp of the revolutionary forces if his countrymen would fully arm "our beloved General." They lamented the shameful neglect of the "illustrious man, who had sacrificed every private view to the public service. ..." "Where is the man," asked a Lancaster, Pennsylvania, essayist in 1778, "who lays claim to the enjoyment of freedom that will not exert himself in assisting our great general to complete what he so disinterestedly engaged in. ..." Early in 1781, the orator commemorating the Boston Massacre lauded Washington, bewailed the languor of the country, and called upon the people to rise up and expel the enemy. "Let justice then be done to our country—let justice be done to our great leader; and, the only means under heaven of our salvation, let his army be replenished."[9]

Public praise poured down upon Washington. Orators and preachers and poets lauded his greatness. Celebrants at patriotic banquets and festivities toasted his name. In 1781, Continental Army officers stationed on Long Island commemorated the Fourth of July, drinking thirteen toasts, among them one to General Washington. They observed the occasion under a flag bearing the likeness of the great man.[10]

Not only military officers and public officials and prominent personages applauded Washington. As a token of their esteem, a family in Delaware sent him a few yards of dimity cloth they had made. Everywhere he went crowds thronged to see and cheer him. The inhabitants of Newport, Rhode Island, illuminated their town in his honor, the town's Council providing candles for the poorer citizens to share in the celebration. Philadelphians likewise lit up their city to mark his arrival.

He "walked through some of the principal streets," reported the *Pennsylvania Packet*, "attended by a numerous concourse of people, eagerly pressing to see their beloved general." Inhabitants of Caroline County, Virginia, daily watched for him to pass by on his way to meet Cornwallis at Yorktown. In Albany and Schenectady, New York, he was greeted with loud roars of cannon fire and joyful pealing of church bells and great crowds of people.[11]

"Through all the land he appears like a benevolent god;" said a French army chaplain, "old men, women, children, they all flock eagerly to catch a glimpse of him when he travels and congratulate themselves because they have seen him. People carrying torches follow him through the cities; his arrival is marked by public illuminations; the Americans, though a cold people . . . have waxed enthusiastic about him and their first songs inspired by spontaneous sentiments have been consecrated to the glorification of Washington."[12]

George Washington represented more than the displacement of George III, for the American revolutionaries had overthrown more than that one king. They had done away with kingship altogether. They had rejected hereditary rule, whether by one man or many. Instead, they created republican governments based on the ideal that the governors would be chosen because of their individual talents and virtue and would remain subject to the laws. This was the utopian idea they fought for, believing themselves the vanguard of a worldwide republican revolutionary movement. Americans fought, they asserted, not simply for their own liberty, but for the liberty of all mankind.

Washington, who is usually thought of as pragmatic, nonideological, even conservative, shared these convictions. The terms *pragmatic* and *conservative* are relative. He may have been less sanguine than, say, a Thomas Jefferson, but he operated within the same republican ideological consensus. He may later have worried about the viability of republican government in America, but even his pessimism about human nature and his sense of the fragility of free government were part of the Whig-republican outlook. When all is said and done, one irreducible fact remains: George Washington was ready to fight for eight long years to root out royal rule in America and replace it with a republican experiment. All of his efforts during the war to subordinate military to civilian authority, to discipline his troops, to enforce and model public virtue, to incarnate the character of the citizen-soldier, must be understood as deriving from that fact. To Washington, as to his fellow revolutionaries, their struggle was charged with worldwide significance. In

February 1776, the patriot general called upon his men to prepare their minds for battle. "It is a noble Cause we are engaged in," he said. "[I]t is the Cause of virtue, and mankind. . . . Freedom, or Slavery must be the result of our conduct. . . ." [13]

Republican government depended upon the virtue of the people. The revolutionaries celebrated Washington's virtue as an embodiment of the nation's virtue and as a model that would help perpetuate it. Francis Hopkinson proposed a "Toast" to the American patriot.

> 'Tis Washington's health—fill a bumper all round,
> For he is our Glory and Pride;
> Our Arms shall in battle with Conquest be crown'd,
> Whilst Virtue and He's on our Side.
>
> 'Tis Washington's health—loud cannon should roar,
> And Trumpets the Truth should proclaim,
> There cannot be found, search all the World o'r,
> His equal in Virtue and Fame.
>
> 'Tis Washington's Health—our Hero to bless
> May Heaven look graciously down,
> O long may He live, our Hearts to possess,
> And FREEDOM still call Him her own. [14]

Other poets and writers likewise proclaimed that he vindicated the superiority of New World republicanism over the corrupt and dying systems of the Old World. "Let venal poets praise a King / For virtues unpossess'd, / A volunteer, unbrib'd I sing / The Hero of the West." Thus wrote a poet-officer of the Continental Army in 1779. Two years later, on the eve of the victory at Yorktown, Philip Freneau imagined Washington's eventual arrival in the heavenly pantheon of heroes. There he would "shine" "with patriot kings and generous chiefs . . . / Whose virtues raised them to be deemed divine. . . ." [15]

Thomas Paine also relied on Washington's image when in *The Rights of Man* he contrasted republicanism with hereditary monarchy. Hereditary institutions produced irrationality, waste, and weak rulers. In republican states, leaders neither exploited the people, nor aggrandized themselves, but were committed to the public business and the public welfare. "I presume," declared Paine, "that no man in his sober senses, will compare the character of any of the kings of Europe with that of General Washington." [16] The standard implicit in Paine's argument was the character of a Patriot King. He, like Freneau and Hopkinson and the anonymous army poet, in effect asserted that George Washington validated republicanism by proving it could produce a leader who matched up to the highest monarchical ideal, an ideal monarchs rarely achieved in fact.

To be sure, Washington had his critics. They questioned his military leadership. More important, they feared the idolatry of him as the indispensable man. There is no room here to examine that criticism in detail, or to recount the so-called Conway Cabal, the clash with and court-martial of Charles Lee, or Washington's public image during the course of the Revolutionary War. Several observations must suffice. Washington had amazingly few critics, and very little of the criticism was made public. More amazing still was the response of Washington's supporters. They treated criticism as a plot against him and, worse, as a kind of betrayal of the Revolution itself. This suggests again the depth of attachment to him. The criticism reached a peak in the winter of 1777–8. By the end of 1778, most of his chief critics and rivals were off the scene, their careers ruined or temporarily eclipsed. To the end of the war, Washington was virtually immune from public criticism. Observers who feared excessive adulation of him had to raise the issue obliquely.

Those who looked to Washington for primary leadership, those who venerated him as the indispensable man were implicitly applying to him the precepts of inherited political ideology. According to Machiavelli, states were rarely founded or reformed except by a great man acting alone. The instability of public "manners" and institutions in such historical moments threatened to subject a commonwealth to the vicissitudes of fortune. A masterful leader exercising extraordinary powers must in the one case establish and in the other reconstitute the principles that would make the polity viable. Bolingbroke borrowed the idea of the great ruler, fleshed it out, gave it a name, and prescribed it as the remedy for Britain's "corruption." Americans had readily adopted this concept, then had awaited a monarch who would incarnate the ideal and rescue them from imminent slavery. When George III failed them, they turned to George Washington, perceiving his conduct through a republican version of the idea of a Patriot King.

Washington strove to embody the "Country Party" ideal of true patriotism, but his fellow Americans found in his conduct something of much greater significance. The public-minded man of the Radical Whigs closely resembled in character Bolingbroke's Patriot King. In one sense, the Patriot King was simply the true patriot writ large. To be sure, the great power entrusted to him, the majesty of his office, and the influence of his moral example made an enormous qualitative difference, but in his principles and personal conduct the Patriot King followed the lineaments of the public-minded man.[17] Washington set out to fulfill the terms of the latter ideal; inadvertently he satisfied the former as well. Because of his central role in the Revolution, the extensive powers granted him by Congress, his symbolic significance, and the needs of the moment, Americans began implicitly to apply Bolingbroke's idea to him. They started to think of him as a kind of republicanized Patriot King. It was as though Bolingbroke's "Standing Miracle" had taken place, not in the character of George III, but in the person of their Patriot General.[18]

The Revolutionary Era in America seemed to offer a case study confirming Machiavellian historical theory. The instabilities of an unformed state threatened. Simultaneously, the infection of "corruption" appeared and began to spread. First it came from Britain and then, as revolutionary virtue seemed to give way to private greed and ambition, it came from within. As the mythmakers began to tell it, George Washington stepped forth and almost singlehandedly established national independence and national union. In effect, he both founded and reformed his country. He put down faction and ambition. He united his people around him. He instructed them by policy and example in the art of making their republic secure.

Bolingbroke had written that "[t]he true image of a free people, governed by a Patriot King, is that of a patriarchal family, where the head and all the members are united by one common interest, and animated by one common spirit. . . . [H]e will . . . be himself the centre of their union. . . ."[19] Americans broke their connections with the British Empire to protect themselves from "corruption." They jettisoned the institution of kingship to safeguard their liberties. They established a republic whose viability would depend, they told themselves, on their own virtue. At the center of this commonwealth, modeling civic virtue to them and occupying the place of Bolingbroke's Patriot King, presided George Washington.

The famous humorous tale of Rip Van Winkle, written by a namesake of the great patriot, viewed the effects of the revolutionary transformation as seen by a New York Dutchman who had slept through it. In his home town, he discovered that the old inn was now the Union Hotel. On the sign out front, "he recognized . . . the ruby face of King George, under which he had smoked so many a peaceful pipe; but even this was singularly metamorphosed. The red coat was changed for one of blue and buff, a sword was held in the hand instead of a sceptre, the head was decorated with a cocked hat, and underneath was painted in large characters, GENERAL WASHINGTON."[20]

In Alexandria, Virginia, the owner of a tavern called the "Royal George" actually "obliterated" the image of the king hanging over its door in favor of a likeness of the retired soldier from nearby Mount Vernon. Princeton College asked Charles Willson Peale to execute the general's portrait. It would replace the "picture of the late king of Great Britain, which was torn away by a ball from the American artillery in the battle of Princeton." An English traveler reported seeing pictures of the American patriot "on every sign-post and over every fireplace." In New York City, when the revolutionary rioters tore down the gilded equestrian statue of the tyrant George, they saved the base on which it had stood. On that pedestal, there was erected in 1792 a statue of George Washington.[21] And when the great leader died, the most famous words ever spoken of him echoed the language and thought of Bolingbroke. Henry Lee eulogized George Washington as "first in war, first in peace, and first in the hearts of his countrymen."

A revolution had taken place in American consciousness, a revolution both nationalist and republican, a transformation that severed political ties with Britain and overthrew the institution of monarchy. Despite this radical break with the past, many lines of continuity spanned the historical disjuncture. Monarchical and "Country Party" ideas in reconstituted form continued to exercise their influence. Prominent among these was the implicit perception of George Washington as the fulfillment of the Patriot King ideal. His presence filled the king-shaped vacuum that followed the overthrow of George III. His conduct supplied a needed propaganda weapon to the revolutionary cause. His career and image bridged the gap between monarchy and republicanism, colonial subordination and nationhood. The myth of Washington completed the national myth of America as a republic of pure virtue.

Throughout his life, Washington marshalled his prodigious energies in a continuous quest for honor, for validation by his society of his personal and public character. "To obtain the applause of deserving men is a heartfelt satisfaction," he said, "to merit it is my highest wish. . . . If my conduct . . . hath merited the approbation of this great country, I shall esteem it one of the most fortunate and happy events of my life." Deliberately, he had labored to embody the Catonic image. His incarnation of that ideal and his perceived fulfillment of the ideal of the Patriot King generated the celebration of his character and deeds. He recognized the importance of those beliefs to his contemporaries.

He understood what was expected of him. Sharing those values, he strove to match them and thus to win the applause of his countrymen and of succeeding generations. Back of George Washington's extraordinary exertions stirred a desire for distinction, a yearning for public esteem that ultimately became a quest for historical immortality. Behind his astounding performance prodded that mixture of egotism and patriotism, selfishness and public-mindedness that historians have come to call the spur of fame.[22]

"The foundations of useful knowledge"

Historians have long assumed that Washington read only for practical purposes related to business, farming, and soldiering. Worthington Chauncey Ford summed up that view: "Washington was no reader, and his only enthusiasm lay in books on agriculture, which he studied and laboriously extracted with a minuteness that was extraordinary. As a young officer in the colonial militia he gave some attention to military books. . . . There is little evidence that he cared for history, even of the War of Independence. . . . [H]e read for a purely commercial purpose; to fit himself for service in the camp, and to conduct his farming on a profitable basis."[1]

Apparently Douglas Southall Freeman agreed. He occasionally noted Washington's acquisition of books but never seriously evaluated the influence of reading and ideas on him. Samuel Eliot Morison and James Thomas Flexner gave slightly greater emphasis to reading, finding significant formative influences in his acquaintance with two widely read works, Roger L'Estrange's popularization of Stoicism, *Seneca's Morals*, and Joseph Addison's play *The Tragedy of Cato*. Still, both historians agreed he was, in Flexner's words, "only a sporadic reader."[2]

Some of Washington's contemporaries agreed with the later assessment that he had little interest in intellectual pursuits. John Adams acidly asserted: "That Washington was not a scholar is certain. That he was too illiterate, unlearned, unread for his station and reputation is equally past dispute." Thomas Jefferson more temperately declared that his fellow Virginian spent his time "in action chiefly, reading little, and that only in agriculture and English history."[3]

Though he accumulated a library of some nine hundred volumes on a wide range of subjects, his letters and papers only rarely contain references to his reading. For that reason and because he was a man of action rather than a man of thought, a man of affairs and not a bookish man, his contemporaries and later students of his life have supposed he read little besides the practical books in his library.

Washington had only limited formal schooling. In later life, he felt somewhat self-conscious about what he considered his "defective education." Spurred by this sense of deficiency, he developed a lifelong habit of reading, reading of the sort he and his culture thought essential to the preparation of virtuous and effective public leadership. Despite this effort, he remained unsure of his learning. Ever guarded in his presentation of himself, he made it a policy to assert his opinions only when he felt himself master of a subject, even then expressing his thoughts with characteristic diffidence.[4]

Unsurprisingly, then, his contemporaries, particularly those sparkling intellects in whose presence he would have felt the greatest inclination to listen rather than talk, as well as historians since that time failed to recognize the importance of reading and ideas in the great man's life. Not that he was a scholar. Nearly always his reading did have a practical intent. But a thorough examination of his papers and library discloses that he gave more thought to reading, learning, and ideas than historians have credited. More important, it makes clear the place of reading in his life.

Washington gave much more thought to education than has been recognized. Chapter 1 examined his own schooling and subsequent tutelage by Lawrence Washington and William Fairfax. His later plans for his stepson Jack Custis reflected the same philosophy of learning. His ward would one day come into a large fortune entailing both social position and public duty. ". . . I think the more conspicuous the point of view a man is to appear in," he told the boy's teacher, "the more pains should be taken to enlarge his mind and qualify him for a useful Member of Society. . . ." Critical of the upbringing accorded many young men of Virginia's upper class, he intended "to make [Jack] fit for more useful purposes, than a horse Racer."[5]

His biographers have asserted that he drew most of his "education" from practical experience, but he himself believed extensive reading should form the foundation of other kinds of learning. For this reason, he opposed Jack's taking the Grand Tour until he had improved more in his academic acquirements. He did not believe that "becoming a mere scholar is a desirable education for a gentleman; but I conceive a knowledge of books is the basis upon which other knowledge is to be built; and that it is men and things more than books he is to be acquainted with by travelling."[6]

The stepfather brought to Mount Vernon a tutor, who supervised the education of Jack and his sister, Patsy, for over six years. Later he boarded the boy at Rev. Jonathan Boucher's school in Maryland. Finally, he sent him to New York, hoping the indolent youth would complete a college education there.[7]

Though he left the direction of Jack's schooling to these instructors, he let them know what he thought essential in the education of a gentleman. "[A]ny man possessed of a large landed estate" must have an acquaintance with arithmetic and mathematics. He believed ". . . Philosophy, Moral, Natural, &c . . . very desireable knowledge for a Gentleman. . . ." He also put strong emphasis on "Classical knowledge," familiarity with the noted authors of antiquity. At least for a time, he thought the study of Greek and Latin useful to enhance such reading. French, having "become a part of polite Education," he considered absolutely necessary "to a Man who has any prospect of mixing in a large Circle. . . ." Most likely Jack's preceptors concurred with this program. They probably also advised Washington on the books he ordered for the children's education, lists including Greek and Latin dictionaries and grammars, volumes in religion and philosophy, and important works of ancient and modern literature and history.[8]

After Jack Custis's death in 1781, two of his young children, Nelly and George Washington Parke Custis, came to live at Mount Vernon. The step-grandfather endeavored "to fit the boy . . . for a University. . . ." Once more he brought a tutor to the plantation, and once more he contended with a lad averse to academic labors. Subsequently he struggled to keep his charge studying at the College of Philadelphia, the College of New Jersey, and other schools.[9]

The program of study Washington intended for the younger Custis again combined practical knowledge and classical learning. The tutor he hired "must be a classical scholar . . . the more universal his knowledge is, the better." The basics should cover arithmetic and mathematics and should particularly emphasize surveying and bookkeeping, penmanship and composition. As to foreign languages, he dropped Greek, still included Latin, and stressed more strongly than ever the importance of French. He thought the youth should keep commonplace notes to improve both his handwriting and his reading. Undoubtedly he expected him to study history and politics, because he proposed that a national university make the science of government an important part of its curriculum.

It particularly pleased him when young Custis announced his intention "to commence a course of reading with Doctor Smith," president of the College of New Jersey, "of such books as he had chosen for the purpose." But Washington warned that "light reading," by which he meant "books of little importance[,] . . . may amuse for the moment, but leave nothing solid behind." As "a man of learning and taste himself," Doctor Smith would "select such authors and subjects, as will lay the foundations of useful knowledge. . . ."[10]

After the Revolution, the American leader also gave thought to the sort of instruction appropriate to youth in a republican society. To G. W. P. Custis he stressed the public, as well as the personal, value of education. With that in mind, he helped finance the education of some of his nephews and the sons of several friends and lent personal and material support to schools in Virginia. As president, he repeatedly advocated and worked toward the creation of a national university, although the idea met heavy resistance in Congress. He made bequests in his will to encourage these and other educational projects. He took an interest in American publications on education and informed himself about academies and colleges in other parts of the Union. He also applauded the attention given to public education by the new nation's legislatures. ". . . I persuade myself," he told an English educational theorist, that they "will leave nothing unessayed to cultivate literature and useful knowledge, for the purpose of qualifying the rising generation for patrons of good government, virtue and happiness."[11]

Washington envisioned two kinds of education, one for the lower classes, the other for the propertied. He endowed a school in Alexandria to instruct the children of the poor in "reading, writing and arithmetic, so as to fit them for mechanical purposes." The national university, and presumably other American institutions of higher learning, would prepare the sons of the upper class to govern the Republic. He expected these future leaders to be "young Gentlemen of good families, liberal education, and high sense of honour. . . ."[12]

The soldier-statesman had striven to win a place in Virginia's ruling class. Thereafter, he worked to keep himself qualified for leadership. Throughout his life, he tried to remedy the deficiencies in his schooling. For instance, following the Revolution he tried to learn French, probably because he intended to travel to France. In June 1783, he ordered a French-English dictionary from New York and the following February sent to Philadelphia for another and for a French grammar. Although he progressed in this study, he did not master the tongue as he wished. More important, he sought to enhance his knowledge through reading. In 1771, he ordered a bookplate bearing his family coat-of-arms and requested that four to five hundred be struck. Since his library numbered many fewer volumes at that date, he made evident his intention to continue purchasing books.[13]

Scholars who have discounted the importance of books to Washington have focused primarily on the inventory made at the time of his death and on the *Catalogue* of that part of the library acquired by the Boston Athenaeum. Several hitherto neglected documents shed important light on how his library grew. In about 1759, the newly married planter began to divide with his stepson, Jack Custis, the library of the boy's father, Daniel Parke Custis, Martha's first husband. Washington probably had the entire library brought to Mount Vernon. He designated some books for the six-year-old lad and some for himself but never completed this allotment. During the next decade and a half, he ordered from England several lists of books for Jack's education, including many important works of history and politics, philosophy and literature. After Jack's death in 1781, he bought part of the young man's library.[14]

His correspondence and ledgers show that throughout his life Washington also bought books, pamphlets, periodicals, and other publications. He ordered many through his commercial agents and bought books and pamphlets in Williamsburg during the Assembly sessions, in Philadelphia during the Constitutional Convention, and in New York and Philadelphia during his presidency. At the close of the Revolution, he indicated one of his intentions for his approaching retirement by having the manager of Mount Vernon compile "A List of Books . . ." at the estate. This inventory includes books he had bought before the war, some from the division of the Custis library, and others from that collection which he had not marked when he divided it with Jack. Meanwhile, he requested the catalogues of New York City booksellers and purchased more than twenty titles. Some items disappeared from his library before his death. For instance, more than a dozen titles on the 1783 list do not appear on the final inventory of 1799, and the index of 1783 itself was incomplete even at that date.[15]

Some writers who have downplayed Washington's interest in reading have pointed out that many of the volumes in his collection came as gifts from the authors, often obscure writers hoping to win wider circulation by obtaining the great man's endorsement or by dedicating their works to him. Hence the presence on his shelves of treatises on everything from education to opium, arithmetic to the history of coat armor. Significantly, most of the volumes by little-known authors came as gifts in the 1780s and 1790s, while the works of celebrated writers, especially those originally published before the Revolution, were usually chosen by Washington himself.[16]

Historians also have at times inferred apathy about books from his failure to mention his reading in his diary. This misunderstands his purpose in making that record. He kept it as a logbook of weather and farm work, travel and social contacts, rather than as a journal of ideas.[17]

In fact, the self-educated American took pride in the library he accumulated. If his demanding life of personal and public business left fewer opportunities for reading than he wished, he still made more time for that pursuit than scholars have realized. One biographer has cited a letter written two months after he retired from the presidency as evidence of the secondary importance of reading to the practical-minded man of affairs. After describing his daily round of activities, Washington observed: "[I]t may strike you, that in this detail no mention is made of any portion of time allotted for reading; the remark would be just, for I have not looked into a book since I came home, nor shall I be able to do it until I have discharged my Workmen; probably not before the nights grow longer. . . ." Rather than indicating inattention to reading, this letter shows that in his second retirement, as in his first during the 1780s, he planned to devote some of his energies to his library. In a few months, as subsequent letters reveal, he was finding the time, particularly to delve into history and politics.[18]

Washington ultimately accumulated a library of over nine hundred volumes on a wide variety of subjects. The ways in which he acquired many of these books remain unknown, but in enough cases we can ascertain that he selected, purchased, or read specific works to gain a clear idea of his literary interests.

In adulthood, he seldom bought books or pamphlets on religious subjects and apparently made those few purchases for other members of the family. He rarely alluded to or quoted the Scriptures. Those occasional references evidence no deep study. The list of books at Mount Vernon compiled in 1783 includes no Bible. The 1799 inventory of his estate mentions three, but one is in Latin and possibly had belonged to Jack Custis, and the others probably came as gifts in the early 1790s. Other religious works popular in Southern colonial libraries are notable by their absence. The overwhelming majority of the religious titles were presentation copies from their authors.[19]

He did read many of the printed sermons sent him but certainly for other than religious reasons. Originally delivered on national fast and thanksgiving days and on the Fourth of July, these discourses both shaped and expressed public opinion on political subjects and often mentioned Washington himself. Even when they lacked overt political content, religious sermons and moralistic essays had public import. The retired sage of Mount Vernon hoped the sentiments and doctrine propounded in a pamphlet entitled "The Philanthropist" would become more prevalent. For sending it he thanked the author, a young Episcopalian parson named Weems.[20]

If Washington showed little appetite for religion, he evidently took a minor interest in philosophy. As a youth he acquired L'Estrange's *Seneca's Morals*. For Jack Custis he purchased, among other philosophical volumes, a set of "All Ciceros Works" and apparently himself read at least some of the compositions of that great Roman. In May 1783, he ordered a copy of Voltaire's *Letters to Several of His Friends*. A few weeks later, he also obtained John Locke's *An Essay Concerning Human Understanding*.[21]

Circumstantial evidence suggests that the statesman read the last-named work. Following the tense struggle over ratification of the Constitution, he avowed a tolerant attitude toward those who had stood on the opposite side of the question. "Men's minds are as varient as their faces, and, where the motives to their actions are pure, the operation of the former is no more to be imputed to them as a crime, than the appearance of the latter; for both, being the work of nature, are equally unavoidable." Drafting his first address to Congress, the newly elected president considered how he might harmonize discordant federalist and antifederalist voices. One fragment of the ravaged manuscript of that undelivered speech begins: "set up my judgement as the standard of perfection? And shall I arrogantly pronounce that whosoever differs from me, must discern the subject through a distorting medium, or be influenced by some nefarious design? The mind is so formed in different persons as to contemplate the same object in different points of view. Hence originates the difference on questions of the greatest import, both human and divine."[22]

If Washington indeed slogged his way through Locke's tome, he did so for a motive other than interest in speculative philosophy. He sought in that treatise what he looked for in all his reading: useful knowledge, greater understanding of the workings of the human mind to enhance his performance as a practical politician and public man.

Approximately 40 percent of the soldier-statesman-planter-entrepreneur's collection consisted of practical books, mostly in law and agriculture. His reference works included a *Dictionary of the Arts and Sciences* in four volumes and the American edition of an *Encyclopaedia* in eighteen volumes, as well as two dictionaries, one of them that of the celebrated Dr. Johnson. He had more than one hundred volumes of legislation and law, among them the journals of the Continental Congress, the debates of the new Federal Senate and House, the laws of the United States, the legislative proceedings and statutes of Virginia as both colony and state, in particular John Mercer's famous *Abridgement*, and laws and judicial proceedings from other colonies and states. In addition, he had several legal handbooks, including, as noted earlier, Richard Burn's *Justice of the Peace and Parish Officer*, designed to guide local public officials in the execution of their duties.[23]

One can perhaps more easily assess the place of agricultural publications in Washington's reading than those on any other subject. Partly this is because he could exchange information and ideas on agriculture with greater freedom than he dared permit himself on most other topics. He talked with visitors about farming and natural history as a means of avoiding politics. He also made his use of reading on agriculture more obvious by his systematic methods of farming. Soon after his retirement from the Virginia Regiment, he began to order handbooks on husbandry and other aspects of farming. After the Revolution, he continued to purchase and welcomed as gifts numerous such volumes and pamphlets. He copied long extracts from the latest works on scientific agriculture, including Arthur Young's *Annals of Agriculture*. He also urged his plantation managers to read these publications attentively.[24]

Farmer Washington's close attention to such works derived from more than the practical needs of a profit-seeking planter and the personal pleasure of one who described farming as his "favourite amusement." It had public, as well as private, use. He carried on an extensive correspondence with the leading agricultural theorists and experimenters in Britain and America. Acting as a sort of intellectual middleman, he received the published accounts of their labors, distributed copies on both sides of the Atlantic, and promoted republication of British writings in the United States. He also contributed his own small share to agricultural experimentation and exchanged information with other farmers. More important, he encouraged them to conduct and report such tests and put his influential support behind the establishment of state societies for the promotion and improvement of agriculture. He believed these endeavors and institutions would promote the economic development and prosperity of the new nation. They would also enable America to contribute its share to the material progress of the human race. In this, he reflected the outlook of the Enlightenment: agriculture and the other physical and social sciences would advance human welfare by experimentally establishing and then disseminating useful knowledge.[25]

Washington's correspondence also evidences an interest in literature. As already noted, at an early age he had obtained copies of Henry Fielding's *Tom Jones* and Tobias Smollett's *Peregrine Pickle*. Later he acquired and read *Don Quixote*, Samuel Butler's popular *Hudibras* (the London edition of 1775 with illustrations by Thomas Hogarth), and excerpts from *Tristram Shandy* in a compendium of selections called *The Beauties of Sterne*. He had a set of the works of Alexander Pope, at least some of which he apparently read. He definitely read the *Fables of Aesop* and Le Sage's popular picaresque novel *Adventures of Gil Blas*. He also owned the works of Jonathan Swift, the poems of John Milton, and a translation of François Fénelon's extremely popular didactic novel *The Adventures of Telemachus*. In all of this, his tastes matched those of his fellow colonials, especially southerners.[26]

As Richard Beale Davis and other scholars have noted, Washington was a "theater-goer par excellence." On a typical visit to Williamsburg in June 1770, he attended performances of the American Company of Comedians five out of seven nights. When the roving troupes came closer to Mount Vernon, he traveled to see them at Alexandria, Dumfries, Fredericksburg, and Annapolis. Throughout the 1760s and 1770s, he attended the theater avidly. Wartime legal restrictions interrupted this activity, with at least one exception. In later years and especially while he resided in New York and Philadelphia, he occupied a prominent place in many audiences.[27]

He saw such plays as John Gay's *The Beggar's Opera, Douglas*, a popular Scottish tragedy with a medieval setting, and George Farquhar's *The Recruiting Officer*, a satire of the British army popular on both sides of the Atlantic throughout the eighteenth century. He probably also attended performances of Shakespeare, since the Virginia Company included his plays in their repertoire. He saw professional productions of *Hamlet* in New York in 1773, *The Tempest* in Philadelphia in 1787, and an amateur presentation of *Julius Caesar* at the presidential residence in New York, probably in the winter of 1790.[28]

He also read plays. In 1790, he subscribed to Royall Tyler's satire *The Contrast*. His library included several volumes of plays, among them the works of Shakespeare. In a number of letters he paraphrased lines from *The Tempest*, *Julius Caesar*, and *Othello*. As mentioned earlier, he shared the general enthusiasm for Joseph Addison's *The Tragedy of Cato* and became thoroughly familiar with it.[29]

Following the Revolution, the American nationalist supported and promoted the works of the young republic's writers. Tyler's *The Contrast*, to which he subscribed, was one of the first significant efforts by an American playwright. He also acquired Jeremy Belknap's *The Foresters*, a satirical history of Anglo-American relations. He showed particular interest in the postwar writings of American poets. He read David Humphreys's "A Poem on the Happiness of America . . ." "with pleasure," telling the author, ". . . it is much admired by all those to whom I have showed it." He praised Timothy Dwight's *The Conquest of Canaan* and commended or patronized poetical productions by Mercy Otis Warren, John Parke, and Robert Treat Paine. He also paid close attention to the reception by English critics of Joel Barlow's epic poem *The Vision of Columbus*, boasting of that young writer as "a genius of the first magnitude. . . ."[30]

Washington's patronage of the arts was regarded at the time as an influential incitement to American cultural development and an appropriate continuation of his wartime guardianship of the new nation.[31] Undoubtedly another major reason for his avid interest in the young nationalist poets was that many of them celebrated his own heroic deeds.

In the spring of 1788, Washington recommended Barlow to Lafayette. This letter suggests that he had read far more widely than has usually been thought. It also offers particular insights into his patronage of American poets, his thoughts about the function of literature, and his own quest for fame. He numbered Barlow among "those Bards who hold the keys of the gate by which Patriots, Sages and Heroes are admitted to immortality. Such are your Antient Bards who are both the priest[s] and door-keepers to the temple of fame. And these . . . are no vulgar functions. Men of real talents in Arms have commonly approved themselves patrons of the liberal arts and friends to the poets of their own as well as former times. In some instances by acting reciprocally, heroes have made poets, and poets heroes."

He reminded Lafayette that the poems of Homer reportedly had enraptured Alexander the Great, who "lamented that he had not a rival muse to celebrate his actions. Julius Caesar is well known to have been a man of a highly cultivated understanding and taste." Augustus magnificently rewarded "poetical merit, nor did he lose the return of having his atcheivments immortalized in song. The Augustan age is proverbial for intellectual refinement and elegance in composition; in it the harvest of laurels and bays was wonderfully mingled together." Just so, the reigns of Louis XIV in France and Queen Anne in Britain would forever stand in memory for producing "a multitude of great Poets and great Captains. . . ." Although America was yet in her infancy, he hoped the productions of her poets and painters might take rank with those of the rest of the world.

After considering the state of the arts in his young country, Washington suddenly seemed to realize that he had let slip his public mask, revealing intellectual and emotional features few ever had a chance to see. "I hardly know how it is that I am drawn thus far in observations on a subject so foreign from those in which we are mostly engaged, farming and politics," he said, "unless because I had little news to tell you." Washington the nationalist sought glory for his country and its achievements. Washington the hero sought historical immortality for himself and intended that America's Barlows should conduct him into the temple of fame.[32]

Besides literature, the Virginian land-hunter and soldier early developed a lifelong interest in maps and books of geography and travel. Eventually he visited each of the United States along the Atlantic seaboard and made half a dozen journeys into the Ohio country. Only once did he voyage beyond the continent, on a brief trip to Barbados in 1752 at the age of eighteen. Following both his provincial and revolutionary military stints, he expressed his "longing desire" to cross the Atlantic and visit Britain and Europe. Unfortunately, public or private responsibilities always forced him to "set Inclination aside."[33] Throughout his life, he had to satisfy his curiosity about foreign lands by sailing in books as his barques, their sails filled with the winds of imagination.

Collecting geographical volumes and travelers' accounts was more than the hobby of an armchair voyager, though. Such books were packed with information about politics and government, history and customs, agriculture and commerce. They supplied knowledge invaluable to the statesman, and Washington made them a significant component of his library. Daniel Defoe's account of his tour through Great Britain, acquired during the Virginian's youth, was only the first of over five dozen such volumes, most selected by himself. They included geographical surveys, voyages round the world, and reports of travels through Britain, Ireland, France, Italy, Switzerland, Germany, Louisiana, and the Near East by popular literary travelers such as Arthur Young and Count Volney.[34]

The American nationalist was also familiar with works about his own country. In June 1788, he offered comments on some half-dozen publications which described the New World and the new nation. He highly recommended " 'Information for those who would wish to remove to America . . . ,' written by the great Philosopher Dr. Franklin. Short as it is, it contains almost every thing, that needs to be known on the subject of migrating to this Country." He noted that this "excellent little Treatise" had first appeared in Europe in 1784 and that Carey's *American Museum* had recently reprinted it. He thought foreign descriptions of America "commonly very defective." The Abbé Raynal, who asserted that all things degenerated in the New World, he dismissed as "quite erroneous." He considered William Guthrie's *A New System of Modern Geography* "somewhat better informed," but "not absolutely correct."

Turning back to American writers, he predicted that "from the pains the Author has taken in travelling through the States and acquiring information from the principal characters in each," the "American Geography," in preparation by the Reverend Mr. Jedidiah Morse of New Haven, "will probably be much more exact and useful." Among "books at present existing," he thought Jefferson's *Notes on the State of Virginia* would "give the best idea of this part of the Continent to a Foreigner." Finally, he believed "the 'American Farmer's Letters,' written by Mr. Crevecoeur (commonly called Mr. St. John) the French Consul in New York (who actually resided twenty years as a farmer in that State) will afford a great deal of profitable and amusing information respecting the *private Life* of the Americans; as well as the progress of agriculture, manufactures, and arts in their Country," but "[p]erhaps the picture he gives, though founded on fact, is in some instances embellished with too flattering circumstances."[35]

When the Father of his Country criticized the Abbé Raynal's theories about America as "quite erroneous," he was commenting on one of the eighteenth century's liveliest intellectual disputes. Raynal had followed the French naturalist George Louis Leclerc, Comte de Buffon, in asserting the inferiority of the New World's productions to those of the Old. In his widely read *Histoire naturelle*, Buffon described the feebleness of native American animals and aborigines and the decline of animals imported into the continent. Raynal extended this argument to include Euro-American culture, disparaging the young societies' literary and intellectual achievements. Oliver Goldsmith propagated the theories of Buffon to a British and American reading public in *An History of the Earth and Animated Nature*. Washington ordered Goldsmith's work from a New York bookseller in June 1783. In the 1790s, he also acquired the abridged English translation of Buffon's natural history.[36]

He read the counterarguments of a fellow American in Jefferson's *Notes on the State of Virginia*, probably deriving from it ammunition to refute these Gallic and British slurs on his native land. In the letter to Lafayette mentioned earlier, he referred to this debate: "Although we are yet in our cradle, as a nation, I think the efforts of the human mind with us are sufficient to refute (by incontestable facts) the doctrines of those who have asserted that every thing degenerates in America. Perhaps we shall be found, at this moment, not inferior to the rest of the world in the performances of our poets and painters; notwithstanding many of the incitements are wanting which operate powerfully among older nations. For it is generally understood, that excellence in those sister Arts have been the results of easy circumstances, public encouragements and an advanced stage of society."[37]

Washington took an interest not only in Anglo-American high culture, but also in North American natural history. He regretted "that we have not in America some general Museum or Cabinet for receiving all the rare Phenomena and unusual productions of nature, which might be collected in this Country: especially as natural History affords, perhaps, a more ample field for investigation here, than in any other part of the world." He also assisted a project to obtain a vocabulary of the languages of American Indians for inclusion in a universal dictionary, believing this would aid research into the origins and interrelationships of languages and peoples. Although no scholar himself, the Virginian read books on lands and cultures vastly different from his own.[38]

In addition, he expressed his geographical inquisitiveness by collecting a wide variety of maps. As a land speculator, he made good use of maps of the British American provinces. As a soldier, he referred to military maps of all parts of the continent, charts of its harbors, and plans of its cities. As a states-man, he gathered maps of the United States as a whole, of the individual mem-ber states, and of many foreign countries. His curiosity defied even terrestrial limits, for in 1790 he bought George Adams's *Essays on the Globes*, recording it in his account book as "Adams on Astronomy." [39] At least two-thirds of the volumes of geography, travel, and natural history in his library came into it at his initiative. His acquisition of these, the number and variety of his maps, charts, and atlases, and his comments on the study of natural history, all evi-dence his eager interest in these fields.

As discussed earlier, Washington kept track of the pamphlet debates during the two decades leading up to the break with Britain. When resistance became revolution, he praised Thomas Paine's *Common Sense*. In the late 1780s and into the 1790s, he followed the argument between British and American writers about the advantages of commerce between the two nations and the commercial policies regulating that trade. [40]

The ardent Federalist followed the debate over ratification of the new Constitution, reading "every performance . . . printed on one side and the other of the great question . . . ," as far as he could obtain them. Correspon-dents sent him the proceedings of the ratifying conventions of Massachusetts, Pennsylvania, and Virginia, as well as other publications from those states and from Maryland and New York. Among other works, he perused the pro-Constitutional essays of John Jay, John Dickinson, Edmund Randolph, Noah Webster, and James Wilson, and the Antifederalist arguments of George Mason, James Monroe, and Richard Henry Lee. In *The Federalist* papers of Madison, Hamilton, and Jay, Washington recognized qualities transcending "the transient circumstances and fugitive performances" of the moment, because the collec-tion "candidly and ably discussed the principles of freedom and the topics of government, which will be always interesting to mankind so long as they will be connected in Civil Society." [41]

President Washington persisted in his habit of reading current political tracts, keeping his finger on the pulse of partisan politics. As he entered retire-ment, he instructed his secretary to purchase "the newly published Pamphlets," explaining that one of his other assistants knew which he already had. From Mount Vernon, he closely watched Federalists and Republicans counterpunch-ing in the press. Among others, he attentively read and circulated Federalist tracts in support of the Alien and Sedition Laws. Throughout his career, he purchased and received as gifts pamphlets on a wide range of public issues. His library contained hundreds. His letters show that he thought them a useful and neces-sary part of his reading. [42]

He also received newspapers from various parts of the country, many of them coming as unsolicited gifts from publishers and admirers. Occasionally he tried to cancel subscriptions. Repeatedly he complained of the inaccuracy of the press. His principal biographers have overemphasized these facts to support the mistaken perception that he was a reluctant politician. The evidence clearly shows that despite his gripes, he read a great many newspapers. They remained for him a principal source of political intelligence. This reading indicates once again his eager involvement in politics.[43]

Washington's program of reading included, as a major component, works on history and politics. According to one estimate, such books constituted approximately one-fourth of his library.[44] When one considers the large number of reference works (encyclopedias, dictionaries, compilations of laws, legislative proceedings, and agricultural guides) and that most of the fifty-three volumes of bound tracts covered contemporary political issues, the importance of history and politics in his reading becomes all the more apparent.

As already noted, he had begun in his teens to read political essays and history, and the Custis estate library had many important volumes in these fields. He also obtained Tobias Smollett's *History of England* and in 1769 Robert Beverley's *History of Virginia*. That same year, he ordered a list of books for Jack Custis's education, including Adam Ferguson's *History of Civil Society*, James Burgh's *The Dignity of Human Nature*, Richard Steele's *The Christian Hero*, Oliver Goldsmith's *History of England in a Series of Letters from a Nobleman to his Son*, the histories of England by David Hume and Catharine Macaulay, and other studies of classical and recent history. His own library had one of the many editions of the *Letters of Junius* by an unidentified contemporary Radical Whig writer. These essays became especially popular in America and were particular favorites of his neighbor, colleague, and probable mentor in political theory, George Mason. As the Revolution began, he subscribed to the American edition of James Burgh's *Political Disquisitions* and acquired Dr. Richard Price's *Observations on the Nature of Civil Liberty*.[45]

His historical interests ranged widely. At the close of the war, he purchased, among other titles, Voltaire's *History of Charles XII, King of Sweden*, Vertot's *History of the Revolutions That Happened in the Government of the Roman Republic*, the *Memoirs of the Duke of Sully*, and William Robertson's *History of the Reign of Charles V*. His library also eventually included Adam Ferguson's *History of the Progress and Termination of the Roman Republic*, Edward Gibbon's *History of the Decline and Fall of the Roman Empire*, and many other volumes of biography and classical and modern history.[46]

The American nationalist again gave attention to his own country and supported the works of native historians. He bought Ebenezer Hazard's collection of state papers and William Robertson's *History of America*. Somewhere he acquired the *History of New England* by the Baptist polemicist Isaac Backus. He received as a gift the first volume of Jeremy Belknap's *History of New-Hampshire*, probably purchased separately the entire three volumes of that work, and aided Belknap in obtaining both information and subscriptions for his *American Biography*. Praising George Richards Minot's *History of the Insurrection in Massachusetts*, he sent a copy across the Atlantic to correct European misimpressions of political conditions in America. His correspondence and library also indicate an interest in accounts of the American Revolution. He circulated subscription forms for William Gordon's history of the Revolution and owned copies of it and David Ramsay's histories of the Revolution in

South Carolina and the nation. From the enemy side, he had Sir Henry Clinton's narrative of the "American Rebellion."[47]

He also obtained books of legal, political, and economic theory and practice. He probably acquired his copy of John Adams's *Defence of the Constitutions of Government of the United States of America* during the Constitutional Convention to aid him in those deliberations. Prior to that meeting, he received from James Madison an abstract of Montesquieu's *Spirit of the Laws*. He also borrowed and copied his brilliant young colleague's memorandum on the constitutions of political confederations, ancient and modern. At other times, he read Adam Smith's *Wealth of Nations* and acquired Jeremy Bentham's *Panopticon*.[48]

Washington's acquisitions evidence strong interest in the study of history and society. He made plain his emphasis on this sort of reading when he inquired about the qualifications of a prospective nominee for high federal office. He asked about the man's "depth in the science of Politicks, or in other words, his acquaintance with history and his *general* knowledge. . . ."[49]

Some have minimized or dismissed the importance of books and ideas to Washington by declaring that he read only for practical reasons. Though he was no intellectual, his curiosity ranged widely. Despite his lack of an extensive formal education, he was far from ignorant. Yet because of his persistent anxiety about others' perceptions of him, he kept his efforts at self-education largely hidden from view.

He read in much the same way his Virginia contemporaries read.[50] He usually did have a utilitarian intent, but this aim encompassed more than the productivity of his farms, the profitability of his businesses, or the effectiveness of his military command. It embraced a significant concern with the realm of ideas. He sought moral and political instruction, looked for guidance in the definition of his social duties, studied to learn the lineaments of just the sort of public self he ought to present and ought to wish to present. His reading was neither scholarly nor speculative nor, usually, recreational. It was deliberate and businesslike and purposeful, whether in agriculture or history, military or political science. He wanted to get in touch with the fundamental ideas of the age and to learn what he must do and ought to do to achieve his personal and political goals.

The holdings of his own and the Custis libraries made available to him many of the important works that shaped the thinking of his generation. As earlier chapters have shown, his perception of the pre-revolutionary Anglo-American political crisis reflected the ideology and rhetoric of the English "Country Party." He read this literature to fit himself for the task of statesmanship. The conventional wisdom had it that history was philosophy teaching by example. When Washington expressed the belief that a knowledge of books was the basis of all other education, he meant that learning had a useful purpose, the proper preparation of gentlemen for public leadership.

His was an age that feared abuses of power, therefore he must prove himself a man capable of wielding that power for the public good and not for his own ambitions. His was a century that distrusted human passions, therefore he must show himself a man of reason and self-restraint, a man who had mastered his own spirit. His was an epoch that valued the harmonious union of philosophical reason and natural simplicity as the golden mean between brute savagery and effete sophistication, therefore he must present himself as one who followed the course prescribed by reason while retaining the pastoral virtues.

He was not a speculative thinker. His gift was not the formulation of ideas, but their incarnation. His genius manifested itself not in profoundly examining the beliefs of his generation, but in embodying them. He gave his closest attention to contemporary ideas and ideals of leadership. He was the eighteenth-century ideal of leadership in the flesh. In significant measure, his understanding of those ideas and ideals came from his reading.

Abbreviations

Diaries   George Washington, *Diaries of George Washington*, ed. Donald Jackson and Dorothy Twohig, Charlottesville, Virginia, 1976–9, 6 volumes.

DSF   Douglas Southall Freeman, *George Washington*, New York, 1948–57, 6 volumes; volume 7 by John A. Carroll and Mary W. Ashworth.

JCC   Worthington C. Ford et al., eds., *Journals of the Continental Congress, 1774–1789*, Washington, D.C., 1904–37, 34 volumes.

JHB   John Pendleton Kennedy and H. R. McIlwaine, eds., *Journals of the House of Burgesses of Virginia*, Richmond, Virginia, 1905–15, 13 volumes.

JTF   James Thomas Flexner, *George Washington*, Boston, 1965–72, 4 volumes.

LDC   Paul H. Smith et al., eds., *Letters of Delegates to Congress, 1774–1789*, Washington, D.C., 1976– , 14 volumes to date.

LTW   S. M. Hamilton, ed., *Letters to Washington, 1752–1775*, Boston and New York, 1898–1902, 5 volumes.

PWC   [George Washington], *Papers of George Washington, Colonial Series*, ed. W. W. Abbot, Dorothy Twohig, et al., Charlottesville, Virginia, 1983– , 6 volumes to date.

PWR   [George Washington], *Papers of George Washington, Revolutionary Series*, ed. W. W. Abbot, Dorothy Twohig, et al., Charlottesville, Virginia, 1985– , 2 volumes to date.

RRD   [Robert Dinwiddie], Robert A. Brock, ed., *Official Records of Robert Dinwiddie, Lieutenant Governor of the Colony of Virginia, 1751–1758*, Richmond, Virginia, 1883, 2 volumes.

RV   William J. Van Schreeven, comp., and Robert Scribner, ed., *Revolutionary Virginia: The Road to Independence*, [Charlottesville, Virginia], 1973, volumes 1–2.

WW   George Washington, *Writings of George Washington*, ed. John C. Fitzpatrick, Washington, D.C., 1931–9, 39 volumes.

Notes

CHAPTER ONE

1. To John Stanwix, 10 April 1758, WW 2:173.

2. On GW's relationship with his mother: to Mary Ball Washington, 7 June 1755, PWC 1:304–5; 14 August, 359–60; to Benjamin Harrison, 21 March 1781, WW 21:340–2; to John A. Washington, 16 January 1783, 26:42–4; to Charles Thomson, 22 January 1784, 27:312; to Mary Washington, 15 February 1787, 29:158–62; to Richard Conway, 6 March 1789, 30:222; to Elizabeth Washington Lewis, 13 September, 30:398–403; DSF 1:190, 193–5, 198–9; 2:17–18; 3:29; 5:281–2, 409–10, 491–2; 6:78–9, 159–60, 228–31; JTF 1:19–20, 30, 46, 114, 116–17, 137, 228, 264–5; 2:417, 471; 3:36–8, 227–8; Bernhard Knollenberg, *George Washington, the Virginia Period, 1732–1775*, Durham, North Carolina, 1976 (originally published 1964), 4–6. On GW's father: "Biographical Memoranda" (October 1783), WW 29:36; to the Mayor and Commonalty of Fredericksburg (14 February 1784), 27:332, in which GW also paid tribute to "my revered Mother; by whose Maternal hand (early deprived of a Father) I was led from Childhood. . . ."; to Burges Ball, 22 September 1799, 37:372.

3. Bertram Wyatt-Brown, *Southern Honor: Ethics and Behavior in the Old South*, New York, 1982, 14–15, 45–7, 155, 157–8.

4. WW 35:421–2; 29:18–19; 30:268–9; 32:166.

5. "Resolves of the Virginia House of Burgesses," 16 May 1769, quoted in RV 1:71; Rhys Isaac, *The Transformation of Virginia, 1740–1790*, Chapel Hill, North Carolina, 1982, 20–1; Gordon Schochet, *Patriarchalism in Political Thought*, New York, 1975.

6. T. H. Breen, *Tobacco Culture: The Mentality of the Great Tidewater Planters on the Eve of Revolution*, Princeton, 1985, 85.

7. Breen, *Tobacco Culture*, 86–8, quote on 86; Isaac, *Transformation*, 131.

8. Quoted in Jack P. Greene, "The Growth of Political Stability: An Interpretation of Political Development in the Anglo-American Colonies, 1660–1760," in John Parker and Carol Urness, eds., *The American Revolution: A Heritage of Change*, Minneapolis, 1975, 29.

9. Breen, *Tobacco Culture*, 89–90.

10. Breen, *Tobacco Culture*, 86–9, quote on 89.

11. DSF 1:57–8, 70–1, 229; PWC 3:202, 203n.1.

12. WW 1:1–5; PWC 1:1–4.

13. Charles Moore, ed. and intro., *George Washington's Rules of Civility and Decent Behaviour in Company and Conversation*, Boston and New York, 1926.

14. WW 29:492–3; 30:245–9; 31:163; 35:294–6, 421–2; Eugene Prussing, *The Estate of George Washington, Deceased*, Boston, 1927, 423, 427; James C. Nicholls, "Lady Henrietta Liston's Journal of Washington's 'Resignation,' Retirement, and Death," *Pennsylvania Magazine of History and Biography*, 95 (1971), 514. On Chesterfield's influence: Richard L. Bushman, "American High-Style and Vernacular Cultures," in Jack P. Greene and J. R. Pole, eds., *Colonial British America: Essays in the New History of the Early Modern Era*, Baltimore and London, 1984, 353–5. Another source of GW's knowledge may have been *A Course of Gallantries*, a translation of a French handbook which he ordered in 1784: WW 27:338–9.

15. WW 1:4–5; Prussing 432–3; Appleton P. C. Griffin, comp., *A Catalogue of the Washington Collection in the Boston Athenaeum*, including William C. Lane, "Inventory of Washington's Library," Boston, 1897, 503–9, 561–5.

16. London, 1747, noted in Griffin 96.

17. The debunkers notwithstanding, GW supervised his aides so closely in drafting and revising his letters and messages that they clearly bear the imprint of his mind. PWR 1:xviii; WW 1:xxxvii–xxxviii, xliv; 36:374–5; DSF 2:14n, 28; 4:72; 5:486; JTF 1:245; 2:412–13; Richard B. Morris, *Seven Who Shaped Our Destiny*, New York, 1973, 36–7; "Liston's Journal," 515. See also from John Parke Custis, 18 August 1771, LTW 4:80. When GW modified his handwriting, he may have used as a model a "Specimen of Penmanship" in his library: Griffin 564; Prussing 433.

18. PWC 1:46; JTF 1:23; Griffin 192, 484, 189, 67, 53, 509, 179 (all these publications in the Boston Athenaeum Collection have GW's autograph between the approximate ages of sixteen and twenty-one); from William Fairfax, 13–14 May 1756, PWC 3:125.

19. PWC 1:39, 45–6.

20. From Landon Carter, 7 October 1755, PWC 2:82.

21. Bushman 352–7; Cecil Wall, "George Washington: Country Gentleman," *Agricultural History*, 43 (1969), 5–6; DSF 3:116.

22. John Shy, "American Society and Its War for Independence," in Don Higginbotham, ed., *Reconsiderations on the Revolutionary War: Selected Essays*, Westport, Connecticut and London, 1978, 72–82; Robert M. Weir, "Who Shall Rule at Home: The American Revolution as a Crisis of Legitimacy for the Colonial Elite," in his *"The Last of American Freemen": Studies in the Political Culture of the Colonial and Revolutionary South*, Macon, Georgia, 1986, 63–88.

23. Isaac, *Transformation*, 99; T. H. Breen, "Horses and Gentlemen: The Cultural Significance of Gambling among the Gentry of Virginia," *William and Mary Quarterly*, third series, 34 (1977), 248–9; Rhys Isaac, "Evangelical Revolt: The Nature of the Baptists' Challenge to the Traditional Order in Virginia, 1765 to 1775," *William and Mary Quarterly*, third series, 31 (1974), 345–9; Jane D. Carson, *Colonial Virginians at Play*, Williamsburg, Virginia, 1965, 102–5; DSF 3:6, quoting a 1760 description of GW; Paul L. Ford, *Washington and the Theatre*, New York, 1899, 49–50.

24. Isaac, *Transformation*, 80–7, 355; Carson 10, 23–35, 257; DSF 1:229; 5:102; Paul L. Ford, *George Washington*, Philadelphia and London, 1924 (originally published as *The True George Washington*, Philadelphia, 1896), 183–5; *Pennsylvania Packet*, 6 March 1779, quoted in Frank Moore, ed., *Diary of the American Revolution, From Newspapers and Original Documents*, New York, 1860, 1859, 2 volumes, 2:133; WW 2:499n; 18:261n; 28:178, 217; 35:397; 37:425n; *Diaries* 1:238; 2:52, 93, 113–14, 120, 127, 246; 3:56, 74, 96, 119, 125, 136, 141, 180, 205, 251–2, 260–1, 287; 4:221; 6:102–3, 116–17, 120, 125, 130, 131, 137–8, 141–2, 146. Later GW studied fencing, an art absolutely useless in eighteenth-century Virginia except as an ornament to distinguish gentlemen from their social inferiors and undoubtedly an expression of his professional military ambition: DSF 2:204; Carson 168–9; Don Higginbotham, *George Washington and the American Military Tradition*, Athens, Georgia, 1985, 16.

25. Wyatt-Brown 48.

26. For a full discussion of GW's interest in the theater see the Appendix.

27. Breen, *Tobacco Culture*, 40–83; Breen, "Horses and Gentlemen," 245.

28. DSF 1:1.

29. DSF 1:197–8, 202–23, 232–3.

30. DSF 1:234.

31. PWC 1:8–37.

32. PWC 1:45, 47–8, 51–2; DSF 1:236–9, 243–4; in the *Virginia Gazette*, 25 April 1751, 4, GW advertised the sale of two lots in Fredericksburg.

33. To John Augustine Washington, 28 May 1755, PWC 1:290, cf. PWC 1:39–44.

34. From Landon Carter, 7 October 1755, PWC 2:82.

35. DSF 1:229–30; "Copy of Poll in Fairfax County," 13 June 1748, Washington Papers, Library of Congress.

36. DSF 1:66–71. At first Lawrence wanted to send George to sea, but the lad's mother, on the sensible advice of her brother, Joseph Ball, vetoed that proposition. As Ball pointed out, a youth such as George, with no "interest," no connections, had little prospect of success in a maritime career, cf. DSF 1:194, 198–9.

CHAPTER TWO

1. Freeman says that at first GW aimed at the adjutancy-general, but cites no evidence for this assertion. I can find none to support it: DSF 1:266–8, 430; to Governor Robert Dinwiddie, 10 June 1752, PWC 1:50–1; John R. Alden, *George Washington*, Baton Rouge, 1984, 9; H. R. McIlwaine and W. L.

Hall, eds., *Executive Journals of the Council of Colonial Virginia*, Richmond, Virginia, 1925–45, 6 volumes, 5:412–13, 6 November 1752; *PWC* 1:53. For the switch to the adjutancy of the Northern Neck, GW secured the support of councillors William Nelson and his brother Thomas, who was secretary of the Colony 1743–76. Undoubtedly he also had the aid of William Fairfax: from William Nelson, 22 February 1753, *PWC* 1:55.

2. *Executive Journals*, 22, 27, 29, 31 October 1753, 5:442–5; Commission, Instructions and Passport, 30 October 1753, *PWC* 1:56–62; Lawrence H. Gipson, *The British Empire before the American Revolution*, Caldwell, Idaho, and New York, 1936–70, 15 volumes, 4:295–6; Charles H. Ambler, *George Washington and the West*, New York, 1971 (originally published Chapel Hill, North Carolina, 1936), 36; DSF 1:273.

3. JTF 1:56; *Diaries* 1:158–60, cf. 126–7.

4. *PWC* 4:79, 91n.3; 1:58; *Diaries* 1:160–1; *Pennsylvania Gazette*, 5 February 1754, 2; 12 March, 1; 26 March, 1; *New York Gazette: or, The Weekly Post-Boy*, 18 February 1754, 2; 25 March, 1; 1 April, 2; *South Carolina Gazette*, 26 February–5 March 1754, 2; 26 March–2 April, 2; Richard Lee Morton, *Colonial Virginia*, Chapel Hill, North Carolina, 1960, 2 volumes, 2:644; Lawrence C. Wroth, *An American Bookshelf, 1755*, New York, 1969 (originally published Philadelphia, 1934), 2–22; *Gentleman's Magazine*, 24 (April 1754), 190; (June), 252–5; (July), 321–2; *Scots Magazine*, 16 (May 1754), 247–8; (June), 301–2; (July), 345–6. Subsequent accounts of the Seven Years' War also mentioned young Washington's embassy: cf. John Entick, *The General History of the Late War*, 3rd edition, London, 1763–64, 5 volumes, 1:96–102; *French Policy Defeated. Being an Account of all the hostile Proceedings of the French, Against the Inhabitants of the British Colonies in North America, For the last Seven Years*, London, 1755, 51–8, cf. 59–61; [William Livingston], *A Review of the Military Operations in North-America*, London, 1757, 6–7. For GW's activities in the spring of 1754 see *Pennsylvania Gazette*, 4 April 1754, 2; 9 May, 2; *New York Gazette*, 8 April, 2; 13 May, 2; *South Carolina Gazette*, 28 May–4 June, 1; 4–11 June, 1.

5. *Executive Journals*, 21 January 1754, 5:458–60; *PWC* 1:63–5, 75–6, 78; to Corbin, February–March 1754, 70–1.

6. To Governor Dinwiddie, 29 May 1754, two letters, *PWC* 1:110–17; *Diaries* 1:191–200; DSF 1:370–6.

7. [Jacob Nicholas Moreau], *A Memorial, Containing A Summary View of Facts, with Their Authorities In Answer to The Observations Sent by the English Ministry to The Courts of Europe*, New York, 1757, translated from the French, 13–15, 70–96 (English retranslation from French translation of GW's captured Journal: see especially 83–5), 97–103; Ambler 65–71; *Diaries* 1:166–73; from Rev. William Smith, 10 November 1757, LTW 2:233–4; Donald H. Kent, ed., "Contrecoeur's Copy of George Washington's Journal for 1754," *Pennsylvania History*, 19 (January 1952), 1–32, another retranslation into English from the French translation of GW's captured Journal of the military campaign of spring 1754; WW 1:36–7n; JTF 1:90–2, 173–4; Hugh Cleland, *George Washington in the Ohio Valley*, Pittsburgh, 1955, 80–3.

8. *PWC* 1:128–9, 142, 178; cf. [Horatio Sharpe], *Correspondence of Gov-*

ernor Horatio Sharpe, ed. William H. Browne, in *Archives of Maryland,* Baltimore, 1883–1972, 72 volumes, volumes 6–8, 6:79–80, 115–16, 198; *Maryland Gazette,* 13 June 1754; *Pennsylvania Gazette,* 27 June 1754, 2; 11 July, 1; *New York Gazette,* 24 June 1754, 3; 15 July, 2; *South Carolina Gazette,* 25 July–1 August 1754, 1; 1–8 August, 1, with dispatches from Williamsburg, Annapolis, and New York; *Gentleman's Magazine,* 24 (July 1754), 93; *Diaries* 1:146–7, 184, 185, 193, 195.

9. *London Magazine,* 23 (August 1754), 370–1; also to John Augustine Washington, 31 May 1754, in *WW* 1:70 and *PWC* 1:118–19 with minor differences of wording. Horace Walpole, *Memoirs of the Reign of King George the Second,* London, 1847, 3 volumes, 1:391–400; Horace Walpole to Sir Horace Mann, 6 October 1754, *The Yale Edition of Horace Walpole's Correspondence,* ed. W.S. Lewis, New Haven, Connecticut, 1937–83, 48 volumes, 20:449–50.

10. *PWC* 1:126–8. I have expanded Dinwiddie's contractions and abbreviations in this and in other cases.

11. To Dinwiddie, 18 May 1754, *PWC* 1:98–100; from Dinwiddie, 25 May, 102–4; to Dinwiddie, 29 May, 107–9.

12. From Dinwiddie, 4 May 1754, *PWC* 1:91–3; to GW, 4 June, 126–7; to Captain Mackay, 4 May 1754, *RRD* 1:149; to Dinwiddie (10 June 1754), *PWC* 1:129–30; cf. Peter Walne, ed., "A Mystery Resolved, George Washington's Letter to Governor Dinwiddie, June 10, 1754," *The Virginia Magazine of History and Biography,* 79 (1971), 131–44. The passage of the letter referred to is on Walne 135–6. Walne has discovered in England what is evidently the recipient's copy. This document shows that Fitzpatrick, following W. C. Ford, printed as two separate letters parts of one continuous and lengthy communication, to Dinwiddie [10 June 1754], *WW* 1:74–6; to Dinwiddie [12 June], 76–84. The original bears no date. These scholars have conjectured the date of 10 June based on knowledge of GW's whereabouts. The statement quoted in the last sentence does not appear in the Sparks, Ford, or Fitzpatrick version of this letter.

13. *PWC* 1:135–8.

14. *PWC* 1:85–7, 87–8, 94, 96–7, 100–1, 104–6, 112, 117–18, 124; *Diaries* 1:177, 181, 182–3, 184, 188; from Dinwiddie, 2 June 1754, *PWC* 1:121, cf. to GW, 1 June, 119–20; 27 June, 150.

15. From Dinwiddie, 4 June 1754, *PWC* 1:126–8; to Dinwiddie, 10 June, 129; Walne 135. On the missing portion of this letter: n.12 above.

16. *PWC* 1:130–1; Walne 136–7. Nothing of this long quote appeared in any of the previously published versions of this letter.

17. *PWC* 1:133, 135.

18. *PWC* 1:131, 138. On 16 June 1754, James Wood of Winchester recorded in his notebook that GW intended to march from Fort Necessity to Redstone Creek and then to attack the French fort, all "contrary to the advice" of the Indian chief, the "Half-King": quoted in *PWC* 1:162. The "Half-King" later complained that the "good-natured" but inexperienced GW had ignored his advice and treated the Indians "as his Slaves": "Journal of the Proceedings of Conrad Weiser," 3 September 1754, in Samuel Hazard et al., eds., *Minutes*

of the Provincial Council, Colonial Records of Pennsylvania, Harrisburg, Pennsylvania, 1851–53, 16 volumes, 6:151–2.

The following newspaper item offers indirect evidence supporting the conclusion that GW hoped to defeat the French single-handed. It first appeared in the *Pennsylvania Gazette,* 11 July 1754, 2. "Since our last a Gentleman arrived here from Alexandria, in Virginia, and informed us, that before he set out, he saw a Letter from Colonel Washington to his Friend there, advising, that he designed to march immediately and attack the French with the Forces he had then under him, being above 500 white Men, besides Indians, and not to wait the Arrival of the other Troops designed for his Camp: That all with him, white Men and Indians, were in high Spirits, and eager for Action, having Plenty of every Thing: And that, on the contrary, he had good Intelligence the Enemy were in Great Want of Provisions, their Number vastly inferior to what it had been represented, and that in general they were dissatisfied, which occasioned a daily Desertion among them; so that he was in great Hopes of getting the better of them without much Bloodshed.

"The Gentleman further added, that 170 of the North-Carolina Men, who came by Water, and the New-York Companies, were at Alexandria when he left it; and that 300 more had marched from North-Carolina by Land, but where they were he had not learnt. He likewise said, that above a Hundred stout Men, from South-Carolina, had gone from Alexandria for the Camp, whether or not they had got to it he could not tell." If GW did write such a letter to a friend in Alexandria, it apparently has not been found. Also in *New York Gazette,* 15 July 1754, 2; *South Carolina Gazette,* 1–8 August 1754, 2. This newspaper item seems to have gone unnoticed previously. For comment on GW's cockiness and his foolhardy advance see DSF 1:379–80; JTF 1:79, 84; Gipson, *British Empire* 6:23–5.

19. PWC 1:143, 155–72; 4:126; *Diaries* 1:201–2; DSF 1:391–411; JTF 1:96–106; Gipson, *British Empire* 6:33–43.

20. For the account by GW and Mackay see: *Virginia Gazette* (Hunter), 19 July 1754, 2–3; *Pennsylvania Gazette,* 1 August 1754, 2; *New York Gazette,* 5 August 1754, 2–3; *South Carolina Gazette,* 22 August 1754, 2 (reprinted in *PWC* 1:159–64). The printer of the *Virginia Gazette* added two paragraphs of editorial comment to this report, blaming the defeat on the delay of the New York Independent Companies. The officers of those units defended themselves in a letter to the *Pennsylvania Gazette,* 10 April 1755, 1. GW and Mackay omitted mention of Van Braam or the humiliating terms of surrender. But on a visit to Philadelphia, Mackay got into several "despuits" about the terms of capitulation and defended himself, GW, and the other officers by blaming Van Braam: from James Mackay, 28 September 1754, *PWC* 1:214. Adam Stephen, an officer in the Virginia Regiment, defended GW and accused Van Braam in a letter published in *Pennsylvania Gazette,* 22 August 1754, 1; *New York Gazette,* 26 August 1754, 2; *Maryland Gazette,* 29 August 1754; *South Carolina Gazette,* 26 September 1754, 1. He continued his defense against the charge of assassination in a second letter, *Pennsylvania Gazette,* 19 September 1754, 2; *New York Gazette,* 7 October 1754, 2. For other reports of the defeat and the publication of the Articles of Capitulation see *Pennsylvania Gazette,* 25 July

1754, 1; *New York Gazette*, 22 July 1754, 3; 29 July, 2; *Maryland Gazette*, 1 August 1754; *South Carolina Gazette*, 19 September 1754, 1. The Articles of Capitulation are reprinted in *PWC* 1:165–8. See also DSF 1:406–8, 413, 420–1, 423; JTF 1:101–5. On Van Braam see *PWC* 1:62n, 67n; to Dinwiddie, 20 March 1754, 78; 29 May, 113; (10 June), 133; [Francis Fauquier], *The Official Papers of Francis Fauquier, Lieutenant Governor of Virginia, 1758–1768*, ed. George Reese, Charlottesville, Virginia, 1980–3, 3 volumes, to William Pitt, 3 April 1761, enclosing resolve of the Burgesses recommending Van Braam to the king's service, 2:502–4; Knollenberg 23–4, 150. GW's only mention of Van Braam's mistranslation is in letter to ——— (circa 1757), *PWC* 1:169–70, 171n.2. In 1786, David Humphreys was working on a biography of GW. The manuscript of that unfinished work has little to say about the defeat. GW's comments written to assist Humphreys include nothing about the controversial aspects of the incident: *PWC* 1:172–3.

21. The author or one of the authors of the "Dinwiddianae," a collection of satirical verse written during the 1750s lampooning Governor Dinwiddie, commented on the defeat in a poem dated 4 November 1754: "Mistakes are easily forgiven, / When honour pricks men on. / I'd not give one of these for seven / of your, Caal heded mon." The last line refers to Dinwiddie's supposed favoritism toward his friend and fellow Scot, Colonel James Innes. The mistake mentioned here probably refers to the signing of the Articles of Capitulation, rather than to GW's hasty advance before Innes and reinforcements arrived. The poem criticizes Dinwiddie for discriminating against Virginia-born men in military appointments. The Virginia officers' "Valour stands unshaken, / who on the beauteous rivers Stream/ too lately were mistaken." Richard Beale Davis has concluded that the author or authors of these verses probably lived in the Northern Neck along the Potomac. Internal evidence suggests that he or they were land speculators whose financial interests had suffered because of Dinwiddie's policy in the Pistole Fee Dispute. All of his "suspects" were acquaintances of GW. Most belonged to the Ohio Company. Richard Beale Davis, ed., "Dinwiddianae," *"The Colonial Virginia Satirist": Mid–Eighteenth Century Commentaries on Politics, Religion, and Society*, in *American Philosophical Society Transactions*, new series, 57 (March 1967), 18–20, 10–16. Landon Carter criticized GW only for having trusted Van Braam: *The Diary of Colonel Landon Carter of Sabine Hall, 1752–1778*, ed. Jack P. Greene, Charlottesville, Virginia, 1965, 2 volumes, 108–11, 115–16; cf. from Carter, 7 October 1755, *PWC* 2:82. From Speaker John Robinson, 15 September 1754, *PWC* 1:209–10, transmitting the Resolve of the Burgesses thanking GW, Mackay, and the officers under their command; published in *Pennsylvania Gazette*, 3 October 1754, 1; *New York Gazette*, 14 October 1754, 2; DSF 1:415–16, 420–3, 432, 438.

22. Huske quoted in Wroth 23–5, 40–1. For some British reactions see *Scots Magazine* 16 (August 1754), 396–8; (September 1754), 446–7; *Gentleman's Magazine* 24 (September 1754), 399–400; *London Magazine* 23 (September 1754), 419–21.

23. From Sharpe, 1 October 1754, *PWC* 1:215–16; Sharpe to Lord Baltimore, 8 August 1754, *Sharpe Correspondence* 6:80; Sharpe to Lord Bury, 5 November, 115–16; Sharpe to John Sharpe, 19 April 1755, 198–9; Thomas

Penn to Governor Robert Hunter Morris, 26 February 1755, Samuel Hazard et al., eds., *Pennsylvania Archives*, first series, Philadelphia, 1851, volumes 2–3, 2:255; Baron Calvert to Governor Sharpe, 10 December 1754, *Sharpe Correspondence* 6:134; Albemarle quoted in JTF 1:108; Johnson to Goldsbrow Banyar, 29 July 1754, [William Johnson], *Papers of Sir William Johnson*, ed. James Sullivan, Albany, New York, 1921–65, 14 volumes, 1:410. Cf. John Lloyd to Henry Lloyd, 10 August 1754, *Papers of the Lloyd Family . . . , Collections of the New York Historical Society*, 60 (1927), 518: "I send Mr Harts paper that you may see the upshot of Washingtons affair." DSF 1:355, 423–4. Although Governor Dinwiddie praised GW publicly, in private letters he was more critical, seeking to shift any blame from himself for having failed to restrain the impetuous young commander: Dinwiddie to Sharpe, 31 July 1754, *Sharpe Correspondence* 6:76–7; to William Allen, 10 March 1755, RRD 1:524.

24. DSF 1:419–20; JTF 1:106–9; Gipson, *British Empire* 6:43.

CHAPTER THREE

1. Landon Carter, *A Letter from a Gentleman in Virginia to the Merchants of Great Britain trading to that Colony* (London, 1754); Griffin 171–2, where it is incorrectly attributed to Peyton Randolph.

2. PWC 1:200, 201–3.

3. PWC 1:148–9, 212–14; RRD 1:213, 221, 223.

4. RRD 1:355, 365, 372–3, 376, 403–4; Gipson, *British Empire* 6:51–2.

5. DSF 1:433–4, 439–41, 443–4; 2:1; JTF 1:112–14; Gipson, *British Empire* 6:52; *Carter Diary*, 115–16; RRD 1:403–4; PWC 1:242n; WW 1:109–10n; DSF 2:12–13; Douglas Edward Leach, *Arms for Empire: A Military History of the British Colonies in North America, 1607–1763*, New York, 1973, 354–5, cf. [Charles Chauncy], *A Letter to a Friend, Giving a Concise, But Just, Account . . . of the Ohio-Defeat*, Boston, 1755, 8–10.

6. From William Fitzhugh, 4 November 1754, PWC 1:223–5; to Fitzhugh, 15 November, 225–7. According to Gipson, Dinwiddie little regretted GW's resignation, because of friction between him and the officers of the Independent Companies and because the Indian allies of the English had come to dislike and even to distrust him, accusing him of foolhardiness and of neglecting to consult with them: Gipson, *British Empire* 6:52–3.

7. To Captain Robert Orme, 15 March 1755, PWC 1:242–5; from Orme, 2 March, 241–2; to Speaker John Robinson, 20 April, 254–7.

8. To Robert Orme, 15 March 1755, PWC 1:243; to Carter Burwell, 20 April, 253, see also to John Robinson, 20 April, 255; to William Byrd, 20 April, 250–1. To John Augustine Washington, 14 May, 278; 28 May, 289, see also to Thomas, Lord Fairfax, 6 May, 265.

9. To John Augustine Washington, 28 May 1755, PWC 1:290–3.

10. To William Fairfax, 7 June 1755, PWC 1:298–9; from Fairfax, 28 June, 1:316–17. For Braddock's complaints about Americans: Stanley M. Pargellis, ed., *Military Affairs in North America, 1748–1765*, New York, 1969 (originally published New York, 1936), 83–5. The author of the "Dinwiddianae" blamed the governor for Braddock's prejudice: Davis, *Colonial Virginia Satirist*, 27.

11. Hayes Baker-Crothers, *Virginia and the French and Indian War*, Chicago, 1928, 73–5; to William Fairfax, 5 May 1755, *PWC* 1:262–4; 7 June, 299.

12. *PWC* 1:267, 272, 278, 312, 320–3; 4:89; DSF 2:52–3, 99–102. For criticism of GW's advice see Alden, *Washington*, 36–8, 41. Braddock also sent GW as a courier to Williamsburg: *PWC* 1:281–9.

13. *PWC* 1:331–43; DSF 2:64–84.

14. "Captain Robert Stewart to his friend at Williamsburg, from Will's Creek," 19 July 1755, *South Carolina Gazette*, 14–21 August 1755, 2; Governor Robert Hunter Morris of Pennsylvania to General William Shirley (no date but probably late July 1755), in George E. Reed, ed., *Pennsylvania Archives*, fourth series, Harrisburg, 1900, 2:434–5; Governor James De Lancey of New York to William Johnson, 3 August 1755, *Johnson Papers* 1:826–7; Governor Dinwiddie to Sir Thomas Robinson, 25 July 1755, *RRD* 2:116; to Governor Sharpe, 29 July, 126; Address of Dinwiddie to the Virginia House of Burgesses (no date but probably 5 August), 135; to Sir Thomas Robinson, 7 August, 139; Lee McCardell, *Ill-Starred General: Braddock of the Coldstream Guards*, Pittsburgh, 1958, 271, quoting Benjamin Franklin's *Autobiography; Universal Magazine*, 17 (August 1755), 92–4; *London Magazine*, 23 (September 1755), 403–5; N. Darnell Davis, "British Newspaper Accounts of Braddock's Defeat," *Pennsylvania Magazine of History and Biography*, 23 (1899), quoting *The Public Advertiser*, 30 September, 17 October, 10 November 1755, 318, 322, 327–8, and *Whitehall Evening Post*, 9–11 October 1755, 321; William Livingston, *A Review of the Military Operations in North America*, London, 1757, 38–40; Entick 1:141–8.

15. *Scots Magazine*, 17 (August 1755), 402; "Letter from Potomack, Maryland, July 27, 1755," *Scots Magazine*, 17 (October 1755), 502; also in *The Public Advertiser*, 3 November 1755, N. D. Davis 327; "Boston in New England, August 18," *Scots Magazine*, 17 (September 1755), 452, with minor differences of wording in *The Public Advertiser*, 3 October 1755, N. D. Davis 319. See also Goldsbrow Banyar to William Johnson, 26 July 1755, *Johnson Papers* 1:772; Richard Walsh, ed., "Braddock on July 9, 1755," *Maryland Historical Magazine*, 60 (1965), 425–6.

16. Orme's letter was circulated widely: Orme to Lieutenant Governor Robert Hunter Morris of Pennsylvania, 18 July 1755, Hazard et al., *Minutes* 6:488; *LTW* 1:71. Morris enclosed it in a report to Secretary of State Sir Thomas Robinson, 30 July 1755, *Pennsylvania Archives*, 4th series, 1900, 2:440. *Pennsylvania Gazette*, 31 July 1755, 3; Goldsbrow Banyar to William Johnson, 26 July 1755, *Johnson Papers* 1:774–5; Orme to Gov. Morris, 18 July 1755, [Cadwallader Colden], *The Letters and Papers of Cadwallader Colden, 1755–1760, Collections of the New York Historical Society*, 54 (1921), 17–19; *New York Gazette*, 4 August 1755, 3; *New York Mercury*, 4 August 1755; Orme to Governor Sharpe, 18 July 1755, *Sharpe Correspondence* 6:252–4; *South Carolina Gazette*, 28 August–4 September, 1755, 3; Orme to Commodore Augustus Keppel, "The Keppel Manuscripts," *American Antiquarian Society Transactions*, 11 (1909), 174–5; *Boston Evening Post*, 11 August 1755; *Boston Gazette*, 11 August 1755; *Boston Weekly News-Letter*, 14 August 1755, 2; Dinwiddie to Orme, 28 July 1755, *RRD* 2:120. Dinwiddie sent Governor William Shirley of Massachusetts copies of Orme's and GW's accounts, 29 July

1755: [William Shirley], *Correspondence of William Shirley*, ed. Charles H. Lincoln, New York, 1912, 2 volumes, 2:211. GW's account to Dinwiddie, 18 July 1755, *PWC* 1:339–42, was published in *Boston Gazette*, 1 September 1755, without attribution and in *Pennsylvania Gazette*, 21 August 1755, 3; *New York Gazette*, 23 August, 2. *Maryland Gazette*, 21 August 1755, composite of Orme's and GW's accounts. Commodore Keppel also received a copy of GW to Dinwiddie, 18 July 1755, "Keppel Manuscripts," 175–7.

Scots Magazine, 17 (September 1755), 451–3, offered extracts of various letters from America explaining the defeat. Though Orme's letter does not appear among them, there is a paraphrase of his one-sentence description of GW's heroism, 452. His account does not seem to have gained wide public circulation in Britain. None of the newspaper dispatches gathered by Davis published it, nor did *London Magazine*, *Gentleman's Magazine*, or *Scots Magazine*. After he returned to England, Orme informed GW that he had written "a true and impartial Narrative of the Affair" that he believed had altered public opinion: from Orme, 2 March 1756, *PWC* 2:320.

17. John Bolling to his son Bob, 13 August 1755, in John A. Schutz, "A Private Report of General Braddock's Defeat," *Pennsylvania Magazine of History and Biography*, 79 (1955), 377; from Dinwiddie, 26 July 1755, *PWC* 1:344–5; from Fairfax, 26 July, 345–6; from Sally Fairfax, Ann Spearing, and Elizabeth Dent, 26 July, 346; from Charles Lewis, 9 August, 357–8; from Philip Ludwell, 8 August, 356–7; from John Martin, 30 August 1755, 2:12; *South Carolina Gazette*, 11–19 September 1755, 2; from Christopher Gist, 15 October 1755, *PWC* 2:115; [Dr. Alexander Hamilton to Gavin Hamilton, August 1755], in Elaine G. Breslaw, "A Dismal Tragedy: Drs. Alexander and John Hamilton Comment on Braddock's Defeat," *Maryland Historical Magazine*, 75 (1980), 118–44, the most thorough contemporaneous analysis; quote from 138–9, for other mention of GW see 132–3, 136.

18. From Joseph Ball, 5 September 1755, *PWC* 2:15; the Earl of Halifax to Sir Charles Hardy, 31 March 1756, "Intercepted Letters to the Duke de Mirepoix, 1756," *American Historical Association Annual Report, 1896*, Washington, D.C., 1897, 1:689. A European correspondent later asked George Mercer, a comrade of GW's, for a description of him. Mercer penned the earliest sketch of GW's appearance and character: William Alfred Bryan, *George Washington in American Literature, 1775–1865*, Westport, Connecticut, 1970 (originally published New York, 1952), 10.

19. John F. Berens, *Providence & Patriotism in Early America, 1640–1815*, Charlottesville, Virginia, 1978, 43; Samuel Davies, *Religion and Patriotism the Constituents of a Good Soldier*, Philadelphia, 1755, 8–9.

20. Whether they praised GW or not, colonial commentators drew the lesson of American superiority in forest fighting: Breslaw 139; [Chauncy]; Higginbotham, *Washington*, 9–10.

21. Peter E. Russell, "Redcoats in the Wilderness: British Officers and Irregular Warfare in Europe and America, 1740 to 1760," *William and Mary Quarterly*, third series, 35 (1978), 629–52, on Braddock's expedition see 642–4.

22. To Adam Stephen, 18 November 1755, *PWC* 2:173, cf. from Stephen,

22 November, 178. GW himself blamed the defeat on the cowardice of the British regular common soldiers. He praised the regular officers and the Virginia troops: *PWC* 1:336–7, 339–40. GW may have alienated himself from influential men in the regular army by having closely associated with Braddock's favorite, Captain Robert Orme. Orme allegedly had cut the senior officers on the expedition out of decision-making and promoted with the general the interests of his friends among the young staff officers. His conniving seems to have ruined his own career and that of another junior officer. There is no evidence that GW consciously joined this scheme, but his affiliations may have added another obstacle to GW's obtaining a regular commission: Stanley Pargellis, "Braddock's Defeat," *American Historical Review*, 41 (1935–36), 253–69.

23. To John Augustine Washington, 14 May 1755, *PWC* 1:278; to Dinwiddie, 18 July 1755, *PWC* 1:340; from Dinwiddie, 26 July, 344–5, cf. *RRD* 1:86–7, 278–9, 281–2, 371.

24. From Christopher Gist, 15 October 1755, *PWC* 2:115; from Charles Lewis, 9 August, 1:358.

25. From Philip Ludwell, 8 August 1755, *PWC* 1:356–7; to Augustine Washington, 2 August, 351–4; from Warner Lewis, 9 August, 358–9; from George Mason, 21 August, 2:9; for GW's new appointment and commission see *PWC* 2:1–8.

26. To Charles Lewis, 14 August 1755, *PWC* 1:364; to Warner Lewis, 14 August, 360–3, cf. to Augustine Washington, 2 August, 351–4.

27. To Warner Lewis, 14 August 1755, *PWC* 1:362–3; to Mary Ball Washington, 14 August, 359–60; see also to John Campbell, Earl of Loudoun, 10 January 1757, 4:89. Compare the letter to his mother with the one to his wife at the time of his appointment as Continental commander-in-chief, expressing the same concern in very similar language: to Martha Washington, 18 June 1775, *PWR* 1:4.

28. GW may have expressed his hope for a regular commission in a letter to Orme, probably written in late September, cf. from Orme, 10 November 1755, *PWC* 2:166. Early in September, Governor Dinwiddie wrote Secretary of State Sir Thomas Robinson soliciting such commissions for GW and the Virginia regimental officers: 6 September 1755, *RRD* 2:191. In their negotiations about the command, Dinwiddie may have promised GW to make this effort: DSF 2:112n. For a detailed reconstruction of the negotiations and the appointment see DSF 2:103–14; *PWC* 2:1–8. GW's appointment was announced in *Virginia Gazette* (Hunter), 5 September 1755, 3; *Pennsylvania Gazette*, 18 September 1755, 2; *New York Gazette*, 22 September 1755, 2; *London Magazine*, 23 (November 1755), 548.

CHAPTER FOUR

1. *PWC* 1:71–4, 129–31, 140–1, 153, 174, 177, 186, 190, 198; 2:83–5, 201, 204; 3:132, 171–4, 227–9, 327–9, 396; 4:66, 68–9, 80–1; DSF 2:115–16, 232; David J. Mays, *Edmund Pendleton, 1721–1803: A Biography*, Cambridge, Massachusetts, 1952, 2 volumes, 1:127–8, 135; WW 2:314–15, 316; *LTW* 3:133–4, 135–6, 137–8; John Ferling, "Soldiers for Virginia: Who

Served in the French and Indian War?" *The Virginia Magazine of History and Biography*, 94 (1986), 307–28; E. Wayne Carp, "Early American Military History: A Review of Recent Work," *The Virginia Magazine of History and Biography*, 94 (1986), 274–5. Ferling argues that the soldiers were a more representative cross-section of Virginia society than historians have thought. Draftees were poor young whites, but he shows that enlistees were young white natives and older immigrants whose economic opportunities were blocked in this slave-based economy. All were landless.

2. *PWC* 1:190–2; 2:102–3, 172; 3:67–167 passim, 414, 430–3; 4:1–4, 11–13; DSF 2:116–26, 130, 132–9, 150–1, 184–5, 189–93, 200–3, 219–20, 232, 254, 258–60; *WW* 1:201, 203–4, 329–31, 492.

3. To Augustine Washington, 2 August 1755, *PWC* 1:352.

4. From Dinwiddie, 14 December 1755, *PWC* 2:214. As colonel of the Regiment, one of GW's perquisites was to be its paymaster: *PWC* 1:132. Also, he continued as district adjutant of the Northern Neck. Dinwiddie appointed a fellow Scot, Colin Campbell, as GW's deputy adjutant. Campbell demanded sixty-five pounds as his share of GW's one-hundred-pound annual salary. GW considered Campbell unqualified and told the governor he preferred to appoint someone of his own training who would accept the forty pounds a year other deputies received. Dinwiddie ordered him to pay Campbell fifty pounds: *PWC* 1:193–4, 207, 355–6 and nn.1, 2; DSF 1:430, 441. One of the poems in the "Dinwiddianae" may have criticized the governor's appointment of Campbell: R. B. Davis, *Colonial Virginia Satirist*, 22–5, cf. 21. In December 1754, GW demanded his back pay as district adjutant, claiming that while a colonel on active duty he had not forfeited that salary: *PWC* 1:235; DSF 2:3–4. He also sought reimbursement for losses at Fort Necessity: *PWC* 1:252–4, 256–7. For GW's negotiations over his pay and perquisites in subsequent years: DSF 2:113, 244–5, 393–4; *PWC* 2:6, 8, 106, 202, 214, 351; 3:367; 4:148, 156, 176, 193, 197n.5, 216, 289, 291, 312; *WW* 2:206–7.

5. *PWC* 2:173, 178; 3:12–13, 42, 88, 110; Dinwiddie to Sir Thomas Robinson, 6 September 1755, *RRD* 2:191–2, cf. 224, 230, 261, 267, 330, 425; *PWC* 3:180–2.

6. To Andrew Lewis, 6 September 1755, *PWC* 2:23–4; to Adam Stephen, 11 September, 27; Memorandum, 11 September, 28; Address, 8 January 1756, 257; Instructions to Company Captains, 29 July 1757, 4:344; to Major Andrew Lewis, 21 May 1758, *WW* 2:202–3. GW tried to train himself as well. On Braddock's expedition he had made copies of the general orders for his future reference: to Robert Orme, 28 July 1755, *PWC* 1:347, 348n.7; Enclosure of Invoice to Richard Washington, 6 December, 2:209, ordering Bland; Higginbotham, *Washington*, 14–15, 18–20; Ira D. Gruber, "British Strategy: The Theory and Practice of Eighteenth-Century Warfare," in Don Higginbotham, ed., *Reconsiderations on the Revolutionary War*, Westport, Connecticut, and London, 1978, 19–20. He also probably had read Julius Caesar's *Commentaries on the Gallic Wars* and perhaps other ancient military writers: from William Fairfax, 13–14 May 1756, *PWC* 3:125; cf. Griffin 537. The regular officers most attentive to their professional education regarded Caesar's

Commentaries as "required reading for any officer who aspired to high command": Gruber 19.

7. *PWC* 3:158, 353–4, 399.

8. *PWC* 2:41, 76; 1:72, cf. 217–9; 2:208–9; 4:343.

9. DSF 2:145–7; Fairfax County Poll, 11 December 1755, Washington Papers, Library of Congress.

10. From Adam Stephen, 23 December 1755, *PWC* 2:226; Frederick County Poll, 10 December 1755, Washington Papers, Library of Congress; Lucille B. Griffith, *The Virginia House of Burgesses, 1750–1774*, University, Alabama, 1970, 159–60.

11. *PWC* 2:72, 74–5n.6, 172–3, 200–1, 204, 213, 218–19, 238; *RRD* 2:309.

12. *RRD* 2:311, 329–30; *PWC* 2:283–6, 291–5, 303; 3:16–17; DSF 2:133–9, 144–5, 148–9, 153–6, cf. *PWC* 2:295–6.

13. DSF 2:156, 158, 162–3, 164, 167; Samuel Eliot Morison, "The Young Man Washington," in his *By Land and by Sea*, New York, 1953, 175. GW ordered fine clothing just before his journey and bought more during it: to Richard Washington, 6 December 1755, *PWC* 2:207–9; "Notes on Journey to Boston," *WW* 1:298–9. *Pennsylvania Gazette*, 12 February 1756, 2; 26 February, 2; 18 March, 2; *New York Mercury*, 16 and 23 February and 22 March 1756; *New York Gazette*, 16 February 1756, 2; 23 February, 3; *Boston News-letter*, 4 March 1756; *Boston Gazette, or Country Journal*, 1 and 22 March 1756.

14. Shirley to Sharpe, 5 March 1756, *Sharpe Correspondence* 6:347–8; [Sharpe to Shirley], 23 March, 380; Orders of General Shirley, 5 March 1756, *PWC* 2:323–4; from Lieutenant Colonel Adam Stephen, 29 March, 324–7; to Robert Hunter Morris, 9 April, 345–6; DSF 2:165–8. That GW expected command of the new expedition himself is indicated by a letter from John Robinson, 27 January 1756, *PWC* 2:303, and suggested by a letter from Colonel Thomas Gage, 10 May, 3:115–16. GW had written to Gage on 14 April: this letter is missing.

15. Sharpe may have endorsed GW's application partly because GW's popularity in Virginia made it politically expedient, but he also noted that GW "really seems a Gentle[ma]n of Merit": [Sharpe to Shirley], 10 April 1756, *Sharpe Correspondence* 6:389; Shirley to Sharpe, 16 May, 415–16; DSF 2:170–1, 196–7.

16. From Dinwiddie, 8 April 1756, *PWC* 2:343–4; from Fairfax, 14 April, 351–2; from Robinson (c. 31 March–2 April), 329; 17 April, 3:12–13; DSF 2:174–5, 178–9.

17. To Dinwiddie, 18 April 1756, *PWC* 3:13–15; 22 April, 33–5; 24 April, 44–7; to Robinson, c. 18 April, 15–17. Some of GW's letters hinting at resigning are now missing, but their contents are evident in the replies. See next note for references.

18. From Charles Carter, 22 April 1756, *PWC* 3:36–8; from William Fairfax, 26 April, 56–8; from Landon Carter, 21 April, 30–2; from Charles Carter, 27 April, 64–5; from Landon Carter (May), 185–8.

19. To Robinson, 27 April 1756, *PWC* 3:62–4; to Dinwiddie, 27 April, 59–60. His letters to Fairfax are missing. From Robinson, 3 May, 87–8; from Fairfax, 13–14 May, 125–6; 20 May, 167–8, cf. from Dinwiddie, 3 May, 85–7; to Dinwiddie, 24 April, 44–7.

20. *PWC* 3:74–84, 95–7, 99, 111–12, 118, 123, 135–6, 142, 147, 151–3, 160, 164, 169, 206, 237–40, 281–2, 334–6, 344–6, 382–4.

21. J. A. Leo LeMay, "The Reverend Samuel Davies' Essay Series: The Virginia Centinel, 1756–1757," in LeMay, ed., *Essays in Early Virginia Literature Honoring Richard Beale Davis*, New York, 1977, 121–63; Richard Beale Davis, *Intellectual Life in the Colonial South*, Knoxville, Tennessee, 1978, 3 volumes, 1:616–7. LeMay argues for Davies as the anonymous author. "Centinel No. I" first appeared in *Virginia Gazette*, 30 April 1756, now missing. The quote is taken from the *New York Gazette: or, The Weekly Post-Boy*, 14 June 1756, 1, cf. LeMay 122–4. "Centinel No. III" probably first appeared in *Virginia Gazette*, 14 or 21 May 1756. Those issues are missing. Reprinted in *New York Gazette*, 28 June 1756, 1, cf. LeMay 125–7.

22. "Centinel No. X," *Virginia Gazette*, 3 September 1756, 1; *Maryland Gazette*, 12 August 1756; *Pennsylvania Gazette*, 16 September 1756, 1, cf. LeMay 130–2.

23. For criticism of Dinwiddie: Davis, *Colonial Virginia Satirist*, 10–16, 19–20, 21–2, 24–5, 27, 31, 36, 40; LeMay 133–4. For GW's reaction: from William Ramsay, 22 September 1756, *PWC* 3:412–13; from John Kirkpatrick, 22 September, 410. GW's letters to these two are missing. Their replies indicate he was considering resigning.

24. From Augustine Washington, 16 October 1756, *PWC* 3:435–8, cf. to Dinwiddie, 10 October, 433; from John Robinson, 16 November, 4:28–9. On Innes: Dinwiddie to Secretary at War Henry Fox, 24 July 1754, *RRD* 1:246; *Carter Diary*, 109, 116; Davis, *Colonial Virginia Satirist*, 19–20; from James Innes, 8 September 1754, *PWC* 1:205–6; to William Fairfax, 7 June 1755, 299; to Robert Jackson, 2 August, 350; from Lt. Col. Adam Stephen, 19 May 1756, 3:165–6; from William Fairfax, 10 July, 247. Dinwiddie's longtime friend Innes held a royal captaincy and had served with Lawrence Washington at Cartagena. Freeman reports that the governor had tried to obtain a regular commission as major for his fellow Scot, but he could find no evidence to support the charge, often repeated by historians, that Dinwiddie was maneuvering to oust GW and replace him with Innes: DSF 1:417–18; 2:6n, 109n, 174, 196n, 221.

25. From William Peachey et al., 12 November 1756, *PWC* 4:18–20; Officers of the Virginia Regiment to Adam Stephen, 6 October, 22–3; Address of the Officers of the Regiment to the Speaker and Gentlemen of the House of Burgesses, 21–22n. Evidently Richard Bland came to the defense of GW and the Regiment, cf. *PWC* 3:437n.3; "Philo Patria," Washington Papers, Library of Congress, and *LTW* 1:386–95; from Bland, 7 June 1757, *PWC* 4:187–9.

26. From Dinwiddie, 27 May 1756, *PWC* 3:180; Dinwiddie to James Abercrombie, 28 May, *RRD* 2:425; Dinwiddie to Loudoun, 1 July, 456; to John Campbell, Earl of Loudoun, 25 July 1756, *PWC* 3:293–4; from William Fairfax, 13–16 August, 347; Proclamation, 15 August, 353–4; from Beverley Rob-

inson, 2 September, 385–6; to Stephen, 6 September, 389; cf. to Dinwiddie, 16 April, 1–6, for GW's plan to reorganize the regiment in a manner more consistent with the regular army.

27. To Dinwiddie, 4 August 1756, *PWC* 3:317–18; to Stephen, 23 October, 440–2; to John Robinson, 9 November, 4:11–18.

28. To Dinwiddie, 4 August 1756, *PWC* 3:314; 14 August, 349–51; from Dinwiddie, 19 August, 359.

29. For other instances of GW's maneuvering: from Robinson, 16 December 1755, *PWC* 2:218–19; 27 January 1756, 303–4; to Robinson, 16 April, 3:6–8; from Dinwiddie, 15 December, 4:57; from Robinson, 17 December, 62; to Dinwiddie, 24 October 1757, *WW* 2:151; to Robinson, 25 October, 153–6; from Robinson, 3 November 1757, *LTW* 2:229–30, cf. to President John Blair, 30 January 1758, *WW* 2:162–3; from Blair, 5 February 1758, *LTW* 2:262; *JTF* 1:165–7, 183; Morton 2:698.

30. To Robinson, 5 August 1756, *PWC* 3:326; from Robinson, 19 August, 366; from Dinwiddie, 19 August, 359.

31. To Dinwiddie, 23 September 1756, *PWC* 3:414–15; to Lieutenant Colonel Adam Stephen, 23 October, 440–2; Remarks on the Council of War, 5 November, 450–2; to Dinwiddie, 24 November, 4:32; 2 December, 34–6; from Dinwiddie, 30 September, 3:424; 26 October, 443; 16 November, 4:26; Minutes of Council, 15 November, 27–8; from Dinwiddie, 10 December, 50–5; to Captain William Bronaugh, 17 December, 59, cf. to Dinwiddie, 19 December, 62–3.

32. To Robinson, 19 December 1756, *PWC* 4:67–9, cf. from Robinson, 31 December, 74.

33. To Dinwiddie, 19 December 1756, *PWC* 4:64–5; from Dinwiddie, 27 December, 72; 2 February 1757, 107.

34. To John Campbell, Earl of Loudoun, 10 January 1757, *PWC* 4:79–93; to Captain James Cuninghame, 28 January, 105–7; from Cuninghame, 27 February, 111–12.

35. *PWC* 4:89–90; Memorial to John Campbell, Earl of Loudoun, Philadelphia, 23 March 1757, 120–1. John Alden reports that GW "attacked" Dinwiddie in this report to Dinwiddie's superior and suggests that this fact may have been communicated to the lieutenant governor by one of his fellow Scots, Loudoun or Loudoun's aide Cuninghame, thus deepening the growing rift between GW and Dinwiddie: *Washington*, 57–9. The passage implicitly criticizing Dinwiddie said in part: "The orders I receive are full of ambiguity. I am left, like a wanderer in a wilderness, to proceed at hazard. I am answerable for consequences, and blamed, without the priviledge of defence!" Alden was apparently relying on the Fitzpatrick edition of GW's writings, which, without editorial comment, includes the statements in the body of the letter seemingly as sent: *WW* 2:17. The editors of *PWC* conclude that GW either added this passage to his recopied letter-book years later, revealing his "lingering bitterness," or, having included it in the original letter-book, "thought better of it and deleted it from the copy he sent to Loudoun": 4:92n.29. The latter seems more likely.

36. *JTF* 1:172.

37. To Dinwiddie, 10 March 1757, *PWC* 4:112–15. For the high opinion of some regulars regarding the Virginia Regiment see the letter from Captain George Mercer, 17 August, 372–4.

38. See the letter from Joseph Chew, 13 July 1757, *PWC* 4:301, in reply to a missing letter from GW, but agreeing with GW's criticisms of "those in Places & Power."

39. *LTW* 2:53; *PWC* 4:127–8n.2; DSF 2:241–2.

CHAPTER FIVE

1. From Dinwiddie, 24 September 1757, *PWC* 4:422; to Dinwiddie, 5 October 1757, *WW* 2:141, cf. *PWC* 4:24–5, 29–33, 199, 386, 397.

2. For Fairfax soliciting appointments: *PWC* 3:109–10, 124–5, 168, 247–8; 4:310–11, 364, 392, 397, 408–9, 422. For other solicitations and GW's increasing resistance see: *PWC* 2:61, 65–8, 81–2, 212–13, 245–6, 279, 319–20; 3:6–8, 101, 170, 185, 190, 242, 259–60, 317, 454–6; 4:123–4, 303, 359–60, 368, 386; *LTW* 2:209–10, 283–4, 287–8, 292–4, 298–300; *WW* 2:178, 197–8, 207, 214, 233. For GW's efforts on behalf of his own friends: *PWC* 1:312, 333; 3:3, 4n; 4:109–10; *LTW* 2:211–12, 248–50, 266, 376–7; 3:5–6, 19–21, 134–5, 137, 151–4; *WW* 2:244–5, 281–2.

3. I am grateful to Robert Middlekauff for first suggesting this to me. See also Higginbotham, *Washington*, 22, 31–3; Orders and Address, 8 January 1756, *PWC* 2:256–8.

4. To Colonel John Stanwix, 4 March 1758, *WW* 2:166–7; 10 April, 172–3; to Colonel Thomas Gage, 12 April, 176–7, cf. *WW* 2:22, 135, 142, 144–5, 150–1, 154–5; Knollenberg 63, 168; from Sir John St. Clair, 20 April 1758, *LTW* 2:279; from Brigade Major Francis Halkett, 25 June, 330.

5. To Robinson, 1 September 1758, *WW* 2:277–8; to Major Francis Halkett, 2 August, 261; to Fauquier, 2 September, 281.

6. *WW* 2:230–2, 235–83 passim, 291, 295, 300; "Coll. Washington is arrived from Williamsburg. . . . I find that the Virgians are disatisfied with the Whole Army taking the route of Pensylvania," Sir John St. Clair to Bouquet, 9 June 1758, [Henry Bouquet], *Papers of Henry Bouquet*, ed. S. K. Stevens et al., Harrisburg, 1951– , 3 volumes to date, 2:60; James Young to Richard Peters, 22 July 1758, Hazard, *Pennsylvania Archives*, 3:489; John Armstrong to Richard Peters, 3 October, 552, "The Virginians are much chagrin'd at the Opening of the Road thro' this Government & Colonel Washington has been a good deal Sanguine & Obstinate upon the Occasion, but the presence of the General has been of Use on this as on other Accounts." At the beginning of September, GW also apparently feared that his fellow Virginians would include him in the blame for the slow progress of the expedition, cf. the letter from William Ramsay, 3 September 1758, *LTW* 3:81.

7. Forbes to Bouquet, 23 September 1758, John Forbes, *Writings of General John Forbes*, ed. Alfred P. James, Menasha, Wisconsin, 1938, 219–21. For evidence of Forbes's and Bouquet's growing irritation with GW: *Forbes Writings*, 171, 173, 199; *Bouquet Papers* 2:277–8, 291, 522–3. On using Braddock's road for supply: to Forbes, 16 November 1758, *WW* 2:303. Other Virginians

agreed with GW's criticism of the Pennsylvanians: *LTW* 2:377–9; 3:33, 156; Robert Munford to Colonel Theodorick Bland, Sr., 4 August 1758, Theodorick Bland, Jr., *The Bland Papers, Being a Selection from the Manuscripts of Colonel Theodorick Bland, Jr.*, ed. Charles Campbell, Petersburg, Virginia, 1840–3, 2 volumes, 1:13–14.

8. To Bouquet, 21 July 1758, *WW* 2:243; 28 August, 275–6; to Robinson, 1 September, 276, cf. *WW* 2:268, 276–8, 278–80.

9. Knollenberg 69; DSF 2:357, 359, cf. JTF 1:217.

10. *LTW* 3:117, 125–6; DSF 2:355–6.

11. DSF 2:353–65.

12. From Joseph Chew, 17 July 1758, *LTW* 2:391–2; from Charles Dick, 25 July, 386; from William Henry Fairfax, 25 July, 387–8; from Robert Rutherford, 26 July, 389–90; from Captain John Hall, 22 December, 3:140. Colonial newspapers mentioned GW after two parties of Virginian troops accidentally fired on one another in November: *Pennsylvania Gazette*, 30 November 1758, 2; *New York Gazette*, 4 December 1758, 2; *South Carolina Gazette*, 8–15 December 1758, 1. *South Carolina Gazette* also reported a skirmish in which GW commanded Virginia reinforcements, 1–8 December 1758, 4. Accounts of the conclusion of the campaign failed to mention him: *Pennsylvania Gazette*, 14 December 1758, 1, 3; 28 December, 2, 3; *New York Gazette*, 18 December 1758, 1–2; 1 January 1759, 1–2; *Boston Gazette, or Country Journal*, 18 December 1758, 2; 25 December, 2; *South Carolina Gazette*, 22–29 December 1758, 1; *Scots Magazine*, 21 (January 1759), 44–5; *Gentleman's Magazine*, 29 (January 1759), 39–40. On GW's resignation see the letter to Governor Fauquier, 9 December 1758, *WW* 2:316–17; DSF 2:398–9; JTF 1:221–3.

13. To William Fairfax, 11 August 1754, *PWC* 1:183–8; to Robert Orme, 28 July 1755, 347, 348n.7; to Andrew Lewis, 6 September, 2:23; Address, 8 January 1756, 256–8; to John Robinson, 24 April, 3:48–52; to Robinson, 5 August, 323–33; to Dinwiddie, 9 November, 4:1–11; to Lord Loudoun, 10 January 1757, 79–93; DSF 1:xv–xvii, 269–70, 289, 428–9; 2:99–102, 180, 198–9, 207, 252, 369–80; Higginbotham, *Washington*, 14–15, 18–20, 39–40.

According to one military historian, GW's solution to one of the tactical problems of Forbes's advancing army clearly reflected some knowledge of current military technique. Evidently he also tried to learn more of the art of soldiering from his experience with General Forbes, for he later acquired the English translation of a recent French military treatise of which Forbes thought highly: Oliver L. Spaulding, Jr., "The Military Studies of George Washington," *American Historical Review*, 29 (1923–4), 677–8; to Forbes, 8 October 1758, *WW* 2:295–8; Griffin 202, 541. For opinions of GW as a soldier: DSF 2:369–80; from Captain George Mercer, 17 August 1757, *PWC* 4:372–3; Ambler 120.

14. To John Campbell, Earl of Loudoun, 10 January 1757, *PWC* 4:83, 85; Higginbotham, *Washington*, 34–7; Carp, "Early American Military," 276–7.

15. Address of the Virginia Regimental Officers to GW, 31 December 1758, *LTW* 3:143–6, cf. 2:247, 389–90, 3:3, 80, 97, 137, 138–9, 142, 150, 151; Robert Munford to Theodorick Bland, Sr., 6 July 1758, *Bland Papers* 1:10;

JHB, 1758–1761, 26 February 1759, 66–67, resolution of thanks to GW for his years of military service to the colony; DSF 2:317, 383–5.

16. Captain George Mercer, GW's military aide, 1760, quoted in Bryan 24; DSF 3:6; JTF 1:191–2. Different sources, including GW himself, give different heights and weights for him. He himself said he was six feet tall, but at his death his secretary Tobias Lear measured him at six feet three and one-half inches. GW may have put on weight by the time of the Revolution, when he weighed in at around 200 pounds: JTF 1:80.

17. Ferling 312–13, analyzing Virginia Regiment size rolls, reports the median height of native Virginians as five feet eight inches; nearly half of the American-born were that height or taller, but the majority of the soldiers were under five feet seven inches.

18. To Fauquier, 2 December 1758, WW 2:312–14.

19. To Sharpe, 24 April 1754, PWC 1:86, cf. 83, 88, 130; 3:353–4.

20. On usage of *country, nation,* and *national: Oxford English Dictionary, s.v.;* Ian R. Christie and Benjamin W. Labaree, *Empire or Independence, 1760–1776,* New York, 1976, 19; PWC 1:127, 200, 207, 221–3, 351; 2:8, 12, 19, 22, 29, 66, 85, 103, 172; to Dinwiddie, 10 March 1757, 4:113.

21. Proclamation, 15 August 1756, PWC 3:353–4. GW's younger contemporaries shared his understanding of the relationship between self-interest and the public good. See the letter from Adam Stephen, 29 March 1756, 2:324–5; from Captain Robert McKenzie (Mackenzie), 18 February 1757, 4:109–10; from Joseph Chew, 13 July, 301.

22. From Robert Orme, 10 November 1755, PWC 2:166; from Thomas Gage, 10 May 1756, 3:115; from Joseph Chew, 14 March 1757, 4:116; 13 July, 301; 10 May 1758, LTW 2:301; from Robert Rutherford, 31 July, 3:4.

23. To Colonel William Fitzhugh, 15 November 1754, PWC 1:226.

24. Knollenberg 44–6, 160–1; JTF 1:112, 121–2; Alden, *Washington,* 34; John Alden, *Robert Dinwiddie, Servant of the Crown,* Williamsburg, Virginia, 1973, 94–5, 100–1; Marcus Cunliffe, *George Washington, Man and Monument,* revised edition, New York, 1982 (originally published Boston, 1958), 43–5; DSF 2:388–96. Higginbotham offers an interpretation similar to the one advanced here: *Washington,* 22, 118, 120.

25. Gwenda Morgan has shown that an angry sense of the neglect and mistreatment of their colony was for Virginians a primary result of the war. "Virginia and the French and Indian War: A Case Study of the War's Effects on Imperial Relations," *The Virginia Magazine of History and Biography,* 81 (1973), 23–48; cf. Baker-Crothers, passim; Curtis P. Nettels, *George Washington and American Independence,* Westport, Conn., 1976 (originally published Boston, 1951), 61–4. Following Braddock's defeat, Charles Chauncy of Massachusetts complained that the "military merit" of colonial officers had been neglected in the distribution of regular army appointments for service in America, that British officers were appointed instead, and that provincial officers were subordinated to them: [Chauncy], *Letter,* 8–10.

26. WW 2:288.

27. To the Officers of the Virginia Regiment, 10 January 1759, reprinted in JTF 1:349–50; to Richard Washington, 7 May 1759, WW 2:322; 20 September, 337.

CHAPTER SIX

1. "Many other men matured after 25," wrote Freeman; "Washington was almost transformed": DSF 3:448. As Freeman described him, GW the provincial officer was diligent, capable, and courageous, but fundamentally rather preoccupied with his own ambition and reputation. From the outset of the Revolution, he displayed the modesty, self-mastery, and public-mindedness that won him lasting fame. Freeman attributed the contrast to a dramatic change in GW's personal character, which he regarded as one of the major surprises in his research. He asserted that GW had given up ambition for public honor and sought office only out of a sense of duty. This perceived transformation resulted from private rather than public experiences. The difficulties of GW's increasingly complicated business enterprises supposedly taught him patience and softened his acquisitive instincts with a growing spirit of charity. The trusteeships and security for debts he undertook for friends and neighbors seemingly fostered tolerance of human foibles and a sense of responsibility for others. His stepdaughter's illness and death and his stepson's troublesome behavior, according to Freeman, engendered compassion toward human suffering. Unnumbered small acts of charity were in reality, Freeman believed, "spiritual exercises" that wrought vast changes in GW's character: DSF 1:xiii–xv; 2:388–99; 3:ix, xii–xiii, xxviii–xxix, xxxvi–xxxvii, 26–7, 35, 63, 71–5, 88, 121n, 184–5, 204, 210, 230, 234–5, 253, 262–5, 270–1, 279–80, 286, 288, 318–20, 325–6, 336, 337, 338, 372, 396–7, 448–50.

Evidently, though, Freeman was dissatisfied with his attempt to account for the change he perceived, for he finally called it "a mystery, . . . beyond documentary explanation": DSF 3:xiii. His interpretation remains dissatisfying for two reasons. He isolated GW from the political, social, and intellectual context that shaped him and in which he moved. His focus on personal rather than public experiences, influences, and concerns forced him to shift GW abruptly from a minor to the major role in the revolutionary drama, offering only his limited previous military experience and his residence in politically strategic Virginia as the reasons his contemporaries suddenly turned to him.

See also JTF 1:229, 249–50, 317–18; Cunliffe, *Washington*, 41; Alden, *Washington*, 71, 81, 83; Robert F. Jones, *George Washington*, Boston, 1979, 36–7; Rupert Hughes, *George Washington*, New York, 1926–30, 3 volumes, 1:336–7, 365–9, 372; 2:34, 160, 186, 212–13. Knollenberg suggested that the biographers have given insufficient attention to politics in this period of GW's life, though he himself did not explore the subject in depth: 101–6. Nathaniel Stephenson and Waldo H. Dunn, *George Washington*, New York, 1940, 2 volumes, 1:208–10, 221–4, 230–2, emphasized GW's political activities and acumen, as did Bernard Faÿ in an otherwise superficial book, *George Washington: Republican Aristocrat*, Boston, 1931, 151–65, 273.

2. DSF 2:316–18; Griffith 90–1, 94; Charles Sydnor, *American Revolutionaries in the Making*, New York, 1965 (originally published as *Gentlemen Freeholders*, Chapel Hill, North Carolina, 1952), 66; from Gabriel Jones, 6 July 1758, *LTW* 2:343–4; from Colonel John Carlyle, 14 July, 360; from Colonel William Fairfax, 25 July, 387.

3. From Lt. Charles Smith, 20 July 1758, *LTW* 2:373; from Gabriel Jones,

6 July, 343–4; from John Kirkpatrick, 6 July, 346; from James Wood, 7 July, 349. Another veteran politician, former governor James Glen of South Carolina, agreed with their counsel. Having visited GW and his command at Fort Cumberland, Glen wrote from Raystown urging the necessity of his presence at Winchester, "for one day at least": Glen to GW and Colonel William Byrd, 19 July, 365–6. Lord Fairfax to George William Fairfax, 5 July 1758, quoted in DSF 2:318.

4. From John Kirkpatrick, 6 July 1758, *LTW* 2:346; from Robert Rutherford, 26 July, 389–90.

5. From Lt. Colonel Adam Stephen, 19 July 1758, *LTW* 2:366–7; to Bouquet, 19 July, *WW* 2:241; DSF 2:318–19.

6. To Bouquet, 21 July 1758, *WW* 2:242–3.

7. GW kept two copies of the polls, alphabetizing one. Both are in Washington Papers, Library of Congress. The alphabetized poll is reprinted in *LTW* 2:400–9. My count of the votes differs from those of others. Joseph Carroll, who was hired by Lieutenant Charles Smith to record the poll for GW, *LTW* 2:398, incorrectly totaled: GW 310, Martin 240, West 199, Van Swearingen 45. Sydnor gives Carroll's totals: 67. When alphabetizing the poll, GW's totals were: GW 309, Martin 239, West 199, Van Swearingen 45. Freeman reports this count: DSF 2:320. Griffith reports those figures and yet another count: 95, 189. I count a total of 397 voters. Flexner gives the total as 396: JTF 1:211. He seems to have arrived at this figure by adding up GW's totals at the end of his alphabetized list and dividing that sum by two. This cannot be correct, because two men voted for only one candidate each. Freeman gives the total number of voters as 391: DSF 2:320.

GW received political intelligence during the election campaign from Jones, 6 July 1758, *LTW* 2:343–4; John Kirkpatrick, 6 July, 345–6; Wood, 7 July, 349–50; Colonel John Carlyle, 14 July, 360; Edward Snickers, 19 July, 367–8; Lt. Charles Smith, 20 July, 372–3 (who helped to run the campaign and to supervise the voting and who often looked after personal business for GW); Robert Rutherford, Esq. (gentleman, town builder, and promoter of development of the navigation of the upper Potomac), 20 July, 374. GW received letters of congratulation from Captain John McNeill, 24 July, 381; Jones, 24 July, 382; Thomas Walker, 24 July, 383; Smith, 24 July, 384–5; Carlyle, 25 July, 385; Charles Dick, 25 July, 386; Colonel William Fairfax, 25 July, 387; Captain Robert Stewart, 25 July, 388; Rutherford, 26 July, 389–90. GW thanked his campaign managers: to Jones, 29 July 1758, *WW* 2:249; to Wood (July 1758), 251.

8. *LTW* 2:397–8; 3:15; Election Accounts, 24 July 1758, 2:398–400; *WW* 2:251.

9. See n.7 above.

10. *WW* 2:333, 334n; [Daniel Parke Custis], "Catalogue of the Library of Daniel Parke Custis," *The Virginia Magazine of History and Biography*, 17 (1909), 406; "A List of Books at Mt. Vernon 23 July 1783," Washington Papers, Library of Congress.

11. To Richard Washington, 20 September 1759, *WW* 2:337; 10 August 1760, 345; 14 July 1761, 361–2; 20 October, 371; to Robert Cary and Com-

pany, 3 November, 373; 30 September 1762, 385; to Capel and Osgood Hanbury, 26 April 1763, 392; to Cary, 26 April, 395. GW's interest in relations with the Indians was also reflected in his acquisition of published copies of the Lancaster Treaty with the Six Nations of 1744 and the Treaty with the Catawbas and Cherokees of 1756: Griffin 198–9. His subsequent vigorous activities in land speculation necessitated knowledge of these matters.

12. From Colonel George Mercer, 16 September 1759, *LTW* 3:158–63; from Captain Robert Mackenzie, 12 August 1760, 193–4; a copy of Attakukulla's Speech to Colonel Byrd, 7 July 1761, 220–2; a series of letters from Captain Robert Stewart, 16 January 1759, 150–3; undated, 157; 28 September, 163–9; 8 March 1760, 176–7; 14 April, 178–80; 14 May, 180–2; 3 June, 183–6; 2 October, 195–200; 13 February 1761, 200–3; 12 March, 204–10; 6 April, 211–13; 10 June, 215–17; 7 July, 218–19; 20 July, 223–4. To Captain Robert Mackenzie, 20 November 1760, *WW* 2:355–6; to Robert Stewart, 27 April 1763, 396–8; 2 May, 399–400; 13 August, 402–4; 1:171–2, 183–4.

13. *JHB, 1758–1761*, 57, 113, 129; DSF 3:7–12.

14. DSF 3:30–3; *JHB, 1758–1761*, 139, 141, 142, 143, 147. GW also served on the committee to tender to Captain Robert Stobo the congratulations of the House on his safe return from captivity in Canada: 150.

15. On the March session: DSF 3:35; from Captain Robert Stewart, 3 June 1760, *LTW* 3:184. Stewart's letter indicates the reason for GW's absence. Overlooking it, Freeman concludes that GW "excused himself" from the session because "he did not think he should interrupt his farm work for what he probably expected to be a brief gathering. . . ." On the October session: DSF 3:48–52; *JHB, 1758–1761*, 188. Freeman thought the Burgesses "probably availed themselves" of GW's experience.

16. From Stewart, 12 March 1761 (two letters), *LTW* 3:203, 204–10. The first letter indicates that GW had requested the information contained in the second. From Stewart, 6 April, 211, refers to GW's letter of 27 March: DSF 3:57, 59. Freeman makes no mention of the letters from Stewart.

17. *JHB, 1758–1761*, 223, 225, 227, 240, 241, 248, 252, 253, 254; DSF 3:58–9; Mays, *Edmund Pendleton*, 1:153–4.

18. To Robert Cary and Company, 3 November 1761, *WW* 2:373; to Peter Stover, 9 November, 373–4; *JHB, 1761–1765*, 7, 10.

19. From Stewart, 25 January 1762, *LTW* 3:231–3; DSF 3:68–72. Freeman concludes that GW probably stayed home because he anticipated the outcome of what he knew would be a brief session, but finds his absence "dramatic evidence of the extent to which he had separated himself from the career that once had held his heart. . . . " He was devoting himself to his private affairs rather than advocating "proper compensation for faithful officers and men who had obeyed his orders."

20. *JHB, 1761–1765*, 45, 92, 94, 97, 100–1, 111, 117, 140; DSF 3:73–5, 82–4.

21. *PWC* 1:236; 4:163, 204, 352; *WW* 2:404; from Captain Robert Stewart, 13 February 1761, *LTW* 3:202; DSF 3:55–6, 61–2. Freeman wrote that Mercer, having declared himself a candidate, "had become in a sense Wash-

ington's associate precisely as Martin had been in 1758. Washington had not then learned that he fared best when he ran alone; he and Mercer consequently made common cause": DSF 3:55. See also Stephenson and Dunn 1:229–30, 255–6; Griffith 96.

22. *LTW* 3:201–2.

23. Jay B. Hubbell and Douglass Adair, "Robert Munford's *The Candidates; or The Humours of a Virginia Election*," *William and Mary Quarterly*, third series, 5 (1948), 217–57, especially 221, 223–4, 237, 238, 243–4, 245, 252, 257. Munford's play depicts a Burgess election in which Worthy, who prefers private to public life, agrees to stand for office and joins interests with Wou'dbe. He calls upon his "interest" with the yeomen freeholders, their trust in him, in order to secure election of his friend and to shut unworthy gentrymen out of office. The voters heed his advice. The play's outcome represents the ideal of traditional deferential politics. Richard R. Beeman, "Robert Munford and the Political Culture of Frontier Virginia," *Journal of American Studies*, 12 (1978), 169–83, compares the play to the rough-and-tumble reality of some elections in recently settled Southside Virginia. Both Munford's play and Beeman's discussion offer intriguing parallels with the 1761 Frederick election.

24. Beeman, "Robert Munford," 177–8.

25. From Stewart, 13 February 1761, *LTW* 3:202, cf. Hubbell and Adair 221.

26. From Stewart, 13 February 1761, *LTW* 3:203 (McNeill was most likely Captain John McNeill, another former comrade from the Virginia Regiment); from Stewart, 12 March, 203–4.

27. See nn.15–17 above.

28. To Captain Thomas Van Swearingen, 15 May 1761, WW 2:358. See Hubbell and Adair 240–1, 242 for Munford's depiction of genuine and feigned gentry regard for common folk.

29. On the election duties of Virginia sheriffs: Sydnor 27–31, 68–9.

30. To Captain Van Swearingen, 15 May 1761, WW 2:358–9. Fitzpatrick misprints "handle" as "trouble." Flexner gives the correct quotation: JTF 1:256. Flexner recognizes the ethically dubious nature of GW's proposal to the sheriff but fails to analyze the incident, choosing simply to quote that part of the letter. He ignores GW's circulation of material against Stephen: 255. Freeman says of GW's suggestion: he was "practical in politics as in everything else." He paraphrases GW's statement that "as Sheriff I know you cannot appear in this, nor would I by any mean have you do any thing that can give so designing a Man as Colo. Stevens the least handle," to read that the "Sheriff should not do any thing that could 'give so designing a man as Colonel Stephen' any ground for making trouble" (following his usual practice, Freeman corrected and modernized GW's orthography). Ignoring GW's violation of the election law, Freeman interpreted GW's entire campaign against Stephen as a defense of his principles in a contest with a man who had proved himself unprincipled: DSF 3:61–62, cf. Hughes 3:210; Stephenson and Dunn 1:230.

31. "A Copy of the Poll taken at the Election of Burgesses in Frederick County this 18th day of May 1761," Washington Papers, Library of Congress. The 1761 poll usually omits titles, but comparison with the 1758 poll reveals

that in addition to Martin, Stephen won the votes of the Rev. Mr. John Hoge, Capt. John Funk, Capt. John Denton, and Col. Morgan Morgan. Martin, Hoge, and Denton all voted for GW, while Funk and Morgan supported Mercer. Col. Morgan had also voted against GW in 1758. Members of the gentry who supported GW and Mercer included Col. James Wood, Col. John Hite, Lt. Charles Smith, Dr. James Craik, and three men identified on the 1758 poll as gentlemen, Alexander Wodrow, Henry Moore, and GW's brother-in-law, Fielding Lewis. The first two voters in 1761 were GW's brothers John and Samuel. A few minutes later, a third brother, Charles, joined them in voting for him and Mercer. Fitzpatrick, Freeman, and Griffith mistakenly credit Mercer with only 399 votes: WW 2:359n; DSF 3:62; Griffith 96, 160. The error originated with Thomas Wood, "One of the poll takers," who copied the poll for GW. Twice listing the totals, he gave Mercer 400 votes in one place and 399 in another. Griffith (190) also mistakenly reports the turnout as 601. This number too originated with Wood, who took the final tallies for each of the candidates and added them together to obtain a total of 1202. For some reason, he divided this figure by two to obtain 601. Three votes were thrown away on Robert Rutherford, Col. John Hite, and Henry Brinker. On GW paying Mercer: DSF 3:62.

32. For further comment on that code and its advantages for the gentry: Sydnor 70–1.

33. Hubbell and Adair 252; "A Letter from George Washington to Andrew Burnaby, 1761," contrib. Henry Field, *William and Mary Quarterly*, second series, 22 (1942), to Burnaby, 27 July, 221–2.

34. Freeman discerned no political ambition in GW. Writing of the impending 1761 reelection campaign, he concluded that "it was not a pleasant prospect for a man who desired most of all to remain at home and to attend to his own affairs; but if it had to be done, Washington would do it. Membership in the House of Burgesses was at once the duty and the avocation of a gentleman. He could not discharge the duty if he shunned the contest": DSF 3:56.

CHAPTER SEVEN

1. WW 2:336–7, 345.

2. To Richard Washington, 15 April 1757, WW 2:22–3; 10 September, 124; to Anthony Bacon and Company, 10 September, 125; to Thomas Knox, 26 December, 159–60; to Washington, 26 December, 160–1; to Knox, January 1758, 161; to Washington, 18 March, 168; 7 May 1759, 321–2; to James Gildart, 12 June, 326; DSF 3:17–18, 22, 34.

3. To Robert Cary and Company, 2 July 1759, WW 2:327; 25 November, 338; to Capel and Osgood Hanbury, 25 November, 338; to Mr. Farrel, 30 July 1760, 343; to Richard Washington, 10 August, 344; to James Gildart, 3 April 1761, 358; to Crosbies and Trafford, 6 March 1765, 421–2; to Cary, 20 September, 429; from Crosbies and Trafford, 3 August 1765, *LTW* 3:271–2; from Thomas Eden and Company, 31 May 1774, 5:7; to Osgood Hanbury and Company, 4 August 1774, WW 3:234–5; DSF 3:368, cf. to Stewart and Campbell, 4 September 1766, 2:442.

4. To Robert Cary and Company, 20 September 1759, WW 2:328; 25 No-

vember, 338; 30 November, 339; 28 April 1760, 342; 24 October, 353; 3 April 1761, 356–7; to James Gildart, 3 April, 358; to Richard Washington, 14 July, 361; to Cary, 12 October, 368; 28 May 1762, 376, 378–9; 20 June, 379; 18 September, 380–2; 30 September, 384; 26 April 1763, 393–4; 27 September, 404–5; DSF 3:23–4, 33–4, 45–7, 52, 60–1, 70, 76, 81, 82–3, 84–5, 88–9.

5. To Robert Cary and Company, 28 September 1760, WW 2:350; 18 September 1762, 380; 27 September 1763, 405–6.

6. WW 2:346, 349, 351, 353, 356–7, 376–8, 379, 381–2, 391–2, 401, 404–5, 412; DSF 3:34, 46–7, 52, 56, 76, 82–3, 84–6, 90, 111–12, 114–15.

7. Breen, *Tobacco Culture*, 40–83.

8. To Robert Cary and Company, 28 May 1762, WW 2:378.

9. See above, n.5, and to Cary, 20 September 1765, WW 2:427–8; DSF 3:88, 144–5.

10. WW 2:335n, 342n; Invoices to Robert Cary and Company, 20 September 1759, 330–6; Invoice, 27 September 1763, 406 and n.; to Charles Lawrence, 10 August 1764, 420–1; Carson 94–6; DSF 3:115–16.

11. Breen, *Tobacco Culture*, 85, 91, 92–3, 124–7, 129–32, 142–7.

12. To Robert Cary and Company, 1 August 1761, WW 2:362–4; 1 May 1764, 414–15; 10 August, 416–18, cf. to Cary, 10 August 1760, 349–50; 26 April 1763, 393; to Robert Stewart, 27 April, 396–8; DSF 3:39, 63–4, 84–6, 88–91, 103, 110–12, 114–16; Breen, *Tobacco Culture*, 148–9.

13. To Robert Cary and Company, 10 August 1764, WW 2:416–18.

14. Griffin 555–61, 172, 25–6, 41–2.

15. To Robert Stewart, 2 May 1763, WW 2:399.

16. Griffin 172, where Peyton Randolph is mistakenly identified as the author.

17. To Stewart, 2 May 1763, WW 2:399–400. During the May session, GW served on a committee to hear petitions from officers and soldiers who had served in the regiment: *JHB, 1761–1765*, 175–6, 179–80, 185–7.

18. To Burwell Bassett, 5 July 1763, WW 2:400–1; to Stewart, 13 August, 402–4; to Richard Washington, 27 September, 408–9; DSF 3:97–8.

19. DSF 3:107–9, 117–20; *JHB, 1761–1765*, 230, 247–8; *Fauquier Papers* 3:1194–6. Among other matters, the commission recommended that Adam Stephen be allowed 10s. per diem, the authorized pay of a county lieutenant on active duty, rather than the 20s. he had requested as county lieutenant of both Hampshire and Frederick. GW also sat on a special committee to investigate charges that Adam Stephen had committed fraud while commanding militia troops. The House convicted Stephen of two minor charges, but otherwise praised his conduct. GW remarked sarcastically about Stephen: to Captain Robert Stewart, 13 August 1763, WW 2:404.

20. DSF 3:127–39. For GW's probable early departure see 139n. *JHB* failed to record his presence.

21. To Burwell Bassett, 2 August 1765, WW 2:424. The results of the vote on 16 July 1765 were: GW 201, West 148, Posey 131. Washington Papers, Library of Congress; Griffith 160; DSF 3:141.

22. To Robert Cary and Company, 20 September 1765, WW 2:427–31. I have rearranged some of GW's repetitious arguments.

23. *WW* 2:427–30; to Crosbies and Trafford, 6 March 1765, 421–2.

24. *WW* 2:429–31; to Capel and Osgood Hanbury, 20 September 1765, 432–3; to James Gildart, 20 September, 433.

25. What is remarkable is the relatively short time GW had devoted to tobacco production and the relative ease and decisiveness of his break with the tobacco regime. He apparently had decided early in 1765 to find alternatives to tobacco but necessarily had to stay with it until he came up with a substitute. Thus, one could argue that he had only committed six years of his own serious effort to the enterprise. He may have been considering shifting to wheat as early as 1763, when he signed a contract to deliver surplus wheat to two Alexandria merchants. For a different view: Breen, *Tobacco Culture*, 81–2.

26. To Robert Cary and Company, 20 September 1765, Washington Papers, Library of Congress, quoted in this and the next three paragraphs. This portion of GW's letter is not printed in *WW* 2:427–31 because the phrasing closely resembles that in a letter to Francis Dandridge, 20 September 1765, *WW* 2:425–6. In fact, GW's language was more pointed to Cary; to Capel and Osgood Hanbury, 25 July 1767, 466.

27. To Francis Dandridge, 20 September 1765, *WW* 2:425–6; DSF 3: 142–4. On scarcity of a circulating medium: Fauquier to Earl of Halifax, 14 June 1765, *Fauquier Papers* 3:1258–9.

28. DSF 3:150; Mason to GW and Fairfax, 23 December 1765, in [George Mason], *The Papers of George Mason*, ed. Robert A. Rutland, Chapel Hill, North Carolina, 1970, 3 volumes, 1:60–1; "Scheme for Replevying Goods and Distress for Rent" (23 December 1765), 61–5; also in *LTW* 3:282–6; originals in Washington Papers, Library of Congress. Freeman is correct that GW's leadership at this time was not "conspicuous," but he fails to note Mason's "Scheme" or GW's involvement with it: DSF 3:153n. GW had trouble collecting at least one debt because of the scarcity of hard money: from Col. Thomas Moore, 21 October 1766, *LTW* 3:288–90.

29. To Robert Cary and Company, 21 July 1766, *WW* 2:440; to Capel and Osgood Hanbury, 25 July 1767, 466.

30. Louise B. Dunbar, "A Study of 'Monarchical' Tendencies in the United States from 1776 to 1801," *University of Illinois Studies in the Social Sciences*, 10 (1922), 9–10; William D. Liddle, "'A Patriot King or None': Lord Bolingbroke and the American Renunciation of George III," *Journal of American History*, 65 (1978–9), 958–60; William D. Liddle, "A Patriot King, or None: American Public Attitudes toward George III and the British Monarchy, 1754–1776," Ph.D. diss., Claremont Graduate School, 1970, 191–222; Pauline Maier, *From Resistance to Revolution, Colonial Radicals and the Development of American Opposition to Britain, 1765–1776*, New York, 1974 (originally published New York, 1972), 100–6, 110.

31. Jack P. Greene, "*Virtus et Libertas*: Political Culture, Social Change, and the Origins of the American Revolution in Virginia, 1763–1776," in Jeffrey J. Crow and Larry E. Tise, eds., *The Southern Experience in the American Revolution*, Chapel Hill, North Carolina, 1979, copyright 1978, 55–108; *JHB*, 1766–1769, 14–15, 22; GW also served on a special committee to consider a bill respecting entailed lands of Ralph Wormeley, 54, cf. 45, 52, 55, 58;

DSF 3:173, 175 and n. For evidence of respect for GW: Francis Fauquier to the Bishop of London, 6 November 1765, *Fauquier Papers* 3:1298.

32. To Cary and Company, 17 May 1767, WW 2:454; 20 July, 461–2; 5 May 1768, 484–5; to Hanbury, 5 May, 485; to Cary, 25 July 1769, 513–14; to Hanbury, 25 July, 515; 1 June 1774, 3:217; to Cary, 1 June, 220; DSF 3:152, 176, 179, 193, 242, 263, 347.

33. On prices and charges: to Cary and Company, 23 June 1766, WW 2:435–6; 21 July, 440; 20 July 1767, 461–2; 5 May 1768, 484–5; 20 June, 491–2, cf. to Stewart and Campbell, 4 September 1766, 442. On damage: to Captain Joshua Pollard, 22 August 1766, 441–2; to James Gildart, 22 September, 443–4; 25 February 1768, 481–2; DSF 3:207.

34. To Cary and Company, 20 September 1765, WW 2:428–9; 23 June 1766, 435–6; 21 July, 439–40; 22 August, 440–1.

35. Griffin 83, 228. Other publications in GW's library also evidence his interest in public affairs. He had a sermon "Upon the Peace" (Williamsburg, 1763), a panegyric on liberty preached at the conclusion of the Seven Years' War by the Reverend Mr. James Horrocks, president of William and Mary College. He followed the proceedings of Parliament and political affairs at the center of the Empire, in 1762 ordering Dodsley's *Annual Register*, "from the beging to the prest year, inclusive," and probably around the same time acquired a published collection of parliamentary debates. He obtained the *Annual Registers* for 1750, 1759, 1760, and 1761. The inventory of his estate records *A Collection of the Parliamentary Debates in England, from the year 1668 to the Present Time*, published in 1741: Griffin 531, 43; "A List of Books at Mt. Vernon 23 July 1783," Washington Papers, Library of Congress; Prussing 421.

36. WW 2:426, 431; DSF 3:179, 196, 242–3, 263; Arthur Pierce Middleton, *Tobacco Coast: A Maritime History of Chesapeake Bay in the Colonial Era*, ed. George Carrington Mason, Baltimore, 1984 (originally published Newport News, Virginia, 1953), 178.

37. On hemp and flax: DSF 3:127n, 140, 145, 152, 168, 179, 263; *LTW* 4:161. On wheat and corn: WW 2:422–3, 424, 444–53; 3:89, 114–15, 142, 147, 186, 219–20; *LTW* 4:135–6, 147, 149, 150, 162–3, 167, 168, 172, 174, 180–3, 200, 222, 228, 238, 239, 394; DSF 3:168, 176, 179, 181–2, 186, 195–6, 263, 296, 347. On flour and biscuit: WW 3:109–10, 112, 116, 143, 167, 186, 204, 212–15, 220; *LTW* 4:38, 159–60, 162–3, 174, 187–8, 207, 216–17, 236, 238, 247, 270, 305–10, 322, 373–4, 394; 5:17–18, 72–4, 144, 157; DSF 3:179, 243–4, 263, 267, 277–8, 295–6, 327, 337, 347. On mills: WW 3:63, 109–10, 165, 174–9; *PWR* 2:306; *LTW* 4:131–2, 147, 167, 180–1, 199, 255, 269; 5:105–6, 151; DSF 3:196, 243–4, 263, 267, 287, 290, 294, 308–9, 324–5, 337, 343.

38. On fishing: WW 2:439, 522; 3:25–6, 62, 82, 89, 90, 96–7, 109, 112, 143, 169, 256; *LTW* 4:67–8, 157–8, 159, 174, 217, 247, 374; 5:18, 157; DSF 3:75, 145–6, 179, 243, 254, 263, 267, 287, 290, 294, 337–8, 347; John C. Pearson, "The Fish and Fisheries of Colonial Virginia, Fourth Installment," *William and Mary Quarterly*, second series, 23 (1943), 130–5; Middleton 224–5. On salt: WW 2:364, 379, 438, 482, 494; 28:389–90; *LTW* 3:272; 4:242; Middleton 227–8.

39. On GW's schooner and brig: WW 3:42, 166 and n., 204, 212; *LTW* 4:140, 374; 5:72–3; DSF 3:145–6, 179, 345. On GW exporting products: WW 2:522; 3:25–6, 98–9, 105–7, 109–10, 143, 147, 167, 204, 212–15, 220, 256; *LTW* 4:131–2, 140, 159–60, 174, 206–7, 216–17, 236, 238, 247; DSF 3:243, 295, 296, 327. On buying slaves: WW 3:98–9; DSF 3:244, 278, 294, 296.

CHAPTER EIGHT

1. To George Washington Parke Custis, 7 January 1798, WW 36:117; to William Pearce, 18 December 1793, 33:195; 5 February 1760, *Diaries* 1:232–4; 1 December 1785, 4:243; 6 December, 245, cf. 256, 266–8, 275, 293–4, 296, 312–13, 327–9, 335–7; 2:7, 9–27; WW 30:265; 32:330, 456–9, 462–8; 35:138; 36:112–13, 285–6; 37:460–1, 471–2; DSF 2:385; 3:110; JTF 1:38, 231–2, 272–4. "Method and Exactness are the *fort* of his character": "An Old Soldier," *Gentleman's Magazine*, 17 August 1778, 369.

2. DSF 3:87, 126–8, 142, 177–8, 295; *Virginia Gazette* (Purdie and Dixon), 19 March 1767, 3; *Diaries* 3:234–5; Vote Count for Vestry Elections for Truro Parish, 25 March and 22 July 1765, and Fairfax Parish, 28 March and 25 July 1765, Washington Papers, Library of Congress.

3. Isaac, *Transformation*, 60–5. GW also wanted to maintain "a Family Pew" at Christ Church in Alexandria. A letter to John Dalton, 15 February 1773, WW 3:112–14, indicates the importance of this status symbol to him.

4. *Executive Journals* 6:298; *Diaries* 2:94–5, 109; DSF 3:209.

5. Invoice to Cary and Company, 18 July 1771, WW 3:61; Griffin 527; Burn, *Justice of the Peace* . . . , London, 1770, 4 volumes. GW also owned copies of John Mercer's famous *Abridgement* of the Acts of the Virginia Assembly and Richard Starke's *Virginia Justice*, a compilation of the laws of the colony. GW agreed to receive subscriptions for the latter in his neighborhood: Griffin 535, 530; *Virginia Gazette* (Purdie and Dixon), 21 December 1769, 2; *Virginia Gazette* (Rind), 18 January 1770, 4. For other legal books probably acquired during these years see Griffin 527–37.

6. According to Freeman, the December 1768 poll was: GW 205, John West 175, John Posey 132: DSF 3:209–10; *Diaries* 2:113–14. On the elections in 1769 and 1771: DSF 3:231–2, 287; *Diaries* 2:180; 3:74.

7. *JHB, 1766–1769*, 165. Washington Papers, Library of Congress, contain the Agreement of the Philadelphia Merchants, 6 February 1769; the Philadelphia Merchants' Association, 10 March 1769; the letter of the Philadelphia Merchants to the Annapolis Merchants, 15 March 1769; the reply of the Annapolis Merchants, March 1769; and the Circular Letter of the Annapolis Merchants, 25 March 1769: all in *LTW* 3:349–54.

8. Next nine paragraphs based on letter to Mason, 5 April 1769, WW 2:500–4; *Mason Papers* 1:96–8.

9. Freeman suggests that GW meant "deprivation" or "depreciation": DSF 3:211n. Rutland prints it as "deprivation." GW might also have meant "deprecation."

10. On mounting planter debts: Breen, *Tobacco Culture*, 170–5, 191–2.

11. Breen, *Tobacco Culture*, 160–2, 196.

12. From Mason, 5 April 1769, *Mason Papers* 1:99–100.

13. From Mason, 23 April 1769, *Mason Papers* 1:102–3; "The Nonimportation Association as Corrected by Mason," 103–6. Traditionally Washington scholars have credited Mason with authorship of the Virginia Association of 1769: DSF 3:214; WW 2:500n; LTW 3:349n; JTF 1:311–14. Robert Rutland, editor of Mason's papers, has shown that someone other than Mason must have drafted the plan. He suggests Richard Henry Lee as a likely candidate: *Mason Papers* 1:95–6. *Diaries* 2:143.

14. *Diaries* 2:148–53. In 1768, entrepreneurs on the frontier who hoped to compete with Pennsylvanians in supplying the garrison at Pittsburgh requested GW to urge the Assembly to support establishment of stopping places on the road. Ever eager to see Virginia get its share of such commerce, he urged Acting Governor Blair to intervene with General Gage about this matter: to Blair, 17 May 1768, WW 37:487–8. In 1771, Arthur Lee solicited his patronage in obtaining appointment as the Burgesses' agent in London. "Knowing what influence you very justly possess; I shall greatly depend for success, on your approbation": from Lee, 10 July 1771, LTW 4:75. As the next chapter will show, the settlers on the frontier relied on that influence, and the province as a whole continued to regard GW as Virginia's foremost expert in matters of defense.

He also continued to be highly regarded outside Virginia. Governor Benedict Calvert and other notables from Maryland visited Mount Vernon in December 1771. In May 1773, on a trip to New York, GW was a guest in the homes of Governor Richard Penn of Pennsylvania, Governor William Franklin of New Jersey, and several prominent merchants: *Diaries* 3:75–6, 179–83.

15. Jack P. Greene and Richard M. Jellison, "The Currency Act of 1764 in Imperial-Colonial Relations, 1764–1776," *William and Mary Quarterly*, third series, 18 (1961), 485–518.

16. On the March–April 1767 session: *JHB, 1766–1769*, 128–9, cf. 115–16, 125–8. The Council disapproved of the plan. The House ordered its London agent to lobby for it with the Crown: DSF 3:180–1. On the July 1771 session: *JHB, 1770–1772*, 125.

17. *JHB, 1766–1769*, 211, 228. GW was regularly appointed to special committees, including several of particular interest to him personally. One in December 1769 and another in April 1772 were appointed to draft bills to make the Potomac navigable, while a third during that latter session was called upon to amend the regulations for the inspection of flour: 289, 314, 332–3, 334, 336, 347; *JHB, 1770–1772*, 125, 204, 209, 210, 241, 291, 292, 302, 304–5, 310, 311, 313, 316; DSF 3:218–21, 237, 252, 274, 289–90, 312–16, 348; *Diaries* 2:58, 148, 150–2, 193–7, 199–202, 239–41, 245–9; 3:40–1, 94–7, 165–6, 250–2, 254–6.

In his classic study of political practices in mid-eighteenth-century Virginia, Charles Sydnor ranked nine men as the most powerful members of the House because they chaired the six standing committees and most of the special committees. He also noted a second group of nine important but somewhat less prominent Burgesses. Although not chairmen, these sat on three of the standing committees, including in every case the Committee of Privileges and Elections and the Committee of Propositions and Grievances. In this second group, Sydnor included GW: Sydnor 98–9.

18. On the significance of the Robinson scandal and the Chiswell case: Greene, *"Virtus et Libertas,"* 55–108. On rise of dissenters: Richard R. Beeman and Rhys Isaac, "Cultural Conflict and Social Change in the Revolutionary South: Lunenburg County, Virginia," *Journal of Southern History,* 46 (1980), 525–50; Isaac, "Evangelical Revolt," 345–68; Rhys Isaac, "Religion and Authority: Problems of the Anglican Establishment in Virginia in the Era of the Great Awakening and the Parsons' Cause," *William and Mary Quarterly,* third series, 30 (1973), 3–36. For the creation of the Committee for Religion: *JHB, 1766–1769,* 190, 211; *JHB, 1770–1772,* 78–9, 204; *JHB, 1773–1776,* 75.

19. For petitions about vestries: *JHB, 1766–1769,* 210, 216, 252, 259–60, 296, 343, 346, 347; *JHB, 1770–1772,* 10, 30, 39, 43, 44, 45, 47, 48, 52, 62, 78, 80, 82, 89, 93–4, 164, 169, 171, 199, 225–32, 242, 257–8, 262–3, 265, 285; *JHB, 1773–1776,* 25, 79–80, 81–2, 86, 104, 128, 131. For bills regulating vestry elections: *JHB, 1770–1772,* 43, 45, 52, 79, 93, 96, 221, 241, 247; H. R. McIlwaine, ed., *Legislative Journals of the Council of Colonial Virginia,* Richmond, Virginia, 1918–19, 3 volumes, 3:1458. On episcopate proposal: *JHB, 1770–1772,* 188, 275; to Rev. Jonathan Boucher, 4 May 1772, *WW* 3:81. On dissenters: *JHB, 1766–1769,* 195, 252, 256, 267; *JHB, 1770–1772* 20, 40, 160–1, 182–3, 185–6, 188, 194, 197, 245, 249; *JHB, 1773–1776,* 92, 102; William Taylor Thom, *The Struggle for Religious Freedom in Virginia: The Baptists,* Baltimore, 1900, 28–9, 44–9.

20. Christie and Labaree, 122, 125.

21. *RV* 1:70–1.

22. *RV* 1:73; *Diaries* 2:151–2; *Mason Papers* 1:103–6, 109–13; DSF 3:220–2.

23. *RV* 1:73–7; *Mason Papers* 1:109–13; *Virginia Gazette* (Purdie and Dixon), 25 May 1769, 1.

24. *RV* 1:77; *Diaries* 2:153; Griffin 68. Probably GW had read Dickinson's essays in the *Virginia Gazette* the previous year. The "Letters" were serialized in Rind's *Gazette,* 24 December 1767 and 18 February 1768, and in Purdie and Dixon's *Gazette,* 7, 14, 21, 28 January 1768; 18, 25 February; 3, 10, 17, 24, 31 March.

25. To Robert Cary and Company, 25 July 1769, *WW* 2:512–14; DSF 3:228–30.

26. *Diaries* 2:239, 241; *Carter Diary,* 418.

27. *Diaries* 2:245.

28. Mason to Lee, 7 June 1770, *Mason Papers* 1:116–20.

29. *Diaries* 2:248–9; *RV* 1:78–83; *Mason Papers* 1:120–4.

30. *Diaries* 2:239–41, 245–8.

31. To Reverend Jonathan Boucher, 30 July 1770, *WW* 3:21–2; to Robert Cary and Company, 20 August 1770, 37:494, cf. to George William Fairfax, 27 June 1770, 3:17.

32. Nonimportation Agreement [22 June 1770], *WW* 3:16; *Diaries* 2:256; Donald M. Sweig, "The Virginia Nonimportation Association Broadside of

1770 and Fairfax County: A Study in Local Participation," *The Virginia Maga-zine of History and Biography*, 87 (1979), 316–25; *Virginia Gazette* (Rind), 11 October 1770, 3.

33. To Robert Cary and Company, 20 August 1770, WW 37:490–4; In-voices, 20 August 1770, 3:22–4; Calvin B. Coulter, Jr., "The Import Trade of Colonial Virginia," *William and Mary Quarterly*, third series, 2 (1945), 300–3, cf. to Cary, 15 July 1772, WW 3:89–90; (10) July 1773, 140.

34. George Mason to [George Brent?], 6 December 1770, *Mason Papers* 1:127–9.

35. Fairfax Committee to Peyton Randolph [18 July 1771], *Mason Papers* 1:132–4; *Virginia Gazette* (Rind), 18 July 1771, 3; *Diaries* 3:20, 33, cf. Com-mittee Chosen by the Associators of Fauquier County to Peyton Randolph, 11 June 1771, *Virginia Gazette* (Rind), 8 July 1771. The exact date of the Fairfax Committee's letter to Randolph is uncertain. Reprinting it from Rind's *Gazette* of 18 July 1771, Rutland uses that date. It was most probably written in late June or early July. The committee had examined the invoices of two merchants, Alexander Henderson and William Balmain, on 18 June. Freeman suggests that GW brought the document with him to Williamsburg when he came to the Assembly session: DSF 3:276. GW left Mount Vernon on 12 July and arrived in town on 15 July, the day of the Association's general meeting: *Diaries* 3:39–40.

36. To Robert Cary and Company, 20 July 1771, WW 3:56–60; to Mat-thew Campbell, 7 August 1772, 99–101.

37. Invoice, 18 July 1771, WW 3:61–2; to John Didsbury, 18 July, 53–4; to [Thomas Gibson], 18 July, 54–5; to Maudiut and Company [20 July], 55–6; *Diaries* 3:41. See also: to Cary and Company, 6 June 1768, WW 2:488–90; Invoices, 15 July 1772, 3:90–4; to John Didsbury, 15 July, 94–5; to Thomas Gibson, 15 July, 95–6; to Gibson, 10 July 1773, 141–2; Invoice, 26 July, 144n.

38. Liddle, "'Patriot King,'" 960–1; Liddle, "Public Attitudes," 236–47; *RV* 1:55; Maier, *From Resistance to Revolution*, 200–5; Dunbar 12–14.

39. *Virginia Gazette* (Purdie and Dixon), 6 September 1770; A. J. Wall, "The Statues of King George III and the Honorable William Pitt Erected in New York City 1770," *New York Historical Society Quarterly Bulletin*, 4 (July 1920), 36–57, see 37–49. Militant members of both the New York and the South Carolina Assembly proposed statues of Pitt, while moderates favored stat-ues of the king: Kenneth Silverman, *A Cultural History of the American Revo-lution*, New York, 1976, 98.

40. *Diaries* 3:108–9; WW 3:83–4 and 84n; DSF 3:292–3.

CHAPTER NINE

1. To Captain John Posey, 24 June 1767, WW 2:458–60. See also Breen, *Tobacco Culture*, 182–5.

2. Thomas Perkins Abernethy, *Western Lands and the American Revolu-tion*, New York and London, 1937, 68.

3. For 18 February 1754, *Executive Journals* 5:461–2; 19 February, 499–500; 25 May 1763, 6:257; from George Mercer, 16 September 1759, *LTW*

3:159–60; Jack M. Sosin, *Whitehall and the Wilderness: The Middle West in British Colonial Policy, 1760–1775*, Lincoln, Nebraska, 1961, 43–6; Knollenberg 1976, 182nn.1–3; *Fauquier Papers* 1:275–7, 331–2, 353, 359, 376–7, 405–6, 439–40; 2:771, 774–6.

4. DSF 3:93–5, 101–3, 109; Knollenberg 87–8; *Fauquier Papers* 3:1132; William Waller Hening, *Statutes at Large, Being a Collection of All the Laws of Virginia, from the First Session of the Legislature, in the Year 1619*, Richmond, Virginia, 1821–3, 13 volumes, 8:18–19.

5. Knollenberg 88–90.

6. To William Crawford, 21 September 1767, WW 2:467–71; DSF 3:188–90.

7. For 15 December 1769, *Executive Journals* 6:337–8; 4 November 1771, 438–41; to Lord Botetourt, 8 December 1769, WW 2:528–32; 3:1–4, 9–12, 26–9, 66–70, 72–7, 85–7, 118–24, 153–4, 158–63, 171–2; 37:494–5, 585; *Virginia Gazette* (Purdie and Dixon), 21 December 1769, 2; 21 June 1770, 2; 31 January 1771, 3; 12 November 1772, 2; *Virginia Gazette* (Rind), 28 December 1769, 1; 31 January 1771, 2; 14 January 1773, 1–2; 25 November 1773, 4; from William Crawford, 12 November 1773, LTW 4:275; to George Muse, 29 January 1774, WW 3:179–80; DSF 3:215–16, 237–40, 245, 247, 252–3, 264, 265–6, 278, 283–5, 290, 297–306, 333–5; Knollenberg 86–7, 91–6; to Presley Neville, 16 June 1794, WW 33:407; Sosin 191–2.

8. To Charles Washington, 30 January 1770, WW 3:1–4; DSF 3:245–8, 317–18, 329, 331–5; Knollenberg 98–9, 135–7.

9. Notes on the Navigation of the Potomac River above the Great Falls (July–August 1754), PWC 1:179–80; to Charles Carter (August 1754), 196–8; DSF 3:177; to Thomas Johnson, 1762, WW 2:391.

10. *JHB, 1766–1769*, 314, 334; *JHB, 1770–1772*, 292, 297, 304–5, 310, 316. GW's name appeared first in a long list of trustees in an announcement in *Virginia Gazette* (Purdie and Dixon), 3 November 1774, 4; *Virginia Gazette* (Pinkney) 10 November 1774, 3. See also LTW 4:30, 122–3; 5:84–6, 109–10, 133; *Diaries* 3:106–7; WW 3:81.

11. Grace L. Nute, ed., "Washington and the Potomac: Manuscripts of the Minnesota Historical Society [1754], 1769–1796, I," *American Historical Review*, 28 (1923), 509–10.

12. To Henry Riddell, 22 February 1774, WW 3:189; to Thomas Johnson, 20 July 1770, 18–20; 5 May 1772, 83.

13. To Thomas Johnson, 20 July 1770, WW 3:19. GW thought the project would fail to obtain the necessary financial backing if it were undertaken at public expense. He proposed that private subscribers be vested by the two legislatures with the right to levy tolls: 18–19. Such an arrangement was incorporated into the expanded plan adopted in the Virginia Assembly in 1772: see above, n.10 and WW 3:81, 83.

14. To William Fairfax, 23 April 1755, PWC 1:258; DSF 3:177; *Diaries* 2:182–3; from Robert Adam, 7 January 1774, LTW 4:303–4; from Robert Carter Nicholas, 9 April, 371–3; from Adam, 17 May, 392–4; to Robert McMickan, 10 May 1774, WW 3:213. In Washington Papers, Library of Congress, are two letters accompanying the petitions from Fairfax County regard-

ing the duty on rum, regulation of the inspection of herring, and extension of Alexandria's boundaries. Both letters were addressed to the two Fairfax Burgesses. The first has no signatures. The second is from William Ramsay, Robert Adam, and John Carlyle, Alexandria merchants. Both are dated 16 May 1774. The first supports repeal of the duty on rum. The second advocates extending the limits of the town of Alexandria because of its burgeoning population: *JHB, 1772–1776*, 119–20, 123.

15. Thomas M. Preisser, "Alexandria and the Evolution of the Northern Virginia Economy, 1749–1776," *The Virginia Magazine of History and Biography*, 89 (1981), 282–93.

16. To Lord Botetourt, 9 September 1770, WW 37:494–5; to Earl Dunmore, 2 November 1773, 3:157; from Thomas Glascock, 22 August 1773, *LTW* 4:251–2; from Daniel Carroll, 1 September, 256–7; from Robert H. Harrison, 8 September, 257–9; from Richard Thompson, 30 September, 265–8. In an advertisement offering 20,000 acres for lease on the Ohio and Great Kanawha rivers, GW assured prospective tenants that even now, without an established government, the land could be settled "in Peace and Safety." He expected the capital of the new colony to be located at the mouth of the Great Kanawha, increasing the value of the property in that vicinity: *Virginia Gazette* (Purdie and Dixon), 29 July 1773, 3; *Virginia Gazette* (Rind), 5 August 1773, 3; DSF 3:327–8; Robert D. Mitchell, *Commercialism and Frontier: Perspectives on the Early Shenandoah Valley*, Charlottesville, Virginia, 1977, 127–8.

17. Christie and Labaree 168; Sosin 142, 155–6, 167–9; 205–10; Order in Council, 7 April 1773, E. B. O'Callaghan, ed., *Documents Relative to the Colonial History of the State of New York*, Albany, New York, 1853–87, 15 volumes, 8:357–8.

18. To William Crawford, 25 September 1773, WW 3:149–51; 25 September, 152–3; from John Armstrong, 17 August 1773, *LTW* 4:248–50; from Peter Hogg, 11 December, 280–1; from Armstrong, 24 December, 290–2; Abernethy 89.

19. To Lord Dunmore, 12 September 1773, "Letters of George Washington to Lord Dunmore," *William and Mary Quarterly*, second series, 20 (1940), 164–5; to John Armstrong, 10 October 1773, WW 3:155–6; to Lord Dunmore, 2 November 1773, 157–8; Abernethy 89.

20. George Washington, *Diaries of George Washington*, ed. John C. Fitzpatrick, New York, 1925, 4 volumes, 1:185n; to James Wood, 13 March 1773, WW 3:124–5; to Governor Peter Chester of West Florida, 25 March, 126–7; to Wood, 30 March, 127–9; to Thomas Lewis, 17 February 1774, 182–5.

21. To Lewis, 17 February 1774, WW 3:185; to James Wood, 20 February, 37:506, cf. to Lewis, 17 February, 3:184; *JHB, 1773–1776*, 127; Abernethy 110–11.

22. To Thomas Lewis, 17 February 1774, WW 3:183–5; to James Tilghman, Jr., 17 February, 185–7; to Henry Riddell, 22 February, 187–90; 1 March, 193–4; 5 March, 195–6; to Valentine Crawford, 30 March, 200–4; Advertisement, *Maryland Gazette*, 26 May 1774, 211–12; from Daniel Carroll, 1 September 1773, *LTW* 4:256–7; from Robert Adam, 14 February 1774, 325–7; from Henry Riddell, 24 February, 337–41; 2 March, 342–4; from William McGachen, 13 March, 354; from Riddell, 18 March, 355–6; from

John David Woelpper, 23 March, 357–63; from James Tilghman, Jr., 7 April, 368–71; DSF 3:343–4, 397–8.

23. From Valentine Crawford, 8 June 1774, *LTW* 5:16–17; from Captain William Crawford, 8 May, 4:389; from Dr. John Connolly, 28 May, 5:4; 7 June, 8. See also: *LTW* 4:379–92, 396–7; 5:3–15, 31–2, 46.

24. Nettels, *Washington and Independence*, 77–80; Christie and Labaree 194–5; Sosin 235–8, 240–1.

CHAPTER TEN

1. *Diaries* 3:250; *JHB, 1772–1776*, 102. GW again sat on the Committees of Privileges and Elections, of Propositions and Grievances, and for Religion.

2. To George William Fairfax, 10 June 1774, *WW* 3:224. GW used that term some three and a half weeks later, in his first extant observations on the crisis. But he undoubtedly held the same views when he first learned of the Boston Port Bill.

3. *Diaries* 3:250–2, 255–6.

4. George Mason to Martin Cockburn, 26 May 1774, *Mason Papers* 1:190–1; Thomas Jefferson, "Autobiography," *The Writings of Thomas Jefferson*, ed. Paul L. Ford, New York, 1892–9, 10 volumes, 1:11–12; *The Papers of Thomas Jefferson*, ed. Julian Boyd et al., Princeton, New Jersey, 1950– , 25 volumes to date, 1:105.

5. *Jefferson Writings* 1:12; *RV* 1:93–4.

6. To George William Fairfax, 10 June 1774, *WW* 3:223; *Diaries* 3:251; *Carter Diary* 2:818–19; DSF 3:353n. Although GW wrote to Fairfax two weeks later, he probably had learned at least by 26 May, the day of the dissolution, that Richard Henry Lee had drafted resolutions and that they would be introduced at the end of the session. If Governor Dunmore had heard about the resolves, it seems improbable GW had heard nothing. Dunmore knew neither the author nor the substance of the resolves. Landon Carter thought Attorney General John Randolph had "traitorously informed" the governor of these things.

7. *WW* 3:223–5; *Diaries* 3:251.

8. *RV* 1:96–8.

9. *Diaries* 3:252; DSF 3:354–5.

10. *RV* 1:99–102; GW saved his copy of this broadside letter, *LTW* 3:354–6; DSF 3:355–7; *Diaries* 3:252.

11. *Diaries* 3:254–5; *Carter Diary* 2:818, cf. 821.

12. *Diaries* 3:255–6; *RV* 1:149.

13. To Robert Cary and Company, 1 June 1774, *WW* 3:220.

14. *WW* 3:223–5.

15. *Diaries* 3:256; *RV* 1:137; from Thomas Johnson, Jr., 28 June 1774, *LTW* 5:18–19.

16. *Diaries* 3:257; *WW* 3:227.

17. *Diaries* 3:259; to Bryan Fairfax, 4 July 1774, *WW* 3:227–8.

18. From Bryan Fairfax, 3 July 1774, *LTW* 5:20–2.

19. Prussing 141.

20. Custis, "Catalogue," 406–10; Butterfield is quoted in Isaac Kramnick, *Bolingbroke and His Circle: The Politics of Nostalgia in the Age of Walpole*,

Cambridge, Massachusetts, 1968, 26; to Capel and Osgood Hanbury, 25 July 1769, *WW* 2:515–17.

21. Bernard Bailyn, *The Ideological Origins of the American Revolution*, Cambridge, Massachusetts, 1967; Caroline Robbins, *The Eighteenth-Century Commonwealthman*, Cambridge, Massachusetts, 1959; John G. A. Pocock, *The Machiavellian Moment*, Princeton, 1975.

22. Kramnick 1–83; John G. A. Pocock, "Virtue and Commerce in the Eighteenth Century," *Journal of Interdisciplinary History*, 3 (1972–3), 119–21.

23. To Bryan Fairfax, 4 July 1774, *WW* 3:228–9. In June 1773, GW inherited through his wife some £8000 from his deceased stepdaughter Patsy Custis. This would easily wipe out his remaining debt. To his exasperation, Cary and Company delayed completing the necessary transactions: *WW* 3:164–5; DSF 3:326, 341–2. On Virginians' debts: Breen, *Tobacco Culture* 38–9, 127, 198; Richard B. Sheridan, "The British Credit Crisis of 1772 and the American Colonies," *Journal of Economic History*, 20 (1960), 161–86; Thad W. Tate, "The Coming of the Revolution in Virginia: Britain's Challenge to Virginia's Ruling Class, 1763–1776," *William and Mary Quarterly*, third series, 19 (1962), 335–7.

CHAPTER ELEVEN

1. "Extract of a Letter to a Gentleman in Boston," Alexandria, Virginia, 6 July 1774, Peter Force, ed., *American Archives*, fourth series, New York, 1837–46, 6 volumes, 1:517–18.

2. *Diaries* 3:260; from Bryan Fairfax, 17 July 1774, *LTW* 5:23; to Fairfax, 20 July 1774, *WW* 3:230–1; GW to Brother (probably John Augustine Washington), 11 July 1774, in Donald M. Sweig, "A New-Found Washington Letter of 1774 and the Fairfax Resolves," *William and Mary Quarterly*, third series, 40 (1983), 283–91. This letter indicates that the committee had drafted the resolves by 11 July: 290. This was probably done in Alexandria on 6 July, since GW was at home throughout the next five days: *Diaries* 3:260. Circulation of the draft prior to the second county meeting on 18 July is indicated by Bryan Fairfax's 17 July letter: *LTW* 5:22–9. He wrote: "Some Resolves being prepared by the Committee, It is now proper to consider them": 23. His general observations and particularly his criticisms of resolutions 3–7 and 23 indicate he had seen a draft: 26–7. There were several public occasions on which reactions to the draft could have been received. Thursday, 14 July, the Assembly election was held in Alexandria. Gentlemen and freeholders would also customarily have been discussing public affairs before and after worship services in the two local parishes on 10 and 17 July. GW attended worship on the seventeenth and was, of course, in Alexandria for the election: *Diaries* 3:260–1.

3. *Diaries* 3:260–1; Nicholas Cresswell, *The Journal of Nicholas Cresswell*, New York, 1924, 27–8.

4. *Diaries* 3:261; *WW* 3:230.

5. On the authorship of the Fairfax Resolves: DSF 3:362; JTF 1:321; Nettels, *Washington and Independence*, 90, 92; Rutland, editorial note, *Mason Papers* 1:199–200; *Diaries* 3:261; *RV* 1:110; Sweig, introductory note,

"Washington Letter," 286, 287. The letter discovered by Sweig, from GW to his brother and dated 11 July 1774, indicates that the committee had agreed at least upon the substance of most of the resolves by that date. The letter briefly enumerates the actions proposed for a new commercial boycott, indicating that the committee had agreed upon a draft, later amended. GW wrote that the committee had resolved to stop exports to Great Britain if American grievances were not fully redressed before September 1775: Sweig 290. The Fairfax Resolves, adopted on 18 July, called for nonexportation to begin in November 1775 under those circumstances: *Mason Papers* 1:207. Also, GW's letter omits mention of perhaps the most controversial of the resolutions, the twenty-third, warning the king "that from our Sovereign there can be but one Appeal": 208–9. GW does say that there were "a number of Resolves too tedious to recite, & Improper to Copy as they cannot, as yet, be calld the Resolves of the County ": Sweig, "Washington Letter," 290. Undoubtedly the committee had also agreed upon the belligerent twenty-third resolve, since Bryan Fairfax protested against it in his letter to GW on 17 July. Fairfax also strenuously disagreed with the resolve denying the authority of Parliament to legislate for the colony and asserting that right as exclusive to the provincial assembly: *LTW* 5:26, 27–9. One of the primary pieces of evidence used to argue for Mason's authorship is the presence in the Washington Papers of a copy of the resolves in his handwriting. As more than one scholar has pointed out, this document does not prove his authorship, since it records the resolves in the form finally adopted.

6. From Bryan Fairfax, 17 July 1774, *LTW* 5:22–9.
7. To Bryan Fairfax, 20 July 1774, *WW* 3:230–1.
8. Fairfax Resolves, *Mason Papers* 1:201–10 and *RV* 1:127–33.
9. From Bryan Fairfax, 17 July 1774, *LTW* 5:22–9.
10. From Bryan Fairfax, 5 August 1774, *LTW* 5:34–5.
11. *RV* 1:133.
12. *Virginia Gazette* (Rind), 4 August 1774, 2; *Boston Gazette, and Country Journal*, 8 August 1774, 2.
13. To Bryan Fairfax, 20 July 1774, *WW* 3:230–4.
14. *RV* 1:109–68, declarations of thirty-one constituencies at meetings June–July 1774 to instruct representatives at the August Convention in Williamsburg.
15. *Diaries* 3:263–4, 266.
16. *RV* 1:223–6; to Thomas Johnson, Jr., 5 August 1774, *WW* 3:235–6.
17. *RV* 2:230–9.
18. The seven delegates and their vote totals were: Randolph 104, Lee 100, Washington 98, Henry 89, Richard Bland 79, Benjamin Harrison 66, Edmund Pendleton 62. Thomas Nelson, Jr., and Thomas Jefferson each garnered 51 votes, while five other men obtained a scattering of votes.

The tabulation was recorded by Edmund Berkeley, a representative of Middlesex County. He recorded the totals on a blank page of *The Virginia Almanac for 1774*. This document has caused some confusion. Berkeley gives two sets of figures. The first column, written in ink, contains the tabulation just given. A second column, in pencil, has different totals. Some historians have suggested that the Convention took a second ballot. The difficulty is that all seven delegates chosen are recorded in the first column as having attained majorities. Why would they have had to stand on a second ballot as well?

In addition, the order of leading candidates is different in the second column. For instance, in the second poll, GW and Henry have 104 votes each, putting them ahead of Lee with 102. Yet the credentials of the Virginia delegation named them in the order given in the first column. In votes of this sort, the order would be used to determine the chairmanship of the delegation and the order of succession to that chairmanship: editorial note, *RV* 1:227–9; DSF 3:370, see also photoreproduction of Berkeley's tabulation with explanatory note following page 373.

The solution to the mystery appears to be that Berkeley recorded the vote total for two separate elections. His first column reports the vote at the Convention of August 1774 for the Virginia delegation to the First Continental Congress. The order of names and most of the vote counts in his second column correspond to the order of the delegation elected at the Richmond Convention of March 1775 to represent Virginia at the Second Continental Congress: Force 2: 170. For discussion of the Richmond Convention vote see Chapter 13 at n.18.

For newspaper reports of the Convention resolutions, the Virginia Association, and the election and instruction of the congressional delegates: *Virginia Gazette* (Purdie and Dixon), 4 August 1774, 2; 11 August, 1; *Virginia Gazette* (Rind), 4 August 1774, 3; 11 August, 3; *Boston Gazette*, 29 August 1774, no. 1011, Supplement, 1; *Pennsylvania Gazette*, 17 August 1774, 2; 24 August, Postscript, 1; *South Carolina and American General Gazette*, 2–9 September 1774, 2; *South Carolina Gazette* (Peter Timothy), 12 September 1774, 2; *South Carolina Gazette, and Country Journal*, 13 September 1774, 2; 20 September, 2.

19. To Thomas Johnson, Jr., 5 August 1774, *WW* 3:235–6; to Lee, 7 August, 236; "Pocket-day-Book or Cash Memorandums," 6 August 1774, Washington Papers, Huntington Library, which also records purchase of "the Association's Papers etc."; 7 August, evidently the nonimportation agreement.

20. [Thomas Jefferson], "A Summary View of the Rights of British America," *Papers of Thomas Jefferson*, ed. Julian P. Boyd, Charles T. Cullen, et al., Princeton, 1950– , 25 volumes to date, 1:121–35 (for the ms. text).

21. *RV* 1:240–2.

22. Liddle, "Public Attitudes," 307–12.

23. Liddle, "Public Attitudes," 316–17, 2–3, 34n, 253–4; Liddle, " 'Patriot King,' " 953; Carson 212–15.

24. Liddle, "Public Attitudes," 313–17; Christopher Marshall, *Extracts from the Diary of Christopher Marshall*, ed. William Duane, New York, 1969 (originally published Albany, New York, 1877), 6; Maier, *From Resistance to Revolution*, 237–9; Stella F. Duff, "The Case against the King: The *Virginia Gazettes* Indict George III," *William and Mary Quarterly*, third series, 6 (1949), 396; Christie and Labaree 204.

25. Committee of Correspondence of Charles County, Maryland, to the Committee of Correspondence of Fairfax County, Virginia, 9 August 1774, *LTW* 5:44–5; 14–29 August 1774, *Diaries* 3:269–71.

26. From Bryan Fairfax, 5 August 1774, *LTW* 5:34–44.

27. To Fairfax, 24 August 1774, *WW* 3:237–42. During the war that followed, GW assured the neutralist Fairfax of his friendship despite their continuing political differences: to Bryan Fairfax, 25 September 1777, in Peter Walne, ed., "George Washington and the Fairfax Family," *The Virginia Magazine of History and Biography*, 77 (1969), 446; to Fairfax, 1 March 1778, *WW* 11:2–5.

28. To Mrs. Sarah Bomford, 28 August 1774, *WW* 3:243; to Bryan Fairfax, 24 August, 242.

29. *Diaries* 3:271–2; *RV* 1:133.

CHAPTER TWELVE

1. John Adams to Abigail Adams, 7 October 1774, [John Adams], *Adams Family Correspondence*, ed. Lyman H. Butterfield et al., Cambridge, Massachusetts, 1963–5, 4 volumes, 1:164–5; 9 October, 166; John Adams, *Diary and Autobiography of John Adams*, ed. Lyman H. Butterfield et al., Cambridge, Massachusetts, 1961–4, 4 volumes, 2:150, 156, cf. 122–57; Edmund Cody Burnett, *The Continental Congress*, New York, 1964 (originally published New York, 1941), 24–31.

2. See, for instance, Samuel Adams to Joseph Warren(?), 25 September 1774, *LDC* 1:100; Burnett 30, 22.

3. Burnett 24–31; Thomas Lynch to Ralph Izard, 26 October 1774, *LDC* 1:247, cf. William Bradford to James Madison, 4 January 1775, *The Papers of James Madison*, ed. William T. Hutchinson, William M. E. Rachal, et al., Chicago and Charlottesville, Virginia, 1962– (15 volumes to present), 1:131.

4. *Diaries* 3:274–87; *Adams Diary* 2:132, 136, 149.

5. Silas Deane to Elizabeth Deane, [10–11 September 1774], *LDC* 1:61–2; Dr. Solomon Drowne to Miss Sally Drowne, 5 October 1774, *Pennsylvania Magazine of History and Biography*, 5 (1881), 110–11, Drowne visiting Philadelphia from Rhode Island; *Diaries* 3:287. Roger Atkinson to Samuel Pleasants, 1 October 1774, "Letters of Roger Atkinson," *The Virginia Magazine of History and Biography*, 15 (1907–8), 356; Pleasants belonged to a prominent Philadelphia Quaker family. GW dined at his home during both the First and the Second Congress, cf. *Diaries* 3:276, 335.

6. Drowne to Drowne, *Pennsylvania Magazine* 110–11; Deane to Deane, *LDC* 1:61–2; Atkinson to Pleasants, *Virginia Magazine* 356; Thomas Lynch to Ralph Izard, 26 October 1774, *LDC* 1:247; 31 August 1774, *Adams Diary* 2:117; William Black to Boston Committee, October 1774, quoted in *WW* 3:247–8n; Ezra Stiles, *The Literary Diary of Ezra Stiles*, ed. Franklin Bowditch Dexter, New York, 1901, 3 volumes, 17 November 1774, 1:485.

7. From Lt. Robert Mackenzie, 13 September 1774, *LTW* 5:49–50.

8. *Diaries* 3:280; *Adams Diary* 2:140–1.

9. To Mackenzie, 9 October 1774, *WW* 3:244–7. Because GW made his points repetitiously in this letter, I have rearranged the order of some of his sentences, to clarify his meaning. Cf. Instructions to Brigadier General John Sullivan, 7 November 1775, *PWR* 2:325, for evidence that GW's statements were not mere rhetoric but settled convictions shaped by Radical Whig ideology.

10. James Kirby Martin, *Men in Rebellion: Higher Governmental Leaders and the Coming of the American Revolution*, New Brunswick, New Jersey, 1973.

11. *LTW* 5:50; *WW* 3:247.

12. Burnett 47–50; Christie and Labaree 209–10; Franklin to Galloway, February 1775, quoted in Christie and Labaree 210.

13. Samuel Adams to Joseph Warren?, 25 September 1774, *LDC* 1:100; John Adams, "Notes on Measures to be Taken up by Congress," September–October 1774, *Adams Diary* 2:145–6. For the view that Samuel Adams did not favor independence until the fall of 1775: Pauline Maier, *The Old Revolutionaries*, New York, 1980, 21–6.

14. Burnett 53–7; Christie and Labaree 211; *JCC* 1:120, 75–80.

15. Washington Papers, Library of Congress, Ledger B, 25 October 1774; Griffin 55; *Diaries* 3:287. At the beginning of the session, GW had bought John Dickinson's *Essay on the Constitutional Power of Great-Britain*, Philadelphia, 1774. Later he purchased three other unidentified pamphlets: "Pocket-day-Book or Cash-Memorandums . . . ," 8 September, 15 October 1774, Washington Papers, Huntington Library.

16. Fairfax County Militia Association [21 September 1774], *Mason Papers* 1:210–11.

17. From William Ramsay, Robert H. Harrison, and John Fitzgerald, 19 October 1774, *LTW* 5:56–7; from William Milnor, 29 November, 65–6; "Pocket-day-Book or Cash-Memorandums . . . ," 15, 20 October 1774, Washington Papers, Huntington Library.

18. William E. White, "The Independent Companies of Virginia, 1774–1775," *The Virginia Magazine of History and Biography*, 86 (1978), 151; Nettels, *Washington and Independence*, 92, incorrectly states that the Virginia Convention called for formation of independent militia companies; *Mason Papers* 1:210–11; *Pennsylvania Gazette*, 5 October 1774, 3.

CHAPTER THIRTEEN

1. *Diaries* 3:291, 309; *RV* 2:317; *LTW* 5:65–6, 68–9, 78–9, 80–1, 100, 112–13, 132–3, 150–1, 158–9; *WW* 3:265–6; Griffin 220; *Diaries*, ed. Fitzpatrick, 2:185n; *Mason Papers* 1:220; Mays 1:306; William Bradford to James Madison, 4 January 1775, *Madison Papers* 1:131–3.

2. *Diaries* 3:289–92, 297–300, 302–5, 307–10, 312–13; *LTW* 5:86, 116.

3. *WW* 3:248; *Diaries* 3:297, 303, 309, 313–14; *Virginia Gazette* (Pinkney), 29 December 1774, 3.

4. *Diaries* 3:303; "Fairfax County Committee of Safety Proceedings" [17 January 1775], *Mason Papers* 1:212–13. There was some confusion as to both the quantity and the method of collection, leading to a dispute between GW and Mason: 219–21, 223, 225–8; *Diaries*, ed. Fitzpatrick, 2:185n.

5. Dunmore quoted in DSF 3:398n.

6. Fairfax County Committee of Safety Proceedings (17 January 1775), *Mason Papers* 1:212; Mason to GW, 6 February, 214–15; Fairfax County

Militia Plan "for Embodying the People," drafted by Mason (enclosure of 6 February 1775), 215.

7. *Pennsylvania Evening Post*, 14 February 1775, 38.

8. The rationale was taken verbatim from the proceedings of the Maryland Provincial Committee, 8–12 December 1774. Charles Lee had helped to formulate this plan and probably had discussed it with GW during his week at Mount Vernon: *RV* 2:187; *Maryland Gazette*, 25 December 1774; *Virginia Gazette* (Purdie and Dixon), 29 December 1774. The Maryland Committee solved the problem of funding the militia forces by setting quotas for each county. They "recommended to the committee of each county to raise [this money] by subscription, or in such other voluntary manner as they think proper, and will be most agreeable to their respective counties": *RV* 2:187.

9. Extract of a Letter from a Gentleman of Philadelphia to a Member of the British Parliament, 24 December 1774, Force 1:1066; Samuel Chase to James Duane, 5 February 1775, *LDC* 1:306, cf. Extract of a Letter from the Earl of Dunmore to the Earl of Dartmouth, 24 December 1774, Force 1:1062; Letter from Annapolis, 31 December 1774, in Margaret Wheeler Willard, ed., *Letters on the American Revolution, 1774–1776*, Boston and New York, 1925, 46; Richard Henry Lee to Arthur Lee, 24 February 1775, *LDC* 1:313–14; James Madison to William Bradford, 20 January 1775, *Madison Papers* 1:135; [early March], 141. See especially Dunmore to Dartmouth for a description of the ways in which Virginia's County Committees and independent companies were already functioning as an extralegal government.

10. Charles Lee to Edmund Burke, 16 December 1774, [Charles Lee], *Papers of Charles Lee, Collections of the New York Historical Society*, New York, 1872–5, volumes 4–7, 4:148.

11. Extract of a Letter from a Gentleman in America to a Member of the British Parliament, 26 December 1774, *London Chronicle*, 25–7 April 1775, Willard 41–2.

12. *Virginia Gazette* (Pinkney), 12 January 1775, 1; from George William Fairfax, 2 March 1775, *LTW* 5:127.

13. William Milnor, the Philadelphia merchant from whom he purchased military equipment for the independent companies, sent him many pamphlets: from Milnor, 29 November 1774, *LTW* 5:65, enclosing "A Friendly Address to All Reasonable Americans, on the Subject of Our Political Confusions," by Dr. Myles Cooper, president of King's College in New York City, and the reply of Charles Lee, "Strictures on a Pamphlet, entitled A 'Friendly Address to All Reasonable Americans, on the Subject of our Political Confusions' ": *Lee Papers* 4:151–66; from Milnor, 27 December 1774, *LTW* 5:74, enclosing seven pamphlets; 7 March 1775, 132–3, sending two pamphlets, one said to be by Joseph Galloway. For other Tory publications acquired by GW, see Griffin 24, 43, 59, 167, 177. On GW's gleaning of political intelligence from private letters: *WW* 3:268; *LTW* 5:145.

14. To Dr. John Connolly, 25 February 1775, *WW* 3:268; Mason to GW, 6 February 1775, *Mason Papers* 1:214.

15. *Mason Papers* 1:211, 214, 216.

16. From Independent Company of Richmond, 17 March 1775, LTW 5:
140–1.
17. Mason to GW, 6 February 1775, Mason Papers 1:214; Diaries 3:309.
18. RV 2:300.
19. RV 2:366–9.
20. RV 2:374–5, 379.
21. RV 2:376, 381–3; LTW 5:75–8, 83–4, 128–9.
22. RV 2:376–7, 380–1. The vote as recorded by John Tazewell, clerk of
the Richmond Convention, is in the first column below.

	Tazewell	Berkeley (second column)
Peyton Randolph	107	107
George Washington	106	104
Patrick Henry	105	104
R. H. Lee	103	102
Edmund Pendleton	100	100
Benjamin Harrison	94	94
Richard Bland	90	90
Thomas Jefferson	18	18
Thomas Nelson	16	16
Francis L. Lee	3	3
James Mercer	3	
Archibald Cary	1	1
Dudley Digges	1	
Robert Carter Nicholas		1

Compare Tazewell's tabulation with that of Edmund Berkeley, right column
above, adapted from RV 1:228 and discussed above, Chapter 11, n.18. Berkeley's Papers contain a list of vote totals in an election of Virginia delegates to
the Continental Congress. That tabulation has two columns. The second is usually thought to record a second ballot at the Williamsburg Convention of August 1774.
    But Berkeley was also at Richmond, again representing Middlesex County.
If the names of the candidates in his second column are listed in the order of
their vote totals, as I have done above, that order corresponds exactly with
Tazewell's tabulation in March 1775 at Richmond. Tazewell's totals and those
in Berkeley's second column are the same for each candidate except GW, Henry,
and Lee. Also, Berkeley gives James Mercer no votes in his second column, but
7 in his first. He gives Robert Carter Nicholas 4 votes in his first column and
1 vote in his second. Instead of Nicholas, Tazewell concludes his tabulation with
Dudley Digges, assigning him 1 vote. Berkeley's first column gives Thomson
Mason 16 votes. His second column records no votes for Mason, and Tazewell
omits Mason's name; this suggests that Mason was a candidate in Williamsburg
but not in Richmond. Berkeley's first column is in ink; his second is in pencil:
RV 1:227–8; 2:325, 337.
    The most likely explanation is that sometime after the election of congres-
sional delegates at Richmond (25 March 1775), Berkeley took the piece of paper on which he had recorded the Williamsburg vote and jotted down from

memory the new figures. This would explain both his reason for recording two columns of figures and the discrepancies between his second column and Tazewell's tabulation.

23. To John Augustine Washington, 25 March 1775, *WW* 3:276–7.

24. *Diaries* 3:316; *WW* 3:268–72. GW obtained a pamphlet copy of the Convention proceedings: Griffin 216.

25. From Major William Crawford, 20 September 1774, *LTW* 5:51–3; from Valentine Crawford, 1 October, 54, cf. from William Crawford, 14 November, 61–4.

26. From Doctor John Connolly, 9 February 1775, *LTW* 5:101–2; *JHB, 1773–1776*, 282; *Virginia Gazette* (Purdie), 23 June 1775, Supplement, 3.

27. *WW* 3:256–61, 268–72; *LTW* 5:102–4, 153–6, 166–74; to Dunmore, 3 April 1775, *WW* 3:280–2; from Dunmore, 18 April 1775, *LTW* 5:158.

28. To Benjamin Harrison, 18 December 1778, *WW* 13:463; *DSF* 3:407–9; Knollenberg 96–8, 184–5. Knollenberg argues that a resurvey would have been in the interests of the other veterans, because they could have made certain GW did not grant himself the cream of the land the second time around and because a licensed surveyor would have refused to violate his oath of office by giving GW an illegal amount of river frontage.

29. *Diaries* 3:320–2, 325.

30. *LTW* 5:150–1, 158–9, 161–2; *Diaries* 3:321–3, 325. Evidently the Fairfax and other county committees had begun regulating prices: Larry Bowman, "The Virginia County Committees of Safety, 1774–1776," *The Virginia Magazine of History and Biography*, 79 (1971), 331.

31. To George Mercer, 5 April 1775, *WW* 3:288.

32. *Mason Papers* 1:215–16.

33. GW apparently agreed with Mason. A year later, he wrote that "frequent appeals to the people can be attended with no bad, but may have very salutary effects": to Joseph Reed, 1 April 1776, *WW* 4:454–5.

34. For 15 April 1775, *Diaries* 3:321: "Went up to Alexandria to the Muster of the Independt. Company. Returnd late at Night." See next note for the basis of this conjectured date.

35. Remarks on Annual Elections for the Fairfax Independent Company (c. 17–26 April 1775), *Mason Papers* 1:229–32; reprinted from Kate Mason Rowland, *The Life of George Mason, 1725–1792*, New York, 1892, 2 volumes, 1:430–3. The location of the original manuscript is unknown. Rutland conjectures that Mason's Remarks were prepared sometime between 17 and 26 April, because by 17 April, Mason and GW had settled the accounts of their collection of the three-shilling levy to buy arms and ammunition. Mason was at Mount Vernon on 17 April, on that date signing a receipt to reimburse GW: *Diaries* 3:322; Account of Fairfax County Weapons Levy (17 April 1775), *Mason Papers* 1:228. On 26 April, the company met to exercise in Alexandria: *Diaries* 3:323. Rutland finds an earlier date unlikely, partly because the company was already functioning "on a loose basis" in January and February, as is indicated by Mason's plan of 6 February "for Embodying the People." Also, during February, Mason was frequently traveling back and forth across the Potomac to

call upon his seriously ill mother-in-law who resided in Maryland, thus making his attendance at militia meetings improbable: *Mason Papers* 1:232.

There is further reason to doubt an earlier dating. Assuming that GW attended all of the meetings of the Fairfax Independent Company, he recorded in his diary only two such gatherings in January and February 1775, on 16 January when he went to Alexandria to "review" the company and on 18 February when he went "to meet & exercise" it: *Diaries* 3:303, 309. The January meeting is too early a date for the reorganization, for Mason's initial proposal for reform was in early February. Also, that plan proposed annual election of officers but made no mention of rotation in office. Furthermore, it is unlikely that Mason attended the February meeting of the militia company, because the day before he had told GW he was ill: *Mason Papers* 1:214–16, 220.

As Rutland notes (1:232), reference in Mason's Remarks to GW as the commanding officer puts the reorganization meeting sometime before his departure for the Second Continental Congress on 4 May 1775: *Diaries* 3:327. According to GW's diary, the company met on three occasions during these weeks: 15 and 26 April, and 1 May: *Diaries* 3:321, 323, 325. It is unnecessary to assume that the meeting to consider reorganization came after Mason and GW had settled their financial accounts.

The language of GW's diary suggests 15 April 1775 as the date of the reorganization meeting. His entry of that day records that he went to Alexandria to the "Muster" of the company: *Diaries* 3:321. In all other instances, he used the words "review," "meet," and "meet & exercise": *Diaries* 3:303, 309, 323, 325; to John Augustine Washington, 25 March 1775, *WW* 3:276–7. Although the word *muster* can mean the meeting of a military organization for exercise or drill, it also means the convening or enrollment of such a body. GW may have used the word in the latter sense to designate a meeting of the military company, not to drill, but to discuss the rules and principles of its constitution.

36. GW apparently never read Machiavelli's *Discourses*; at least, the various inventories of his library fail to list it. But from Mason and others and from his own reading he adopted the ideology of the Whig-republican tradition, a tradition in which the language and ideas of Machiavelli were pervasive. In the midst of the Revolutionary War, GW wrote Mason lamenting the peculations of moneymakers and stock-jobbers, the prevalence of parties in Congress, and the absence of the ablest men from the national scene. "Friends and foes seem now to combine to pull down the goodly fabric we have hitherto been raising at the expence of so much time, blood, and treasure; and unless the bodies politick will exert themselves *to bring things back to first principles*, correct abuses, and punish our internal foes, inevitable ruin must follow [emphasis added]": 27 March 1779, *WW* 14:300–1.

37. From Edmund Pendleton, 21 April 1775, *LTW* 5:160; from Spotsylvania Independent Company, 26 April, 162–3; from Prince William Independent Company, 26 April, 163–4; from Albemarle Independent Company, 29 April, 165; DSF 3:410–12; White 155–7.

38. DSF 3:414–15, 421–3; White 157–8; James Madison to William Bradford, 9 May 1775, *Madison Papers* 1:144–5; Address to Captain Patrick Henry and the Gentlemen Independents of Hanover (9 May), 146–8; from

Alexander Spotswood, 30 April 1775, *LTW* 5:166. Young James Madison thought Henry's bold move would be "disapproved" by the Virginia congressional delegates who had urged their armed countrymen to return home. In addition to Peyton Randolph, these included the moderate Edmund Pendleton and the militant Richard Henry Lee. Madison praised Henry and criticized "[t]he Gentlemen below whose property will be exposed in case of a civil war...." He thought that "some of them [had] discovered a pusilanimity little comporting with their professions or the name of Virginian." Contrary to Flexner, Madison was not including GW in this charge. "[T]he Gentlemen below" referred to planters living along the lower York and James rivers: *Madison Papers* 1:145 and n.7; JTF 1:330.

39. From Spotswood, 30 April 1775, *LTW* 5:166.

40. *Diaries* 3:325–8; DSF 418; Richard Caswell to William Caswell, 11 May 1775, *LDC* 1:339–40.

41. Charles Royster, *A Revolutionary People at War: The Continental Army and American Character, 1775–1783*, Chapel Hill, North Carolina, 1979, 25; Willard 86, 91–2, 98–105; Caswell to Caswell, 11 May 1775, *LDC* 1:339–41; Joseph Hewes to Samuel Johnston, 11 May, 342–3; Silas Deane to Elizabeth Deane, 12 May, 346–7; 21 May, 365; John Adams to Abigail Adams, 29 May, 417. See also *LDC* 1:356–7, 364, 365, 413–14, 415; *Madison Papers* 1:149.

42. Joseph Hewes to Samuel Johnston, 11 May 1775, *LDC* 1:342–3.

43. Samuel Curwen, *The Journal of Samuel Curwen, Loyalist*, ed. Andrew Oliver, Cambridge, Massachusetts, 1972, 2 volumes, 1:3–9.

44. To the Fairfax County Committee, 16 May 1775, *LDC* 1:354.

45. To George William Fairfax, 31 May 1775, *WW* 3:291. Sam Adams was still describing the British troops in Boston as "the ministerial Army," but some Americans were already calling them "the Kings Troops": Adams to James Warren, 28 June 1775, *LDC* 1:553; Richard Caswell to William Caswell, 11 May, 340; letter from Charles-Town, South Carolina, 10 May 1775, Willard 105.

46. *WW* 3:291–2.

CHAPTER FOURTEEN

1. DSF 3:431–8; JTF 1:332–45; 2:10–18; Hughes 2:234–54; Stephenson and Dunn 1:324–8. Bernhard Knollenberg agreed that sectional differences prompted election of GW, but concluded that contemporary and "strong circumstantial evidence" indicated that a great majority of GW's fellow delegates preferred him to anyone else from the outset: 113–16. See also Alden, *Washington*, 109–13.

2. For a critique of Adams's autobiography as a source regarding GW's appointment see n.25 below.

3. To the Officers of Five Virginia Independent Companies, 20 June 1775, *PWR* 1:17.

4. *JCC* 2:13, 22–45.

5. John Adams to James Warren, 21 May 1775, *LDC* 1:364.

6. *JCC* 2:49–53, 57–66; *LDC* 1:351; *Diaries* 3:330–1; DSF 3:421, 425.

7. *JCC* 2:67, 74; *LDC* 1:412; *Diaries* 3:331, 333–4; DSF 3:429, 430; Massachusetts Provincial Congress to Continental Congress, 16 May 1775, Force 2:620–1.

8. *JCC* 2:79–80.

9. *JCC* 2:89–90; *Diaries* 3:334–6; Nettels, *Washington and Independence*, 87; *Rules and Articles, for the Better Government of the Troops raised, or to be raised, and kept in pay by and at the joint expence of the Thirteen united English Colonies of North America* (Philadelphia, 1775); Griffin 57.

10. On these committees were Samuel Adams and Thomas Cushing of Massachusetts, Silas Deane of Connecticut, Lewis Morris of New Jersey, Thomas Mifflin of Pennsylvania, Joseph Hewes of North Carolina, Thomas Lynch of South Carolina, and all of the New Yorkers. GW also conferred with these and other colleagues over dinner. When he had no other dinner invitation, he dined at the City Tavern with Randolph, Lee, and Harrison of Virginia, John Alsop of New York, Samuel Chase of Maryland, and Caesar Rodney and George Read of Delaware. On other occasions, he dined or spent the evening with John Rutledge and Thomas Lynch of South Carolina, John Dickinson and Thomas Mifflin of Pennsylvania, and the Massachusetts delegation. As during the First Congress, GW was also a guest in the homes of Philadelphians prominent in politics and commerce, including Joseph Reed and Robert Morris: George Read to Gertrude Read, 18 May 1775, *LDC* 1:358; *Diaries* 3:328–32, 333–6; John Adams to Abigail Adams, 29 May 1775, *LDC* 1:417.

11. Extract of a letter from one of the Virginia delegates to his friend now in this city, dated 14 June 1775, *Virginia Gazette* (Purdie), 23 June 1775, Supplement, 2, and *LDC* 1:486–7.

12. *JCC* 2:91–4. Freeman and Flexner both assert that GW stayed away from Congress on 15 June, the day of his election, but neither documents this assertion: DSF 3:436; JTF 1:339. I have found no evidence to indicate GW's absence. John Adams recalled that he moved that Congress "adopt" the army at Boston and simultaneously suggested, without officially nominating, GW for the chief command: *Adams Diary* 3:322–3. Although Adams's memory of these events was often unreliable, there is no reason to doubt this particular recollection. This probably took place on 14 June. Freeman and Flexner may have conjectured GW's absence on 15 June because the minutes record that the president announced his election to him on 16 June. His election was the last item of business on the fifteenth; his acceptance speech was the first on the sixteenth. It was customary on such occasions to allow time for the preparation of public addresses. Also, it is highly unlikely that they elected him without being certain he would accept the commission. For them to have chosen a commanding general only to have him turn them down would have seriously injured the cause.

13. DSF 3:433.

14. Warren to Adams, 7 May 1775, [John Adams], *Papers of John Adams*, ed. Robert J. Taylor et al., Cambridge, Massachusetts, 1977–83, 6 volumes, 3:4; Gerry to Massachusetts Delegates, 4 June 1775, in James T. Austin, *The Life of Elbridge Gerry*, Boston, 1828–9, 2 volumes, 1:79. In his diary entry of 4 May 1775, Ezra Stiles recorded: "It is said that the Mass. Prov. Congress have

sent to Col. Washington of Virginia to be Generalissimo of the American army, & Gen. Lee to be second in Command: perhaps it may be true": *Stiles Literary Diary* 1:544.

15. James Warren to John Adams, 20 June 1775, *Warren-Adams Letters, Being Chiefly a Correspondence Among John Adams, Samuel Adams, and James Warren, 1743–1814, Massachusetts Historical Society Collections, Volumes 72–73*, Boston, 1917–25, 72:63; Elbridge Gerry to Massachusetts Delegates to Congress, 20 June 1775, *Adams Papers* 3:40–1; Samuel Adams to James Warren, 28 June 1775, *LDC* 1:553, see also 503, 518, 519.

16. *Adams Diary* 3:322–3. Flexner and Rupert Hughes also conclude that Ward was a contender against GW: JTF 1:334; Hughes 2:234–5. Freeman concludes that Pendleton opposed GW's election at GW's urging, but cites no documentary evidence: DSF 3:434n. Flexner follows this interpretation, but repeatedly misidentifies Pendleton as "Isaac Pemberton": JTF 1:336, 340.

17. DSF 3:433, cf. JTF 1:334; Hughes 2:236–8.

18. Gerry to Massachusetts Delegates, 4 June 1775, in Austin 1:79.

19. Gerry to Massachusetts Delegates to Congress, 20 June 1775, *Adams Papers* 3:40–1.

20. John Adams to Elbridge Gerry, 18 June 1775, *LDC* 1:503; John Adams to James Warren, 20 June, 518; Samuel Adams to Joseph Warren, 20 June, 519; Samuel Adams to James Warren, 28 June, 553. John Adams recollected that Lee had been "most strenuously Urged by many," especially Thomas Mifflin of Pennsylvania, for appointment as the first major general. Mifflin had argued that because of "his Rank, Character and Experience," Lee would refuse to accept any position other than second in command. Adams had objected that "it would be a great deal to expect of General Ward that he should serve under any Man, but that under a *stranger* [emphasis added] he ought not to serve." Despite Lee's experience and expertise, it would "humiliate" Ward and Massachusetts to subordinate the native to the newcomer: *Adams Diary* 3:323–4. Adams and his Massachusetts colleagues were working strenuously to replace Ward with Washington and to defeat fear in the Bay Colony of Lee as an outsider. Adams had to justify his vote for Lee to opinion back home: Adams to Gerry, 18 June 1775, *LDC* 1:503, cf. Adams to James Warren, 20 June, 518. Appointing Ward as the first major general was probably a necessary compromise.

21. To illustrate this usage of the word, the Oxford English Dictionary quotes as its one example from the eighteenth century Lord Bolingbroke's *Dissertation Upon Parties*. "There is a plain and real Difference between Jealousy and Distrust," he wrote. "Men may be jealous, on account of their Liberties, and I Think they ought to be so, even when They have no immediate Distrust that the persons, who govern, design to invade them."

22. Lee to Edmund Burke, 16 December 1774, *Lee Papers* 4:148–9; Fragment of a Letter to the Public (undated but follows letter to Burke of 16 December 1774), 149, cf. Letter from A Gentleman in Philadelphia, to a Member of the British Parliament, 26 December 1774, Force 1:1066, and *Virginia Gazette* (Dixon and Hunter), 1 July 1775, 1–2.

For the application of this idea to the selection of Continental generals: New York Delegates to the New York Provincial Congress, 3 June 1775, *LDC*

1:442–3; New York Provincial Congress to New York Delegates to Congress, 7 June 1775, Force 2:1281–2. See also: to the Commanding Officer of the Fourteenth Virginia Regiment, 4 June 1777, *WW* 8:178–9, cf. to Colonel Alexander Spotswood, 30 April 1777, 7:494–5; to President James Bowdoin, 17 March 1778, 11:98–9; to Henry Laurens, 24 July 1778, 12:223–6; to Gouverneur Morris, 24 July 1778, 12:226–8.

23. Charles Lee to Sir Charles Davers, 28 September 1774, *Lee Papers* 4: 135; to [Benjamin Rush], 15 December, 143–4; Fragment of a Letter to the Public (undated but follows letter to Burke of 16 December 1774), 150; to the Gentlemen of the Provincial Congress of Virginia (no date but probably early 1775), 172–8. On indemnification of Lee: John Adams to Elbridge Gerry, 18 June 1775, *LDC* 1:503; John Hancock to Joseph Warren, 18 June, 508; Samuel Adams to Joseph Warren, 20 June, 519; Samuel Adams to James Warren, 28 June, 553. In the last letter, Sam Adams suggested that it might be imprudent to make this arrangement known publicly.

24. John Adams to James Warren, 24 July 1775, *LDC* 1:658, cf. Mercy Otis Warren to John Adams, October 1775, *Adams Papers* 3:269.

25. John Adams reported the "earnest desire" of GW to have Lee with him: Adams to Gerry, 18 June 1775, *LDC* 1:503, cf. 518, 519, 553. George Cuthbert said that Congress had appointed Lee "more to please Washington" than from "any opinion or confidence they had in Mr. Lee" (quoted in Nettels, *Washington and Independence*, 148).

Samuel Adams told James Warren: "We have appointed the Generals you ask for. . . . The Experience of Washington & Lee may make good all Deficiencies": 28 June 1775, *LDC* 1:553. See also Silas Deane to Samuel B. Webb, 22 June 1775, [Samuel Blachley Webb], *Correspondence and Journals of Samuel Blachley Webb*, collected and ed. Worthington Chauncey Ford, New York, 1893, 3 volumes, 1:71–2; John Adams to William Tudor, 20 June 1775, *LDC* 1:517.

The story of Lee's appointment illustrates some of the problems with John Adams's autobiography as a source on GW's selection. As Adams remembered it, the Massachusetts and other New England delegations had been divided about appointing GW. John Hancock had thought he himself should at least be offered the post, as a compliment due him. Thomas Cushing and several others had "faintly expressed their Opposition" to a non–New Englander. Robert Treat Paine had spoken highly of Artemas Ward but had not taken a stand on GW's appointment: *Adams Diary* 3:321–3, 325.

No contemporary evidence corroborates Adams's recollections. Probably he confused the politicking over the appointments of GW and Lee. In his correspondence of June and July 1775, as in that of his fellow delegates, there is no mention of Hancock wanting the appointment, nor is anything said of Cushing, Hancock, or Paine resisting election of GW. But Adams did report that "C and H and P have given us a great deal of Trouble, in the Election of Lee, and I expect will avail themselves of all the Whims and Prejudices, of our People." In contemporaneous letters, Hancock and Cushing wrote lukewarmly of Lee's election, while they and Paine spoke positively, even enthusiastically, of GW: John Adams to Cotton Tufts, 21 June 1775, *LDC* 1:529; John Hancock to Elbridge Gerry, 18 June, 507; Hancock to Joseph Warren, 18 June, 507–8;

Robert Treat Paine to Artemas Ward, 18 June, 509; Thomas Cushing to James Bowdoin, Sr., 21 June, 530.

In this section of his autobiography Adams's memory played tricks on him regarding other matters. He remembered having met Joseph Reed during the summer of 1775 when the Philadelphian was GW's secretary. He had in fact become closely acquainted with Reed during the First Congress in September–November 1774. He attributed to the moderate Reed the view in mid-1775 that independence was "inevitable," a conclusion Reed had yet to reach. He also confused Henry Middleton, delegate to Congress from South Carolina, 1774–6, with his son Arthur, who succeeded him in the spring of 1776. His account of debates and divisions within Congress regarding independence was similarly anachronistic. Although he was recollecting the situation during the first half of 1775, he was, as the editors of his autobiography point out, "to some extent anticipating the events and opinions of early 1776": *Adams Diary* 2:113, 115, 116, 121–2, 131, 132, 136, 146, 151, 155–7; 3:314–20.

The question of sectional rivalry offers the clearest instance of the difficulty with this source regarding GW's appointment. He remembered in 1804 that a "Southern Party" had existed in Congress in 1775. "[T]he Intention was very visible to me, that Col. Washington was their Object, and so many of our staunchest Men were in the Plan that We could carry nothing without conceeding to it." A few sentences later Adams contradicted himself. "In several Conversations" with delegates from Virginia, "I found more than one very cool about the Appointment of Washington, and particularly Mr. Pendleton was very clear and full against": *Adams Diary* 3:321–3.

The purpose of Adams's autobiographical recollections seems to have been to establish his own central role in these events. He reported that Congress was split by various factions, most importantly a southern party against a northern party. Also, "[t]he Massachusetts Delegates and other New England Delegates were divided. Mr. Hancock and Mr. Cushing hung back. Mr. Paine did not come forward, and even Mr. Samuel Adams was irresolute." The Virginia delegation likewise was in disagreement about GW's election. Seizing the initiative, Adams determined to move "that Congress should adopt the Army before Boston and appoint Colonel Washington Commander of it." There was some opposition, but these dissenters were persuaded to change their minds. Washington was "unanimously elected, and the Army adopted": *Adams Diary* 3:321–3. In other words, according to John Adams, John Adams was chiefly responsible for the creation of the Continental Army and of George Washington as a national leader.

    26. Eliphalet Dyer to Jonathan Trumbull, Sr., 16 June 1775, *LDC* 1:496; John Adams to Abigail Adams, 17 June, 497; Dyer to Joseph Trumbull, 17 June, 499; John Adams to James Warren, 6 [July], 591; *Adams Diary* 3:321.

    27. *LDC* 1:87, 201–3, 227, 252, 268, 291, 301–2, 303, 310–11, 317–18, 337, 354, 408, 436.

    28. Dyer to Governor Jonathan Trumbull, Sr., 16 June 1775, *LDC* 1:496; Dyer to Joseph Trumbull, 17 June, 499; John Adams to Abigail Adams, 17 June, 497; Adams to James Warren, 6 [July], 591; Alden, *Washington*, 25.

    29. Extract of a Letter from a Gentleman of Philadelphia, to a Member of the British Parliament, 26 December 1774, *London Chronicle*, 25–27 April

1775, in Force 1:1066–7, also in *Virginia Gazette* (Dixon and Hunter), 1 July 1775, 1–2; to Martha Washington, 18 June 1775, *PWR* 1:4 (it is unclear precisely when GW had Pendleton draft the will. He told Martha only that it had been "since I came to this place (for I had not time to do it before I left home). . . ." This suggests that he had gotten Pendleton to draft the will prior to his election as commander-in-chief); Richard Caswell to William Caswell, 11 May 1775, *LDC* 1:340.

30. To the Fairfax County Committee, 16 May 1775, *WW* 37:510–12 and *LDC* 1:354. (Angle brackets indicate illegible or mutilated copy.) GW urged the Fairfax Committee to choose someone to replace him "Pro:tem," but offered no hint of when he might return to Virginia: to Martha Washington, 18 June 1775, *PWR* 1:4. He told Martha he did not doubt "but that I shall return safe to you in the fall" (cf. to Martha Washington, 23 June, 27), but at the same time he told Burwell Bassett, ". . . I have no expectations of returning till Winter . . .": 19 June, 13.

Another indication that GW anticipated such an appointment was his purchase on 7 June 1775 of "5 books—military": Cash Memoranda, Washington Papers, Library of Congress. The titles are unknown, but General Washington recommended five works of military science to Colonel William Woodford, 10 November 1775, *PWR* 2:347. These included: Humphrey Bland, *A Treatise of Military Discipline*, London, 1727, 9th edition 1762, with GW recommending "the newest edition," the ninth; Count Turpin de Crissé, *An Essay on the Art of War*, translated by Captain Joseph Otway, London, 1761; "Instructions for Officers, lately published at Philadelphia," which may be either Roger Stevenson's *Military Instructions for officers detached in the field*, Philadelphia, 1775, or Thomas Simes's *The Military Guide for Young Officers*, London, 1775; Jeney, *The Partisan: Or, the Art of making War in Detachment*, London, 1760; and Major William Young, *Manoeuvres, or Practical Observations on the Art of War*, London, 1771. One military historian considered this a balanced and varied introduction to works of military science which "could never have been prepared by one unfamiliar with military literature": Spaulding 678–9. GW, whose reading on most subjects has been considered meager, may have been unfairly slighted regarding even his reading on the art of war. For a corrective see *WW* 3:293n; 8:29; Griffin 111, 202, 232–3, 537–42; Spaulding 675–80; Robert K. Wright, "'Nor Is Their Standing Army to Be Despised': The Emergence of the Continental Army as a Military Institution," in Ronald Hoffman and Peter J. Albert, eds., *Arms and Independence: The Military Character of the American Revolution*, Charlottesville, Virginia, 1984, 65–8; Higginbotham, *Washington*, 78. See Chapter 4 at n. 6.

GW also acquired a number of publications on political subjects. *A Declaration . . . seting forth the Causes and Necessity of their taking up Arms*, Philadelphia, 1775, drafted by John Dickinson and published by order of Congress; GW had it read to the army at Boston, 15 July 1775, and sent a copy to George William Fairfax in England, along with the second address of Congress to the inhabitants of Great Britain: Griffin 56–7; to Fairfax, 25 July 1775, *PWR* 1:171. GW also acquired a copy of "An Address to the twelve united Colonies of North-America by their Representatives in Congress, to the People of Ireland," Philadelphia, 1775; "A Sermon on the present Situation of American Affairs," by the Reverend Doctor William Smith, Provost of the College and Academy of Philadelphia, preached 23 June 1775, Philadelphia, 1775; and a sermon for the congressionally appointed fast day, 20 July 1775, by the Reverend Dr. Thomas Coombe, Philadelphia, 1775. From New York City, he obtained two copies of a pamphlet giving the substance of the testimony of Richard Glover to the House of Commons on behalf of West Indian planters and merchants petitioning for redress because of the harmful effects they apprehended from the non-importation association established by Congress, New York, 1775 (originally published London, 1775): Griffin 56, 184–5, 58–9, 85. Heading the list of "Encouragers of the work" for the Philadelphia edition of James Burgh's *Political Disquisitions*, 1775, was "His Excellency, George Washington, Esq.; Generalissimo of all the Forces in America." The original London edition had appeared only the year before: Charles Evans, comp., *American Bibliography*, Chicago, 1903–59, 14 volumes, 5:107; H. Trevor Colbourn, *The Lamp of Experience: Whig History and the Intellectual Origins of the American Revolution*, New York, 1974 (originally published Chapel Hill, North Carolina, 1965), 19.

31. To Martha Washington, 18 June, *PWR* 1:3–4; to John Augustine Washington, 20 June 1775, 19–20.

32. Address to the Continental Congress (16 June 1775), *PWR* 1:1; to Burwell Bassett, 19 June, 12–13; to John Parke Custis, 19 June, 15; to the Officers of Five Virginia Independent Companies, 20 June, 16–17; to John Augustine Washington, 20 June, 19.

33. To Robert Jackson, 2 August 1755, *PWC* 1:350; to Bassett, 19 June 1775, *PWR* 1:13.

34. To Martha Washington, 18 June 1775, *PWR* 1:4 (in August 1755, when offered command of the Virginia Regiment the second time, GW had used almost identical language to justify his acceptance to his mother: to Mary Ball Washington, [14 August 1755], *PWC* 1:359); to John Augustine Washington, 20 June, *PWR* 1:19. In his autobiography, written decades later, Benjamin Rush recalled that about the time of GW's appointment Patrick Henry told Rush of a conversation with the general in which GW declared his inadequacy for the command and his expectation of the ruin of his reputation: George W. Corner, ed., *The Autobiography of Benjamin Rush*, Princeton, New Jersey, 1948, 112–13. Although this secondhand story describes GW's anxieties as somewhat more intense than his own contemporaneous written expressions conveyed them, the anecdote does not fundamentally contradict GW's own words. This reference is included in a note rather than in the text because it was secondhand and was recorded long after the event.

35. To Mrs. George William Fairfax, 12 September 1758, *WW* 2:288; to Martha Washington, 18 June 1775, *PWR* 1:4.

36. To John Augustine Washington, 25 March 1775, *WW* 3:277.

CHAPTER FIFTEEN

1. *PWR* 1:17.

2. Bernard Bailyn, *The Origins of American Politics*, New York, 1968, 41–8, 53–6, 139–46; Bailyn, *Ideological Origins*, 56–63.

3. Bailyn, *Ideological Origins*, 43–4. See also: Silverman 82–3, 105–7, for Whig literary as well as political influences.

4. Joseph Addison, *The Tragedy of Cato*, in John S. P. Tatlock and R. G. Martin, eds., *Representative English Plays*, New York, 1938, second edition, 543–76.

5. Fredric M. Litto, "Addison's *Cato* in the Colonies," *William and Mary Quarterly*, third series, 23 (1966), 431–49; Ford, *Washington and Theatre*, 25–6; Davis, *Intellectual Life in the Colonial South* 3:1301–2; to Mrs. George William Fairfax, 25 September 1758, *WW* 2:293. In many letters, GW quoted or paraphrased lines from the play: to Governor Jonathan Trumbull, Sr., 18 July 1775, *PWR* 1:132; to Brigadier General John Thomas, 23 July, 160; to Governor Nicholas Cooke, 29 October, 2:250; to the Comte de Grasse, 15 May 1784, *WW* 27:401; to Timothy Pickering, 27 July 1795, 34:251; to David Humphreys, 12 June 1796, 35:92; to Alexander Hamilton, 26 June, 103. See also n.6 below. Joseph Reed drafted the letter to Thomas. Thomas Mifflin drafted the first letter to Arnold. The draftsmen of the other letters written in 1775 have not been identified. Paraphrases and quotes from *Cato* occur in many contemporaneous American letters, so it is possible that one of GW's military secretaries inserted those lines. GW drafted the other letters himself.

6. Instructions to Colonel Benedict Arnold, 14 September 1775, *PWR* 1:458; to Arnold, 5 December, 2:493. In 1778, Jonathan Mitchell Sewall wrote an epilogue for a Portsmouth, New Hampshire, production of *Cato* in which he compared Washington to the noble Roman. Thomas Dawes, Jr., the Boston Massacre orator in 1781, also identified GW with Cato: Bryan 144–5; Hezekiah Niles, ed., *Principles and Acts of the Revolution in America*, New York, 1876 (originally published Baltimore, 1822), 70.

7. To the Officers of Five Virginia Independent Companies, 20 June 1775, *PWR* 1:16, cf. 12–13, 19. (GW had made the same assertion of insufficient experience using similar language when, in 1755, he was offered the command of the Virginia Regiment: to Charles Lewis, 14 August 1755, *PWC* 1:364.) *Virginia Gazette* (Purdie), 14 July 1775, Supplement, 2; *Pennsylvania Evening Post*, 25 July 1775, 321; *Pennsylvania Gazette*, 26 July 1775, 2; *Boston Gazette, and Country Journal*, 14 August 1775, 4; *Massachusetts Gazette and Boston Weekly News-Letter*, 31 August 1775, 2.

8. Silas Deane to Elizabeth Deane, 16 June 1775, *LDC* 1:494; *Adams Diary* 3:323; Eliphalet Dyer to Joseph Trumbull, 17 June 1775, *LDC* 1:499–500; Deane to Deane, 18 June, 505, cf. 497, 506, 530. GW's practice of speaking little, especially in public assemblies, and then only with great forethought and in moments when his opinion would carry weight, probably also had its intended effect at this moment in his career. According to one contemporary commentator, the rashness of Patrick Henry's oratory and actions at this time had cost him the confidence of moderates: Mays 2:21. In his autobiography, John Adams observed: "Eloquence in public Assemblies is not the surest road, to Fame and Preferment, at least unless it be used with great caution, very rarely, and with great Reserve. The Examples of Washington, Franklin and Jefferson are enough to shew that Silence and reserve in public are more Efficacious than Argumentation or Oratory": *Adams Diary* 3:336.

9. John Adams to Abigail Adams, 17 June 1775, *LDC* 1:497; Robert Treat

Paine to Artemas Ward, 18 June, 509; Silas Deane to Joseph Trumbull, 18 June, 506; Adams to William Tudor, 20 June, 517; Adams to James Warren, 20 June, 518; Thomas Cushing to James Bowdoin, Sr., 21 June, 530.

10. To John Augustine Washington, 20 June 1775, *PWR* 1:19, cf. 3, 12–13, 15, 16; Answer to an Address from the Massachusetts Legislature, [29 March 1776], *WW* 4:440–1.

11. *Adams Diary* 3:323; New York Provincial Congress to New York Delegates, 7 June 1775, Force 2:1281–2.

12. Address to the Continental Congress (16 June 1775), *PWR* 1:1. The New England delegates opposed the pay voted for all of the general officers as far too high. They feared that the people back home would find it disturbingly extravagant, but the representatives of the other provinces insisted upon the necessity of establishing and upholding the dignity and status of Continental generals: *LDC* 1:500, 504, 529, 530. GW's refusal of pay, his request that Congress instead simply underwrite his expenses in the service, was probably in part a response to these misgivings. See also to Lund Washington, 26 November 1775, *PWR* 2:432, for GW's instructions to his estate manager to practice economy "at home," because he would earn nothing in the service.

13. Adams to Elbridge Gerry, 18 June 1775, *LDC* 1:504.

14. Deane to Elizabeth Deane, 16 June 1775, *LDC* 1:494.

15. Benjamin Franklin to Silas Deane, 27 August 1775, *LDC* 1:710. On mercenaries see *Constitutional Gazette*, 30 September 1775, quoted in Moore, *Diary of Revolution*, 1:144–5; Willard 154, 207–8, 214, 220.

16. *Pennsylvania Evening Post*, 14 October 1775, 467; *Pennsylvania Packet*, 16 October 1775, 2; *Massachusetts Spy*, 20 October 1775, 2; *South Carolina Gazette* (Timothy), 28 November 1775, 1.

17. Address of Massachusetts Council and House, 29 March 1776, Washington Papers, Library of Congress, published in *Boston Gazette, and Country Journal*, 1 April 1776, 2; *Providence Gazette*, 6 April 1776, 1; *Virginia Gazette* (Dixon and Hunter), 20 April 1776, 2; Address of John Hancock to GW on Behalf of Congress, 2 April 1776, Washington Papers, Library of Congress; draft by John Jay in [John Jay], *John Jay, the Making of a Revolutionary: Unpublished Papers, 1745–1780*, ed. Richard B. Morris, New York, 1975, 247; [Thomas Paine], *The Writings of Thomas Paine*, ed. Moncure D. Conway, New York, 1894–9, 4 volumes, 2:434. For other comments on GW's refusal of pay, his independent fortune, and his leaving private affluence to take the command see "Extract of a letter to a Gentleman in London, dated Philadelphia, June 20, 1775," Force 2:1033; Address from the Massachusetts Provincial Congress to GW on his arrival at Cambridge, 3 July 1775, *PWR* 1:52; Elbridge Gerry to Samuel Adams, 13 December 1775, quoted in Nettels, *Washington and Independence*, 197; Honorary Degree Conferred by Harvard College, 3 April 1776, *Boston Gazette, and Country Journal*, 15 April 1776, 1; 22 April, 4; 31 March 1777, 1–2; "The Spectator to the People of Massachusetts-Bay," 27 January, 1; "On General Washington," 23 September 1782, 3; "A Poem Containing Some Remarks on the Present War," ballad written by a New Englander following the victory at Boston, in Burton Egbert Stevenson, ed., *Poems of American History*, Boston and New York, 1922, 174; "A Political Catechism," by Francis Hopkinson, January 1777, in George Everett Hastings, *The Life and Works of Francis*

Hopkinson, Chicago, 1926, 286; *Freeman's Journal,* 12 April 1777, in Moore, *Diary of Revolution* 1:381; *New Jersey Gazette,* 6 December 1780, in *ibid.* 2:300; *Gazette of the State of South Carolina,* 14 April 1777, 2; Boston Massacre Oration by Jonathan Mason, Jr., 5 March 1780, Niles 64; Ezra Stiles, "The United States Elevated to Glory and Honor," election sermon preached before Connecticut General Assembly, 8 May 1783, New Haven, in John Wingate Thornton, ed., *The Pulpit of the American Revolution,* New York, 1970 (originally published Boston, 1860), 448–9; *Pennsylvania Gazette,* 25 February 1784, 2, noting GW's delivery of his accounts of his expenditures during the war.

American newspapers also reprinted items from the British press praising GW's disinterested virtue. See for instance *Pennsylvania Gazette, and Weekly Advertiser,* 19 May 1779, 2; 29 November 1780, 1; 28 November 1781, 2; *New Jersey Gazette,* 6 December 1780, in Moore, *Diary of Revolution* 2:300; *Boston Gazette, and Country Journal,* 24 November 1783, 1.

18. Higginbotham, *Washington,* 41–2; Carp, "Early American Military," 276–7.

19. DSF 3:426 and n.

20. Address from the New York Provincial Congress, 26 June 1775, *PWR* 1: 40. Three weeks earlier, this same body had enumerated to its congressional delegation the qualifications of a Continental major or brigadier general. They preferred a man of property, kindred, and connections, "that his country . . . may have sure pledges that he will faithfully perform the duties of his high office, and readily lay down his power when the general weal shall require it": New York Provincial Congress to New York Delegates, 7 June 1775, Force 2:1281–2.

21. Address to the New York Provincial Congress, 26 June 1775, *PWR* 1:41.

22. Minutes of the New York Provincial Congress, 26 June 1775, Force 2:1322; *New York Gazette; and the Weekly Mercury,* 3 July 1775, 3; *Pennsylvania Evening Post,* 1 July 1775, 277; *Dunlap's Pennsylvania Packet,* 3 July 1775, 2; *Pennsylvania Journal,* 5 July 1775, in Moore, *Diary of Revolution* 1:104; *Massachusetts Spy,* 5 July 1775, 3; *Pennsylvania Gazette,* 5 July 1775, 1; *Virginia Gazette* (Pinkney), 13 July 1775, 2; *Virginia Gazette* (Purdie), 14 July 1775, 3; *Virginia Gazette* (Dixon and Hunter), 15 July 1775, 3; *South Carolina Gazette, and Country Journal,* 18 July 1775, 2; 25 July, 3; from Landon Carter, 9 May 1776, Washington Papers, Library of Congress, cf. *Carter Diary* 2:1042–3.

23. See, for instance, to John Hancock, 10 July 1775, *PWR* 1:87, 88, 91; [31 August], 390–1; 19 November, 2:398–9; 18 December, 573; 19 January 1776, *WW* 4:259–60; 9 February, 315–18; 7 March, 374; to John Adams, 7 January 1776, 219–20; to Joseph Reed, 3 March, 4:366–8. These examples are taken only from the first year of the war. Illustrations from GW's military correspondence during succeeding years could easily be multiplied to superfluity. For orders against plundering and fraud and commanding cooperation with civilian officials: General Orders, 5 July 1775, *PWR* 1:63; 10 August, 281; 5 September, 414–15; 16 September, 2:1; 23 October, 220; 17 November, 388; 23 July 1776, *WW* 5:327; 1 January 1777, 6:466; 21 January, 7:46–7; to Col. Benedict Arnold, 14 September 1775, *PWR* 1:456–60; Proclamation, 21

March 1776, *WW* 4:412–13. In response to the fear of standing armies and mercenary soldiers, see GW's observations on the danger of suspicion of the American army and his argument that it could be trusted because it was made up of citizen-soldiers: to John Banister, Virginia Delegate to Congress, 21 April 1778, *WW* 11:290–2. For an excellent analysis of GW's ideological and pragmatic reasons for seeking to prevent plundering: E. Wayne Carp, *To Starve the Army at Pleasure: Continental Army Administration and American Political Culture, 1775–1783*, Chapel Hill, North Carolina, 1984, 82–84.

24. *Boston Gazette, and Country Journal*, 1 April 1776, 1; *New York Gazette and Weekly Mercury*, 8 April 1776, 3; *Virginia Gazette* (Dixon and Hunter), 11 May 1776, 1; *South Carolina and American General Gazette*, 17 April– 1 May 1776, 3; *Pennsylvania Evening Post*, 14 January 1777, in William S. Stryker et al., eds., *New Jersey Archives, Documents Relating to the Revolutionary History of the State of New Jersey, Newspaper Extracts, 1776–1782*, Paterson and Trenton, 1901–17, 2nd series, 5 volumes, 1:257–8; *Virginia Gazette* (Purdie), 7 February 1777, 1; *Pennsylvania Gazette*, 12 February 1777, 3; *South Carolina and American General Gazette*, 20 February 1777, 2; 13 March, 1.

25. Address of Massachusetts Council and House to GW, 29 March 1776, Washington Papers, Library of Congress, and *Boston Gazette, and Country Journal*, 1 April 1776, 2; *Providence Gazette*, 6 April 1776, 1; *Virginia Gazette* (Dixon and Hunter), 20 April 1776, 2; Answer to an Address from the Massachusetts Legislature, [28 March 1776], *WW* 4:441.

26. Marquis de Chastellux, *Travels in North America in the Years 1780, 1781, and 1782*, trans. and ed. Howard C. Rice, Chapel Hill, North Carolina, 1963, 2 volumes, 1:113–14; from Mason, 19 March 1783, *Mason Papers* 2:765; Jefferson to Dr. Walter Jones, 2 January 1814, Thomas Jefferson, *The Writings of Thomas Jefferson*, ed. Andrew A. Lipscomb and Albert Bergh, Washington, D.C., 1903, 20 volumes, 14:50. See also Resolves of New York Committee of Safety, 18 April 1776; New York Committee of Safety to GW, 18, 25, 29 April and 23 November; Resolve of the New York Provincial Congress, 8 June; Address of the Governor, Council, and General Assembly of New Jersey, 6 December 1783, all in Washington Papers, Library of Congress; *Virginia Gazette* (Dixon and Hunter), 13 July 1776, 4, 5; Boston Massacre Oration by Benjamin Hichborn, 5 March 1777, Niles 47–50; Address of Ministers et al. of the Dutch Reformed Church at Raritan, New Jersey, to GW and GW's reply, 1 June 1779, Stryker 3:441–3; Address of the Magistrates of the City of Philadelphia to GW and GW's reply, *Pennsylvania Gazette*, 25 December 1781, 3; Address of the Massachusetts General Court to GW, 3 September 1783, 2, and *Boston Gazette, and Country Journal*, 29 September 1783, 2. Alexandre Gérard, first French minister to the United States, wrote to Comte de Vergennes, 8 March 1779: "It is certain that if General Washington were ambitious and scheming, it would have been entirely in his power to make a revolution; but nothing on the part of the General or the Army has justified the shadow of a suspicion. The General sets forth constantly this principle that one must be a Citizen first and an officer afterwards": Gilbert Chinard, ed. and trans., *George Washington as the French Knew Him*, New York, 1969 (originally published Princeton, 1940), 73–4.

27. *WW* 2:444–53; 3:179–80; *PWR* 1:334–6; *LTW* 4:224; 5:110–12, 146–50.

28. Isaac Weld, *Travels through the States of North America* ... *1795–1796, and 1797*, New York, 1970, 2 volumes, 1:105–6; Jefferson to Dr. Walter Jones, 2 January 1814, *Jefferson Writings*, ed. Lipscomb and Bergh, 14:49; Henrietta Liston, "Liston's Journal," 515.

29. "Liston's Journal," 516. In 1783, GW advised his nephew Bushrod to "[b]e courteous to all but intimate with few, and let those few be well tried before you give them your confidence": 15 January 1783, *WW* 26:39–40.

30. Morris to John Marshall, 26 June 1807, Anne C. Morris, ed., *The Diary and Letters of Gouverneur Morris*, New York, 1888, 2 volumes, 2:492.

31. Jefferson to Jones, 2 January 1814, *Jefferson Writings*, ed. Lipscomb and Bergh, 14:49.

32. Abigail Adams to John Adams, 16 July 1775, *Adams Family Correspondence* 1:246; Rush to Thomas Ruston, 29 October 1775, Benjamin Rush, *Letters of Benjamin Rush*, ed. Lyman H. Butterfield, Princeton, 1951, 2 volumes, 1:92. See also Chinard 52, 56–7, 62–3, 75; *WW* 14:63–4n, quoting a German mercenary serving with the British; *WW* 26:321n., quoting an English observer; Benjamin Henry Latrobe, *The Virginia Journals of Benjamin Henry Latrobe, 1795–1798*, ed. Edward C. Carter II et al., New Haven, Connecticut, 1977, 2 volumes, 1:171–2; Lydia Post Diary, 27 November 1776, quoted in Catherine L. Albanese, *Sons of the Fathers: The Civil Religion of the American Revolution*, Philadelphia, 1976, 149; "Liston's Journal," 514; Julian Ursyn Niemcewicz, *Under Their Vine and Fig Tree: Travels through America in 1797–1799, 1805* ... , trans. and ed. Metchie J. E. Budka, Elizabeth, New Jersey, 1965, 84; *Pennsylvania Gazette*, 29 November 1780, 1; 3 September 1783, 2; Baron Ludwig Von Closen, *Revolutionary Journal, 1780–1783*, trans. and ed. Evelyn M. Acomb, Chapel Hill, North Carolina, 1958, 241.

33. *Jefferson Writings*, ed. Lipscomb and Bergh, 14:49; John Adams to Abigail Adams, 23 June 1775, *Adams Family Correspondence* 1:226; DSF 3:459–60, 463, 466.

34. *WW* 4:155, 387–8; 7:452–3, 494–5; 8:178–9; 9:124–30; 12:257–8; 20:349–50; 21:162n; 26:205–6; 37:109–12, 230–1; *Diaries* 6:4. GW frequently used theatrical metaphors to describe his and others' participation in public affairs and even to describe life itself: *PWR* 1:374; *WW* 26:334, 433; 27:285; 30:73, 288; 34:109; 35:205, 246, 324, 341, 399, 403, 411, 412, 418, 437, 447, 452; 36:4, 169, 305, 311, 326, 345, 367; 37:138, 161. During his presidency, GW indicated that he thought of himself as playing a role: speaking in the third person, he considered how "the President" should conduct himself: *WW* 30:355, 394; 32:153, 163; 33:161, 353; 34:224, 228, 482; 35:245; *Diaries* 5:476, 483, 487, cf. *WW* 35:252n; *PWR* 1:98.

CHAPTER SIXTEEN

1. Liddle, " 'Patriot King,' " 951–70; Liddle, "Public Attitudes."

2. Kramnick 157–77; Bailyn, *Ideological Origins*, 50–1.

3. Niccolò Machiavelli, *Chief Works and Others*, trans. Allan Gilbert, Dur-

ham, North Carolina, 1965, 3 volumes, *The Discourses*, Book I, Chapter 10, 1:223.

4. Kramnick 244–5; Henry St. John, 1st Viscount Bolingbroke, *The Works of the Late Right Honorable Henry St. John, Lord Viscount Bolingbroke*, London, 1754, 5 volumes, "The Idea of a Patriot King," 3:35–125.

5. *Works of Bolingbroke*, 3:40, 73, 77–82, 108–9, 65–8, 82–3; Liddle, "'Patriot King,'" 955.

6. *Works of Bolingbroke*, 3:75–7, 55–6, 69–70, 91, 124–5.

7. David Hume, *Political Essays of David Hume*, ed. Charles W. Hendel, Indianapolis, 1953, 12; Governor Francis Bernard to Massachusetts Assembly, May 1765, quoted in Lawrence H. Gipson, *The Coming of the Revolution, 1763–1775*, New York, 1954, 88; John Brown, *An Estimate of the Manners and Principles of the Times*, London, 1757–8, 2 volumes in 1, 2:252–9; James Burgh, *Political Disquisitions*, London, 1774–5, 3 volumes, 2:456–7; 3:125, 190; Richard Price, *Observations on the Nature of Civil Liberty*, London, 1776, 70; Liddle, "'Patriot King,'" 953, 956–7; Liddle, "Public Attitudes," 91–6, 102n, 127n; Richard Beale Davis, *A Colonial Southern Bookshelf*, Athens, Georgia, 1979, 59–61; Robert M. Weir, "The Role of the Newspaper Press in the Southern Colonies on the Eve of the Revolution: An Interpretation," in his *"The Last of American Freemen,"* 180–3.

8. Liddle, "'Patriot King,'" 957–8; Liddle, "Public Attitudes," 134–66.

9. Liddle, "Public Attitudes," 208–16.

10. Liddle, "'Patriot King,'" 962–3; Liddle, "Public Attitudes," 247–53. Liddle argues that virtually all attacks on monarchy in general and on George III in particular originated in Britain. This is borne out by the evidence cited by other historians who have studied the American resistance movement during these years, although they do not make that point, cf. Maier, *From Resistance to Revolution*, 205–19; Dunbar 12–19; Duff 383–97.

11. Maier, *From Resistance to Revolution*, 205–19; Liddle, "Public Attitudes," 257–81, 293n.

12. *JCC* 2:160; to George William Fairfax, 31 May 1775, *WW* 3:291–2. For instances from July to December 1775 of GW calling the British army "Ministerial Troops" and blaming the crisis on a ministerial conspiracy: *PWR* 1:116, 171, 184, 189, 226, 274, 280, 284, 398, 419, 421, 438, 447, 448; 2:47, 70, 101, 161, 179, 180, 187, 199, 214, 225–6, 239, 252, 282, 301, 303, 325, 345, 387, 392, 408, 462, 489, 490, 562, 576, 579, 585, 600, 618, 623. See also Liddle, "'Patriot King,'" 966, 970; John Richard Alden, *The American Revolution, 1775–1783*, New York, 1954, 74; Philip Davidson, *Propaganda and the American Revolution, 1763–1783*, New York, 1973 (originally published Chapel Hill, North Carolina, 1941), 149–50; Duff 396–7; Willard 123, 143, 145, 163, 166–7, 175–8, 180, 189–94, 213–14; *South Carolina and American General Gazette*, 18–25 August 1775, 2; *Virginia Gazette* (Purdie), 20 October 1775, Supplement, 2.

13. For the most thorough examination of GW's role see Nettels, *Washington and Independence*.

14. *PWR* 1:54, 88–9, 132, 223–4, 240–1, 245–6, 265–6, 361, 372–3, 376–7, 384; 2:55–6, 73, 192, 331, 335, 450, 528–9.

15. To Lewis Morris, 4 August 1775, *PWR* 1:241; to Governor Jonathan Trumbull, 18 July, 131, 132 (two letters); to Brigadier General John Thomas, 23 July, 159–62, cf. to Nicholas Cooke, 4 August, 221; to New York Provincial Congress, 8 August, 274; to Brigadier General Joseph Spencer, 26 September, 2:55–6; to Major Benjamin Tupper, [20 October], 214; General Orders, 22 October, 216–17; General Orders, 28 November, 443–4.

16. To Lieutenant General Thomas Gage, 11 August 1775, *PWR* 1:289.

17. From Lieutenant General Thomas Gage, 13 August 1775, *PWR* 1: 301–2.

18. To Gage, 19 August 1775, *PWR* 1:326–8. This letter, obviously designed for public consumption, was carefully composed and polished. General Charles Lee framed an early draft, parts of which made it to the final version. The draft in Washington Papers, Library of Congress, is in the hand of Joseph Reed, one of GW's secretaries: "Draft—to General Gage" [August 1775], *Lee Papers* 4:200–2; *WW* 3:431–2n; Nettels, *Washington and Independence*, 150–1.

19. To John Hancock, 31 August 1775, *PWR* 1:392; *Virginia Gazette* (Purdie), 22 September 1775, 2, "Extract of a Letter from the Camp at Cambridge, August 21," probably reprinted from a Philadelphia newspaper of 6 September. GW-Gage letters published in: *Boston-Gazette, and Country Journal*, 23 October 1775, 1; *Massachusetts Gazette and Boston Weekly News-Letter*, 19 October 1775, 1–2; *Massachusetts Spy*, 13 October 1775, 2; *New York Gazette and Weekly Mercury*, 9 October 1775, 1; *Pennsylvania Evening Post*, 28 September 1775, 440–1; 16 December, 580; *Pennsylvania Gazette*, 4 October 1775, 4; *South Carolina and American General Gazette*, 16–20 October 1775, 3; *South Carolina Gazette* (Timothy), 17 October 1775, 3; *Virginia Gazette* (Pinkney), 12 October 1775, 1; *Virginia Gazette* (Purdie), 13 October 1775, Supplement, 1; *Virginia Gazette* (Dixon and Hunter), 14 October 1775, 3; *Pennsylvania Magazine: Or, American Monthly Museum*, volume I, number 10 (October 1775), 486–8. Benjamin Rush to Thomas Ruston, 29 October 1775, *Rush Letters* 1:92, cf. to William Ramsay, 10–16 November 1775, *PWR* 2:344, responding to public "approbation" in Virginia.

For another example of skillfully fashioned American propaganda originating from GW's headquarters see GW's address "To the Inhabitants of Canada" (c. 14 September 1775), *PWR* 1:461–3. This broadside once again made GW the voice of the American cause: *Boston Gazette, and Country Journal*, 2 October 1775, 2; *Massachusetts Gazette and Boston Weekly News-Letter*, 26 October 1775, 1; *Pennsylvania Evening Post*, 7 October 1775, 456–7; *Virginia Gazette* (Purdie), 20 October 1775, Supplement, 1. In the last paper, a writer issuing a call to arms quoted "the words of our noble WASHINGTON in his address to the people of Canada": 20 October, Supplement, 2.

20. "Proceedings of the Committee of Conference" (18–24 October 1775), *PWR* 2:185–205, see especially 194–5; Nettels, *Washington and Independence*, 164–8.

21. Liddle, "Public Attitudes," 363–90; Liddle, "'Patriot King,'" 965; Samuel Ward to Henry Ward, 2 November 1775, *LDC* 2:291; Rhode Island Delegates to Governor Nicholas Cooke, 4 November, 301; Joseph Hewes to James Iredell, 9 November, 322; Joseph Hewes to Samuel Johnston, 9 November, 324; John DeHart to the New Jersey Assembly, 13 November, 334–5.

22. Liddle, "Public Attitudes," 391–2; Liddle, "'Patriot King,'" 966.

23. To Joseph Reed, 10 February 1776, *WW* 4:321; Circular Instructions for the Seizure of Certain Royal Officials, 5(–12) November 1775, *PWR* 2:301–2; Instructions to Brigadier General John Sullivan, 7 November, 325; to Governor Jonathan Trumbull, Sr., 15 November, 379–80; to Governor Nicholas Cooke, 15 November, 379; to Joseph Reed, 20 November, 408; to William Ramsay, [4–11] December, 489.

24. Liddle, "'Patriot King,'" 967–8; Liddle, "Public Attitudes," 405–24; Winthrop D. Jordan, "Familial Politics: Thomas Paine and the Killing of the King, 1776," *The Journal of American History*, 60 (September 1973–4), 299–301; Davidson 149–50; from Fielding Lewis, 6 March 1776, Washington Papers, Library of Congress; Willard 274–5, 300–1, 306; Griffin 156–7, for GW's copy.

25. On *Common Sense*: to Joseph Reed, 31 January 1776, *WW* 4:297; to Reed, 1 April, 455. On Independence: to Reed, 14 January 1776, 244; to President of Congress, 9 February, 313, 315–18; to Reed, 10 February, 321; to President, 14 February, 330–1; to Reed, 7 March, 383; to President, 24 March, 427–8 and n.6; to John Augustine Washington, 31 March, 447–51; to John Adams, 15 April, 483–4. On the king: to President, 4 January, 209–10. On "King's" troops: *WW* 4:215–17, 281, 288, 321, 332, 366, 384, 449, 469, 474, 530, 533–4; 5:3–4, 20, 121, 167, 169–70, 193, 281, 321.

26. To Joseph Reed, 1 April 1776, *WW* 4:455; 20 November 1775, *PWR* 2:408–9.

27. On GW's nationalism: to Joseph Reed, 31 January 1776, *WW* 4:297; to Major General Charles Lee, 14 March, 397; to Reed, 1 April, 454–5, cf. 5:251, 316. On handling Tories: to Governor Nicholas Cooke, 6 January 1776, 4:216; to Governor Trumbull, 7 January, 217–19; Instructions to Major General Charles Lee, 8 January, 221–2; 23 January, 266; 30 January, 293; to Major General Schuyler, 27 January, 281; to John Augustine Washington, 31 March, 449; to the Committee of Suffolk, Long Island, 16 May, 5:48–9; to Major General Putnam, 21 May, 69–70; to New York Legislature, 21 May, 70; to Major General Schuyler, 22 May, 75; to President of Congress, 20 June, 159; 28 June, 193; to the Committee of Essex County, New Jersey, 30 June, 203–4; to the Captain of Governor Franklin's Guard, 30 June, 204–5; to Brigadier General Livingston, 5 July, 225; 6 July, 226–7.

28. Liddle, "Public Attitudes," 438–41; "Declaration of Independence," *Jefferson Papers*, ed. Boyd, Cullen, et al., 1:429–32.

29. *Boston Gazette, and Country Journal*, 22 July 1776, 2, 3; *Pennsylvania Gazette*, 17 July 1776, 2; 24 July, 2; 9 October, 3; *Virginia Gazette* (Dixon and Hunter), 29 July 1776, 4; *Pennsylvania Journal*, 17 July, 20 August 1776, and *Universal Intelligencer, and Pennsylvania Evening Post*, 8 October 1776, both quoted in Moore, *Diary of Revolution*, 1:270–1, 279, 283–4; Isaac Bangs, *Journal of Lieutenant Isaac Bangs, April 1 to July 29, 1776*, ed. Edward Bangs, Cambridge, Massachusetts, 1880, 57; *Marshall Diary*, 80–1; Liddle, "Public Attitudes," 442–3.

30. Liddle, "'Patriot King,'" 951, 968; Maier, *From Resistance to Revolution*, 288–95, cf. Liddle, "Public Attitudes," 426–34, 444–6.

31. Curtis P. Nettels, "The Washington Theme in American History," *Mas-*

sachusetts Historical Society Proceedings, 68 (1952), 175; DSF 3:xii–xiii.

32. To Richard Henry Lee, 10 July 1775, PWR 1:98.

33. On GW's journey to Cambridge: Boston Gazette, and Country Journal, 3 July 1775, 3; Massachusetts Spy, 5 July 1775, 3; Pennsylvania Evening Post, 24 June 1775, 265; 27 June, 269; 11 July, 298; 13 July, 301; Pennsylvania Gazette, 21 June 1775, 3; 28 June, 2, 3; 12 July, 3; 19 July, 4; South Carolina and American General Gazette, 7–14 July 1775, 3; 14–21 July, 3; 4–11 August, 1; South Carolina Gazette, and Country Journal (Charles Crouch), Extraordinary, Sunday Evening, 9 July 1775; 11 July, 2; Extraordinary, Saturday, 22 July, 2; Virginia Gazette (Purdie), 7 July 1775, 2, 3; 14 July, Supplement, 1; 4 August, 2; Virginia Gazette (Pinkney), 6 July 1775, 3; 13 July, 2, 3; 3 August, 2; Virginia Gazette (Dixon and Hunter), 8 July 1775, 3; 15 July, 1, 2; 5 August, 2; Extract of Minutes of the New York Provincial Congress, 25 June 1775, Force 2:1318; Thomas Jones, History of New York during the Revolutionary War..., New York, 1968 (originally published New York, 1879), 2 volumes, 1:55–8, 555–6, a loyalist account that sniggers at the timorousness of New York's leaders; Nineteenth Annual Report, 1914, American Scenic and Historic Preservation Society, Albany, New York, 1914, 261, 265, 266. For a detailed account of GW's journey see DSF 3:459–76. For New Englanders' opinions of GW: Joseph Webb to Silas Deane, 22 June 1775, Webb Correspondence and Journals 1:71; Pennsylvania Gazette, 28 June 1775, 3; Virginia Gazette (Pinkney), 13 July 1775, 3; (Purdie), 14 July 1775, Supplement, 1; (Dixon and Hunter), 15 July 1775, 1; William Tudor to John Adams, 26 June 1775, Adams Papers 3:48; James Warren to Adams, 27 June, 52; John Thaxter to Adams, 28 June 1775, Adams Family Correspondence 1:234.

34. Pennsylvania Packet, 12 June 1775, in Moore, Diary of Revolution 1:96; Virginia Gazette (Purdie), 30 June 1775, 3; New York Gazette and Weekly Mercury, 19 June 1775, 2, cf. 3 July, 2.

35. From the Fairfax Independent Company, 8 July 1775, PWR 1:77–8; Virginia Gazette (Purdie), 4 August 1775, Postscript, 1.

36. David Freeman Hawke, Benjamin Rush, Revolutionary Gadfly, Indianapolis and New York, 1971, 21; Dunlap's Pennsylvania Packet, 26 June 1775, 3.

37. "American Liberty, a Poem," appeared as a pamphlet in New York, July 1775; advertised in New York Journal (Holt), 6 July 1775; Philip Freneau, Poems of Philip Freneau, ed. Fred Lewis Pattee, Princeton, 1902–7, 3 volumes, 1:142n, 148, 149; Philip M. Marsh, Philip Freneau, Poet and Journalist, Minneapolis, 1968, copyright 1967, 45. Despite his prose attacks on the Washington administration during the 1790s, Freneau wrote a greater quantity of verse praising GW than any other poet of the era: Bryan 121–7. For another poetic reference to GW's heroism at Braddock's defeat: Kent A. Bowman, Voices of Combat: A Century of Liberty and War Songs, 1765–1865, Westport, Connecticut, 1987, 19, quoting Pennsylvania Packet, 14 September 1775. [John Leacock], The Fall of British Tyranny; or, American Liberty Triumphant, Philadelphia, 1776, was the first dramatic fiction in which GW appeared as a character. Internal evidence indicates that this play was written following publication of Common Sense in January 1776 and before news had arrived in Philadelphia of the victory at Boston on 17 March. In one of its disconnected

scenes "Lord Hypocrite" recalls one of GW's heroic exploits in the previous war: p. 12. GW appears in several scenes with Lee and Putnam. GW does not stand apart from or above his colleagues, but no character in any scene has a distinctive individual personality. The patriots simply declaim against British tyranny: pp. 58–65.

38. Extract of a Letter from a Gentleman of this City, dated Cambridge, 9 August, *Pennsylvania Gazette*, 23 August 1775, 3; *Pennsylvania Evening Post*, 24 August 1775, 374–5; *Virginia Gazette* (Purdie), 8 September 1775, Supplement, 1; Jonathan Williams Austin to John Adams, 7 July 1775, *Adams Papers* 3:66; *Stiles Literary Diary* 1:614; Hannah Winthrop to Mercy Warren, 17 August 1775, *Warren-Adams Letters* 72:102, see also Mercy Warren to John Adams, 5 July 1775, *Adams Papers* 3:58; James Warren to John Adams, 7 July, 68; William Tudor to Adams, 19 July, 79; Abigail Adams to John Adams, 16 July 1775, *Adams Family Correspondence* 1:246; Thomas Lynch to GW, 13 November 1775, *PWR* 2:366.

39. From Phillis Wheatley, 26 October 1775, *PWR* 2:242–4; James Warren to John Adams, 16 November 1775, *Adams Papers* 3:306, see also 305–6; Warren to Adams, 3 December, 3:347; from Charles Carroll of Carrollton, 26 September 1775, *PWR* 2:45; from Richard Henry Lee, 26 September, 52.

40. Dedications: Rev. Mr. Jacob Duché, "The Duty of Standing Fast in Our Spiritual and Temporal Liberties," advertised in *Virginia Gazette* (Dixon and Hunter), 9 September 1775, 3; from Jacob Duché, 5 August 1775, *PWR* 1:246–7; Roger Stevenson, *Military Instructions for Officers . . . Containing, a Scheme for Forming a Corps of Partisans*, advertised in *Boston Gazette, and Country Journal*, 30 October 1775, 1. Naming ships: Lawrence Martin, "The Dates of Naming Places and Things for George Washington," *History of the George Washington Bicentennial Celebration, Literature Series*, Washington, D.C., 1932, 3 volumes, 3:309; *PWR* 2:47n.1, 178, 267; *Pennsylvania Evening Post*, 13 August 1776, 401; Roger P. Bristol, *Supplement to Charles Evans' American Bibliography*, Charlottesville, Virginia, 1970, 246, B4300, broadside announcing outfitting of brigantine "Washington" as privateer, 17 September 1776. Naming children: *Virginia Gazette* (Pinkney), 24 August 1775, 3; 5 October, 3; *Virginia Gazette* (Dixon and Hunter), 7 October 1775, 3; *Pennsylvania Gazette*, 8 November 1775, 3; *Constitutional Gazette*, 23 August 1775, and *New England Chronicle*, 2 November 1775, both in Moore, *Diary of Revolution* 1:121, 159. For later examples of naming children for GW and even for Martha see *Essex Gazette*, 18 January 1776, quoted in *ibid.* 1:192; *Boston Gazette, and Country Journal*, 22 January 1776, 3; 22 April, 3; 27 May, 3; 28 December 1778, 3; *Virginia Gazette* (Purdie), 17 May 1776, 2; Robert A. Gross, *The Minutemen and Their World*, New York, 1976, 139; *Pennsylvania Gazette*, 25 September 1776, 3; from Ebenezer Hancock, 30 January 1777; from Matthew Neely, 8 December 1783, both in Washington Papers, Library of Congress; *South Carolina and American General Gazette*, 26 March 1778, 2; to Joseph Reed, 4 July 1780, *WW* 19:115; to Mrs. Nathanael Greene, 15 December 1780, 20:480.

41. *Boston Gazette, and Country Journal*, 4 December 1775, 3; *Massachusetts Spy*, 8 December 1775, 2; *Pennsylvania Evening Post*, 21 November 1775,

535; 26 December, 594; *Pennsylvania Gazette*, 22 November 1775, 3; 29 November, 3; 6 December, 2; *Pennsylvania Packet*, 27 November 1775, 3; *Virginia Gazette* (Purdie), 8 December 1775, 2; *Virginia Gazette* (Dixon and Hunter), 9 December 1775, 2; *Marshall Diary*, 51–3; DSF 3:581, cf. 4:77; *Massachusetts Spy*, 26 January 1776, 3.

42. Vote of "Meeting of the Freeholders and other Inhabitants of the district of Stoughtonham," 11 March 1776, Washington Papers, Library of Congress. Heretofore scholars of geographical place-names have believed that the first place named for GW was Mount Washington on Manhattan Island and the first town Washington, New Hampshire. The former place was named during the spring or early summer of 1776 when Fort Washington was constructed there. The petition to establish the Town of Washington, New Hampshire, was dated 22 September 1776. The town was incorporated 13 December 1776. In North Carolina, a petition to establish the "Washington District" was received by the Council of Safety on 22 August 1776. The petition may have been composed as early as 5 July. Representatives of the District were seated in the revolutionary legislature on 19 November 1776. The District became Washington County on 18 December 1777. A vast territory, it eventually became the State of Tennessee. Maryland established Washington County on 6 December 1776, but the name may have been used as early as 31 August. Washington County, Virginia, was established 21 December 1776. The petition to create the county dated from June, but the name Washington was proposed and then adopted probably sometime after 11 October, when the petition was first considered by the House of Delegates: L. Martin 3:308–10; George R. Stewart, *Names on the Land*, revised edition, Boston, 1968, 164. The first fort named for GW was not on Manhattan, but near Portsmouth, New Hampshire, designated sometime before the end of October 1775: *PWR* 2:252.

43. *Boston Gazette, and Country Journal*, 22 January 1776, 1, from *Pennsylvania Packet*; Peter Thacher, *An Oration Delivered at Watertown, March 5, 1776. To Commemorate the Bloody Massacre at Boston: Perpetrated March 5, 1770*, Watertown, Massachusetts, 1776, 13–14. See also "Smile Massachusetts, Smile," *Connecticut Gazette*, 23 February 1776, 3, listed in Gillian B. Anderson, ed., *Freedom's Voice in Poetry and Song*, Wilmington, Delaware, 1977, 23; reprinted in Frank Moore, *Songs and Ballads of the American Revolution*, New York, 1856, 118–21.

44. *Boston Gazette, and Country Journal*, 18 March 1776, 3; 25 March, 3; 1 April, 2, 3; 8 April, 2; 15 April, 1; 22 April, 4; *New York Packet*, 28 March 1776, in Moore, *Diary of Revolution* 1:222, 226–7; *Pennsylvania Evening Post*, 30 March 1776, 162–3; 2 April, 166–7; 9 April, 177, 179; 16 April, 189; *Pennsylvania Gazette*, 3 April 1776, 2; *Pennsylvania Packet*, 22 April 1776, 5; *Providence Gazette*, 6 April 1776, 1; *South Carolina and American General Gazette*, 17 April–1 May 1776, 2; *Virginia Gazette* (Dixon and Hunter), 20 April 1776, 2; 11 May, 4. Congress voted that a gold medal be struck and presented to Washington to commemorate his great victory: from President Hancock, 2 April 1776, and from John Adams, 1 April, both in Washington Papers, Library of Congress, cf. *South Carolina and American General Gazette*, 1–8 May 1776, 3. For other praise of GW see: from George Mason, 2 April

1776, *Mason Papers* 1:266; Abigail Adams to John Adams, 31 March 1776, *Adams Family Correspondence* 1:369; John Winthrop to John Adams, 5 April 1776, *Adams Papers* 4:109; "Extracts from the Diary of Dr. James Clitherall, 1776," 13 May 1776, *Pennsylvania Magazine of History and Biography*, 22 (1898), 471 (this entry is in the past tense, which suggests it was written sometime later).

45. Wheatley's poem appeared in *Virginia Gazette* (Dixon and Hunter), 30 March 1776, 1, and *Pennsylvania Magazine* 17 (April 1776); Phillis Wheatley, *Poems of Phillis Wheatley*, ed. Julian D. Mason, Jr., Chapel Hill, North Carolina, 1966, 87–8. For the New Englander's "Remarks" see B. E. Stevenson 174. "[A]wake, awake": *Virginia Gazette* (Dixon and Hunter), 25 May 1776, 3; *Pennsylvania Packet*, 13 May 1776, 3. See also Elisha Rich, "A Poem On the Late distress of the Town of Boston," Chelmsford, Massachusetts, 1776, broadside, in Georgia B. Bumgardner, ed., *American Broadsides*, Barre, Massachusetts, 1971, plate 12. Another poem praising GW's success over the British at Boston was written in the spring of 1776 by young David Humphreys, who later became one of GW's secretaries and in the 1780s began a kind of official biography of GW which he never completed. He became noted at the time as a poet and served as a diplomat. His "Ode" to GW was transmitted to the general in July 1776, somehow was mislaid, and remained unpublished until 1971: Julian D. Mason, "David Humphreys' Lost Ode to George Washington, 1776," *Quarterly Journal of the Library of Congress*, 28 (January 1971), 29–37.

46. *Webb Correspondence and Journals* 1:148–9; Jedediah Huntington to Jabez Huntington, 24–25 June 1776, Josiah Huntington and Jedediah Huntington, *Huntington Papers: Correspondence of the Brothers Josiah and Jedediah Huntington . . . 1771–1783, Connecticut Historical Society Collections*, Hartford, Connecticut, 1923, 20:302; *Massachusetts Spy*, 5 and 10 July 1776, 3; *Pennsylvania Journal*, 26 June 1776; *Pennsylvania Evening Post*, 2 July 1776, both in Moore, *Diary of Revolution* 1:255–7; *Pennsylvania Gazette*, 26 June 1776, 2–3; 3 July, 2; *Virginia Gazette* (Purdie), 5 July 1776, 2; *Virginia Gazette* (Dixon and Hunter), 6 July 1776, 8; 20 July, 4; Willard 328–9.

47. "Memorial of Sundry inhabitants of the city of New York and other friends to the peace and safety of the United States of America," 9–14 July 1776; Address of Officers and Soldiers of Several Regiments of the Second Brigade Stationed at New York City, 29 June 1776, both in Washington Papers, Library of Congress; Jedediah Huntington to Jabez Huntington, 24–25 June 1776, *Huntington Papers* 20:302. The Massachusetts legislature issued a proclamation for a day of public humiliation, fasting, and prayer to supplicate God that "he would commend his blessing upon all our public Counsels in this important crisis of our political affairs; protect and preserve the Life of our General, his Officers and Soldiers; succeed and prosper their arms, where ever employed": *Boston Gazette, and Country Journal*, 15 July 1776, 1.

48. *Boston Gazette, and Country Journal*, 29 July 1776, 2; 5 August, 1; 12 August, 2; *Massachusetts Spy*, 24 July 1776, 3; 14 August, 4; *New York Gazette and Weekly Mercury*, 29 July 1776, 1; 5 August, 1; *Pennsylvania Evening Post*, 16, 18, 23, 25, 27 July 1776, 352, 356, 357, 363, 369, 373; *Pennsylvania Gazette*, 24 July 1776, 2, 3; 31 July, 3; *Pennsylvania Journal*, 31 July 1776, in

F. Moore, *Diary of the Revolution* 1:272–5; *Pennsylvania Magazine: Or, American Monthly Museum*, volume II (July 1776), 343–4; *Virginia Gazette* (Dixon and Hunter), 3 August 1776, 1; 10 August, 5; 17 August, 1; *Virginia Gazette* (Purdie), 9 August 1776, 2; 16 August, 1; *Bangs Journal*, 62; *Webb Correspondence and Journals* 1:155–6; DSF 4:140–1. For the American general's account: *Massachusetts Spy*, 7 August 1776, 3; Resolve of Congress, 17 July 1776, Washington Papers, Library of Congress. Cf. Garry Wills, *Cincinnatus: George Washington and the Enlightenment*, New York, 1984, xix–xxi.

49. "War and Washington!" by Jonathan Mitchell Sewall, in B. E. Stevenson 170. Bristol lists a broadside under the title "Gen. Washington, a new favourite song, at the American camp. To the tune of the British Grenadiers," 1776. There is no place of publication, but it was most probably Boston: Bristol, 250, B4361. This is probably Sewall's song. It possibly first appeared in *Massachusetts Spy*, 2 February 1776: Arthur M. Schlesinger, Sr., "A Note on Songs as Patriot Propaganda, 1765–1776," *William and Mary Quarterly*, third series, 11 (1954), 87. Also as "A New Song," *Virginia Gazette* (Dixon and Hunter), 24 February 1776, 3. For another example of a song that implicitly contrasted the two Georges and prophesied a far-flung and wealthy American empire see "Washington and Common Sense," to the tune of "Smile, Britannia," *Freeman's Journal, or New Hampshire Gazette*, 22 October 1776, author unidentified, dated Bordeaux, 1 July 1776, in George L. Duyckinck and Evert A. Duyckinck, *Cyclopaedia of American Literature*, New York, 1855, 2 volumes, 1:464.

50. Dr. Albigence Waldo, "Valley Forge, 1777–1778. Diary of Surgeon Albigence Waldo, of the Connecticut Line," *Pennsylvania Magazine of History and Biography*, 21 (1897), 306–7; Thomas Hughes, *A Journal by Thos: Hughes*, intro. E. A. Benians, ed. R. W. David, Cambridge, England, 1947, 28 January 1779, 63, see also *Pennsylvania Packet*, 21 January 1778, listed in Anderson 194; "War and Washington," broadside, Philadelphia, 1779, Evans 6:43, 16520; Marvin L. Brown, trans. and ed., *Baroness von Riedesel and the American Revolution: Journal and Correspondence of a Tour of Duty, 1776–1783*, Chapel Hill, North Carolina, 1965, 92–3.

CHAPTER SEVENTEEN

1. John Shy, "The American Revolution: The Military Conflict Considered as a Revolutionary War," in Stephen G. Kurtz and James H. Hutson, eds., *Essays on the American Revolution*, New York, 1973, 146–8.

2. Shy, "American Revolution," 134, 135n, 142–3, 145–6n.

3. Davidson 312–37. In areas under British army control, loyalists continued to celebrate royal birthdays: *Royal Gazette* (New York), 5 June 1779, in Stryker 3:400–1; *South Carolina and American General Gazette*, 17 January 1781, 3; 20 January, 3; *Royal Gazette* (Charlestown), 6–9 June 1781, 3; 28 July–1 August, 2; 24–27 July 1782, 3; *Royal South Carolina Gazette*, 6 June 1782, 3.

4. *Boston Gazette, and Country Journal*, 9 October 1780, 1; *South Carolina and American General Gazette*, 24 December 1778, 4. See also *Constitutional Gazette*, 31 July 1776, *Freeman's Journal*, 29 October 1776, *New York*

Journal, 15 September 1777, all in Moore, *Diary of Revolution,* 1:278, 318–19, 435–6; *Boston Gazette, and Country Journal,* 3 February 1777, 2; 4 August, 1; 8 May 1780, 1; 5 March 1781, 2; 2 April, 2; 3 June 1782, 1; 31 March 1783, 1–2; *Gazette of the State of South Carolina,* 26 May 1777, 1; *Pennsylvania Gazette,* 21 February 1778, 4; 28 February, 1–2; Stryker 2:17–18, 50–4; 102, 121–4, 135, 158–9, 231–2, 281–2, 486; Freneau 1:273, 274; 2:3–6, 9–18, 32, 112–14, 117–19, 126–7, 165–7, 167–9, 217–19, 219–20; Davidson 373–4.

5. *Virginia Gazette* (Dixon and Hunter), 24 August 1776, 8.

6. "A New Catechism," *Pennsylvania Journal,* 19 February 1777, in Moore, *Diary of Revolution* 1:391–7; *Boston Gazette, and Country Journal,* 31 March 1777, 1–2; *Gazette of the State of South Carolina,* 14 April 1777, 2; Hastings 286.

7. From Levi Allen, 27 January 1776, Washington Papers, Library of Congress; James Morton Smith, comp., *George Washington: A Profile,* New York, 1969, 14; Liddle, "Public Attitudes," 443. GW's birthday was first celebrated by civilians in Williamsburg, Virginia, and in Milton, Connecticut, in 1779. In 1780, birthday celebrations were held in Williamsburg and Fredericksburg, Virginia. The French and American armies observed it at Providence, Rhode Island, in 1781. Inhabitants of Virginia and gentlemen and army officers in Boston held celebrations in 1782: *Virginia Gazette* (Dixon and Nicolson), 26 February 1779, 3; 19 February 1780, 2; 26 February, 2; *Pennsylvania Gazette, and Weekly Advertiser,* 10 March 1779, 2; *South Carolina and American General Gazette,* 18 March 1779, 2; *Stiles Literary Diary,* 3 March 1779, quoted in Hughes 1:497, cf. 3:325; to Rochambeau, 24 February 1781, WW 21:286; Edmund Pendleton to James Madison, 11 February 1782, *Pendleton Papers* 1:386; *Boston Gazette, and Country Journal,* 18 February 1782, 1. Early in 1775, a broadsheet appeared entitled "Alphabet for Little Masters and Misses," containing the following lines: "G, stands for George, may God give him wisdom and grace. . . . W, stands for Wilkes, who us from warrants saved." In May 1778, a Boston newspaper published "The Political A.B.C." in which "the E stands for England, for virtue once fam'd, / Till curst with a Prince who all virtue disclaim'd. . . . The W stands for our brave WASHINGTON / And worlds that rejoice for the honor he's won": Moore, *Songs and Ballads,* 88–9; *Boston-Gazette, and Country Journal,* 18 May 1778, 5.

8. "To His Excellency General Washington," Hortentius, Stryker 2:135–7; "On General Washington," *Boston Gazette, and Country Journal,* 23 September 1782, 3; "A Song. To The Tune of Pepperell and Pumpkinshire People," *Pennsylvania Gazette,* 4 April 1778, 2. This song by Francis Hopkinson depicted GW surrounded by heroes and guarding America. Also in *Pennsylvania Packet,* 8 April 1778, and *Pennsylvania Evening Post,* 30 June 1778: Hastings 298–9. A poem in *New Hampshire Gazette,* 12 October 1779, depicts America's military chiefs thronging around GW and directed by him: Duyckinck and Duyckinck 1:474.

9. "To the PRINTER . . . ," *Boston Gazette, and Country Journal,* 8 June 1778, 3; Lancaster, Pennsylvania, newspaper, 22 April 1778, in Moore, *Diary of Revolution* 2:37; Boston Massacre Oration by Thomas Dawes, Jr., 5 March

1781, in Niles 70–2. See also "The Spectator to the People of the Massachusetts Bay," *Boston Gazette, and Country Journal,* 20 January 1777, 1; 27 January, 1; "To the GENEROUS and BRAVE," 20 April 1778, 2; *Freeman's Journal,* 12 April 1777; *New Jersey Gazette,* 21 January 1778, both in Moore, *Diary of Revolution* 1:379–83; 2:4; "A Soldier," *Virginia Gazette* (Dixon and Hunter), 7 February 1777, 1–2; "From the New Jersey Gazette, January 21. Thoughts on the situation of affairs," *Pennsylvania Gazette,* 14 February 1778, 1; "The Sentiments of an American Woman," 21 June 1780, 1; "Cato," 2 August 1780, 3; "An Address from the Legislature of the State of New York to Their Constituents," 9 May 1781, 1. In 1782, members of opposing political factions in Pennsylvania accused one another of having betrayed the American cause by having betrayed GW: 11 December 1782, 2; 18 December, 4. "To the Brave Americans," 7 March 1778, 4; also in *Virginia Gazette* (Purdie), 3 April 1778, 1; Extracts from a Message of Governor William Livingston to the New Jersey Assembly, Princeton, 29 May 1778, Stryker 2:236.

10. Addresses of Pennsylvania Executive Council and Magistrates of Philadelphia and GW's replies in *Pennsylvania Gazette, and Weekly Advertiser,* 5 January 1779, 3; *South Carolina and American General Gazette,* 28 January 1779, 2. Soon after, the Pennsylvania Executive Council commissioned Charles Willson Peale to do GW's portrait to hang in the Council Chamber. The Spanish envoy ordered five copies: *Pennsylvania Gazette, and Weekly Advertiser,* 27 January 1779, 3; *Pennsylvania Packet,* 4 February 1779, in Moore, *Diary of Revolution* 2:126; *Virginia Gazette* (Dixon and Nicolson), 9 April 1779, 2. At the close of the war, Congress commissioned an equestrian statue of GW to be erected at the residence of Congress when it should be established: *Boston Gazette, and Country Journal,* 22 September 1783, 1. The American Philosophical Society and the American Academy of Arts and Sciences both elected him to their memberships: to Joseph Reed, 15 February 1780, *WW* 18:11–12; from Dr. William Smith, 1 November 1780, 20:348n; to Rev. Joseph Willard, 22 March 1781, 21:351–2. Harvard, Yale, and the University of Pennsylvania conferred honorary doctorates on him, while a newly founded college in Maryland named itself after him: *Boston Gazette, and Country Journal,* 15 April 1776, 1; *New Haven Journal,* 2 May 1781, in Moore, *Diary of Revolution* 2:420; to Ezra Stiles, 15 May 1781, *WW* 22:90; Address of the Trustees and Faculty of the University of Pennsylvania, 13 December 1783, Washington Papers, Library of Congress; GW's reply, 13 December 1783, *WW* 27:267–8; *Pennsylvania Gazette,* 23 July 1783, 1; to Rev. William Smith, President of Washington College, 18 August 1782, *WW* 25:37–8; *Pennsylvania Gazette, and Weekly Advertiser,* 1 January 1783, 1.

For orations and dedications: *South Carolina and American General Gazette,* 3 December 1779, 4; *Virginia Gazette* (Purdie), 21 August 1778, 2; to Rev. Nathaniel Whitaker, 20 December 1777, *WW* 10:175–6; to Rev. Israel Evans, 13 March 1778, 11:78; to Rev. Timothy Dwight, Jr., 18 March, 105–6; to Elias Boudinot, 28 February 1779, 14:162; to Rev. Uzal Ogden, 5 August, 16:51; to Mrs. Richard Stockton, 22 July 1782, 24:437–8; to James Mitchell Varnum, 10 March 1783, 26:202–3.

For toasts: Jeremiah Greenman, *Diary of a Common Soldier in the American*

Revolution, 1775–1783, ed. Robert Bray and Paul E. Bushnell, DeKalb, Illinois, 1978, 212; *Virginia Gazette* (Purdie), 22 July 1775, Supplement, 2; 12 July 1776, 1; 16 August, 2; 5 December 1777, 2; *Virginia Gazette* (Dixon and Hunter), 29 July 1775, 3; *Boston-Gazette and Country Journal*, 9 July 1781, 3; *Pennsylvania Gazette, and Weekly Advertiser*, 25 July 1781, 4; *Pennsylvania Gazette*, 30 July 1783, 2.

11. To David Finney, 5 May 1780, WW 18:328–9; *Pennsylvania Gazette, and Weekly Advertiser*, 11 April 1781, 1; DSF 5:267–8; *Pennsylvania Packet*, 1 September 1781, in Moore, *Diary of Revolution* 2:475–6; Mays, *Edmund Pendleton*, 2:174; *Pennsylvania Gazette*, 17 July 1782, 2–3. See also *Pennsylvania Gazette*, 16 May 1778, 3; *South Carolina and American General Gazette*, 11 June 1778, 3; *Gazette of the State of South Carolina*, 10 February 1779, 2.

12. Chinard 69. See also to Governor William Livingston, 14 March 1778, WW 11:79; Thomas Anburey, *Travels through the Interior Parts of America*, New York, 1922, 2 volumes, 2:232; from Elisha Boudinot, April 1783, in Jane J. Boudinot, ed., *The Life, . . . and Letters of Elias Boudinot*, New York, 1971, (originally published Boston and New York, 1896), 2 volumes, 1:305–6.

13. General Orders, 27 February 1776, WW 4:355. See also General Orders, 4 July 1775, 3:310; General Orders, 12 November, 4:85–6; to Governor Trumbull, 7 July 1776, 5:235; to Brigadier General de Borre, 3 August 1777, 9:7; General Orders, 1 March 1778, 11:8–10; to the Irish in New York City, 2 December 1783, 27:253–4.

14. *Pennsylvania Gazette*, 4 April 1778, 2, *Pennsylvania Packet*, 8 April 1778, *Pennsylvania Evening Post*, 30 June 1778, 2, *Connecticut Journal*, 21 April 1778, 3, all listed in Anderson 217, 213, 195, 15, 711–12; *Hastings* 299–300. See also "A Song. To the Tune of Pepperell and Pumpkinshire People," *Pennsylvania Gazette*, 4 April 1778, 2; *Pennsylvania Packet*, 8 April 1778; *Pennsylvania Evening Post*, 30 June 1778; "The Ballad," probably early 1778, *Hastings* 298–303.

15. For army poet: Duycinck and Duycinck 1:474; *New Jersey Gazette*, 18 August 1779, 1, *Boston Evening Post*, 11 September 1779, 4, *Exeter Journal, or New Hampshire Gazette*, 12 October 1779, 4, *New Hampshire Gazette*, 12 October 1779, 4, all listed in Anderson 139, 65, 117, 128. For Freneau: "An Address to the Commander-in-Chief, Officers, and Soldiers of the American Army," Freneau 2:83. First appeared in *Freeman's Journal*, 5 September 1781, less than a week after GW and his army passed through Philadelphia on their way to Yorktown, titled "To His Excellency General Washington," and addressed wholly to him. The opening line in the original newspaper version began "Accept, great chief, that share of honest praise / A grateful nation to your merit pays." In the 1786 edition of Freneau's poems, it appears without change, but in the 1795 edition it was given a new title and the opening words were altered to read "Accept, great men . . .": 81n. By the mid-1790s, Freneau would become the leading polemicist against the Washington administration, but during the war he shared the general enthusiasm for him. See also "Verses Occasioned by General Washington's arrival in Philadelphia, on his way to his seat in Virginia," December 1783, 225–9, in which victorious GW, about to resign his commission, shuns power and thereby sets an example for the Old World and

its monarchs; "Rivington's Confessions . . . ," December 1783, 229–38, reflects the shift of affection and allegiance from George III to GW. Tory newspaperman Rivington declares that for him the "monarch has lost all his charms," and so he will publish "An ode or a sonnet in Washington's praise" (232).

16. *Paine Writings* 2:413–18, see especially 427–8.

17. Historians of Anglo-American political thought have noted the free and frequent borrowing of ideas and rhetoric between the Radical Whigs and Radical Tories who jointly constituted the "Country Party" opposition to the Walpole Administration: Kramnick 169–77, 236–60; Bailyn, *Ideological Origins*, 39. Much that Bolingbroke said in his weekly paper *The Craftsman* might have come from Trenchard and Gordon's *Cato's Letters*. Several of these short pieces contained the seeds of the later "Idea of a Patriot King." *The Craftsman*, number 213, makes clear the connection between the concept of the Patriot King and that of the public-minded man: Saturday, 1 August 1730, London, 1731 edition, 6:250–9, cf. Kramnick 80–1, 167–8. GW had a copy of these essays. See above, Chapter 10 at n.20. For the view that the Patriot King concept shaped GW's conduct as president and that of his next five successors: Ralph Ketcham, *Presidents above Party: The First American Presidency, 1789–1829*, Chapel Hill, North Carolina, 1984, see especially 4–5, 89–93.

18. Douglas Southall Freeman noted a significant difference between the young provincial and the mature revolutionary leader. Though GW had made many sacrifices during the French and Indian War, Freeman found him intensely ambitious and at times self-serving. In contrast, contemporary descriptions of him from the beginning of the Revolution through the remainder of his career perceived him as an utterly selfless patriot. Freeman concluded that GW had undergone a virtual transformation of character induced by private experiences between 1758 and 1775: DSF 3:xii–xiii, cf. 1:xiii–xv; 2:388–99; 3:ix, xxviii–xxix, xxxvi–xxxviii, 448. Surely, he had matured emotionally, but Freeman failed to note that he had also matured as a politician and leader. Nor did he take account of how political ideology and revolutionary fervor affected both GW's actions and public perceptions of him. Not to detract from his real involvement and noble contribution, but the transformation observed by Freeman was less in his personal character than in his and his fellow Americans' political consciousness and conduct. The phenomenon Freeman sought to explain was in fact the revolutionary substitution of GW for George III and the perception of him as a kind of republicanized Patriot King.

19. *Works of Bolingbroke* 3:82–3.

20. Washington Irving, *The Sketch Book*, New York, 1961, 48.

21. Helen Hill, *George Mason: Constitutionalist*, Cambridge, Massachusetts, 1938, 43; Cunliffe 10; John Bernard, *Retrospections of America, 1797–1811*, New York, 1887, 87; Margaret Brown Klapthor and Howard Alexander Morrison, *G. Washington: A Figure upon the Stage*, Washington, D.C., 1982, 18, 21.

22. To Josiah Quincy, 24 March 1776, WW 4:421–2; Douglass G. Adair, *Fame and the Founding Fathers*, ed. H. Trevor Colbourn, New York, 1974, 8.

APPENDIX

1. W. C. Ford, "Prefatory Notes to the Inventory of the Contents of Mount Vernon," 1909, reprinted in Prussing, Appendix II, 402–3. See Chapter 14 n.30.

2. DSF 1:229; 3:20, 80, 367; 6:3, 328n; Morison, "Young Man Washington," 168–72; JTF 1:240–2; 4:469. Morison also found the hallmarks of Marcus Aurelius's philosophy in GW's conduct, but no evidence indicates that he owned or read those writings. Other historians have agreed that GW gave little time to books and reading, except possibly on agriculture and warfare: Alden, *Washington*, 86, 219; Ambler 16–17; Philip A. Bruce, *The Virginia Plutarch*, New York, 1971 (originally published Chapel Hill, North Carolina, 1929), 2 volumes, 1:156; Cunliffe 25–9, 152–4; Richard Beale Davis, *Intellectual Life of Jefferson's Virginia, 1790–1830*, Knoxville, Tennessee, 1964, 89–90; Davis, *Intellectual Life in the Colonial South* 2:545; Ford, *George Washington*, 203–8; Hughes 1:44, 436; 2:210; 3:114; Morris 36; Nettels, *Washington and Independence*, 58–9; Saul K. Padover, "George Washington: Portrait of a True Conservative," *Social Research*, 22 (1955), 203–11; Prussing 137–8; Dixon Wecter, *The Hero in America*, New York, 1941, 101. Henry Cabot Lodge differed from the consensus by describing GW as a lover of reading, but he made little attempt to examine the nature of that reading or its influence on GW's life and thought: *George Washington*, Boston and New York, 1898, 2 volumes, 1:62; 2:340–1, cf. Stephenson and Dunn 1:243, 336; 2:140, 199, 216.

3. Adams quoted in Cunliffe 25; Jefferson to Dr. Walter Jones, 2 January 1814, *Jefferson Writings*, ed. Lipscomb and Bergh, 14:50, cf. Hughes 3:113.

4. To David Humphreys, 25 July 1785, WW 28:203. One of the reasons Washington may have felt anxious to compensate for his educational shortcomings was the importance of literary skills in reinforcing the power of the upper classes in Virginia by distinguishing between a "high" literary culture and the oral culture of the lower classes: Isaac, *Transformation*, 121–35, 355, see also Hubbell and Adair 223, 240, 241.

5. To the Reverend Jonathan Boucher, 5 June 1771, WW 3:43; to Boucher, 30 May 1768, 2:488.

6. To Boucher, 9 July 1771, WW 3:50–1.

7. DSF 3:79–80, 202–3, 311–12, 323, 336.

8. To Boucher, 13 May 1770, WW 3:14; 16 December, 35; 2 January 1771, 36–7; 5 June, 45; 9 July, 51; Invoice, 12 October 1761, 2:371; "Catalogue of Books for Master Custis," 25 July 1769, 515–17.

9. WW 28:157–8, 309–10, 311–12; *Diaries* 4:337; WW 35:282, 284–5; 36:421–2.

10. To George William Fairfax, 10 November 1785, WW 28:311–12; to Samuel Hanson, 26 July 1788, 30:24–5; to the Reverend William McWhir, 12 October 1789, 30:433–4; to G. W. P. Custis, 19 December 1796, 35:341; 23 July 1797, 511; to McDowell, 2 September 1798, 36:421–2. The letters to Hanson and McWhir concern the education of GW's nephews, George Steptoe Washington and Lawrence Augustine Washington. He had the same expectations for them as for G. W. P. Custis. Young Custis's letters from school show

that he took the subjects prescribed by his stepgrandfather: "Letters from G. W. P. Custis to George Washington, 1797–1798," *The Virginia Magazine of History and Biography,* 20 (1912), 296–311.

11. To G. W. P. Custis, 15 November 1796, WW 35:282, cf. to John Mc-Dowell, 5 March 1798, 36:180–1. On national university see n.12 below. On his gifts to Virginia schools see: 28:321–2, 356–8, 471; 29:481–2; 35:212–13; 36:293. On aid to individuals see: *Diaries* 4:188, 195; WW 29:25; 31:162–3. For GW's advocacy of a national university: 30:493–4; 34:22–3, 59–60, 106–8, 146–9; 35:198–201, 204–5, 230, 248, 292, 303–5, 316–17; Latrobe, 19 July 1796, 1:171, describing GW's disappointment at failing to secure establishment of a national university; DSF 7:401, 421; JTF 4:199–201. For GW's educational bequests: Extracts from Will, WW 34:59–60n; Last Will and Testament (9 July 1799), 37:278–81. For GW's interest in educational publications: 28:13–14, 27; 29:272; 34:44–45, 119–20; 35:458; 36:487–8; 37:140; Griffin 77, 116–18.

12. On Alexandria Academy: WW 28:356–8; 33:281–2. On national university and upper-class education: 34:147; 35:199, 316–17; 36:490–1, 513, 516, see also 35:282; 36:180–1; 37:163.

13. On learning French: WW 27:24–5, 338–9, 401; 28:522; 30:130–1; 31:381; 35:468–9; *Diaries* 4:72–3; Griffin 496. On bookplates: to Robert Adam, 22 November 1771, WW 3:77.

14. 1799 Inventory of GW's estate is in Washington Papers, Mount Vernon Ladies' Association; printed in Prussing 418–33; Griffin, *Catalogue,* has detailed annotations by Griffin and an appendix by William C. Lane with additional notes on many of the books in the 1799 inventory; "Custis Catalogue," 404–12; DSF 3:20; to John Didsbury, 12 October 1761, WW 2:370, 371, 515–17; 3:155; 24:143. Some of the titles he bought for Jack and some Jack had inherited from his father appear on the 1799 Inventory. Compare that list with the "Custis Catalogue" mentioned above and "The Library of John Parke Custis . . . ," *Tyler's Quarterly Historical and Genealogical Magazine,* 9 (1928), 97–103.

15. See Griffin's and Lane's notes; "A List of Books at Mt. Vernon 23 July 1783," in the handwriting of Lund Washington, Washington Papers, Library of Congress; to Lt. Col. William S. Smith, 15 May 1783, WW 26:435; 21 May, 449–50; 18 June, 27:22; 20 June, 24–5. GW's ledger shows that on 3 November 1772, he bought Jean Bernard Bossu's *Travels through Louisiana* and John Byron's *Voyage 'Round the World, in 1764–5–6.* Bossu shows up on the 1783 "List"; Byron does not: Griffin 28–9, 504, 507; Prussing 423. Although the list includes most of the books GW acquired as a youth, it leaves out the *Panegyrick to the Memory of Frederick, Late Duke of Schomberg:* JTF 1:31. In 1771, he had purchased a popular legal guide, Richard Burn's *The Justice of the Peace and Parish Officer,* London, 1770, 11th edition, four volumes. This title appears in the 1799 Inventory, but not in the 1783 catalogue: Invoice, 18 July 1771, WW 3:61; Griffin 527; Prussing 425.

16. Cf. W. C. Ford quoted in Prussing 402. WW 28:13, 463–4; 29:138; Griffin 18.

17. Prussing 403; Ford, *George Washington,* 202–3.

18. To Lawrence Lewis, 4 August 1797, WW 36:3; Ford, *George Washington*, 204; to James McHenry, 29 May 1797, WW 35:455–6. For post-Presidential reading see discussion and references below and Niemcewicz 102–3.

19. Griffin 497–503. GW definitely received one of the English-language Bibles as a gift: to the Reverend Mr. Clement Crutwell, 10 July 1795, WW 34:234. On popular religious works in southern colonial libraries see Davis, *Intellectual Life in the Colonial South* 2:528, 714–15; Davis, *A Colonial Southern Bookshelf*, especially 24, 68–9, 77–9.

20. WW 33:75; 34:172n, 176n; 36:281; 37:140, 215, 216–17, cf. Griffin 125–6, 145–7, 195–6, 246; to Reverend Mason Locke Weems, 29 August 1799, WW 37:347.

21. To Capel and Osgood Hanbury, 25 July 1769, "Catalogue of Books for Master Custis . . . ," WW 2:515; to Annis Boudinot Stockton, 31 August 1788, 30:76; to Lt. Col. William S. Smith, 21 May 1783, 26:450; to Smith, 20 June, 27:25; Griffin 490, 553; Prussing 419, 427.

22. To Harrison, 9 March 1789, WW 30:223; "Proposed Address to Congress," [April?, 1789], 299. Written in GW's hand, this orginally lengthy document was intended either as his first inaugural address or his first annual message to Congress. In both cases, he decided on much shorter and more general statements. Subsequently, this invaluable paper suffered from the vandalism of Jared Sparks, who gave away in bits and pieces more than half of it, cf. WW 30:296–7n.

23. Griffin 496–7, 527–37; WW 36:11, 27. See Chapter 8 n.5.

24. For GW's talk of agriculture and natural history: "Liston's Journal," 514; Niemcewicz 86. For acquisition of agricultural publications: WW 2:321, 323, 354, 436n; 31:340; 33:436–7; 34:118–19, 121, 232, 234–6, 406; 35:321, 371, 419, 431, 506; 36:322; 37:96; Griffin 26–7, 102, 117, 230–1. For GW's urging his managers to read: WW 32:216–17, 249, 283; 34:214, 342–3; 35:43, 207.

25. On agriculture as GW's "favourite amusement": WW 28:510; 30:47; 35:246. GW genuinely did love farming, but occasionally he described this interest to make it fit his image as the Cincinnatus of the West: WW 29:414; 30:150. On agricultural experiments: WW 28:200–1, 394–5, 524; 29:297–8, 388–9, 414–17, 455; 30:47, 150; 31:340; 32:337; 33:436–7; 34:118–19; 35:245–7, 253–4, 315–16, 321–2, 323–4, 371, 419, 506; 37:97. GW belonged to Virginia's Philosophical Society for the Advancement of Useful Knowledge: *Diaries* 3:256; "Pocket-day-Book or Cash Memorandums," 15 June 1774, Washington Papers, Huntington Library.

26. For *Tom Jones* and *Peregrine Pickle*: "A List of Books at Mt. Vernon 23 July 1783," Washington Papers, Library of Congress. He purchased a copy of *Don Quixote* in Philadelphia following adjournment of the Convention. The Spanish minister to the United States gave him a copy a few months later. Since he had first alluded to the novel three years earlier, he probably had read the copy in the Custis library, which he had not assigned to either Jack or himself. Griffin 482–3: he bought Tobias Smollett's 1786 translation; to Diego de Gardoqui, 28 November 1787, WW 29:321; to Reverend Mr. William Gor-

don, 20 December 1784, 28:15; to Tobias Lear, 3 October 1790, 31:130; "Custis Catalogue," 407. For references to *Hudibras*: to Warner Lewis, 19 December 1788, *WW* 30:166; to Thomas Marshall, 25 March 1795, 34:158; to George Gilpin, 29 March 1795, 163; to William B. Harrison, 10 April 1799, 37:180; Griffin 482; Prussing 427. On two occasions of mourning GW referred to or quoted *Tristram Shandy*, but he probably had never read the entire novel since it appears on none of the inventories and he seems never to have ordered it. He did own *The Beauties of Sterne*: to Jonathan Trumbull, Jr., 6 November 1781, *WW* 37:555; 1 October 1785, 28:284; Griffin 488; Prussing 426. On Pope: "Custis Catalogue," 407; 1783 "List"; to Joseph Reed, 7 March 1776, *WW* 4:380–1. On Aesop's fables: "Custis Catalogue," 404; Sir Roger L'Estrange, *Fables of Aesop and other Eminent Mythologists*, London, 1699. GW refers to the morals of Fables XXXIII, "A Daw and Borrow'd Feathers," 32; CXXIX, "A Fox and Grapes," 120; CC, "Jupiter and a Herds-Man," 178, in letters to John Armstrong, 18 May 1779, *WW* 15:99; to Lafayette, 28 April 1788, 29:479–80; to Henry Lee, 22 September, 30:98; to G. W. P. Custis, 15 November 1796, 35:282. On *Gil Blas*: "Liston's Journal," 515–16; Griffin 486; Prussing 427. For Milton, Pope's translations of *The Iliad* and *The Odyssey*, *Gulliver's Travels*, and the works of Swift: "Custis Catalogue," 407, 410; "A List of Books at Mt. Vernon 23 July 1783," Washington Papers, Library of Congress; Prussing 423, 424, 427, 429. For a possible reference to Swift see a letter to Alexander Spotswood, 25 March 1799, *WW* 37:156. For *Telemachus*: "Custis Catalogue," 409; 1783 "List"; Prussing 424, 431. On colonial southern literary tastes: Davis, *A Colonial Southern Bookshelf*, especially 23, 54–5, 103, 106–10, 118–21.

27. Davis, *Intellectual Life in the Colonial South* 3:1302, see also 1292; for the most thorough discussion of GW's love of the theater see Ford, *Washington and the Theatre*; *Diaries* 2:247–8; 1:81; 2:58, 239; 3:4, 25, 41, 56, 63, 65, 67–8, 136–7, 205. A few months after the victory at Yorktown, GW attended a program in Philadelphia that included Beaumarchais's *Eugénie*, Garrick's *The Lying Valet*, and Francis Hopkinson's oratorio *The Temple of Minerva*, the last of which praised GW: Joseph Jackson, "Washington in Philadelphia," *Pennsylvania Magazine of History and Biography*, 56 (1932), 135–6; *Diaries* 5:500–2; 6:229, 230, 233, 235.

28. *Diaries* 2:58, 95, 247; 3:3, 182; 5:176; Ford, *Washington and the Theatre*, 44.

29. Tobias Lear to Thomas Wignell, 30 May 1790, *WW* 31:42n; Griffin 488–9, 24, 559; Prussing 419, 421, 422, 424. For paraphrases of Shakespearean lines: to Henry Laurens, 3 October 1778, *WW* 13:15; to Elizabeth Willing Powel, 23 April 1792, 32:23; to John Jay, 1–[5] November 1794, 34:16; to G. W. P. Custis, 28 November 1796, 35:296. In Philadelphia in July 1787, he saw a performance of James Thomson's *Edward and Eleanora* and three weeks later he purchased a copy of that Scottish poet's more famous work, *The Seasons*: *Diaries* 5:176; *WW* 29:258; Griffin 491. On *Cato* see above, Chapter 15 at n.5.

30. Prussing 427; to Humphreys, 30 October 1785, *WW* 28:305; to Dwight, 1 April 1786, 399; to Warren, 4 November 1790, 31:144–5; to Parke, 23

March 1787, 29:182n; to Paine, 7 September 1795, 34:301–2; to the Marquis de la Luzerne, 28 May 1788, 29:503–4; to Lafayette, 28 May, 506–7; Griffin 105, 156, 159–60, 219. GW subscribed for twenty copies of Barlow's work while in Philadelphia for the Convention: Griffin 16. GW also had "Poems on Several Occasions," by "A Gentleman of Virginia" (William Dawson), Williamsburg, Virginia, 1736: James Southall Wilson, "Best-Sellers in Jefferson's Day," *Virginia Quarterly Review*, 36 (1960), 227–8.

31. Silverman 489.

32. To Lafayette, 28 May 1788, WW 29:506–7. GW's interest in ancient culture and history is also suggested by his comments on music in ancient times to Francis Hopkinson, 5 February 1789, WW 30:196–7.

33. WW 2:336–7, 345; 26:299, 418; 27:89, 190, 319–20, 457; 28:419; 29:205. Political and diplomatic considerations also entered into GW's wish to visit France.

34. Griffin 13, 28–9, 86, 149, 231–2, 503–8, 548; "Custis Catalogue" 405, 407; "A List of Books at Mt. Vernon 23 July 1783," Washington Papers, Library of Congress; Ledger A, 3 November 1772, Washington Papers, Library of Congress; WW 26:435n; 27:24–5, 338–9; 28:56, 384, 429, 459, 484; 29:522; 30:70; 35:36; Prussing 418, 420, 423, 426, 429.

These works included: *A Voyage Round the World, in the Years 1740–1744*, London, 1749, 6th edition, compiled from the papers of George Anson, later Admiral Lord Anson, who had commanded an English expedition to the South Seas; Patrick Gordon, *Geography Anatomiz'd, or, The Geographical Grammar*, London, 1749, 19th edition, a survey comprehending a general view of the globe and particular information about the physical and human geography of many countries; *Travels through that Part of North America formerly called Louisiana*, London, 1771, 2 volumes, by Jean Bernard Bossu, captain in the French Marines; John Byron, *Voyage 'Round the World, in 1764–5–6 in His Majesty's Sloop the Dolphin*; Arthur Young, *A Tour in Ireland ... 1776 to 1779*, Dublin, 1780, 2 volumes; *The World Displayed* (probably 4th edition, n.p., 1774–8, 20 volumes), "A curious collection of voyages and travels, selected from the writers of all nations," in 20 pocket volumes; the Duke of Hamilton's account of his travels through France. (Although Hamilton's *Travels* is absent from the 1799 Inventory, GW had received it, because he reported to his agent in New York that "the Gazette you sent me" advertised a later edition "than the one you sent me before," one comprehending Hamilton's subsequent travels through Denmark and other countries. He requested purchase of these as well: to Smith, 20 June 1783, WW 27:25.) John Moore, *A View of Society and Manners in Italy*, London, 1783, 2 volumes, and its companion work, *A View of Society and Manners in France, Switzerland, and Germany*, London, 1783, 2 volumes; Count Volney, *Travels through Syria and Egypt*, London, 1788, 2 volumes; and William Guthrie's *A New System of Modern Geography* (probably London, 1782).

GW hoped to obtain but may never have gotten Arthur Young's *Six Months' Tour Through England* and an edition of Captain Cook's voyages. As president, he obtained the first edition of Young's report of his travels in France (London, 1792). The author sent him a copy of the second edition (1794): Griffin 231–2,

548; Prussing 418, 420. GW may have read one of them. The *Oxford English Dictionary* lists Young's *Travels* . . . [*in*] *France* (1792) as the first example of the use of the word *capitalist*. GW used that term in two letters written in July 1797: to the Earl of Buchan, 4 July 1797, *WW* 35:487; to William Strickland, 15 July 1797, 500.

35. To Richard Henderson, 19 June 1788, *WW* 29:519–22. Morse had stopped at Mount Vernon two years earlier while gathering material for this work: *Diaries* 5:72. GW probably bought the first edition of the *American Geography*, Boston, 1789. Morse presented him with a copy of the second edition, *The American Universal Geography*, Boston, 1793, 2 volumes: to Morse, 17 July 1793, *WW* 33:12–13. GW ordered Morse's *American Gazetteer*, Boston, 1797, and then received a presentation copy from the author: to Biddle, 28 May 1797, *WW* 35:455; to Morse, 20 June, 468; to Biddle, 3 July, 484; Griffin 144–6, 506; Prussing 422, 423, 430.

A copy of the second edition of Jefferson's *Notes*, Philadelphia, 1794, with GW's customary autograph was sold in 1876: Griffin 521. Clearly he had read the book when he wrote this letter in 1788. Either he had borrowed a copy or owned the first edition for a time. The 1799 Inventory lists the title: Prussing 423.

Crevecoeur first published *Letters from an American Farmer* in English in 1782. In 1787, he presented GW with a copy of the Paris edition in French, 1787, 3 volumes: to Crevecoeur, 9 July 1787, *WW* 29:245; Griffin 61, 517; Prussing 431. Because of the limitations of GW's French, he either had someone read and evaluate the work for him, or he borrowed or bought the English edition before he wrote the 1788 letter quoted in the text. His comments suggest direct acquaintance.

GW omitted from this list the Marquis de Chastellux, *Travels in North America in the Years 1780, 1781, and 1782*. In mid-1786, that gentleman, who had served with the French expeditionary force in the American Revolution, presented GW with a copy of the original French edition, Paris, 1786, 2 volumes: Griffin 106, 505; Prussing 431. David Humphreys, GW's former military secretary, read and reviewed the book for him and translated its noted portrait of the American hero. GW modestly suggested that his French compatriot's "friendship and partiality" might have, "in this one instance, acquired an ascendency over your cooler judgement": to Chastellux, 18 August 1786, *WW* 28:522–3. The following year, he purchased the English translation in Philadelphia: Griffin 504; Prussing 420. For a modern translation see the edition by Howard L. Rice, Chapel Hill, North Carolina, 1963, 2 volumes.

36. *WW* 27:24–5; Griffin 549, 550; Prussing 419. The 1799 Inventory also lists "Abbe Rynals [*sic*] discourse on the advantage of the discovery of America." This refers to a pamphlet in French by the Marquis de Chastellux replying to Raynal, Paris, 1787: Griffin 44; Prussing 431.

37. To Lafayette, 28 May 1788, *WW* 29:507. Compare this with Jefferson's refutation of Raynal. The Frenchman had declared that America had yet to produce "one man of genius in a single art or a single science." Jefferson pointed to GW, "whose memory will be adored while liberty shall have her votaries, whose name will triumph over time, and will in future ages assume its just station among the most celebrated worthies of the world, when that wretched

philosophy shall be forgotten which would have arranged him among the degeneracies of nature." He noted also the genius of Franklin in physics and Rittenhouse in astronomy and waved a hand toward unnamed numbers of American statesmen, orators, painters, and sculptors. All of these showed "that America, though but a child of yesterday, has already given hopeful proofs of genius. . . ." In proportion to its age and population, the new nation had contributed "its full share" of "the geniuses which adorn the present age," especially when compared with France and England "where genius is most cultivated, where are the most excellent models for art, and scaffoldings for the attainment of science . . .": Thomas Jefferson, *Notes on the State of Virginia*, ed. William Peden, New York, 1972 (originally published Chapel Hill, North Carolina, 1954), 64–5. Jefferson also questioned both Buffon's reasoning and his data and marshalled a fund of biological and anthropological information to disprove his assertions: 47–64.

38. On natural history: Niemcewicz 86; to Gustavus Scott, 15 July 1788, *WW* 30:13–14; *LTW* 4:152–5, 208–16. For the project on Indian languages, he enlisted the superintendent of Indian Affairs for the Northwest Territory, the U.S. commissioner to the Southern Indians, two missionaries, and a geographer: *WW* 28:425, 525; 29:88–9, 183, 191, 369–70, 374–7; 30:63–4; Griffin 73. For other reading: *WW* 27:338–9; 28:238–9; 30:63–4; 34:232; Griffin 73.

39. Among other maps of the American colonies, GW had Lewis Evans's "A General Map of the Middle British Colonies in America," William Scull's "Map of the Province of Pennsylvania," and Fry and Jefferson's "Map of Virginia." He had two elegant charts of the seacoast of North America from the Gulf of Florida to the Bay of Fundy, a plan of the Mississippi from the river Iberville to the river Yazoo, maps of the world, Holland, India, Spain, and a chart of France. The inventory of his estate recorded many individual maps and charts, some that he had bound together, "1 large Globe," and five atlases including Thomas Jefferys's *The West-India Atlas*, containing forty-one charts and maps and historical accounts of the several countries and islands, Jefferys's *General Topography of North America and the West Indies*, containing ninety-three maps, charts, plans, and surveys, and Herman Moll's *Geographia Classica; or, The Geography of the Antients as Contained in the Greek and Latin Classics*: Griffin 561–5; Prussing 432–3; *Diaries* 4:62–4, 70n.17; *WW* 30:381; 31:283; 32:252; 37:193. For Adams's *Essays on the Globes*, London, 1789: Griffin 549; Prussing 423.

40. On GW's pamphlet reading in the 1760s and 1770s: Chapter 3 n.1; Chapter 7 at nn.14, 16, and n.35; Chapter 8 n.24; Chapter 11 nn.19–20; Chapter 12 n.15; Chapter 13 nn.13, 24; Chapter 14 n.30. On Paine: *WW* 4:297, 455. Paine told John Adams he had derived some of his arguments against monarchy from John Milton, probably from *Pro Populo Anglicano Defensio*, written in 1651 to justify the overthrow and execution of Charles I and published in English in 1692 following the Glorious Revolution. The catalogue of the Custis library includes "Milton's Defence," probably the English edition of that same essay. GW may then have read it: Paine to Adams quoted in Jordan 302; "Custis Catalogue," 409.

The debate about Anglo-American commerce began with John Baker Holyroyd, Lord Sheffield, *Observations on the Commerce of the American States,* London, 1783. It is unclear whether GW read it, but he showed familiarity with it, saw a number of the replies to it, and evinced acquaintance with contemporary ideas about international commerce: to Edmund Pendleton, 22 January 1795, *WW* 34:98; to James Warren, 7 October 1785, 28:290–1; to Richard Champion, 19 July 1791, 31:314–15 (on Champion's *Considerations on the Present Situation of Great Britain and the United States of America, with a View to Their Future Commercial Connexions,* London, 1784, cf. Griffin 42–3, 516). GW had William Bingham, *A Letter from an American . . . on the Subject of the Restraining Proclamation; and Containing Strictures on Lord Sheffield's Pamphlet on the Commerce of the American States,* first published London, 1784. GW had the Philadelphia reprint of 1784. The copy in the Boston Athenaeum has the autographs of John Augustine Washington and Bushrod Washington and may not have belonged to GW. He also owned Tench Coxe, "A Brief Examination of Lord Sheffield's Observations . . . ," Philadelphia, 1791; Coxe, *A View of the United States of America, in a Series of Papers, Written at Various Times, between the Years 1787 and 1794,* Philadelphia, 1794; Thomas Ruston, *Remarks on Lord Sheffield's Observations on the Commerce of the American States, by an American,* London, 1784: Griffin 24, 60, 560.

41. To Alexander Hamilton, 28 August 1788, *WW* 30:66; Griffin 97, 109, 160–1, 217, 220, 518–20, 531, 532, 534–5, 557, 558; Prussing 423, 425; *WW* 29:287, 327–8, 332, 334–5, 357, 400, 404, 458, 468, 499; 30:63.

42. He praised Hamilton's "Camillus" essays in defense of Jay's Treaty: to Hamilton, 29 July 1795, *WW* 34:263–4. He also circulated a speech by Senator Fisher Ames of Massachusetts supporting implementation of that pact: to Thomas Pinckney, 22 May 1796, 35:62; Griffin 8. He asked his secretary to obtain Thomas Paine's reply to Edmund Burke's *Reflections on the Revolution in France*: to Tobias Lear, 19 June 1791, *WW* 31:302. Subsequently Paine sent fifty copies of his response to Burke, which became Part I of *The Rights of Man*: to Paine, 6 May 1792, 32:38–9; Griffin 523, 560; Prussing 430. GW seems never to have read Burke's work itself. Catharine Macaulay Graham sent her own *Observations* on Burke's *Reflections*: to Graham, 19 July 1791, *WW* 31:316; Griffin 129. GW also noted Paine's attack on him in his "Letter to George Washington," the criticism of GW by Pierre Adet, the recently departed French minister to the United States, in his "Note" in French, and the replies to Paine by Peter Porcupine and Charles L. Pinckney Horry: to David Stuart, 8 January 1797, *WW* 35:357–60; to Horry, 6 May 1798, 36:255–6; Griffin 158. For GW's pamphlet-reading in retirement: to Tobias Lear, 9 March 1797, *WW* 37:577; to Alexander Spotswood, 22 November, 23; to Judge Alexander Addison, 6 December, 27; to John Marshall, 30 December, 76; to Bushrod Washington, 31 December, 80–1; to Addison, 4 March 1799, 145–6; Griffin 3–4, 77. For other important pamphlets acquired during GW's retirement see: to Clement Biddle, 28 May 1797, *WW* 35:455; 15 September, 36:33; to Timothy Pickering, 6 February 1798, 155–6. In his will, GW bequeathed "my library of Books and Pamphlets of every kind" to his nephew Bushrod Washington: "Last Will and Testament" 9 July 1799, 37:284.

43. For evidence that GW read many newspapers: *PWC* 4:387–8, 399–400; *PWR* 2:552, 570–1; *WW* 3:222, 240, 296, 297, 300; 21:350; 28:10, 142, 329, 349, 384, 419–20, 437; 29:122, 125; 30:7–8, 16; 32:163; 33: 102, 221, 469; 34:62, 101, 158, 214, 250, 263–4, 339–40, 364, 473, 481; 35:91–2, 208, 349, 486; 36:8, 17, 89, 92, 119, 126, 253, 384, 389, 403, 474, 496; 37:93, 102, 143, 156, 161, 162, 183, 188, 221, 323, 438, 510, 577; *LTW* 3:15; George Mason to GW, 6 February 1775, *Mason Papers* 1:214; DSF 3: 426; 19 July 1796, Latrobe 1:171, reporting that in the morning "in the sitting room . . . all the latest Newspapers were laid out"; 5 June 1798, Niemcewicz 102–3, reporting that GW read about ten different newspapers each evening; JTF 4:457, GW was reading newspapers on the last evening he spent with his wife and Tobias Lear. For GW's attempts to discontinue subscriptions: *WW* 28:56, 142, 211, 419–20, 430; 33:173n; 35:488. For GW's complaints about newspapers: *WW* 35:126, 430, 447. He also subscribed to many periodical magazines: Griffin 491–6.

44. Prussing 141, tabulating and adding to the count of William C. Lane in Griffin. Lane classified and annotated the items in a defective copy of the 1799 Inventory. In some cases, we might quibble with Lane and shift titles to "History" and "Politics, Political Economy, etc." from "Law," "Legislation," "Literature," or "Geography and Travels."

45. "A List of Books at Mt. Vernon 23 July 1783," Washington Papers, Library of Congress; Griffin 23, 189–90; Prussing 426, 433; to Capel and Osgood Hanbury, 25 July 1769, *WW* 2:516–17. On the *Letters of Junius*: Griffin 521; Prussing 419; Clinton Rossiter, *The Political Thought of the American Revolution*, New York, 1963 (originally Part 3 of *Seedtime of the Republic*, New York, 1953), 72; Rowland 2:369. On Burgh and Price: Colbourn 19; Griffin 168.

46. *WW* 26:449–50; 27:22, 24–5; Griffin 510–15; Prussing 419, 420, 427. GW also requested but may not have obtained a biography of Peter the Great and Vertot's "Revolution of Portugal." He received Robert Watson's *History of the Reign of Phillip II, King of Spain*, Walter Harte's *History of the Life of Gustavus Adolphus, King of Sweden*, and a biography of Louis XV. In February 1784, he requested booksellers in Philadelphia to send several works of history and current politics, including a history of the United Provinces of the Netherlands and "A review of the characters of the principal Nations of Europe": *WW* 27:338–9. In Philadelphia during the Convention, he bought "Baron Haller's Letters": Ledger B, 12 September 1787, Washington Papers, Library of Congress. Probably during his presidency, he acquired the works of Frederick II, King of Prussia, John Gillies's history of that monarch's reign, Volney's *The Ruins, or a Survey of the Revolutions of Empires*, and histories of the city of Rome and the nation of Spain. At unknown dates, he also obtained Crawford's *History of Ireland* and Temple Stanyan's *Grecian History*: Griffin 61, 508, 510–15; Prussing 419, 420, 430.

47. On Hazard: *WW* 31:225. On Robertson: 26:449–50. On Backus: Prussing 426. On Belknap: *WW* 33:361; 36:290–1, 292, 295, 296, 327, 485, 486. On Minot: 30:62, 64–5, 68–9, see also Griffin 98–9, 508–9, 520. On Gordon and Ramsay: *Diaries* 4:275–6; to Ramsay, 3 June 1790, *WW* 31:47n;

Griffin 510–11, 513; Prussing 419, 420. On Clinton: 423. In the 1790s, GW welcomed the first volume of Minot's *Continuation of the History of the Province of Massachusetts Bay, from the Year 1748*, a study that comprehended events in which the hero himself had taken part: to Minot, 5 March 1798, *WW* 36:181–2; Griffin 512; Prussing 422–3. He read Dr. Richard Price's *Observations on the Importance of the American Revolution* and had other English publications on that conflict, including *A View of the History of Great Britain during the Administration of Lord North*; *An Impartial History of the Present War in America*, published as a series of seventeen pamphlets; and the records of the parliamentary debate on the Treaty of Peace: *WW* 28:62–3; Griffin 168–9, 513, 515, 519. He promised to aid William Smith in gathering public papers for a history of the Revolution: to Smith, 8 May 1792, *WW* 32:41. He told William Heath he wished to purchase that comrade's memoirs when published. GW later thanked him for sending an "elegantly bound" copy, promising to "avail myself of the liberty you allow me, to express my sentiments with the utmost candour and freedom," if in reading it he should have occasion "to make any observations thereon": 20 May 1797, 35:449–50; 1 March 1799, 37:140–1; Griffin 99, 511.

48. E. P. G. Bourne, "The Use of History Made by the Framers of the Constitution," *American Historical Association Annual Report, 1896*, Washington, D.C., 1897, 1:226; Prussing 427, 403, 419; Griffin 2, 524, 22.

49. To Edward Carrington, 28 September 1795, *WW* 34:317.

50. On the purposes of reading in GW's Virginia: Robert Dawidoff, *The Education of John Randolph*, New York, 1979, see especially 115–63; Jack P. Greene, "Society, Ideology, and Politics: An Analysis of the Political Culture of Mid-Eighteenth-Century Virginia," in Richard M. Jellison, ed., *Society, Freedom, and Conscience: The American Revolution in Virginia, Massachusetts, and New York*, New York, 1976, 43–4.

Selected Bibliography

DOCUMENTARY

[Adams, John]. *Adams Family Correspondence*, ed. Lyman H. Butterfield et al. Cambridge, Massachusetts, 1963–5, 4 volumes.

Adams, John. *Diary and Autobiography of John Adams*, ed. Lyman H. Butterfield et al. Cambridge, Massachusetts, 1961–4, 4 volumes.

[Adams, John]. *Papers of John Adams*, ed. Robert J. Taylor et al. Cambridge, Massachusetts, 1977–83, 6 volumes.

Addison, Joseph. *The Tragedy of Cato*. In J. S. P. Tatlock and R. G. Martin, eds., *Representative English Plays*. New York, 1938, 543–76.

Anderson, Gillian B., comp. *Freedom's Voice in Poetry and Song*. Wilmington, Delaware, 1977.

Bangs, Isaac. *Journal of Lieutenant Isaac Bangs, April 1 to July 29, 1776*, ed. Edward Bangs. Cambridge, Massachusetts, 1880.

Bernard, John. *Retrospections of America, 1797–1811*. New York, 1887.

Bland, Theodorick, Jr. *The Bland Papers, Being a Selection from the Manuscripts of Colonel Theodorick Bland, Jr.*, ed. Charles Campbell. Petersburg, Virginia, 1840–3, 2 volumes.

Boston Evening Post.

Boston Gazette, or Country Journal; Boston Gazette, and Country Journal.

Boston Newsletter.

Boudinot, Jane J., ed. *The Life, . . . and Letters of Elias Boudinot*. New York, 1971 (originally published Boston and New York, 1896), 2 volumes.

[Bouquet, Henry]. *Papers of Henry Bouquet*, ed. S. K. Stevens et al. Harrisburg, Pennsylvania, 1951– , 3 volumes.

Bumgardner, Georgia B., ed. *American Broadsides*. Barre, Massachusetts, 1971.

Burnett, Edmund C., ed. *Letters of Members of the Continental Congress*. Washington, D.C., 1921–36, 8 volumes.

Carter, Landon. *Diary of Colonel Landon Carter of Sabine Hall, 1752–1778,* ed. Jack P. Greene. Charlottesville, Virginia, 1965, 2 volumes.

Chastellux, Marquis de. *Travels in North America in the Years 1780, 1781, and 1782,* trans. and ed. Howard C. Rice. Chapel Hill, North Carolina, 1963, 2 volumes.

[Chauncy, Charles]. *A Letter to a Friend, Giving a Concise, But Just, Account . . . of the Ohio Defeat.* Boston, 1755.

Chinard, Gilbert, ed. *George Washington as the French Knew Him.* New York, 1969 (originally published Princeton, 1940).

[Colden, Cadwallader]. *The Letters and Papers of Cadwallader Colden, 1755– 1760, Collections of the New York Historical Society,* 54 (1921).

Curwen, Samuel. *The Journal of Samuel Curwen, Loyalist,* ed. Andrew Oliver. Cambridge, Massachusetts, 1972, 2 volumes.

[Custis, Daniel Parke]. "Catalogue of the Library of Daniel Parke Custis," *Virginia Magazine of History and Biography,* 17 (1909), 404–12.

Custis, G. W. P. "Letters from G. W. P. Custis to George Washington, 1797– 1798," *Virginia Magazine of History and Biography,* 20 (1912), 296–311.

[Custis, John Parke]. "Library of John Parke Custis," *Tyler's Quarterly Historical and Genealogical Magazine,* 9 (1928), 97–103.

Davies, Samuel. *Religion and Patriotism the Constituents of a Good Soldier.* Philadelphia, 1755.

Davis, N. Darnell. "British Newspaper Accounts of Braddock's Defeat," *Pennsylvania Magazine of History and Biography,* 23 (1899), 316–28.

Davis, Richard Beale, ed., *"The Colonial Virginia Satirist": Mid-Eighteenth Century Commentaries on Politics, Religion, and Society,* "Dinwiddianae." In *American Philosophical Society Transactions,* new series, 57 (March 1967).

[Dinwiddie, Robert]. *Official Records of Robert Dinwiddie, Lieutenant Governor of the Colony of Virginia, 1751–1758,* ed. Robert A. Brock. Richmond, Virginia, 1883, 2 volumes.

Duyckinck, George L., and Duyckinck, Evert A. *Cyclopaedia of American Literature.* New York, 1855, 2 volumes.

Entick, John. *The General History of the Late War.* Third edition, London, 1763–4, 5 volumes.

[Fauquier, Francis]. *Official Papers of Francis Fauquier, Lieutenant Governor of Virginia, 1758–1768,* ed. George Reese. Charlottesville, Virginia, 1980–3, 3 volumes.

Forbes, John. *Writings of General John Forbes,* ed. Alfred P. James. Menasha, Wisconsin, 1938.

Force, Peter, ed. *American Archives.* New York, 1837–46, fourth series, 6 volumes.

Ford, Worthington C., et al., eds. *Journals of the Continental Congress, 1774– 1789.* Washington, D.C., 1904–37, 34 volumes.

French Policy Defeated. Being an Account of all the hostile Proceedings of the French, Against the Inhabitants of the British Colonies in North America, For the Last Seven Years. London, 1755.

Freneau, Philip. *Poems of Philip Freneau,* ed. Fred Lewis Pattee. Princeton, 1902–7, 3 volumes.

Gazette of the State of South Carolina.

Gentleman's Magazine.

Greenman, Jeremiah. *Diary of a Common Soldier in the American Revolution, 1775–1783,* ed. Robert Bray and Paul E. Bushnell. DeKalb, Illinois, 1978.

[Hamilton, Alexander, and Hamilton, John]. "A Dismal Tragedy: Drs. Alexander and John Hamilton Comment on Braddock's Defeat," ed. Elaine G. Breslaw, *Maryland Historical Magazine,* 75 (1980), 118–44.

Hamilton, Stanislaus M., ed. *Letters to Washington, 1752–1775.* Boston and New York, 1898–1902, 5 volumes.

Hazard, Samuel, et al., eds. *Minutes of the Provincial Council, Colonial Records of Pennsylvania.* Harrisburg, Pennsylvania, 1851–53, 16 volumes.

Hazard, Samuel, ed. *Pennsylvania Archives.* Philadelphia, 1852–6, first series, 12 volumes; George E. Reed, ed., Harrisburg, fourth series, 1900–2, 12 volumes.

Hubbell, Jay B., and Adair, Douglass. "Robert Munford's *The Candidates; or The Humours of a Virginia Election," William and Mary Quarterly,* third series, 5 (1948), 217–57.

Hughes, Thomas. *Journal by Thos: Hughes,* intro. E. A. Benians, ed. R. W. David. Cambridge, England, 1947.

Huntington, Josiah, and Huntington, Jedediah. *Huntington Papers: Correspondence of the Brothers Josiah and Jedediah Huntington, 1771–1783, Connecticut Historical Society Collections.* Hartford, Connecticut, 1923.

Irving, Washington. *The Sketch Book.* New York, 1961, "Rip Van Winkle," 37–55.

Jefferson, Thomas. *Notes on the State of Virginia,* ed. William Peden. New York, 1972 (originally published Chapel Hill, North Carolina, 1954).

[Jefferson, Thomas]. *Papers of Thomas Jefferson,* ed. Julian P. Boyd, Charles T. Cullen, et al. Princeton, 1950– , 25 volumes to date.

Jefferson, Thomas. *Writings of Thomas Jefferson,* ed. Paul L. Ford. New York, 1892, 10 volumes.

Jefferson, Thomas. *Writings of Thomas Jefferson,* ed. Andrew A. Lipscomb and Albert Bergh. Washington, D.C., 1903, 20 volumes.

[Johnson, William]. *Papers of Sir William Johnson,* ed. James Sullivan. Albany, New York, 1921–65, 13 volumes.

Jones, Thomas. *History of New York during the Revolutionary War . . .* New York, 1968 (originally published New York, 1879), 2 volumes.

Kennedy, John Pendleton, and McIlwaine, H. R., eds. *Journals of the House of Burgesses of Virginia.* Richmond, Virginia, 1905–15, 13 volumes.

Kent, Donald H. "Contrecoeur's Copy of George Washington's Journal," *Pennsylvania History,* 19 (January 1952), 1–32.

Latrobe, Benjamin Henry. *The Virginia Journals of Benjamin Henry Latrobe, 1795–1798,* ed. Edward C. Carter II et al. New Haven, Connecticut, 1977, 2 volumes.

Leacock, John. *The Fall of British Tyranny; or, American Liberty Triumphant.* Philadelphia, 1776. In Montrose J. Moses, ed., *Representative Plays by American Dramatists.* New York, 1918–25, 3 volumes, 1:277–350.

[Lee, Charles]. *Papers of Charles Lee, Collections of the New York Historical Society,* New York, 1872–5, volumes 4–7.

L'Estrange, Sir Roger. *Fables of Aesop and Other Eminent Mythologists.* London, 1699.

Liston, Henrietta. "Lady Henrietta Liston's Journal of Washington's 'Resignation,' Retirement, and Death," ed. James C. Nicholls. *Pennsylvania Magazine of History and Biography,* 95 (1971), 511–20.

Livingston, William. *A Review of the Military Operations in North America.* London, 1757.

London Magazine.

Machiavelli, Niccolò. *Chief Works and Others,* trans. Allan Gilbert. Durham, North Carolina, 1965, 3 volumes.

McIlwaine, H. R., ed. *Legislative Journals of the Council of Colonial Virginia.* Richmond, Virginia, 1918–19, 3 volumes.

McIlwaine, H. R., and W. L. Hall, eds. *Executive Journals of the Council of Colonial Virginia.* Richmond, Virginia, 1925–45, 6 volumes.

Marshall, Christopher. *Extracts from the Diary of Christopher Marshall,* ed. William Duane. New York, 1969 (originally published Albany, New York, 1877).

Maryland Gazette.

[Mason, George]. *The Papers of George Mason,* ed. Robert A. Rutland. Chapel Hill, North Carolina, 1970, 3 volumes.

Moore, Charles, ed. and intro. *George Washington's Rules of Civility and Decent Behaviour in Company and Conversation.* Boston and New York, 1926.

Moore, Frank, ed. *Diary of the American Revolution, From Newspapers and Original Documents.* New York, 1860, 1859, 2 volumes.

Moore, Frank. *Songs and Ballads of the American Revolution.* New York, 1856.

[Moreau, Jacob Nicholas]. *A Memorial, Containing A Summary View of Facts, with Their Authorities In Answer to The Observations Sent by the English Ministry to The Courts of Europe.* New York, 1757.

Morris, Anne C., ed. *The Diary and Letters of Gouverneur Morris.* New York, 1888, 2 volumes.

New York Gazette.

New York Gazette and Weekly Mercury.

New York Gazette: or, The Weekly Post-Boy.

New York Mercury.

Niemcewicz, Julian Ursyn. *Under Their Vine and Fig Tree: Travels through America in 1797–1799, 1805,* trans. and ed. Metchie J. E. Budka. Elizabeth, New Jersey, 1965.

Niles, Hezekiah, ed. *Principles and Acts of the Revolution in America.* New York, 1876 (originally published Baltimore, 1822).

Nute, Grace L., ed. "Washington and the Potomac: Manuscripts of the Minnesota Historical Society," *American Historical Review,* 28 (1922–3), 497–519, 705–22.

Paine, Thomas. *The Writings of Thomas Paine,* ed. Moncure D. Conway. New York, 1894–9, 4 volumes.

Pargellis, Stanley M., ed. *Military Affairs in North America, 1748–1765.* New York, 1969 (originally published New York, 1936).

[Pendleton, Edmund]. *The Letters and Papers of Edmund Pendleton, 1734–1803,* collected and ed. David S. Mays. Charlottesville, Virginia, 1967, 2 volumes.

Pennsylvania Gazette.

Pennsylvania Magazine: Or, American Monthly Museum. Philadelphia, 1775–6.

Providence Gazette.

[Riedesel, Friederike Charlotte Luise, Freifrau von]. *Baroness von Riedesel and the American Revolution: Journal and Correspondence of a Tour of Duty, 1776–1783,* trans. and ed. Marvin L. Brown. Chapel Hill, North Carolina, 1965.

Royal Gazette (Charles Town, South Carolina).

Royal South Carolina Gazette.

Rush, Benjamin. *Letters of Benjamin Rush,* ed. Lyman H. Butterfield. Princeton, 1951, 2 volumes.

St. John, Henry, Lord Viscount Bolingbroke. *Works of the Late Right Honorable Henry St. John, Lord Viscount Bolingbroke.* London, 1754, 5 volumes.

Schutz, John A. "A Private Report of General Braddock's Defeat," *Pennsylvania Magazine of History and Biography,* 79 (1955), 374–7.

Scots Magazine.

[Sharpe, Horatio]. *Correspondence of Governor Horatio Sharpe,* ed. William H. Browne. In *Archives of Maryland,* Baltimore, 1883–1972, 72 volumes, volumes 6–8.

[Shirley, William]. *Correspondence of William Shirley,* ed. Charles H. Lincoln. New York, 1912, 2 volumes.

Smith, Paul H., et al., eds. *Letters of Delegates to Congress, 1774–1789.* Washington, D.C., 1978– , 14 volumes to date.

South Carolina and American General Gazette.

South Carolina Gazette.

South Carolina Gazette, and Country Journal.

Stevenson, Burton Egbert, ed. *Poems of American History.* Boston and New York, 1922.

Stiles, Ezra. *Literary Diary of Ezra Stiles,* ed. Franklin Bowditch Dexter. New York, 1909, 3 volumes.

Stryker, William S., et al., eds. *New Jersey Archives, Documents Relating to the Revolutionary History of the State of New Jersey, Newspaper Extracts, 1776–1782.* Paterson and Trenton, 1901–17, 2nd series, 5 volumes, F. B. Lee, ed., volume 2; W. Nelson, ed., volume 3.

Thornton, John Wingate, ed. *The Pulpit of the American Revolution.* New York, 1970 (originally published Boston, 1860).

Universal Magazine.

Van Schreeven, William J., comp., and Robert Scribner, ed. *Revolutionary Virginia: The Road to Independence.* University Press of Virginia [Charlottesville], 1973, volumes 1–2.

Virginia Gazette (various publishers).

Waldo, Dr. Albigence. "Valley Forge, 1777–1778. Diary of Surgeon Albigence

Waldo, of the Connecticut Line,"*Pennsylvania Magazine of History and Biography*, 21 (1897), 299–323.

Walpole, Horace. *Memoirs of the Reign of King George the Second*. London, 1847, 3 volumes.

Walsh, Richard, ed. "Braddock on July 9, 1755," *Maryland Historical Magazine*, 60 (1965), 425–6.

Warren-Adams Letters, Being Chiefly a Correspondence Among John Adams, Samuel Adams, and James Warren, 1743–1814, Massachusetts Historical Society Collections, Volumes 72–73. Boston, 1917–25.

Washington, George. *Diaries of George Washington*, ed. John C. Fitzpatrick. Boston, 1925, 4 volumes.

Washington, George. *Diaries of George Washington*, ed. Donald Jackson and Dorothy Twohig. Charlottesville, Virginia, 1976–9, 6 volumes.

[Washington, George]. "George Washington and the Fairfax Family," ed. Peter Walne, *Virginia Magazine of History and Biography*, 77 (1969), 441–63.

Washington, George. "George Washington's 'Marble colour'd folio Book': A Newly Identified Ledger," ed. Joseph Horrell and Richard W. Oram, *William and Mary Quarterly*, third series, 43 (1986), 252–66.

Washington, George. "A Letter from George Washington to Andrew Burnaby," July 27, 1761, *William and Mary Quarterly*, second series, 22 (1942), 221–2.

Washington, George. "Letters of George Washington to Lord Dunmore," *William and Mary Quarterly*, second series, 20 (1940), 161–6.

Washington, George. "A Mystery Resolved, George Washington's Letter to Governor Dinwiddie, June 10, 1754," ed. Peter Walne, *Virginia Magazine of History and Biography*, 79 (1971), 131–44.

Washington, George. "A New-Found Washington Letter of 1774 and the Fairfax Resolves," ed. Donald M. Sweig, *William and Mary Quarterly*, third series, 40 (April 1983), 283–91.

[Washington, George]. *Papers of George Washington, Colonial Series*, ed. W. W. Abbot, Dorothy Twohig, et al. Charlottesville, Virginia, 1983– , 6 volumes to date.

[Washington, George]. *Papers of George Washington, Revolutionary Series*, ed. W. W. Abbot, Dorothy Twohig, et al. Charlottesville, Virginia, 1985– , 2 volumes to date.

Washington, George. *Writings of George Washington*, ed. John C. Fitzpatrick. Washington, D.C., 1931–9, 39 volumes.

Washington Papers, Huntington Library.

Washington Papers, Library of Congress.

[Webb, Samuel Blachley]. *Correspondence and Journals of Samuel Blachley Webb*, ed. Worthington Chauncey Ford. New York, 1893, 3 volumes.

Wheatley, Phillis. *Poems of Phillis Wheatley*, ed. Julian D. Mason, Jr. Chapel Hill, North Carolina, 1966.

Willard, Margaret Wheeler, ed. *Letters on the American Revolution, 1774–1776*. Boston and New York, 1925.

HISTORICAL STUDIES

Abernethy, Thomas Perkins. *Western Lands and the American Revolution*. New York and London, 1937.

Adair, Douglass G. *Fame and the Founding Fathers*, ed. H. Trevor Colbourn. New York, 1974.

Albanese, Catherine. *Sons of the Fathers: The Civil Religion of the American Revolution*. Philadelphia, 1976.

Alden, John R. *George Washington*. Baton Rouge, Louisiana, 1984.

Alden, John R. *Robert Dinwiddie, Servant of the Crown*. Williamsburg, Virginia, 1973.

Ambler, Charles H. *Washington and the West*. New York, 1971 (originally published Chapel Hill, North Carolina, 1936).

Austin, James T. *The Life of Elbridge Gerry*. Boston, 1828–9, 2 volumes.

Bailyn, Bernard. *The Ideological Origins of the American Revolution*. Cambridge, Massachusetts, 1967.

Bailyn, Bernard. *The Origins of American Politics*. New York, 1968.

Baker-Crothers, Hayes. *Virginia and the French and Indian War*. Chicago, 1928.

Beeman, Richard R. "Robert Munford and the Political Culture of Frontier Virginia," *Journal of American Studies*, 12 (1978), 169–83.

Beeman, Richard R. "Social Change and Cultural Conflict in Virginia: Lunenburg County, 1746 to 1774," *William and Mary Quarterly*, third series, 35 (1978), 455–76.

Beeman, Richard R., and Rhys Isaac. "Cultural Conflict and Social Change in the Revolutionary South: Lunenburg County, Virginia," *Journal of Southern History*, 46 (1980), 525–50.

Berens, John F. *Providence & Patriotism in Early America, 1640–1815*. Charlottesville, Virginia, 1978.

Bliss, Willard F. "The Rise of Tenancy in Virginia," *Virginia Magazine of History and Biography*, 58 (1950), 427–41.

Boorstin, Daniel J. *The Americans: The National Experience*. New York, 1965, "The Mythologizing of George Washington," 337–55.

Bowman, Kent A. *Voices of Combat: A Century of Liberty and War Songs, 1765–1865*. Westport, Connecticut, 1987.

Bowman, Larry. "The Virginia County Committees of Safety, 1774–1776," *Virginia Magazine of History and Biography*, 79 (1971), 322–37.

Bradley, Harold W. "The Political Thinking of George Washington," *Journal of Southern History*, 11 (1945), 469–86.

Breen, T. H. "Horses and Gentlemen: The Cultural Significance of Gambling among the Gentry of Virginia," *William and Mary Quarterly*, third series, 34 (1977), 239–57.

Breen, T. H. *Tobacco Culture: The Mentality of the Great Tidewater Planters on the Eve of Revolution*. Princeton, 1985.

Bryan, William Alfred. *George Washington in American Literature, 1775–1865*. Westport, Connecticut, 1970 (originally published New York, 1952).

Burnett, Edmund Cody. _The Continental Congress._ New York, 1964 (originally published New York, 1941).

Carp, E. Wayne. "Early American Military History: A Review of Recent Work," _Virginia Magazine of History and Biography,_ 94 (1986), 259–84.

Carp, E. Wayne. _To Starve the Army at Pleasure: Continental Army Administration and American Political Culture, 1775–1783._ Chapel Hill, North Carolina, 1984.

Carson, Jane D. _Colonial Virginians at Play._ Williamsburg, Virginia, 1965.

Christie, Ian R., and Labaree, Benjamin W. _Empire or Independence, 1760–1776._ New York, 1976.

Cleland, Hugh. _George Washington in the Ohio Valley._ Pittsburgh, 1955.

Clemens, Paul G. W. _The Atlantic Economy and Colonial Maryland's Eastern Shore: From Tobacco to Grain._ Ithaca, New York, 1980.

Clemens, Paul G. W. "The Operation of an Eighteenth-Century Chesapeake Tobacco Plantation," _Agricultural History,_ 49 (1975), 517–31.

Colbourn, H. Trevor. _The Lamp of Experience: Whig History and the Intellectual Origins of the American Revolution._ New York, 1974 (originally published Chapel Hill, North Carolina, 1965).

Copeland, Pamela, and MacMaster, Richard K. _The Five George Masons._ Charlottesville, Virginia, 1975.

Cunliffe, Marcus. _George Washington, Man and Monument._ Revised edition New York, 1982 (originally published Boston, 1958).

Cunliffe, Marcus. "The Two Georges: The President and the King," _American Studies International,_ 24 (1986), 53–73.

Davidson, Philip. _Propaganda and the American Revolution, 1763–1783._ New York, 1973 (originally published Chapel Hill, North Carolina, 1941).

Davis, Richard Beale. _A Colonial Southern Bookshelf._ Athens, Georgia, 1979.

Davis, Richard Beale. _Intellectual Life in the Colonial South._ Knoxville, Tennessee, 1979, 3 volumes.

Davis, Richard Beale. _Intellectual Life of Jefferson's Virginia, 1790–1830._ Knoxville, Tennessee, 1964.

Dawidoff, Robert. _The Education of John Randolph._ New York, 1979.

Duff, Stella F. "The Case against the King: The _Virginia Gazettes_ Indict George III," _William and Mary Quarterly,_ third series, 6 (1949), 383–97.

Dunbar, Louise B. "A Study of 'Monarchical' Tendencies in the United States from 1776 to 1801," _University of Illinois Studies in the Social Sciences,_ 10 (1922).

Earle, Carville, and Hoffman, Ronald. "Staple Crops and Urban Development in the Eighteenth-Century South," _Perspectives in American History,_ 10 (1976), 7–76.

Ernst, Joseph A. "Robinson Scandal Redivivus: Money, Debts, and Politics in Revolutionary Virginia," _Virginia Magazine of History and Biography,_ 77 (1969), 146–73.

Evans, Emory G. "Planter Indebtedness and the Coming of the Revolution," _William and Mary Quarterly,_ third series, 19 (1962), 511–53.

Ferling, John. "Soldiers for Virginia: Who Served in the French and Indian War?" _Virginia Magazine of History and Biography,_ 94 (1986), 307–28.

Fishwick, Marshall. *American Heroes: Myth and Reality.* Washington, D.C., 1954.

Flexner, James Thomas. *George Washington.* Boston, 1965–72, 4 volumes.

Fliegelman, Jay. *Prodigals and Pilgrims: The American Revolution Against Patriarchal Authority, 1750–1800.* Cambridge, England, 1982.

Ford, Paul L. *George Washington.* Philadelphia, 1924 (originally published as *The True George Washington,* Philadelphia, 1896).

Ford, Paul L. *Washington and the Theatre.* New York, 1899.

Ford, Worthington Chauncey. "Washington and Centinel X," *Pennsylvania Magazine of History and Biography,* 22 (1898), 436–51.

Freeman, Douglas Southall. *George Washington.* New York, 1948–57, 6 volumes; volume 7 by John A. Carroll and Mary W. Ashworth.

Friedman, Lawrence J. *Inventors of the Promised Land.* New York, 1975, "The Flawless American, The Invention of George Washington," 44–78.

Furtwangler, Albert. *American Silhouettes: Rhetorical Identities of the Founders.* New Haven, Connecticut, 1987, "Cato at Valley Forge," 64–84.

Gipson, Lawrence H. *The British Empire before the American Revolution.* Caldwell, Idaho, and New York, 1936–70, 15 volumes.

Gipson, Lawrence H. "Virginia Planter Debt before the American Revolution," *Virginia Magazine of History and Biography,* 69 (1961), 259–77.

Greene, Jack P. "The Attempts to Separate the Offices of Speaker and Treasurer in Virginia, 1758–1766," *Virginia Magazine of History and Biography,* 71 (1963), 11–18.

Greene, Jack P. "The Case of the Pistole Fee," *Virginia Magazine of History and Biography,* 66 (1958), 399–422.

Greene, Jack P. "Foundations of Political Power in the Virginia House of Burgesses, 1720 to 1776," *William and Mary Quarterly,* third series, 16 (1959), 485–506.

Greene, Jack P. "The Growth of Political Stability: An Interpretation of Political Development in the Anglo-American Colonies, 1660–1760." In John Parker and Carol Urness, eds., *The American Revolution: A Heritage of Change,* Minneapolis, 1975, 26–52.

Greene, Jack P. *The Quest for Power: The Lower Houses of Assembly in the Southern Royal Colonies, 1689–1776.* New York, 1972 (originally published Chapel Hill, North Carolina, 1963).

Greene, Jack P. "Society, Ideology, and Politics: An Analysis of the Political Culture of Mid-Eighteenth Century Virginia." In Richard M. Jellison, ed., *Society, Freedom and Conscience: The American Revolution in Virginia, Massachusetts, and New York.* New York, 1976.

Greene, Jack P. " *Virtus et Libertas:* Political Culture, Social Change, and the Origins of the American Revolution in Virginia, 1763–1776." In Jeffrey J. Crow and Larry E. Tise, eds., *The Southern Experience in the American Revolution.* Chapel Hill, North Carolina, 1979, copyright 1978, 55–108.

Greene, Jack P., and Jellison, Richard M. "The Currency Act of 1764 in Imperial-Colonial Relations, 1764–1776," *William and Mary Quarterly,* third series, 18 (1961), 485–518.

Greene, Jack P., and Pole, J. R., eds. *Colonial British America: Essays in the New History of the Early Modern Era*. Baltimore, 1984.

Griffin, Appleton P. C., comp. *A Catalogue of the Washington Collection in the Boston Athenaeum*. Boston, 1897.

Griffith, Lucille. *The Virginia House of Burgesses, 1750–1774*. University, Alabama, 1968.

Hastings, George Everett. *The Life and Works of Francis Hopkinson*. Chicago, 1926.

Hay, Robert P. "George Washington, American Moses," *American Quarterly*, 21 (Winter 1969), 780–91.

Herndon, G. Melvin. "Hemp in Colonial Virginia," *Agricultural History*, 37 (1963), 86–93.

Higginbotham, Don. *George Washington and the American Military Tradition*. Athens, Georgia, 1985.

Hill, Helen. *George Mason: Constitutionalist*. Cambridge, Massachusetts, 1938.

Horrell, Joseph. "George Mason in the Fairfax Court," *Virginia Magazine of History and Biography*, 91 (1983), 418–39.

Hughes, Rupert. *George Washington*. New York, 1926–30, 3 volumes.

Isaac, Rhys. "Dramatizing the Ideology of Revolution: Popular Mobilization in Virginia, 1774–1776," *William and Mary Quarterly*, third series, 33 (1976), 357–85.

Isaac, Rhys. "Evangelical Revolt: The Nature of the Baptists' Challenge to the Traditional Order in Virginia, 1765–1775," *William and Mary Quarterly*, third series, 31 (1974), 348–65.

Isaac, Rhys. "Religion and Authority: Problems of the Anglican Establishment in Virginia in the Era of the Great Awakening and the Parsons' Cause," *William and Mary Quarterly*, third series, 30 (1973), 3–36.

Isaac, Rhys. *The Transformation of Virginia, 1740–1790*. Chapel Hill, North Carolina, 1982.

Jordan, Winthrop D. "Familial Politics: Thomas Paine and the Killing of the King, 1776," *Journal of American History*, 60 (September 1973), 294–308.

Kammen, Michael. *A Season of Youth: The American Revolution and the Historical Imagination*. New York, 1978.

Ketcham, Ralph. *Presidents above Party: The First American Presidency, 1789–1829*. Chapel Hill, North Carolina, 1984.

Klapthor, Margaret Brown, and Morrison, Howard Alexander. *G. Washington: A Figure upon the Stage*. Washington, D.C., 1982.

Klingaman, David C. *Colonial Virginia's Coastwise and Grain Trade*. New York, 1975.

Klingaman, David C. "The Significance of Grain in the Development of the Tobacco Colonies," *Journal of Economic History*, 29 (1969), 268–78.

Knollenberg, Bernhard. *George Washington, the Virginia Period, 1732–1775*. Durham, North Carolina, 1976 (originally published 1964).

Koontz, Louis K. *Robert Dinwiddie*. Glendale, California, 1941.

Kopperman, Paul E. *Braddock at the Monongahela*. Pittsburgh, 1977.

Kramnick, Isaac. *Bolingbroke and His Circle: The Politics of Nostalgia in the Age of Walpole*. Cambridge, Massachusetts, 1968.

Kulikoff, Allan. *Tobacco and Slaves: The Development of Southern Cultures in the Chesapeake, 1680–1800.* Chapel Hill, North Carolina, 1986.

LeMay, J. A. Leo. "The Reverend Samuel Davies' Essay Series: The Virginia Centinel, 1756–1757." In J. A. Leo LeMay, ed., *Essays in Early Virginia Literature Honoring Richard Beale Davis.* New York, 1977, 121–63.

Liddle, William D. "A Patriot King, or None: American Public Attitudes toward George III and the British Monarchy, 1754–1776," Ph.D. thesis, Claremont Graduate School, 1970.

Liddle, William D. "'A Patriot King, or None': Lord Bolingbroke and the American Renunciation of George III," *Journal of American History,* 65 (1978–9), 951–70.

Lipset, Seymour Martin. *The First New Nation: The United States in Historical and Comparative Perspective.* New York, 1963, "The Crisis of Legitimacy and the Role of the Charismatic Leader," 16–23.

Litto, Fredric M. "Addison's *Cato* in the Colonies," *William and Mary Quarterly,* third series, 23 (1966), 431–49.

Longmore, Paul K. "The Enigma of George Washington: How Did the Man Become the Myth?" *Reviews in American History,* 13 (June 1985), 184–90.

McCardell, Lee. *Ill-Starred General: Braddock of the Coldstream Guards.* Pittsburgh, 1958.

Maier, Pauline. *From Resistance to Revolution: Colonial Radicals and the Development of American Opposition to Britain, 1765–1776.* New York, 1974 (originally published New York, 1972).

Maier, Pauline. *The Old Revolutionaries.* New York, 1980.

Marsh, Philip M. *Philip Freneau, Poet and Journalist.* Minneapolis, 1968, copyright 1967.

Martin, Lawrence. "The Dates of Naming Places and Things for George Washington." In *History of the George Washington Bicentennial Celebration, Literature Series.* Washington, D.C., 1932, 3 volumes, 3:308–12.

Mason, Julian D. "David Humphreys' Lost Ode to George Washington, 1776," *Quarterly Journal of the Library of Congress,* 28 (January 1971), 29–37.

Mayo, Bernard. "George Washington," *Georgia Review,* 13 (1959), 135–50; reprinted in Mayo, *Myths and Men,* Athens, Georgia, 1959.

Mays, David J. *Edmund Pendleton, 1721–1803: A Biography.* Cambridge, Massachusetts, 1952, 2 volumes.

Middleton, Arthur Pierce. *Tobacco Coast: A Maritime History of Chesapeake Bay in the Colonial Era,* ed. George Carrington Mason. Baltimore, 1984 (originally published Newport News, Virginia, 1953).

Mitchell, Robert D. *Commercialism and Frontier: Perspectives on the Early Shenandoah Valley.* Charlottesville, Virginia, 1977.

Morgan, Edmund S. *The Genius of George Washington.* New York, 1980.

Morgan, Gwenda. "Virginia and the French and Indian War: A Case Study of the War's Effects on Imperial Relations," *Virginia Magazine of History and Biography,* 81 (1973), 23–48.

Morison, Samuel Eliot. "The Young Man Washington." In his *By Land and by Sea.* New York, 1953.

Morris, Richard B. *Seven Who Shaped Our Destiny.* New York, 1973, "George Washington, Surrogate Father to a Revolutionary Generation," 31–71.

Morton, Richard Lee. *Colonial Virginia.* Chapel Hill, North Carolina, 1960, 2 volumes.

Nettels, Curtis P. *George Washington and American Independence.* Westport, Connecticut, 1976 (originally published Boston, 1951).

Nettels, Curtis P. "The Washington Theme in American History," *Massachusetts Historical Society Proceedings,* 66 (1952), 171–98.

Padover, Saul K. "George Washington: Portrait of a True Conservative," *Social Research,* 22 (1955), 199–222.

Papenfuse, Edward C., Jr. "Planter Behavior and Economic Opportunity in a Staple Economy," *Agricultural History,* 46 (1972), 297–312.

Pargellis, Stanley. "Braddock's Defeat," *American Historical Review,* 41 (1936), 253–69.

Pearson, John C. "The Fish and Fisheries of Colonial Virginia, Fourth Installment," *William and Mary Quarterly,* second series, 23 (1943), 130–5.

Pocock, John G. A. *The Machiavellian Moment.* Princeton, 1975.

Pocock, John G. A. "Virtue and Commerce in the Eighteenth Century," *Journal of Interdisciplinary History,* 3 (1972), 119–34.

Preisser, Thomas M. "Alexandria and the Evolution of the Northern Virginia Economy, 1749–1776," *The Virginia Magazine of History and Biography,* 89 (1981), 282–93.

Price, Jacob M. *Capital and Credit in British Overseas Trade: The View from the Chesapeake, 1770–1776.* Cambridge, Massachusetts, 1980.

Price, Jacob M. "Economic Function and the Growth of American Port Towns in the Eighteenth Century," *Perspectives in American History,* 8 (1974), 121–86.

Price, Jacob M. "The Economic Growth of the Chesapeake and the European Market, 1697–1775," *Journal of Economic History,* 24 (1964), 496–511.

Prussing, Eugene. *The Estate of George Washington, Deceased.* Boston, 1927.

Robbins, Caroline. *The Eighteenth-Century Commonwealthman.* Cambridge, Massachusetts, 1959.

Rowland, Kate Mason. *The Life of George Mason, 1725–1792.* New York, 1892, 2 volumes.

Royster, Charles. *A Revolutionary People at War: The Continental Army and American Character, 1775–1783.* Chapel Hill, North Carolina, 1979.

Russell, Peter E. "Redcoats in the Wilderness: British Officers and Irregular Warfare in Europe and America, 1740 to 1760," *William and Mary Quarterly,* third series, 35 (1978), 629–52.

Schochet, Gordon J. *Patriarchalism in Political Thought.* New York, 1975.

Schwartz, Barry. "The Character of Washington: A Study in Republican Culture," *American Quarterly,* 38 (Summer 1986), 202–22.

Schwartz, Barry. *George Washington: The Making of an American Symbol.* New York, 1987.

Sheridan, Richard B. "The British Credit Crisis of 1772 and the American Colonies," *Journal of Economic History,* 20 (1960), 161–86.

Shy, John. "The American Revolution: The Military Conflict Considered as a

Revolutionary War." In Stephen G. Kurtz and James H. Huston, eds., *Essays on the American Revolution*. New York, 1973, 121–56.

Shy, John. "American Society and Its War for Independence." In Don Higginbotham, ed., *Reconsiderations on the Revolutionary War: Selected Essays*. Westport, Connecticut, 1978, 72–82.

Silverman, Kenneth. *A Cultural History of the American Revolution*. New York, 1976.

Smith, James Morton, comp. *George Washington: A Profile*. New York, 1969.

Smylie, James H. "The President as Republican Prophet and King: Critical Reflections on the Death of Washington," *Journal of Church and State*, 18 (1976), 232–52.

Sosin, Jack M. *Whitehall and the Wilderness: The Middle West in British Colonial Policy, 1760–1775*. Lincoln, Nebraska, 1961.

Spaulding, Oliver L., Jr. "The Military Studies of George Washington," *American Historical Review*, 29 (1923–4), 675–80.

Stephenson, Nathaniel, and Dunn, Waldo H. *George Washington*. New York, 1940.

Stewart, George R. *Names on the Land*. Revised edition, Boston, 1968.

Sweig, Donald M. "The Virginia Nonimportation Association Broadside of 1770 and Fairfax County: A Study in Local Participation," *The Virginia Magazine of History and Biography*, 87 (1979), 316–25.

Sydnor, Charles. *American Revolutionaries in the Making*. New York, 1965 (originally published as *Gentlemen Freeholders*, Chapel Hill, North Carolina, 1952).

Tate, Thad W. "The Coming of the Revolution in Virginia: Britain's Challenge to Virginia's Ruling Class, 1763–1776," *William and Mary Quarterly*, third series, 19 (1962), 323–43.

Thom, William Taylor. *The Struggle for Religious Freedom in Virginia: The Baptists*. Baltimore, 1900.

Tillson, Albert H. "The Militia and Popular Political Culture in the Upper Valley of Virginia, 1740–1775," *Virginia Magazine of History and Biography*, 94 (1986), 285–306.

Wall, A. J. "The Statues of King George III and the Honorable William Pitt Erected in New York City 1770," *New York Historical Society Quarterly Bulletin*, 4 (July 1920), 36–57.

Wall, Cecil. "George Washington: Country Gentleman," *Agricultural History*, 43 (1969), 5–6.

Wecter, Dixon. *The Hero in America*. New York, 1941.

Weir, Robert M. *"The Last of American Freemen": Studies in the Political Culture of the Colonial and Revolutionary South*. Macon, Georgia, 1985.

White, William E. "The Independent Companies of Virginia, 1774–1775," *Virginia Magazine of History and Biography*, 86 (1978), 149–62.

Wills, Garry. *Cincinnatus: George Washington and the Enlightenment*. New York, 1984.

Acknowledgments

Completion of the work reflected in these pages would have been impossible without the assistance and encouragement of a great many people. Moral support has come from many friends, most especially David and Ellen Brown, Christine Davis, Carol Gill, Suellen Hoy, Molly Johnston, Walter Nugent, Dale and Juanita Ryan, Larry Voss, and Barbara Waxman.

Library research and other work received important aid from Stephen Cave, Russell Dees, Pat Delana, Chris Lane, Thomas Martinez, Patricia Tracy, and Ginger Yiao. I am grateful for the generous assistance of the staffs of the Honnold Library at the Claremont Colleges, the Mary Norton Clapp Library at Occidental College, and the Huntington Library.

This work has also called into service a battalion of typists. I wish to thank Ellen Brown, Donna Kelly, Kathy Korenny, JoAnn Mitchell, Sue Neal, Rhen Pixlee, Joy Siglar, Dyana Vukovich, and most especially Howard Bresner and Diane Reichwein.

Carol Pearson caught and corrected many of the errors that seem inevitably to creep like weeds into historians' work. Whatever mistakes remain survive despite her meticulous checking and are due to my own failure.

Mitch Marich, a godsend, expedited the last stages of writing with his knowledge and advice, on one occasion saving me from probable computer-generated madness.

Lynne Withey of the University of California Press went out of her way to find solutions to problems few publishers confront when dealing with authors.

Grants from the Huntington Library and the Earhart Foundation enabled me to complete research and the final draft.

This study is immeasurably better because of the searching questions and helpful criticism of E. Wayne Carp, Marcus Cunliffe, Don Higginbotham, Leonard Levy, Robert Middlekauff, and John Niven.

319

Robert Dawidoff first suggested the subject and guided the work as a doctoral dissertation. He encouraged, urged, cajoled, and demanded the best from me. He has taught me much about the study and writing of history and even more about friendship.

My mother and father, Evelyn and Kenneth Longmore, have worried and worked on my behalf through all of this, as in everything.

Index

Actor/Acting (GW's), 7–11, 32, 51–2, 56–7, 79–80, 141, 181–3; Catonic image in, 173, 174–83 passim, 210; as Continental Army commander, 171, 174–83 passim, 189–90, 195; in Continental Congress, 138; in political tactics/style, 42–3, 79–80, 138, 200; in protests of inadequacy, 19, 32, 160, 168, 174–5, 277n.34. *See also* Physical appearance; Plays; Self-mastery

Adams, Abigail, on GW's appearance and manner, 182

Adams, John, 158, 182, 196, 225, 301n.40; and First Continental Congress, 137, 138, 139, 144, 145; on George III, 186; on GW's education, 213; military enthusiasm of, 158; on speechmaking, 137, 278n.8; role in GW's election as Continental Army commander, 160–7 passim, 175–6, 272n.12, 273n.20, 274–5n.25

Adams, Samuel: and Boston Port Bill, 112, 115; and First Continental Congress, 139, 144, 145; and Second Continental Congress, 164, 165, 166, 272n.10, 274nn. 23, 25, 275n.25

Addison, Joseph, *Tragedy of Cato*, 173–4, 188, 213, 220, 278nn. 5, 6

Adjutancy: GW's, 17, 231–2n.1, 240n.4; Lawrence Washington's, 16, 17

Agrarian social order, Bolingbroke and, 5, 120–1, 185–6

Agriculture. *See* Corn; Flax; Flour; Food-stuffs; Hemp; Reading, GW's; Tobacco; Wheat

Albemarle, William Anne Keppel, Lord: on GW at Fort Necessity, 24

Albemarle County: revolutionary militia of, 157; protest meeting in (1774), 129, 130

Alden, John, on GW's address to Loudoun, 243n.35

Alexander the Great, described by GW as patron of arts, 220; GW orders bust of, 60

Alexandria: boundaries of, 260n.14; commercial importance of, 12–13, 107; establishment of, 12–13

American Academy of Arts and Sciences, GW honorary member of, 292n.10

American Philosophical Society, GW honorary member of, 292n.10

American Revolution. *See* Revolution

Amherst, Jeffery, boasting to subdue colonies, 195

Anne, Queen, GW on arts during reign of, 220–1

Anticolonial bias, 41, 54; of Braddock, 28, 31, 236n.10; commercial (*see* Commerce; Taxes); conspiracy theory re, 90, 122, 126, 135, 139–43, 169; GW's response to, 20–1, 26, 43–54 passim, 68–9, 76, 78–81, 81, 89, 90, 117, 121–2, 135, 139–43, 169–70 (*see also* Militancy; Nationalism); military, 20–1, 26, 35, 41–54 passim, 142, 195, 246n.25; political,

321